TREATISE ON INSTRUMENTATION

HECTOR BERLIOZ
&
RICHARD STRAUSS

Translated by Theodore Front

DOVER PUBLICATIONS, INC., New York

This Dover edition, first published in 1991, is an unabridged republication of the edition originally published by Edwin F. Kalmus, New York, 1948.

Library of Congress Cataloging-in-Publication Data

Berlioz, Hector, 1803–1869.
[Grand traité d'instrumentation et d'orchestration modernes. English]
Treatise on instrumentation / Hector Berlioz & Richard Strauss ; translated by Theodore Front.
p. cm.
Translation of: Grand traité d'instrumentation et d'orchestration modernes.
Reprint. Originally published: New York : E. F. Kalmus, c1948. Including Berlioz' Essay on conducting.
Includes index.
ISBN-13: 978-0-486-26903-0 (pbk.)
ISBN-10: 0-486-26903-5 (pbk.)
1. Instrumentation and orchestration. I. Strauss, Richard, 1864–1949. II. Title.
MT70.B4813 1991
781.3'74—dc20 91-24083
CIP
MN

Manufactured in the United States by RR Donnelley
26903510 2016
www.doverpublications.com

CONTENTS

FOREWORD

When I was asked by the publishers to enlarge and revise the "Treatise on Instrumentation" by Hector Berlioz, I thought at first that the masterwork of the great Frenchman did not need such help to be even today a source of enjoyment and stimulation for all musicians. It appeared to me complete in itself and full of ingenious visions, whose realization by Richard Wagner is obvious to every connoisseur.

Upon closer study, however, I could not help noticing the gaps in this work, completed in the middle of the last century. I became aware of the danger that important parts of Berlioz' work might be considered obsolete and that its lasting value might therefore be overlooked, especially since many other excellent books had developed the subject in the meantime with scientific accuracy (particularly the textbook on instrumentation by the outstanding Belgian authority, Gevaert).

Berlioz was the first to arrange and organize this complicated subject with the supreme industry of a collector. Yet the everlasting value of his work lies in the fact that he not only treated questions of mechanics, but stressed above all the esthetic aspects of orchestral technique. These permanent qualities in the work and its prophetic power, which in a few lines often gives the careful reader a vision of the whole Wagner, may justify this revision. To keep Berlioz' work alive even for the superficial reader, it was necessary to supplement technical details and to point out new achievements, especially in Wagner's work.

The respect for Berlioz' completely unified masterwork demanded that nothing be changed in his text (with the sole exception of the chapter on the organ, which was partly revised and enlarged by Prof. Ph. Wolfrum in accordance with latest developments). My additions are indicated by an undulating line at the side of the text. There is always an abundance of material for musical examples; hence I have avoided important and interesting examples which were quoted by Gevaert. Gevaert's book contains so much worth reading concerning the technique and acoustics of instruments that I should urgently recommend its study in addition to Berlioz' work.

In the art of instrumentation, as in other arts, the question of theoretical books is highly problematic. I claim that a musician with talent for composition, who plays the violin or some wind instrument in an orchestra, will have more skill in instrumentation (without any knowledge of its theory) than the equally gifted pianist or music critic who has diligently studied textbooks, but has never come closer to orchestral instruments than the first row of a concert hall.

Therefore, if the student wants to achieve more in the art of instrumentation than just writing a few pleasant-sounding pieces ("excellently scored", as our critics would call them), and if he has no opportunity to conduct an orchestra and be in daily contact with its magic powers, then he should not only study the scores of the great masters, but above all ask instrumentalists of all kinds to familiarize him with the exact technique of their instruments and with the timbre of their registers. He should, so to speak, try to find out the secrets of the orchestra tuning-room. There are improvements which an inventive player may have discovered for his mouthpiece, for the arrangement of the valves, for other details in the construction or the material of his instrument, technical tricks, devised in an idle hour for the player's own amusement. All this may open unexpected vistas to a creator in search of new forms of expression for new ideas. It may be more valuable for progress than any treatise which is primarily based on the achievements of the past.

Thus, the practical instrumentalist, through his skill, stimulates the composer to new ideas. Great ideas, on the other hand, which at first do not seem feasible, gradually lift the ambitious instrumentalist to their level. They have had the greatest influence on progress in the construction of instruments, on improvements in their technique, and on the enrichment of their expressive possibilities.

The development of the orchestra until the appearance of Berlioz is sufficiently known and need not detain us here too long. I should like to refer the reader to Richard Wagner's magnificent interpretations in his writings, especially in "Opera and Drama". It would not be appropriate to try to cover here in a few lines a great chapter in the history of music and to show in detail and with all its fine articulations an organic development which was influenced by thousands of seeds, stimuli, mistakes and successes. All I can venture to give here is a brief, compressed survey. I trust the sympathetic reader will understand my intention: not to offer an esthetic system, cleanly divided into separate categories like so many drawers, but simply to develop certain important points, leaving it to the educated reader to fill in the connecting details with the help of his own knowledge and of his feelings. With this reservation, I should like to follow the two main roads of orchestral development from Handel, Gluck and Haydn to Wagner. I might be permitted to call them in brief the *symphonic* (*polyphonic*) and the *dramatic* (*homophonic*) roads.

The origin of the *symphonic* orchestra is to be found mainly in Haydn's and Mozart's string quartets (as well as in Bach's organ fugues). The symphonic works of these two masters reveal in their style, in their themes, melodies and figurations the character of the string quartet with all its polyphonic possibilities. One might almost call them string quartets with obbligato wood-wind and noise instruments to reinforce the tutti (French horns, trumpets, kettledrums).

In spite of the greater number of wind instruments used in his Fifth and Ninth Symphonies, even Beethoven cannot hide the mark of chamber music. In Beethoven, more than in Haydn and Mozart, the spirit of the piano injects its characteristic elements—the same spirit which later completely dominates Schumann's and Brahms' orchestral works (unfortunately, not always to their advantage or to the listener's enjoyment). Only Liszt with his instinct for tone colors succeeded in filling this spirit of the piano in the orchestra with new poetic life.

The beautiful melodic contours of the four equally important parts in the classical string quartet attained their highest freedom, worthy of Bach's choral polyphony, in Beethoven's last ten quartets. There is none of this freedom in Beethoven's nine symphonies. But Wagner found in it the style for his "Tristan" and "Meistersinger" orchestra; he owes to it the unheard-of, miraculous sounds of his string quintet.

It should be added, of course, that the melodic development from Haydn to Beethoven automatically raised the technical demands upon the orchestra and stimulated coloristic effects alien to the style of chamber music. Thus the orchestra approached more and more the second road of development, which we have already named the *dramatic* one.

Handel and Haydn, as well as Gluck in his operas, consciously stressed the coloristic elements in their predominantly homophonic style (which our dear, easy-going opera audiences even today prefer to polyphony). It was their aim to reinforce poetry and stage by the expressive forces of the orchestra. This transformed the choir of instruments gradually into sensitive groups and finally into "speaking" individuals.

The subjects chosen by the composers of the Romantic School, especially Weber (in "Freischuetz", "Oberon", "Euryanthe"), led to further discoveries in this direction. The genius of Richard Wagner finally achieved a synthesis of the two directions. He combined the *symphonic* (polyphonic) technique of composition and orchestration with the rich expressive resources of the *dramatic* (homophonic) style.

Hector Berlioz' aim may have been the same. At the risk of being misunderstood, one might say in short that he was not dramatic enough for the stage, and not symphonic enough for the concert hall. Still, in his attempt to combine stage and concert hall he discovered new and splendid expressive resources for the orchestra. To be sure, he failed to justify his use of dramatic effects in symphonic works by coining his ideas in a dramatic form (which is impossible without rich polyphony): his works were always lyric or epic. But he was the first to derive his inspiration consistently from the character of the orchestral instruments. Endowed with a special gift for conceiving new combinations of sound, he discovered many new coloristic possibilities and subtle shadings.

No doubt this bold innovator, so ingenious in blending colors, this real creator of the modern orchestra had no feeling at all for polyphony. We do not know whether he was acquainted with the polyphonic mysteries of J. S. Bach's miraculous scores. But it is certain that his, musically speaking, somewhat primitive sense of melody lacked the understanding for polyphony, the culmination of musical genius, which we admire in Bach's cantatas, in Beethoven's last quartets, in the poetic construction of the third act of "Tristan", as the highest emanation of an unrestrained melodic wealth. And only truly meaningful polyphony can disclose the loftiest tone-miracles of the orchestra. A score with awkward or just indifferent inner parts and basses will rarely lack a certain harshness; it will never have the brilliant sonority of a piece in which the second wind instruments, the second violins, violas, violoncelli and basses also take part in the soulful enunciation of beautifully curved melodic lines. This is the secret of the wonderful tone-poetry in the scores of "Tristan" and "Meistersinger" as well as of the "Siegfried Idyll", which was written for "small orchestra". On the other hand, even Berlioz' orchestral dramas, constructed with such mastery of sound, as well as Weber's and Liszt's scores show by the brittleness of their colors that the choir of accompanying and filling parts was not deemed worthy of melodic independence by the composer; (and each of these masters was, in his way, a great instrumental poet and interpreter of orchestral colors). Hence the conductor cannot achieve that spiritual participation of all parts in the whole which is indispensable for producing a uniformly warm sound.

The superiority of Wagner, who perfected the modern orchestra, over Berlioz, who created it, is usually said to consist exclusively in the more profound meaning of his poetic and musical ideas. Yet there are three technical points which should be stressed (of course with reasonable reservations), for they are the basis for the perfection of Wagner's ideas in the modern orchestra: first, the employment of the richest polyphonic style; secondly, the accomplishment of this through the invention and introduction of the valve horn; thirdly, taking over the virtuoso technique of the solo-concerto for all instruments of the orchestra (Beethoven already required this in his last string quartets, but not in his symphonies).

Thus, Richard Wagner's scores are the alpha and omega of my additions to this work; they embody the only important progress in the art of instrumentation since Berlioz. But I must warn the student to approach this study with great caution. Generally the score of "Lohengrin" should be considered a basic textbook for the advanced student; only after studying it thoroughly may he proceed to the polyphony of "Meistersinger" and "Tristan", and to the fairy-tale world of the "Ring". Esthetically, the treatment of the wind instruments in "Lohengrin" is the apex of true perfection, never before reached. The so-called third wood wind (English horn and bass clarinet), added for the first time, are employed here in manifold combinations of sound. The second, third and fourth horns, the trumpets and trombones have already attained polyphonic independence. The doubling of melodic parts, so characteristic for Wagner, is used with a sure sense for tonal balance and for beauty of sound, which even today arouses deep admiration. I particularly recommend the study of the scene between Ortrud and Telramund at the beginning of the second act; the wonderful wood-wind passage when Elsa appears on the terrace; the Procession to the Minster; and the end of the second act, where Wagner succeeds in drawing organ sounds from the orchestra, which even surpass the "king of the instruments".

But before the beginner in the technique of composition and instrumentation starts his first timid swimming exercises in the stormy sea of the orchestra, he must be warned against one danger: the phenomenal sound combinations which a Berlioz or Wagner drew from the orchestra must not be misused. These masters used them for giving expression to unheard-of, great, poetic ideas, feelings and pictures of nature; they must not be reduced to the common property of bunglers, like a child's toy. I wish it were possible to force everybody desirous of attempting orchestral composition to start his career with a number of string quartets. These string quartets he should have to submit to the judgment of two violinists, a violist and a cellist. If the four instrumentalists declare, "yes, this is well set for the instruments", then the disciple of the muses may follow his impulse to write for orchestra (at first preferably for a small one). Finally, when the "young master" can no longer contain his urge for the large orchestra, he should compare Wagner's eleven scores with each other. Let him observe how each of these works has its own combination of instruments, its own orchestral style; how each says what it wants to say in the simplest possible way, and how this noble moderation in the use of means is to be found in all of them. On the other hand, let him be warned against the procedure of one modern composer who once showed me the score of a comedy overture, in which the four "Nibelung" tubas carried on a most lively dance with the rest of the brass—simply as reinforcement of the tutti. Dismayed, I asked the author—otherwise an excellent, highly educated musician—what business the tubas had in this gay overture. Had not Wagner really "invented" them with such wisdom and sure imagination to depict the somber world of the Nibelungs? He answered quite innocently: "Why, nowadays every major orchestra has tubas; why should I not use them?" That silenced me; this man was beyond help.

Berlin, Christmas 1904.

Richard Strauss

INSTRUMENTATION

Introduction

In no period of music history has Instrumentation been discussed so much as at present. This was probably due to the swift development of this branch of art in recent times; perhaps also to the great amount of criticism, of different theories and contradictory opinions, for which the most inferior compositions frequently served as a pretext. Nowadays a great deal of attention is paid to the art of instrumentation, which was still unknown at the beginning of the 18th century; only sixty years ago* its rise was vigorously opposed even by supposedly true friends of music. In more recent times musical progress has again been obstructed, but in a different way. This need not surprise us; it has always been thus.

At first a succession of consonant chords, with a few suspensions here and there, was considered "music". When later Monteverde dared to introduce the dominant seventh chord without preparation, he was violently blamed and abused for this innovation. In spite of all this, the chord was soon generally accepted; and so-called learned composers eventually came to look down with contempt upon any harmonic sequence which was simple, clear and natural. They admitted only compositions which, from beginning to end, abounded in the harshest dissonances (minor and major seconds, sevenths, ninths, etc.). That these chords were used without reason or method did not matter; it almost seemed as if there were only one intention: to make this music as unpleasant as possible to the ear. These musicians took a fancy to dissonant chords, as certain animals prefer salt, prickly plants or thorny shrubs. What originally was mere reaction had grown into exaggeration.

Melody did not exist in these supposedly beautiful musical combinations. Yet, when it gradually started appearing here and there, people decried the decline and ruin of art and of its sacred rules; they believed that everything was lost. But in the course of time melody gained its place, and the usual exaggerations did not fail to appear. Soon there were fanatics of melody who abhorred any piece of music in more than three voice-parts. Some even demanded that the melody should be accompanied only by a bass. Apparently they wanted to give the hearer the pleasure of guessing the missing inner voices. Others went still further and rejected any kind of accompaniment; to them, harmony was a barbarous invention.

Then came *modulation's* turn. At the time when modulation was limited to nearly-related keys, the first who ventured into more distant keys were censured. One might have expected this. Whatever the effect of these new modulations, the masters rejected them vigorously. The innovator pleaded vainly: "Listen to it attentively; convince yourselves how smoothly it is introduced, how well prepared, how skillfully linked with the preceding and following passages, and how wonderful it sounds!" "That does not matter", was the answer; "this modulation is prohibited and that's why it cannot be used." However, modulations into distant keys soon appeared in important works, producing effects as felicitous as they were unexpected. Almost immediately a new kind of pedantry arose: there were people who considered any modulation to the dominant a weakness; even in the simplest rondo they sauntered gaily from C major to F♯ major.

By and by, time restored a reasonable balance. People learned to distinguish use from misuse, reactionary vanity from stupidity and obstinacy. Concerning harmony, melody and modulation, there is now general agreement to approve whatever produces a good effect, and to reject what has a poor effect. Even the authority of a hundred old men (be they as old as a hundred and twenty years) will not persuade us that what is ugly, is beautiful; and what is beautiful, ugly.

Concerning *instrumentation, expression* and *rhythm,* the situation is still different. Their turn came much later for being observed, rejected, admitted, limited, liberated and exaggerated. They have not as yet reached the stage of development achieved by the other branches of music. We can only state that instrumentation leads the others and is close to the stage of exaggeration.

Much time is needed to find the oceans of music; still more, to learn how to navigate in them.

THE INSTRUMENTS

Any sonorous body employed by a composer is a musical instrument. The following is a list of means available at present.

1. Stringed instruments.
   a. Strings set in vibration by a bow: Violin, Viola, Viola d'amore, Violoncello, Double-bass.
   b. Strings plucked: Harp, Guitar, Mandolin.
   c. With keyboard: Pianoforte.
2. Wind instruments.
   a. With reeds: Oboe, English horn, Bassoon, Tenoroon (Basson quinte), Double bassoon, Clarinet, Basset-horn, Bass clarinet, Saxophone, etc.
   b. Without reeds: Flute (large and small).
   c. With keyboard: Organ, Melodium (American organ), Harmonium, Concertina.
   d. Brass instruments, with mouthpiece: French horn, Trumpet, Cornet, Bugle, Trombone, Ophicleide, Bombardon, Bass tuba.

*All time indications in this work refer to the middle of the 19th century.

e. Wooden instruments, with mouthpiece: Russian bassoon, Serpent.
f. Voices of men, women, children, and artificial sopranos and altos.

3. Percussion instruments.
   a. With definite pitch: Kettledrum, Ancient cymbal, Chime, Glockenspiel, Keyboard harmonica, Bells.
   b. With indefinite pitch, producing only noises of different timbre: Drum, Bass drum, Tambourine, Cymbals, Triangle, Gong, Crescent.

To this list are now to be added:

To 1 b: Zither.
To 2 a: Oboe d'amore, Double-bass oboe, Heckelphon, Double-bass clarinet.
To 2 b: Alto flute.
To 2 d: Tuba in F, Tuba in B♭, Euphonium (Barytone).
To 3 a: Xylophone, Celesta.
To 3 b: Birch rod, Small bells.

The art of instrumentation consists in the employment of these sound elements: either to give a particular color to melody, harmony and rhythm; or—independently of these three great musical forces—to produce special effects (which may, or may not, serve some purpose of expression).

Considered in its poetical aspect, this art can be taught as little as the art of inventing beautiful melodies, beautiful chord successions, and powerful rhythmical forms. One can only learn what is suitable for the various instruments, what is practicable or not, what is easy or difficult, what is weak or sonorous. It can also be indicated that one instrument is more appropriate than another for creating certain effects or expressing certain feelings. But as for their blending in groups, in small orchestras or large masses; as for uniting and combining them so that the tone of some instruments is modified by that of others, producing an ensemble tone unobtainable by one instrument or by a group of similar instruments: all this can be demonstrated only by studying the achievements realized in the works of the masters and by analyzing their methods. Their results can doubtless be modified in a thousand ways, good or bad, by composers with similar aims.

The object of this work is, therefore, to indicate the *range* of the instruments and certain features of their *mechanism;* then to examine the nature of their *timbre,* their peculiar *character* and *range of expression*—matters greatly neglected up to now; and finally to study the best known methods for combining them appropriately. To go beyond this would mean to enter the realm of creative inspiration where only a genius can roam and make his own discoveries.

Stringed Instruments

The Violin

The four strings of the violin are usually tuned in fifths:

first string
second string
third string
fourth string

The highest string, E, is generally known as the chanterelle.

These strings are called *open* strings if the fingers of the left hand do not modify the sound by shortening the part of the string which is set in vibration by the bow. The notes to be played on an open string are indicated by a zero (0) placed above or below them.

Some great virtuosos and composers have deviated from this system of tuning the violin. Paganini raised all strings a semitone in order to give more brilliance to the instrument: Consequently, he transposed the solo part, playing for instance in D when the orchestra played in E♭, or in A when the orchestra played in B♭. Open strings being more sonorous than those stopped by fingers, he could thus frequently use them also in keys in which they would otherwise not be possible. De Bériot frequently raised only the G-string a semitone in his concertos. Baillot, on the other hand, sometimes tuned the G-string a semitone lower for the sake of tender or somber effects. Winter, for the same reason, used even the lower F instead of G.

In view of the high degree of skill attained nowadays by our young violinists, the violin may be assigned the following range in a good and fully staffed orchestra:

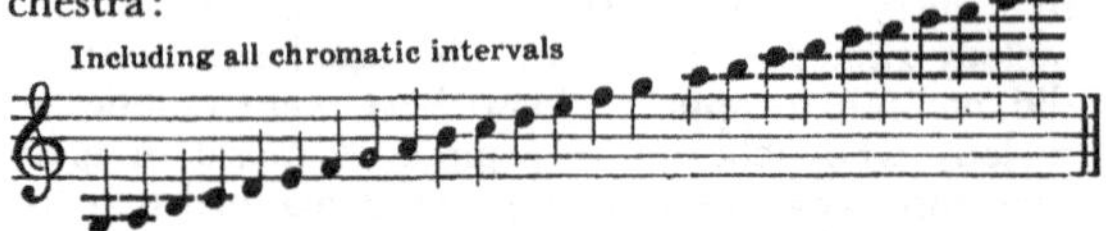

Great virtuosos carry the range several tones higher. By means of harmonics considerably higher notes can be reached, even in the orchestra (more about this below).

In the meantime this range has been frequently extended in the orchestra to

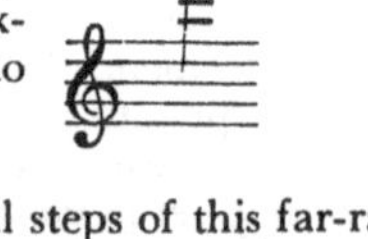

Trills are practicable on all steps of this far-ranging scale of three and a half octaves. But those on the three highest notes, A, B, C, are very difficult; it is advisable not to use them in the orchestra.

See the wonderful trill passage in the third act of "Siegfried" during Bruennhilde's awakening as she looks into the light of the sun, enchanted and at the same time blinded by the unwonted radiance (Example 1).

No. 1. Siegfried, Act III.

Fl.
Ob.
Klar. in B.
Engl. Hrn.
Hrnr.
Baßklar. in B.
Fag.
Tromp. in F.
Pos.
Kontrab.-Tuba.
Pken.
Hrfn. I.
Hrfn. II.
Viol. I.
Viol. II.
Brünh.
cresc.
dim.
più p
(einfach)
1. in D.
rallent.
(tremolo)

The minor trill on the fourth string between G and A♭ is to be avoided as much as possible; it is harsh and has an unpleasant effect.

Numerous *chords* of two, three and four notes can be played on the violin, simultaneously or arpeggio; they vary considerably in their effect.

Chords of two notes, produced by so-called *double stopping* on two strings, are well suited, both in forte and in piano, to melodic phrases as well as to all kinds of accompaniments and tremolos.

The chords of three and four notes, however, are not of a good effect when played piano. They have vitality only in forte; for then only can the bow strike the strings together and make them sound well simultaneously. It should not be forgotten that in these three and four-part chords two tones at most can be sustained, the bow having to quit the others as soon as they are struck. In a moderate or slow tempo it is therefore useless to write:

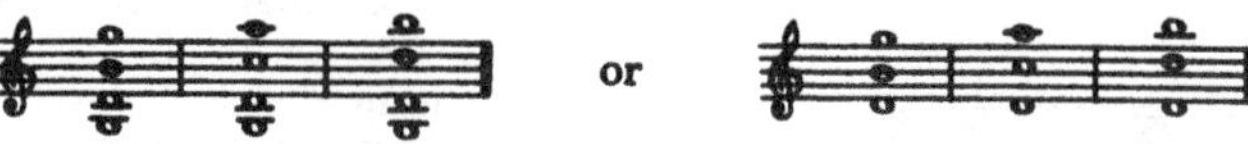

for only the two upper notes can be sustained. In this case it is better to write

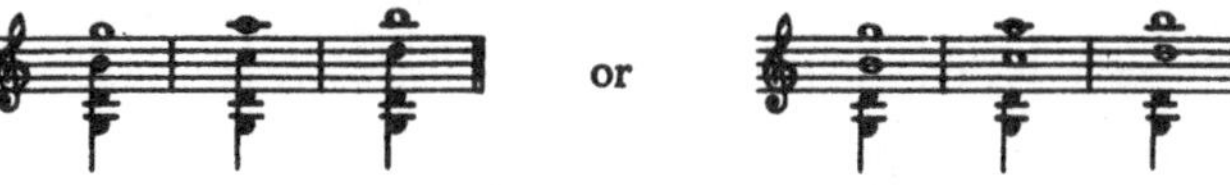

Of course, between the low G and D all chords are impossible since there is only one string (G) to produce the two tones. Should it be necessary to use chords at this extreme end of the scale, they can be obtained in the orchestra only by dividing the violins. This division is indicated in Italian by *divisi* or *a due,* in French by *divisés* or *à deux,* in German by *geteilt,* written over the passage:

The violins are then divided, one group playing the upper and the other the lower part. Starting from the third (D) string upward, all chords of two notes in seconds, thirds, fourths, fifths, sixths, sevenths and octaves are playable; but they become progressively more difficult on the two higher strings.

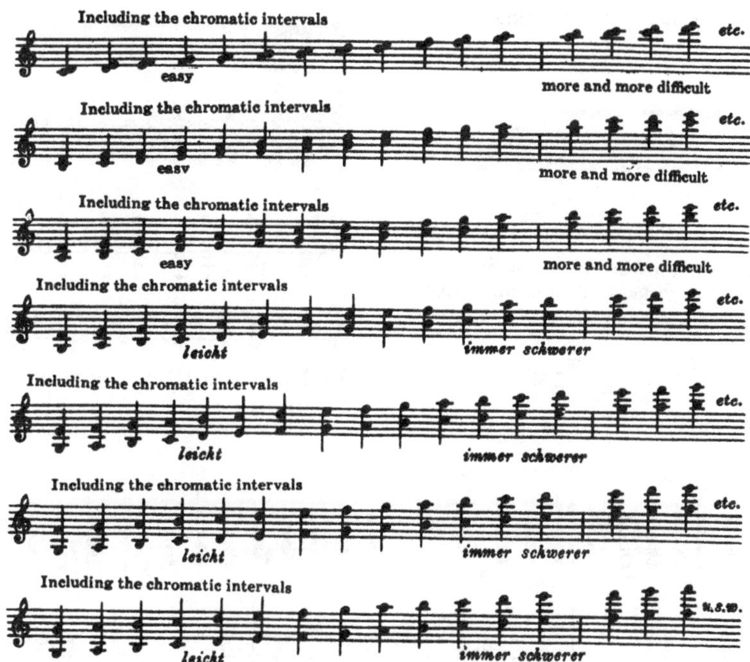

Occasionally one note is played on two strings simultaneously. It is advisable to limit this effect to D, A and E. Only these three notes are easy to execute on two strings; they have a different timbre on each and a full tone, due to the open string:

There is no open string in the other unisons:

Their execution is rather difficult and, hence, their intonation rarely exact.

A lower string can cross a higher open string if it is given an ascending movement while the open string continues in the manner of a pedal-point:

The D remains open while the ascending scale is played on the fourth string throughout.

Ninths and tenths are possible, but far less easy than the preceding intervals. It is better to write them for the orchestra only if the lower string remains open; in this case they offer no difficulty:

Leaps between double stops are to be avoided because they are extremely difficult if not impossible. They demand too great a change in the position of the hand:

Generally such leaps can be used only if the two higher notes and the two lower notes form one chord which could also be played together, for instance:

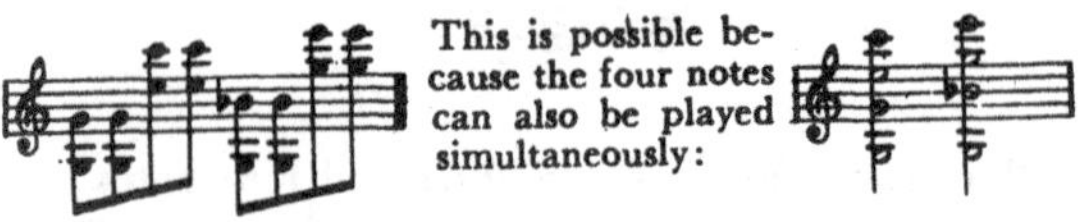

In the following example the four notes could be played simultaneously only with considerable difficulty (except in the last chord). Nevertheless, the leap is here easy because the two lower notes are played on open strings, the two upper ones with the first and third fingers:

Among the chords of three and especially four notes those are always the best and most sonorous which contain most open strings. I consider it even better to confine oneself to chords of three notes if no open string is available for the four-part chord.

The following lists furnish a summary of the most frequently used, most sonorous and least difficult chords of this kind:

In those marked * it is better to omit the lowest note.

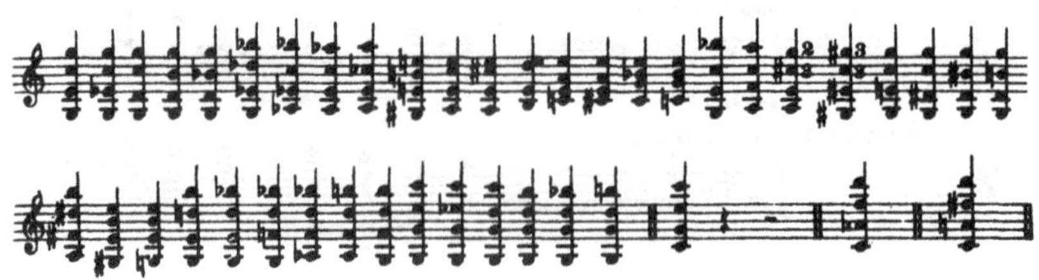

Easy in a moderate tempo:

All sequences of chords combined in this fashion are not difficult. They can also be executed in arpeggio, i.e. consecutively; particularly in pianissimo this often creates the most agreeable effects:

There are furthermore combinations similar to those above, in which the four notes could be played simultaneously only with great difficulty, whereas they are easily executed in arpeggio by means of the first or second fingers passing from the fourth string to the first in order to play the lowest and then the highest note:

By omitting the lowest or highest notes in the preceding examples, one obtains as many three-part chords. To these are to be added the chords which result from combining the various tones of the E-string with the two open center strings, or those of the E and A-strings with the open D-string:

If it is desired to strike one isolated D-minor or major chord, it is not advisable to choose the position marked NB in the foregoing example because it is too difficult without similar chords preceding it. It is better to use the following position, which is easy to play and more sonorous because of the two open strings:

The preceding examples show that all three-part chords are possible on the violin if one takes care, in those without open strings, to spread their tones sufficiently to allow intervals of a fifth or sixth between them. The sixth may be placed either above or below, or both.

Sequences of diminished seventh chords are also easy because the fingering remains the same while the chord changes to the next position:

Certain chords of three notes are practicable in two ways, and it is better to choose the one containing an open string, for instance:

Double trills in thirds can be executed, starting from the low B♭:

But as they are more difficult than simple trills and the same effect can be obtained by dividing the violins, it is usually advisable to avoid them in the orchestra.

The *tremolo* (simple or double) produces various excellent effects. It expresses unrest, excitement, terror in all nuances of piano, mezzoforte or fortissimo if it is employed on one or two of the three strings, G, D, A, and if it is not carried much above the middle B♭:

(Double stops)

The tremolo was used with the greatest effect by Weber and Wagner, perhaps most significantly in the first act of "Walkuere" with Siegmund's call, "Waelse, Waelse!" (Example 2.)

No. 2. Walkuere, Act I.

Horn III u. IV in D.
I. Viol. II.
Viola.
Siegm.
der mich nun Sehnsucht zieht, die mit sü-ßem Zau-ber sehrt, im Zwan-ge hält sie der Mann, der
Alle Vlc. unis.
Kontrab.
poco a poco cresc.
p molto cresc.
in F.
I. II. Hörner. III. IV.
3 Fag.
Pauke II. (tief F)
(trem.)
mich Wehr-losen höhnt! Wäl-se! Wäl-se! Wo ist dein Schwert, das starke Schwert, das im Sturm ich
Vlc.
Kontrab.

2 Fl.
2 Ob.
2 Klar. in B.
4 Hörner in F.
2 Fag.
1 Tromp. in C.
3 Pos.
Kontrab.-Pos.
Pauke.
Viol. I.
Viol. II.
Viola.
Siegm.
Vlc.
Kontrab.
cresc.
dim.
tr
(sehr bestimmt)
acceler.
Tempo I.
(geteilt)
(geteilt)
(Das Feuer bricht zusammen; es fällt aus der sprühenden Glut plötzlich ein greller Schein auf die Stelle des Eschenstammes, welche Sieglindes Blick bezeichnet hatte, und an der man jetzt deutlich einen Schwertgriff haften sieht.)
schwän - ge, bricht mir hervor aus der Brust, was wütend das Herz noch hegt? Was

What a magnificent idea is the picture of the monotonously raging storm at the beginning of "Walkuere". The whipping of the rain and hail by the wind is wonderfully depicted by the following sound-conception (Example 3).

No. 3. Walkuere, Beginning

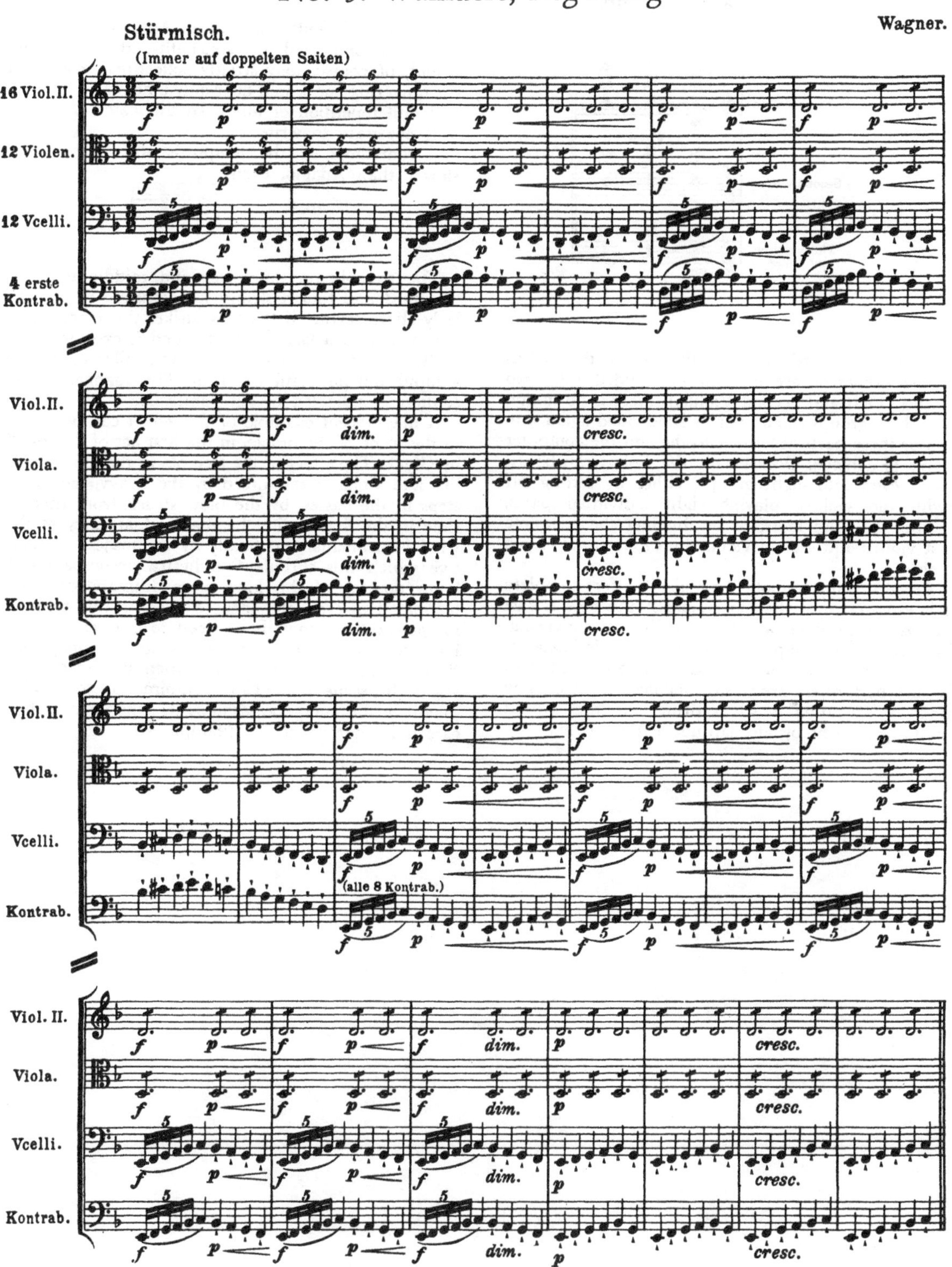

The tremolo has a stormy and vehement character on the medium tones of the E and A-strings in fortissimo.

It becomes ethereal and seraphic when employed in several voices and pianissimo on the high tones of the E-string:

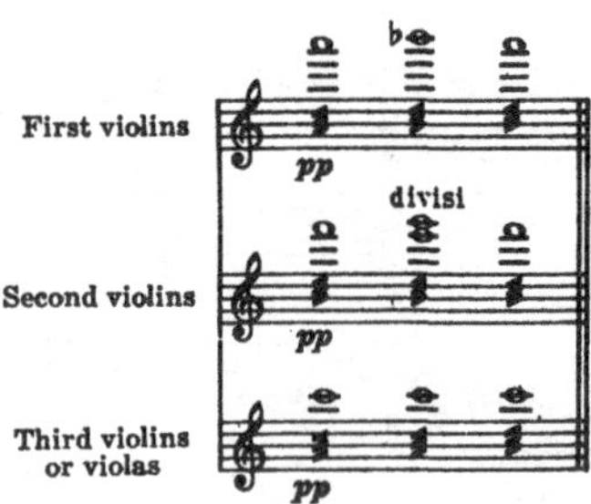

It may be mentioned here that, while the violins in the orchestra are customarily divided into two groups (First and Second Violins), there is no reason why these groups should not be subdivided again into two or three parts according to the aim the composer wants to achieve. Occasionally the violins can be divided even into eight groups, either by setting off eight solo violins, playing eight individual parts, against the solid mass, or by dividing the complete first violins and second violins into four equal choirs each.

I revert to the tremolo. To make its effect complete it is essential that the movement of the bow is fast enough to produce a real trembling or quivering. Therefore, the composer must precisely indicate its execution in accordance with the tempo of the piece; for the performers are always inclined to avoid any mode of execution which is tiring, and they would not fail to profit by any latitude left to them.

In an Allegro assai a tremolo indicated: and executed:

is entirely sufficient. But if in an Adagio the tremolo were also indicated by sixteenths, the performer would, of course, play strictly sixteenths; instead of the quivering one would hear only a heavy and dull repetition of tones. In this case it is necessary to write and sometimes, if the tempo is still slower than Adagio, even

The tremolo on the lower and middle tones of the third and fourth strings in fortissimo is particularly characteristic if the bow strikes the strings near the bridge. In a large orchestra and if executed well by the players, it produces a sound similar to that of a rapid and powerful waterfall. This manner of execution is indicated by *sul ponticello.*

A magnificent example of this effect can be found in the scene of the oracle, in the first act of "Alceste" by Gluck. The effect of the tremolo in the second violins and violas is reinforced by the heavy, menacing steps in the basses, by the blow struck from time to time in the first violins, by the gradual entry of the wind instruments, and finally by the majestic recitative which this turbulent orchestra accompanies. I know nothing of this kind more dramatic or more terrible. However, the idea to execute this tremolo *sul ponticello* cannot be ascribed to Gluck; it is not indicated in his score. The honor for it belongs entirely to M. Habeneck, who, when rehearsing this wonderful scene at the Conservatoire, had the violins play it in this energetic fashion; its superiority in this case is incontrovertible. (Example 4.)

No. 4. Alceste, Act I.

Moderato.
Oboen.
I.
Viol.
II.
Viola.
S.
Bassi.
ver au des-sus d'un mor-tel.
Hauch scheint mein Herz zu durch-wehn.
Quel-le lumière é-cla-
Ha! welches Glanzes Ent-
Ob.
tan - te en - tou - re la sta-tu - e et bril-le sur l'au-tel!
zün - dung! ver - klärt ist Phö - bos Bild-nis, hell-strahlend sein Al - tar!
Tout m'an-non - ce du Dieu la pré-sen - ce su - prê - me, ce
Glän - - zend kün-det er uns, daß er sich jetzt ge - na - het. Der
Dieu sur nos des-tins veut s'ex-pli - quer lui - mê - me; l'horreur d'u-ne sainte é - pou-van - te
Gott verhei-ßet selbst des Göt-terspruchs Ver - kündung. Mit hei - li-ger Schreckens-em-pfin-dung

Flöten.
unis.
Ob.
I.
Viol.
II.
Viola.
S.
se ré-pand au-tour de moi,
hat er-füllt er mei-ne Brust!
la ter-re sous mes
Des heil'-gen Tem-pels
Bassi.
Fl.
pas fuit et se pré-ci-pi-te,
Grund wird unter mir er-schüttert!
le marbre est a-ni-mé,
Das Bild scheinet be-seelt!
Klar. in C.
Hörner in G.
Pos.
le saint tré-pied s'a-gi-te,
Der heil'ge Dreifuß zit-tert!
tout se rem-plit d'un juste ef-
Al-les bebt ah-nungsvoll zu-

Fl.
Ob.
Klar. in C.
Hrnr. in G.
Pos.
I. Viol. II.
Viola.
S.
froi, il va par - ler: Sai - si de
rück! Bald spricht der Gott! Ver - ehrt die
Bassi.
I. Viol. II.
Viola.
S.
crainte et de re - spect, peu - ple! ob - serve un pro - fond si - len - ce!
Fül - le sei - ner Macht, Völ - ker! ver - ehrt sie durch from - mes Schwei - gen!
Bassi.
I. Viol. II.
Viola.
S.
Rei - ne, dé - pose à son as - pect le vain or - gueil de la puis - san - ce! trem - - ble!
Für - stin! menschli - cher Hoheit Pracht und eit - ler Stolz muß sich hier beu - gen! Zitt' - - re!
Bassi.

At the beginning of the second act of "Tristan" this tremolo effect near the bridge (depicting the rustling of the leaves and the blowing of the wind) produces a feeling of awe and apprehension in the listener. (Example 5.)

No. 5. Tristan, Act II.

Wagner.

Flöte II u. III.
Klar. I u. II. in B.
I u. II.
Hrnr. in F.
III.
Fag. I u. II.
Viol. I.
Viol. II.
Violen.
Isolde.
dich täuscht des Lau - - bes säuselnd Ge - -
Vcelli.
Ob.
Engl. Hrn.
Klar. in B.
Fag.
Baßklar. in B.
Viol. I. (geteilt)
Viol. II. (get.)
Violen. (get.)
Isolde.
tön, das la - chend schüt - telt der Wind.
Vcelli. (get.)
Kontrab.
pp
sfp
p
cresc.
(am Stege)
(natürlich)
molto cresc.
etc.

For certain accompaniments of a dramatic and agitated character a *broken tremolo* is sometimes used with good effect, either on one string:

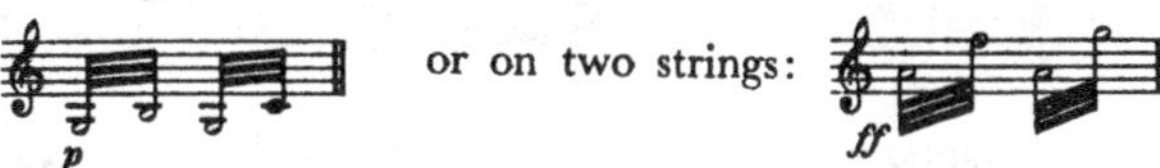

Finally, there is a kind of tremolo which is no longer used, but which Gluck employed admirably in his recitatives. It may be called the *undulating tremolo.* It consists in playing a number of slurred notes on the same tone at a slow speed while the bow does not leave the string. In these not strictly measured accompaniments it is hardly possible for all the performers to play the same number of notes in a bar; some play more and some less. This difference causes a kind of wavering or indecision in the orchestra, perfectly adapted to render the uneasiness and anxiety in certain scenes. Gluck wrote it thus:

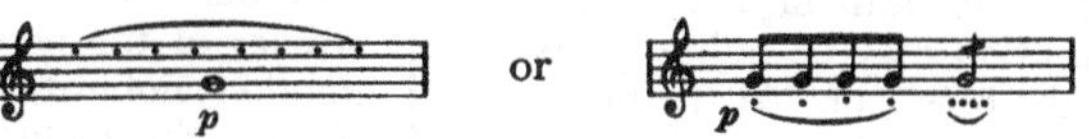

The manner of *bowing* is very important and greatly influences the sonority and expression of motives and melodies. It must be carefully indicated according to the nature of the idea to be rendered. The following signs should be used:

For the *staccato* or light détaché, which is executed over the whole length of the bow by a succession of small strokes, moving the bow only a little at a time:

For the grand, broad staccato (*grand détaché porté*), which is intended to give the string as much sonority as possible by letting it vibrate after the bow has struck it vigorously (this is particularly suitable for pieces of a proud, magnificent character and of moderate speed):

Notes repeated two, three or four times (according to the tempo) give more power and vividness to the tone of the violins and are suitable for various orchestral effects in all kinds of shadings:

However, in phrases of a broad tempo and vigorous character simple notes in *grand détaché* produce a much better effect, unless one wants to employ a real tremolo on each note.

The following phrase

if played in the indicated slow tempo, will sound much more nobly and vigorously than the following:

I believe composers would be too meticulous if they indicated down-bows and up-bows in their scores (as it is done in violin etudes and concertos). But if particular lightness or power or breadth of tone is required, the manner of execution may be indicated as follows: "At the point of the bow", or "At the heel" (lower end of the bow), or "Whole bow on each note". Likewise, "Near the bridge" or "On the finger-board" designate the spot close to or at a distance from the bridge where the bow should strike the strings. The metallic, somewhat rough tones produced near the bridge differ greatly from the soft, veiled tones played over the finger-board.

I should like to cite some practical experiences regarding bowing and fingering. It is customary in many orchestras to indicate uniform bowing for the violins (as well as the other string instruments). Of course, the resulting evenness of bowing gives elegance to the playing of the violin group and is restful to the eyes of the audience. Nevertheless, I would not recommend using this device indiscriminately, for the following reasons.

To curb the different temperaments in bowing means to destroy the soulful expression in the rendering of a melody. One violinist, in accordance with his feelings and technical skill, may need four strokes of the bow to play a melody expressively; another violinist, only two. If the first one is forced to play this melody also with two strokes, his performance will obviously lose its intensity and become poor and dull. Furthermore, if a composer has indicated one bow for a phrase of, let us say, four or more bars, its broad character would be destroyed if it were broken up uniformly into four to six parts by all violinists. In such cases it is my principle to follow strictly the composer's phrase-marks (breathing-marks) only at the beginning and end of a phrase; within the phrase I let each violinist change the bow as he wishes.

For composers it is very important to consider carefully the problem of up-bows and down-bows when they want to achieve certain nuances. For instance, during the first rehearsal of my "Sinfonia Domestica" in New York the theme

did not produce the intended impression of serene gaiety with the indicated bowing, but sounded lame and dull. At last I conceived the idea of having it played in this way:

At once the theme had the cheerfulness desired by me, the dot on the second and fourth eighths was observed automatically, and the passage, whether in upper or inner parts or in the bass, sparkled through the whole orchestra with the same intensity. I had the second theme of the piece phrased accordingly and obtained the same effect:

Therefore, dear fellow composers, watch the up-bow and down-bow! A small bowing-mark at the right place is often more effective than the most eloquent expression marks such as "gay", "grazioso", "spirited", "smiling", "defiant", "furious" etc. Our worthy instrumentalists and their dear conductors pay very little attention to them.

As to fingering, I found, when rehearsing Berlioz' "Fête chez Capulet", that the beginning of the partly chromatic phrase for the violins never sounded quite clear as long as but one violinist played the chromatic scale by sliding up or down with his finger. Finally I prescribed a separate finger for each note. At once the disturbing sounds caused by the sliding stopped and the passage became faultless. This experience gave me the idea to mark this fast violin passage from my "Sinfonia Domestica"

with the following fingering:

This passage is absolutely unclear and blurred with the usual fingering, which would be more appropriate for the howling of the storm in the Pastoral Symphony.

In a symphonic work where the terrible is combined with the grotesque, the back of the bow has been used to strike the strings. This is called *col legno* (with the wood). This strange device should be employed very rarely and only for a very definite purpose. Only in a large orchestra is its effect sufficiently noticeable. The numerous bows quickly falling on the strings produce a kind of crackling sound which would be scarcely audible with a small number of violins, so weak and short is the sound in this case.

This *col legno* symbolizes the snorting of the horse in Liszt's "Mazeppa", the devilish giggling of Mime in Wagner's "Siegfried". (Examples 6, 7.)

No. 6. Mazeppa

Fl.
Ob.
Engl. Hrn.
Klar. in D.
Klar. in A.
Baßkl. in C.
Fag.
Trp. in Es.
Viol. I.
Viol. II.
Violen.
Vcelli.
Kontrab.
marc.
rf
simile

a 2
Fl.
Ob.
Engl. Hrn.
Klar. in D.
Klar. in A.
Baßkl. in C.
Fag.
Trp. in Es.
Viol. I.
Viol. II.
Violen.
Vcelli.
Kontrab.

No. 7. Siegfried, Act II.

Wagner.

(stacc.)
Engl. Hrn.
cresc.
Klar. II. in B.
(stacc.)
Klar. III. in A.
p cresc.
Baßklar. in B.
3 Fag.
(geteilt) (ohne Dämpfer)
Viol. I.
(col legno)
p cresc.
(ohne Dämpfer) pizz.
Viol. II.
(ohne Dämpfer)
Viola.
fz p
Mime.
bald; ohne Wach und Wissen stracks streckst du die Glie - der. Liegst du nun da,
(ohne Dämpfer) pizz.
Vlc.
(ohne Dämpfer)
(col legno)
pizz.
K. B.
(geteilt) (nur 4)
(ohne Dämpfer)
(col legno)
pizz.
p cresc.
Engl. Hrn.
Klar. II. in B.
Klar. III. in A.
Fag. I. II.
(col legno)
Viol. I.
Viol. II.
Viola.
Mime.
leicht könnt ich die Beu - te neh-men und ber - gen; doch er - wach - test du
(col legno)
Vlc.
K. B.
cresc.

Kl. Fl.
Gr. Fl. I.
3 Ob.
Engl. Hrn.
Klar. I. II. in B.
Klar. III. in A.
Baßklar. in B.
I. II. in F.
Hörner.
III. in E.
3 Fag.
I.
Viol.
II.
Viola.
Mime.
Vlc.
K.B.
p cresc.
cresc.
fp
f
dim.
2 u. 3.
1.
(zu 2)
sfz
(geteilt)
pizz.
(Bog.)
je, nir-gends wär' ich si-cher vor dir, hätt' ich selbst auch den Ring.

Kl. Fl.
Gr. Fl. I.
3 Ob.
Engl. Hrn.
Klar. I. II. in B.
Klar. III. in A.
Baßklar. in B.
Hörner.
3 Fag.
Viol. I.
II.
Viola.
Mime.
Vlc.
K. B.
dim.
p
cresc.
sfz
(zu 2)
col legno
pizz.
D'rum mit dem Schwert, das so scharf du schuf'st, hau ich dem Kind' den Kopf erst ab:

The so-called *harmonics* (flageolet tones) are produced by touching the strings lightly with the fingers of the left hand. Thereby the fingers divide the length of the strings at certain spots (the nodal points) without, however, pressing them down upon the fingerboard. These harmonics have a peculiar character of mysterious softness; some are very high and thus greatly extend the upper range of the violin. A distinction is made between *natural* and *artificial* harmonics. The *natural* harmonics are produced by touching lightly certain spots on the *open* strings. Those responding most safely and sonorously are listed below. The black (quarter) notes represent the real pitch of the harmonics; the white (whole) notes indicate the points touched on the open string.

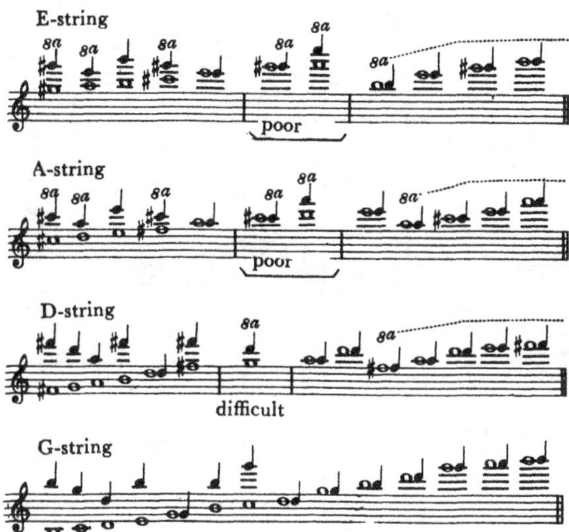

The *artificial* harmonics are obtained very clearly over the whole range of the scale by pressing the first finger firmly on the string (as a kind of movable nut) and touching the indicated point on the string lightly with the other finger.

The octave, lightly touched, produces its unison:

This fingering is not easy and is used almost only on the fourth string.

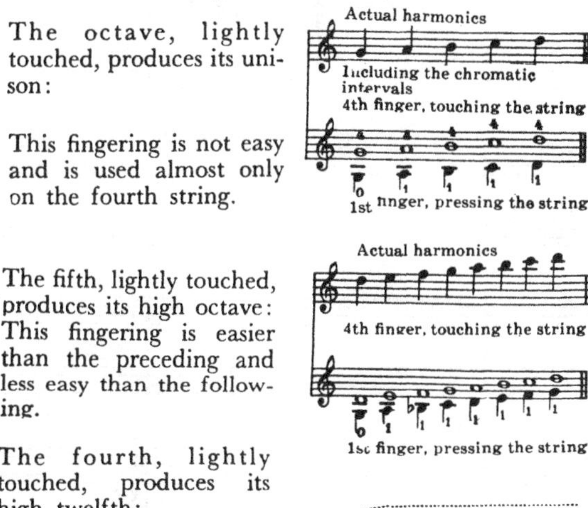

The fifth, lightly touched, produces its high octave: This fingering is easier than the preceding and less easy than the following.

The fourth, lightly touched, produces its high twelfth:

Actual harmonics
Fingers touching
Finger pressing

This fingering is the easiest and therefore to be preferred, except when the harmonic is the twelfth of an open string; in that case the fingering with the fifth is preferable. Thus, to sound a single high B, it is better to use this position: ; the open E-string, whose fifth lightly touched produces its higher octave (B), sounds better than a string pressed down by the first finger, as e.g.:

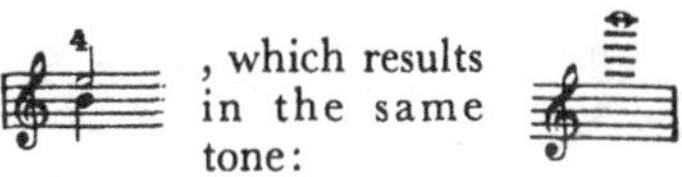

, which results in the same tone:

The fingerings with a touched major or minor third are used very little; the harmonics produced do not sound well.

The major third, lightly touched, produces its high double octave:

The minor third, lightly touched, produces its high major seventeenth:

The major sixth, lightly touched, produces its high twelfth:

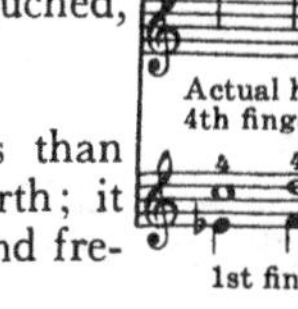

This fingering is used less than that with the touched fourth; it is nevertheless quite good and frequently useful.

I repeat, the positions with touched fourths and fifths are by far the most advantageous.

Some virtuosos produce double stops in harmonics; but this effect is so difficult and therefore dangerous that composers are to be warned against using it.

The harmonics on the fourth string have a flute-like character; they are preferable for a *cantabile* execution of a slow melody. Paganini used them with wonderful success in the prayer from "Moses". The harmonics on the other strings become increasingly more delicate and soft as they rise in pitch. This, as well as their crystalline sound, makes them especially appropriate for those chords which may be called fairy-like: harmonic effects which fill our imagination with radiant dreams and conjure the most delicate images of a poetic, supernatural world. Although our young violinists have become quite familiar with these effects, they should not be used in fast movements or at least not in rapid successions of notes if their perfect execution is to be ensured.

Of course, the composer can employ them in two, three or four parts according to the number of violin parts. The effect of such sustained chords is very impressive if they are warranted by the subject of the piece and well combined with the rest of the orchestra. I have used such chords for the first time, in three parts, in the scherzo of a symphony, sustained above a fourth violin part not in harmonics, which trills continuously on the lowest note. The extraordinary delicacy of the harmonics is enhanced here by the use of mutes; thus softened they rise to the extreme heights of the musical scale, which could hardly be reached by ordinary tones. (Example 8.)

No. 8. Roméo et Juliette, Scherzo de la Reine Mab
Berlioz.
Allegretto.
Solo.
Flöten.
Engl. Horn.
Viol. I. (geteilt)
Flageolettöne.
wirklicher Klang...
leichter Finger...
fester Finger......
Viol. II. (geteilt)
leicht F.
fester F.
Soli.
Violen.
Vcelli I.
Vcelli II.
Fl.
Engl. Hrn.
Flageoletton.
Harfe I.
Harfe II.
Viol. I.
Viol. II.
Violen.
Vcelli.

Fl.
Engl. H.
Viol. I.
Viol. II.
Violen.
Vcelli.
Klar. in B.
Harfe I.
Harfe II.
Flageolettöne.
pizz.
ppp
8va
tr

In writing such chords in harmonics, it is absolutely necessary to indicate by notes of different size and shape, placed one above the other: *the note for the finger touching the string* and that of *the actual harmonic* (on open strings); and *the note for the pressing finger, the touching finger* and *the actual harmonic* (in the other cases). This sometimes results in three notes for a single tone, but without this precaution the execution might easily become a hodgepodge, in which even the composer would have difficulty to recognize his own intentions.

This is no longer necessary. The sign ° above the note (the actual pitch) is now sufficient to indicate the execution in harmonics. The older notation makes the score too complicated.

Mutes (sordines) are small wooden devices which are placed on the bridge of string instruments in order to diminish their volume of sound. They give the instrument at the same time a mournful, mysterious and soft expression, which is frequently and felicitously used in all styles of music. Mutes are usually employed in slow movements; but they are just as appropriate for fast and light pieces or for accompaniments in quick rhythms if the character of the piece demands them. Gluck proved this admirably in his sublime monologue of Alceste (Italian version), "Chi mi parla". (Example 9.)

No. 9. Alceste, Act II

Gluck.

When mutes are indicated, they are generally used by the whole string section. But more frequently than it is usually assumed there are circumstances where only a part of the strings (e.g. the first violins) employ mutes; the mixture of bright and muted tones produces a peculiar color. Sometimes the character of the melody is so different from that of the accompaniment that the use of mutes has to be planned accordingly.

The composer, when indicating the use of mutes in the middle of a piece (by the words *con sordini*), must not forget to allow sufficient time for putting them on. He should provide a rest in the violins, equal in length to about two bars in 4-4 time, moderato. The rest may be shorter when the words *senza sordini* indicate that the mutes are to be removed; this can be done in much less time. The sudden transition from the muted tones to bright, natural ones (without mutes) is sometimes immensely effective in a large orchestra. (Example 10.)

No. 10. Romeo et Juliette, Scherzo de la Reine Mab

In the third act of "Meistersinger" (scene of Sachs and Walter) the mood of the dreamy young man in his conversation with Sachs is wonderfully painted by the entrance of the muted second violins. The device is as simple as it is ingenious (the two words are frequently synonymous). An equally wonderful example is the final scene of "Tristan" where Isolde rises from the prostration of despair to her last enchanted vision. The first violins had been silent for a long time and left the lead to the second violins; then, before Brangaene's words, "Sie wacht, sie lebt", they enter con sordini over muted horns with the theme of Isolde's Liebestod. The theme, the orchestration and the poetic idea combine into one of the most sublime effects.

There are new mutes which are fastened to the lower part of the bridge and which only have to be turned into position; but the tone of the violins suffers considerably.

The *pizzicato* (plucking of the strings) is generally used with bowed instruments. The resulting sounds serve as accompaniments and are very popular with the singers because they do not cover their voices. They are also important for symphonic effects and even in vigorous outbursts of the whole orchestra, where they may be employed in the whole choir of strings or only by one or two sections.

The Adagio of the Symphony in B♭ by Beethoven offers a charming example of pizzicato in the second violins, violas and basses while the first violins are played with the bow. The contrasting sounds are here blended in truly marvelous fashion with the melodic sighs of the clarinet, enhancing its expression. (Example 11.)

No. 11. Symphony in B♭, 2nd movement

If the pizzicato is employed in forte, it should be written neither too high nor too low. Extremely high tones are harsh and dry; the low ones are hollow. In a powerful tutti of wind instruments a pizzicato of all string instruments, like the following, will produce a striking impression:

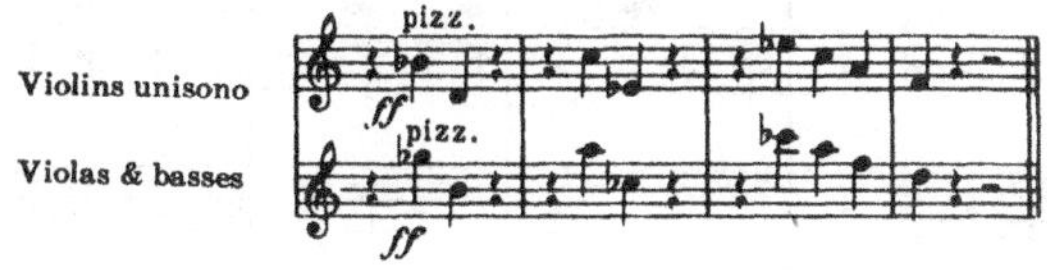

Pizzicato chords of two, three and four notes in fortissimo are equally valuable. The one finger employed glides so quickly across the strings that they sound almost simultaneously and seem to have been plucked at the same time. The various kinds of pizzicato accompaniments in piano have always a delicate effect. They afford a sense of relief to the listener and—if not abused—give a pleasing variety to the sound of the orchestra.

In the future the pizzicato will doubtless be used in even more original and attractive effects than heretofore. Violinists, not considering the pizzicato an integral part of violin technique, have given it hardly any serious attention. They are accustomed to use only the thumb and forefinger for pizzicato and hence are not able to play passages and arpeggios faster than sixteenths in 4-4 time of a very moderate tempo. If, instead, they were to lay down the bow, the little finger of the right hand could rest on the body of the violin and they could use the thumb and the other three fingers like guitar players. Thus they would soon acquire the skill to execute passages like those in the following example, which are impossible at the present time:

The figures above the notes refer to the fingers of the right hand, the letter T indicating the thumb

The repetition of the upper notes in these examples becomes quite easy if the first and second fingers are used alternatingly on the same string.

Short appoggiaturas are by no means impracticable in pizzicato. The following passage from the Scherzo of Beethoven's C-minor Symphony is always executed very well.

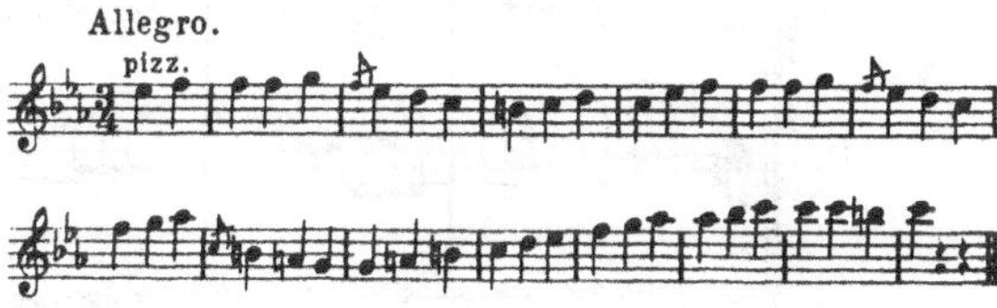

Some of our young violinists have learned from Paganini to play rapid descending scales in pizzicato by plucking the strings with the fingers of the left hand, which rests firmly on the neck of the violin. They sometimes combine pizzicato notes (always

played with the left hand) with bowed tones, even using the pizzicato as an accompaniment of a melody played by the bow. All players will doubtless become familiar with these various techniques in the course of time. Then composers will be able to take full advantage of them.

The following quotation from the overture to King Lear by Berlioz shows an ingenious employment of the pizzicato (Example 12).

No. 12. King Lear, Overture

Fl.
Ob.
a 2
Klar. in C.
I. II. in Es.
Hrnr.
III. IV. in C.
Fag.
sf
Trp. in E.
II.
Pos.
Tuba.
Pkn.
I.
Viol.
II.
Viola.
Vlc.
K.B.

Fl.
Ob.
Klar. in C.
I II in Es.
Hrnr.
III IV. in C.
Fag.
Trp. in E.
Pos.
Tuba.
Pkn.
I.
Viol.
II.
Viola.
Vlc.
K.B.
a2
pizz.
f

In this place I always have a feeling as if a string had burst in Lear's heart or, more realistically, a vein in the half-mad king's brain.

The possibilities of using the pizzicato in the orchestra for characterization are unlimited. To quote a few examples more, I mention: "Tristan", third act (Example 13); "Rheingold" (Example 14); "Meistersinger", Beckmesser's pantomime in the third act (Example 15).

No. 13. Tristan, Act III

No. 14. Rheingold

No. 15. Meistersinger, Act III

With their bows violinists are nowadays able to execute almost anything required. They play in the upper region almost as easily as in the middle; the most rapid runs, the most eccentric designs offer no difficulty. In an orchestra where they are sufficiently numerous, what one of them misses is executed by the others. Thus mistakes are hardly noticed and the final result is exactly as the author intended it. However, sometimes the rapidity, complexity or high position of tones would make a piece too dangerous; or else the author may want to be sure of a secure and neat execution: in such cases the violins should be divided, some playing one part of the passage, the rest another. Thus the notes of each section are interspersed with short rests, not noticed by the listener, which allow, as it were, a breathing space to the players and afford them time to reach difficult positions securely and to strike the strings with the necessary vigor.

If it is desired to have similar or still more difficult passages executed by all the violins, it will always be preferable to divide the first violins into two groups (as in the preceding example) and to let the second violins, also divided into two groups, simply double the two parts of the first violins, instead of giving one part to all the first violins and the other part to all the second violins. The distance between the two sections would disrupt the even flow of the passage and would make the joints between the parts too obvious. But if the parts are divided between the two players at each desk and each part is thus played on both sides of the orchestra, the fragments will connect smoothly and it will be impossible to notice the division of the passage. The listeners will believe to hear it executed by all the violins without interruption. Accordingly, the passage is written as follows:

Moreover, this procedure is applicable to all instruments of the orchestra which have the same quality and lightness of tone. It should be applied whenever a phrase is too difficult to be played well by a single instrument or a single group.

This conception applies to the style of instrumentation which I would call the classical. It stems from the spirit of chamber music and was transferred to the treatment of orchestras. Its main characteristic is that every figure can be executed with absolute clarity by all the instruments. Its opposite is the al-fresco treatment of the orchestra as introduced by Wagner. The classical stands in the same relation to the al-fresco style as that of the Florentine painters of the 14th and 15th centuries (which stems from miniature painting) to the broad manner of a Velasquez, Rembrandt, Franz Hals and Turner with their wonderfully shaded color combinations and differentiated light effects. The most obvious example of the fresco style is the treatment of the violins in the Magic Fire Music in the third act of "Walkuere" (Example 16). Executed by 16 to 32 violinists, this passage achieves a wonderful, exciting effect. A better musical description of the seething flames flickering in a thousand tints cannot be imagined. An easier, perhaps somewhat slower figuration would probably have made an impression of stiffness such as I cannot help noticing in the "Rheingold" during the song of the Rhine Maidens swimming around the reef:

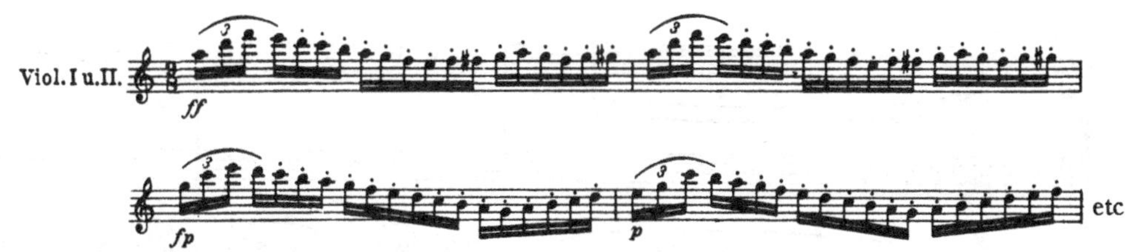

No. 16. Walkuere, Magic Fire Music

2 kl. Fl.
2 gr. Fl.
3 Ob.
Klar. III in D.
I. Klar. in A. II.
Engl. Hrn.
Horn I.II. in E.
Baßklar. in A.
3 Harfen.
p stacc.
Glocken-spiel.
Viol. I.
Viol. II.
(Hier bricht die lichte Flackerlche aus)
pizz.
Viola.

2 kl. Fl.
p
cresc.
poco a poco
a 2
2 gr. Fl.
cre - scen - do
1.
2 Ob.
2.3.
Klar. in D.
2 Klar. in A.
Engl. Hrn.
Horn I. II. in E.
cre - scen - do poco
Baßklar. in A.
2 Harfen
cresc.
Glocksp.
Viol. I.
Viol. II.
arco
Violen.
(geteilt)
arco
p

stacc.
poco a poco cresc.
2 kl. Fl.
2 gr. Fl.
3 Ob.
Klar. in D.
2 Klar. in A.
Engl. Hrn.
4 Hrnr. in E.
p cresc. poco a poco
Baßklar. in A.
3 Hrfn. I. II. III.
3 Hrfn. IV. V. VI.
p stacc.
Glockenspiel.
Viol. I.
Viol. II.
Violen.
p
cresc.
pizz.

3 kl. Fl.
f
3 gr. Fl.
3 Ob.
Klar. in D.
2 Klar. in A.
Engl. Hrn.
4 Hrnr. in E.
Baßklar. in A.
Hrfn. I. II. III.
Hrfn. IV. V. VI.
Viol. I.
Viol. II.
Violen.
(8)
p cresc.
p cresc.

2 kl.Fl.
2 gr.Fl.
3 Ob.
Klar. in D.
2 Klar. in A.
Engl.Hrn.
I. II. in F.
4 Hörner
III. IV. in E.
(zu 2)
2 Fag.
Baßklar. in A.
Hrfn. I. II. III.
Hrfn. IV. V. VI.
Glocksp.
Viol. I.
Viol. II.
Violen.
f
più f

2 kl. Fl.
2 gr. Fl.
3 Ob.
Klar. in D.
2 Klar. in A.
Engl. Hrn.
I. II. in F.
4 Hörner
III. IV. in E.
2 Fag.
Hrfn. I. II. III.
Hrfn. IV. V. VI.
Glocksp.
Triangl.
Viol. I.
Viol. II.
Violen.
Kontrab.
ff stacc.
pizz.
(Lichte Brunst umgibt Wotan mit wildem Flackern.
Er weis't mit dem Speere gebieterisch dem Feuermeere

2 kl.Fl.
2 gr.Fl
3 Ob.
Klar. in D.
3 Klar. in A.
Engl.Hrn.
I.II.in F.
4 Hrnr.
III.IV.in E.
(3tes allein)
3 Fag.
Baßklar. in A.
Hrfn. I.II.III.
Hrfn. IV.V.VI.
Glocksp.
Triangl.
Becken mit Paukenschlägeln.
Viol.I.
Viol.II.
Violen.
Kontrab.
dim.
pizz.
den Umkreis des Felsenrandes zur Strömung an; alsbald zieht es sich nach dem Hintergrunde, wo es nun fort-

2 kl. Fl.
2 gr. Fl.
3 Ob.
Klar. in D.
2 Klar. in A.
Engl. Hrn.
Horn III in E.
3 Fag.
Baßklar. in A.
Hrfn. I. II. III.
Hrfn. IV. V. VI.
Glocksp.
Viol. I.
Viol. II.
Violen. (geteilt)
Vcelli. (geteilt)
Kontrab.
dim.
mf
(mit Dämpfern)
(6)(mit Dämpfern)
während den Bergsaum umlodert.)

I believe that passages on the fourth string and, for certain melodies, also the high tones on the third string could be used to much better advantage than has been the case heretofore. If a particular string is to be used for special effects, the point for changing the string should be clearly indicated. Otherwise the players would soon revert to the ordinary manner of execution, out of habit as well as for the sake of greater facility.

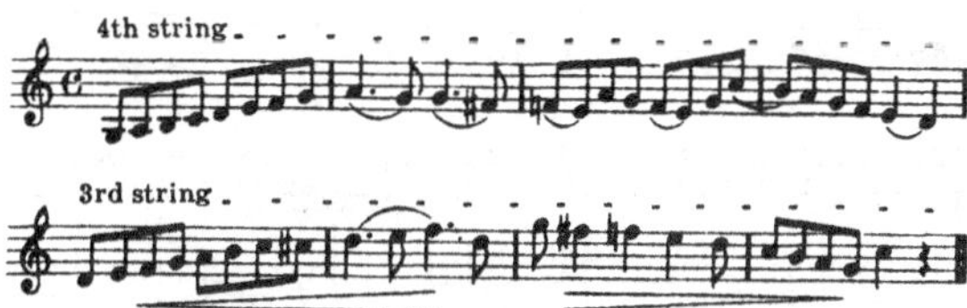

Frequently the first violins are doubled one octave lower by the second violins in order to give greater power to a passage. But unless the tones are extremely high, it is much better to double them in unison; the effect is incomparably stronger and finer. The overwhelmingly powerful effect shortly before the end of the first movement of the C-minor Symphony by Beethoven is due to the unison of the violins. In such cases it is not advisable to reinforce the violins by adding the violas in the lower octave. The low tones of the violas, being much weaker than those of the violins, would only produce an ineffective drone which would darken rather than reinforce the high tones of the violins.* Unless the viola part can be made more prominent, it is better to use the violas for reinforcing the violoncellos in the unison, insofar as their range permits, instead of in octaves. This is what Beethoven did in the C-minor Symphony. (Example 17.)

*Very true! This applies also to French horns and trumpets.

No. 17. Symphony in C minor, 1st movement

Violins have more brilliance and are played more easily in keys which permit the use of the open strings. Only the key of C appears to form an exception to this rule. It sounds less bright than the keys of A and E although all four open strings are available in C whereas only three remain in A, and but two in E.

I think it is possible to define the characteristic timbre of the different keys on the violin and their ease of execution, as follows:

Major keys

C	easy	grave, but dull and pallid
C♯	very difficult	less pallid, and more pronounced
D♭	difficult, but less so than C♯	majestic
D	easy	gay, noisy, somewhat commonplace
D♯	almost impracticable	dull
E♭	easy	majestic, rather bright, soft, grave
E	not very difficult	brilliant, gorgeous, noble
F♭	impracticable	
F	easy	energetic, vigorous
F♯	very difficult	brilliant, incisive
G♭	very difficult	less brilliant, softer
G	easy	rather gay, somewhat commonplace
G♯	almost impracticable	dull, but noble
A♭	not very difficult	soft, veiled, very noble
A	easy	brilliant, elegant, joyful
A♯	impracticable	
B♭	easy	noble, but without brilliance
B	not very difficult	noble, bright, radiant
C♭	almost impracticable	noble, but not very sonorous

Minor keys

C	easy	somber, not very sonorous
C♯	rather easy	tragic, bright, distinguished
D♭	very difficult	somber, not very sonorous
D	easy	plaintive, sonorous, somewhat commonplace
D♯	almost impracticable	dull
E♭	difficult	very dim and mournful
E	easy	shrill, commonplace
F♭	impracticable	
F	rather difficult	not very sonorous, somber, violent
F♯	less difficult	tragic, sonorous, incisive

G♭	impracticable	
G	easy	melancholy, rather sonorous, soft
G♯	very difficult	not very sonorous, sad, distinguished
A♭	very difficult, almost impracticable	very dull, sad, but noble
A	easy	rather sonorous, soft, sad, rather noble
A♯	impracticable	
B♭	difficult	somber, dull, rough, but noble
B	easy	very sonorous, wild, harsh, sinister, violent
C♭	impracticable	

The string instruments, the combination of which forms what is rather improperly called the quartet, are the basis and the constituent element of the whole orchestra. They possess the greatest power of expression and an indisputable wealth of timbres. Particularly the violins are capable of a great number of seemingly incompatible nuances. They convey (in a mass) force, lightness, grace, somber seriousness and bright joy, reverie and passion. The problem is only to know how to make them speak. Moreover, it is not necessary to calculate for them the duration of a sustained tone (as for the wind instruments) and to relieve them by occasional rests; one can be sure that they will never be out of breath. The violins are faithful, sensible, active and indefatigable servants.

Tender and slow melodies, confided too often nowadays to the wind instruments, are never rendered better than by a mass of violins. Nothing can equal the stirring sweetness of some twenty E-strings vibrated by as many skilled bows. Here is the true female voice of the orchestra, a voice at once passionate and chaste, penetrating and soft; whether it weeps, laments, prays or jubilates—no other voice possesses its range of expression. A minute movement of the arm, an unconscious impulse in the player, hardly noticeable with a single instrument, produce in a group the most wonderful shadings and arouse feelings which penetrate to the depth of the heart.

I need hardly mention here the angelic purity of the violins in the Prelude to "Lohengrin". The same violins, in a stirring passage in the third act of "Walkuere", reveal the human bliss of motherlove. (Example 18.) Then again, in the third act of "Siegfried", they depict the "selige Oede auf wonniger Hoeh" (haven of bliss on the mountainous height) in cloudless brilliance. (Example 19.)

No. 18. Walkuere, Act III

No. 19. Siegfried, Act III

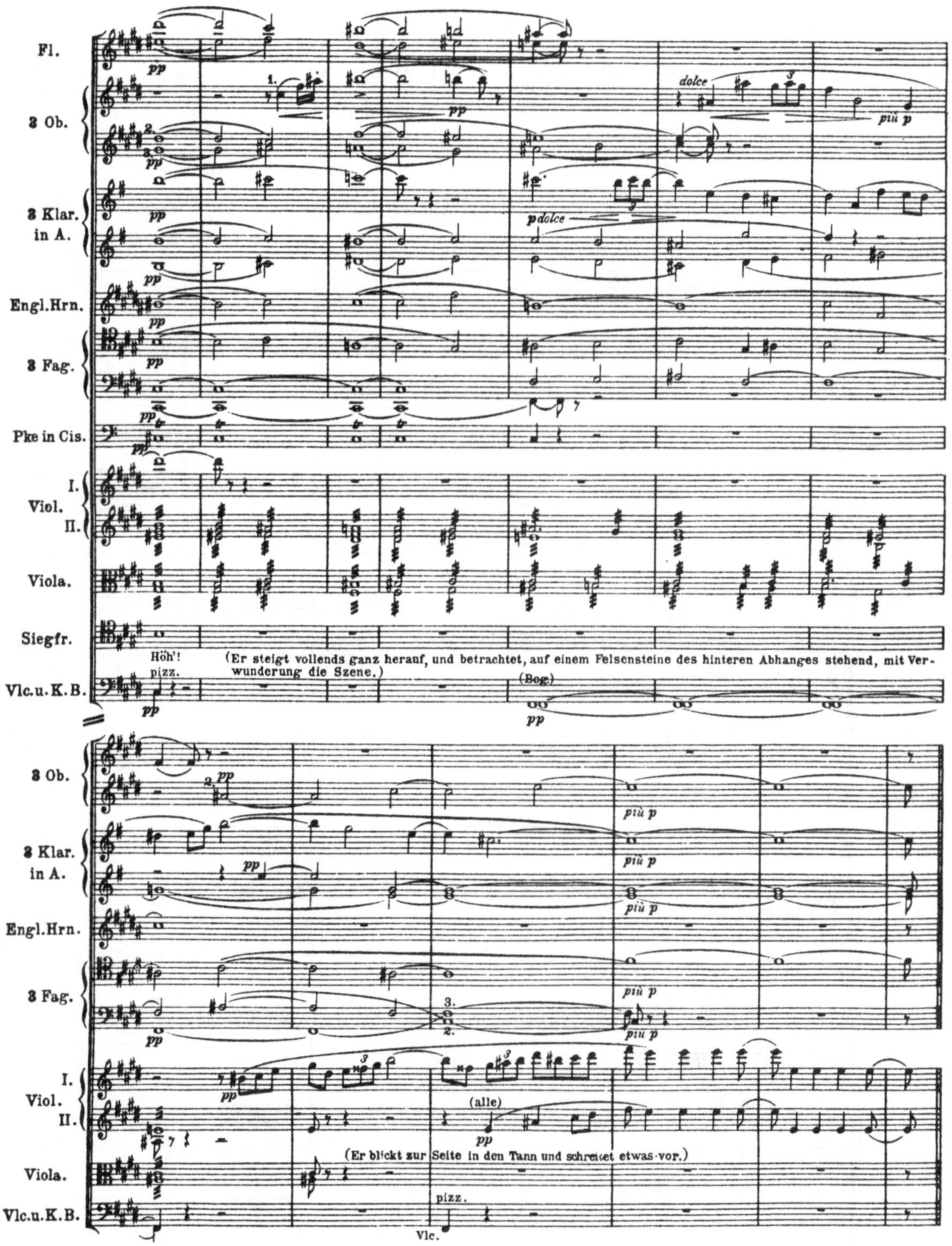
Fl.
3 Ob.
3 Klar. in A.
Engl.Hrn.
3 Fag.
Pke in Cis.
I. Viol. II.
Viola.
Siegfr.
Höh'!
(Er steigt vollends ganz herauf, und betrachtet, auf einem Felsensteine des hinteren Abhanges stehend, mit Verwunderung die Szene.)
Vlc.u.K.B.
pizz.
(Bog.)
dolce
più p
pdolce
(alle)
(Er blickt zur Seite in den Tann und schreitet etwas vor.)
Vlc.

With the same fidelity the violins lend their tones to express the apprentice's love (David in "Meistersinger"):

(Was war nur der Lene?)

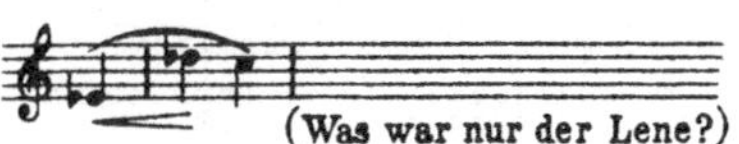

Wagner, inexhaustible in the symbolic use of the orchestral language, even individualized the first and second violins in "Tristan". The second violins, customarily somewhat inferior in execution and tone, serve as accompaniments for the secondary figures, Kurwenal, Brangaene and King Marke; while the warmer and nobler first violins—accustomed to lead—jubilate and suffer with the two heroes of the action.

At the close of this chapter I should like to warn against the so frequent misuse of the solo violin in the orchestra. The effect of a solo violin is so peculiar and conspicuous that it should never be employed without a compelling poetic motive. The great masters used it exclusively as a meaningful symbol: Beethoven, in the Benedictus of his Missa Solemnis, to let a pure soul praise the Lord in a fervent song; and Wagner, in "Rheingold", to unveil the innermost secrets of a woman's heart. (Example 20.)

No. 20. Rheingold

Wagner.

The economical use of the solo violin in Wagner's scores may serve to exemplify once more the old truth that a device becomes the more effective the less it is used.

The Viola

The four strings of the viola are tuned in fifths, like those of the violin, but a fifth lower:

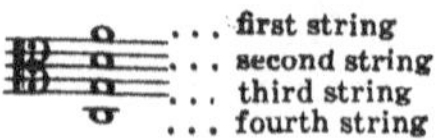

Its ordinary range is at least three octaves:

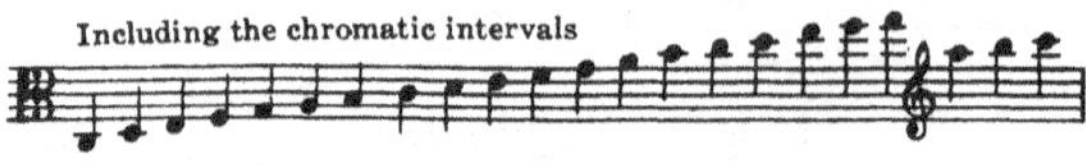

It is written in the alto-clef (C-clef on the third line); the G-clef is used for its highest notes.

All that has been said in the preceding chapter about trills, bowing, chords, arpeggios, harmonics etc., applies equally to the viola, which can simply be considered a violin tuned a fifth lower.

Of all the instruments in the orchestra it is the viola whose excellent qualities have been unappreciated for the longest time. It is just as agile as the violin. Its low strings have a characteristic, husky timbre while its high notes are distinguished by their mournfully passionate sound. The general character of its tones is one of profound melancholy and is notably different from that of the other string instruments. Nevertheless, it has long been neglected—or used, senselessly and ineffectually, for doubling the basses in the higher octave. The unjust treatment of this noble instrument has been due to several causes. In the first place, the masters of the 18th century, rarely writing four real voices, generally did not know what to do with the viola. Whenever they could not give it a few notes to fill up the harmony, they did not hesitate to write the odious *col basso*—often so carelessly that the resulting octaves conflicted either with the harmony or with the melody or with both. Furthermore, it was unfortunately impossible at that time to write any important passage for the viola requiring the most ordinary skill for its execution. Violists were always selected from the weaker violinists. If a musician was unable to fill creditably the post of a violinist, he was relegated to the violas. Thus, violists eventually could play neither the violin nor the viola. I must admit that even in our own time this prejudice against the viola has not disappeared completely. Even in our best orchestras we still find viola players who are no more proficient on that instrument than on the violin. But the harm caused by tolerating them is being recognized more and more; and little by little the viola will be entrusted only to skilled hands, just as the other instruments. Its timbre attracts and captivates one's attention so vividly that it is not necessary for an orchestra to have as many violas as second violins. The expressive powers of its timbre are so marked that, on the very rare occasions afforded by the old masters for its display, it never fails to answer their purpose.

It is the timbre of the viola which creates the deep impression in the famous scene in "Iphigénie en Tauride" where Orestes, exhausted, panting, tortured by remorse, falls asleep with the words: "Calm comes back to my heart"—while the orchestra, in somber excitement, utters sobs and convulsive sighs which are accompanied throughout by the terrible, persevering murmur of the violas. This incomparable piece of inspiration contains not a single note, either in the singer's part or in the instruments, without its own sublime intention; yet, the fascination which it exercises over the listeners, the awe which causes their eyes to dilate and fill with tears, are mainly attributable to the viola part and, particularly, to the timbre of its third string, to its syncopated rhythm and to the strange effect of the unison between its syncopated A and the A of the basses, whose different rhythm abruptly cuts through the syncope. (Example 21.)

No. 21. Iphigénie en Tauride, Act II

Ob.
I. Viol. II.
Viola.
Or.
rer le par - ri - ci - de O - res - te? Dieux
mal dem Mut - ter - mör - der Frie - den? O
Bassi.
Ob.
I. Viol. II.
Viola.
Or.
jus - tes! Ciel ven - geur! Oui,
Göt - ter! welch ein Glück! Ja,
Bassi.
I. Viol. II.
Viola.
Or.
oui! le cal - me ren - tre dans mon
ja, die Ru - he keh - ret mir zu -
Bassi.
I. Viol. II.
Viola.
Or.
coeur! (Il s'endort d'accablement.)
rück! (Er schläft ermattet ein.)
Bassi.

One of the first to discover the demonic possibilities of the viola was Meyerbeer. In his "Robert le Diable" he employed it ingeniously for the expression of pious awe and painful remorse.

In the Overture to "Iphigénie en Aulide" Gluck used the violas as the sole basis of the harmony, in this case not on account of its timbre but to accompany the melody of the violins as softly as possible; this makes the entrance of the basses in forte, after a long rest, much more formidable. Sacchini also gave the lower part to the violas alone in Oepidus' aria, "Your court became my refuge", without, however, intending to prepare a similar outburst; on the contrary, the instrumentation gives here a pleasant freshness and calm to the melody it accompanies. Melodies on the high strings of the viola achieve miracles in scenes of a religious or ancient character.

Cf. Wolfram's "Blick ich umher" ("Tannhaeuser", second act) and Lohengrin's Narration ("Lohengrin", third act)—divided violas in high position unisono with the violins; also the violas sounding like a distant organ, before Walther's Prize Song ("Meistersinger", third act). (Examples 22, 23, 24.)

No. 22. Tannhaeuser, Act II

Harfe.
Violen.
Wolfr.
und hold und tugendsam er-blick' ich Frauen, lieb-li-cher Blü-ten düf-te-reichster Kranz.
Harfe.
Violen.
Wolfr.
Es wird der Blick wohl trunken mir vom Schauen, mein Lied verstummt vor solcher An-mut
Vlc.
Harfe.
cresc.
dimin.
ritard.
Violen.
cresc.
dimin.
Wolfr.
Glanz.
Vlc.
cresc.
dimin.

No. 23. Lohengrin, Act III

*) Durch Flageolet hervorzubringen.

No. 24. Meistersinger, Act III

Wagner.

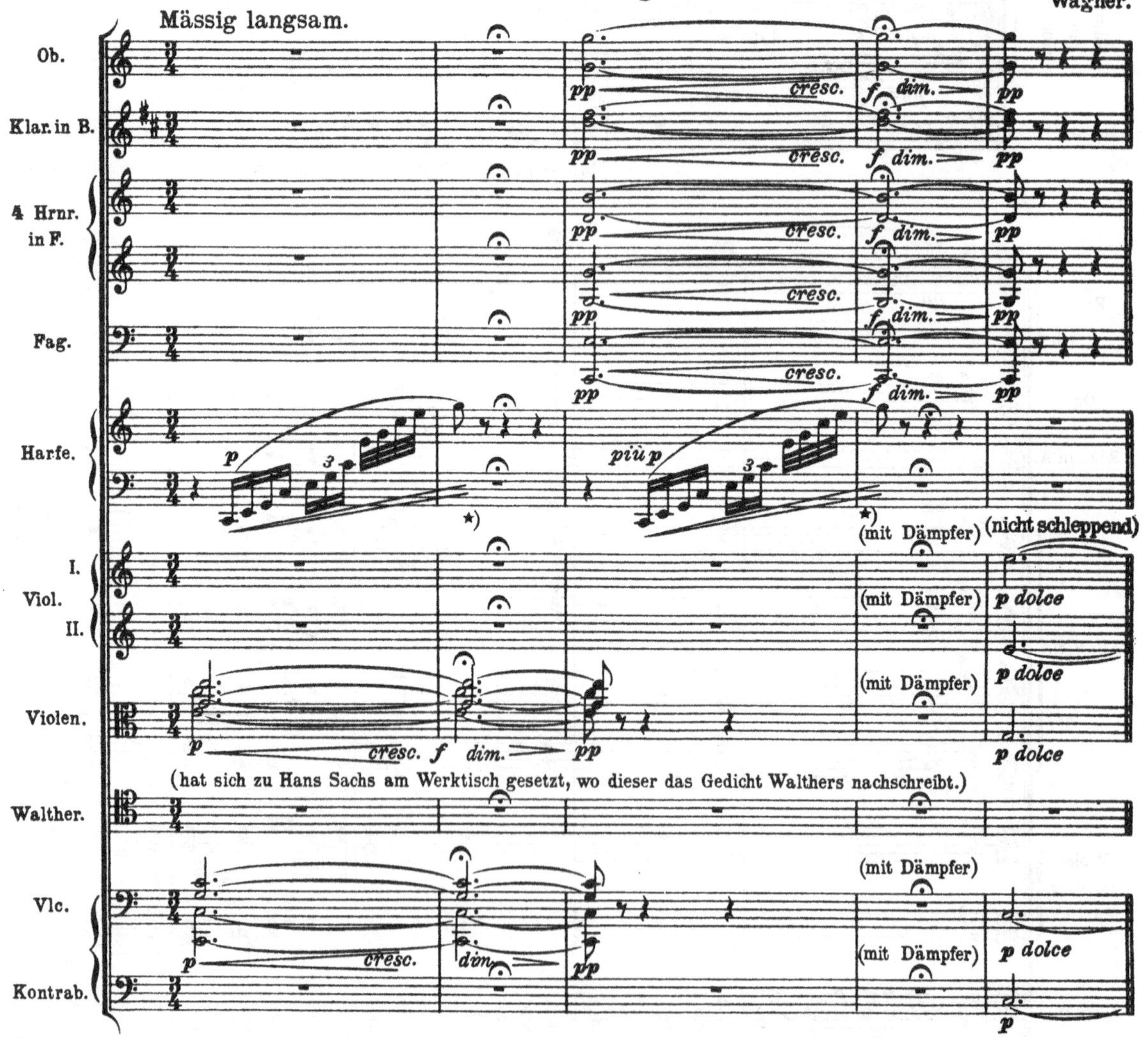

Mässig langsam.

Ob.
Klar. in B.
4 Hrnr. in F.
Fag.
Harfe.
Viol. I.
Viol. II.
Violen.
Walther.
Vlc.
Kontrab.

pp cresc. f dim. pp

p piùp

*) (mit Dämpfer) (nicht schleppend)

p dolce

p cresc. f dim. pp

(hat sich zu Hans Sachs am Werktisch gesetzt, wo dieser das Gedicht Walthers nachschreibt.)

p

*) Die beiden Fermaten müssen von besonders langer Dauer sein, um nach dem schnelleren Anschwellen ein sehr allmähliches Abnehmen ausführen zu lassen.

Spontini was the first to conceive the idea of assigning the melody in part to the violas in his wonderful prayer in "La Vestale". Méhul, allured by the sympathy between the tone of the violas and the dreamy character of Ossianic poetry, used them exclusively, without any violins, in his opera "Uthal". According to the critics of the time, this caused an unbearable monotony detrimental to the success of the work. It was this work which caused Grétry to exclaim: "I would give a Louis d'or for an E-string!" In fact, the viola timbre—so beautiful when judiciously employed and skillfully contrasted with that of the violins and other instruments—is bound to become tiresome; it is too unvaried for any other result.

In a scene of profound sadness (after Bruennhilde's words, "Weh, mein Waelsung" in the second act of "Walkuere") the violas, on the higher octave of the bass clarinets, express Wotan's dejection; an interesting contrast to this is the cowardly-gay dancing figure of the violas in the first act of "Siegfried" when Mime answers the menacing Wotan. (Examples 25, 26.)

No. 25. Walkuere, Act II

No. 26. Siegfried, Act I

Hrnr. in F.
Baßtrp. in Es.
Pke.
Viol. II.
Viola.
Mime.
Vlc.
K. B.
stärksten Helden keiner bestand's; Sieg - mund, der küh - ne, konnt's al - lein: — fechtend führt' er's im Streit, bis an
Hrnr. in F.
2 Fag.
4 Pos.
Viol. II.
Viola.
Mime.
Vlc.
K. B.
Wo - tans Speer es zersprang. Nun verwahrt die Stücken ein wei - ser Schmied, denn er weiß,
4 Hörner in F.
2 Fag.
Pke.
Viol. II.
Viola.
Mime.
Vlc.
K. B.
daß al - lein mit dem Wo - tans - Schwert — ein küh - - nes dum - - mes Kind,

Trp. I in C.
4 Hrnr. in F.
Fag.
Pke.
Viol.
Viola.
Mime.
Sieg - fried, den Wurm versehrt.
Vlc.
K. B.
Ob. I. II.
Engl. H.
Hrnr. in F.
Fag.
Pke.
Viol.
Viola.
Mime.
(ganz vergnügt)
Be - halt' ich Zwerg auch zwei - tens mein Haupt?
Wandrer.
(lachend)
Ha ha, haha
Vlc.
K. B.

The beautiful sound of the violas in the last movement of Beethoven's Ninth Symphony (with "Ihr stuerzt nieder, Millionen") and the comically gruesome solo viola in Aennchen's aria ("Freischuetz", second act) are quoted in Gevaert's work; the solemn introduction to the quartet in "Fidelio" I presume to be generally known and admired. Here I should like to quote the ecstatic solo viola which tells of the miracle of the love potion ("Tristan", first act); and the strange entrance of the violas in "Fidelio" (with "wie ein Schatten schwebt")—(fades like a shadow) where the interval of a third calls forth the picture of the languishing Florestan. (Examples 27, 28.)

No. 27. Tristan, Act I

a tempo (Mäßig.)
Ob.
2 Klar. in B.
Hrn. I in F.
Baßkl. in B.
3 Fag.
3 Pos.
Baßtuba.
Viol.
Violen.
Brang.
(sie zieht ein Fläschchen hervor.)
Den hehr - sten Trank, - ich halt' - ihn hier. —
Isolde.
Du irrst,
Vlc.
K. B.
p dolce
più p
pp
trem.
(Bog.)

No. 28. Fidelio, Act I

At present the violas are frequently divided into first and second violas. In orchestras like that of the Paris Opera, where they are sufficiently numerous, this procedure is not disadvantageous. But in other orchestras which have scarcely four or five violas such a division can only be detrimental, since the weak viola group is in any case in constant danger of being overpowered by the other instruments. In this connection it must also be remarked that most of the violas currently used in our French orchestras are not of requisite proportions; neither in size nor in, tonal volume are they real violas. They are more like violins strung with viola strings. Conductors should absolutely prohibit the use of these mongrel instruments. Their weak sound deprives the orchestra of one of its most interesting tone elements and robs it of sonority, especially on its deep tones.

Professor Hermann Ritter constructed a "Viola alta" which has a fifth string above the four strings of the ordinary viola. Because of its larger size the instrument has a considerably greater volume of tone; besides, it has the additional high tones, very advantageous for modern orchestral works.

Unfortunately, up to now it has been used only to a very limited extent, mainly because it requires considerable physical power. Especially viola players with short arms or fingers may hesitate to give up the more comfortable ordinary viola.

Two other new instruments which try to extend the lower range of the viola and violoncello should be mentioned here: the Violotta and Cellone, constructed by Stelzner. Their practical achievements are still too unimportant to make it worth-while to introduce them into the orchestra. The fact that they are tuned differently, i.e. have lower strings than the violas and violoncellos, makes their use for existing tasks illusory; otherwise, new parts would have to be composed for them.

When the violoncellos have the melody, it is sometimes excellent to double them in unison in the violas; their tone thereby gains in roundness and clarity without losing its preponderance. The theme of the Andante in Beethoven's C-minor Symphony offers an example of this. (Example 29.)

No. 29. Symphony in C minor, 2nd movement

The Viola d'amore

This instrument is somewhat larger than the viola. It has fallen into disuse almost everywhere. Were it not for M. Urban—the only player of the instrument in Paris—it would be known to us only in name.

It has seven gut strings; the lowest three are covered with silver wire, like the C and G on the viola. Below the fingerboard and passing below the bridge are seven more strings of metal. They are tuned in unison with the strings above; vibrating in sympathy with them, they lend the instrument a second resonance, full of sweetness and mystery. It was formerly tuned in several odd ways. M. Urban has adopted the following mode of tuning, in thirds and fourths, as the simplest and most rational:

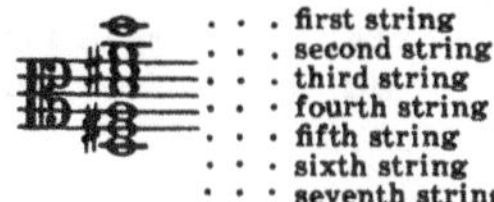

The range of the viola d'amore is at least three and a half octaves. It is written—like the viola—in two clefs.

As the arrangement of the strings indicates, the viola d'amore is appropriate mainly for chords of three, four or more tones, whether arpeggiated, struck simultaneously or sustained; and above all for melodies in double stops. For chords, a different system has to be used from the one for the violin, viola and violoncello, which are tuned in fifths. One must be careful to avoid greater intervals in chords than thirds and fourths—unless at least the lowest tone is played on an open string. Thus, the A of the second string can be combined with any tone over the entire length of the high D-string.

Needless to say, chords of minor thirds and of seconds over the lowest tone of the instrument, such as are impossible, as the tones can be played only on the D-string. Similar limitations on the lowest strings of the other stringed instruments are easily determined.

Harmonics on the viola d'amore have a wonderful effect. They are obtained in the same way as those on the violin and viola. Since the seven open strings of the viola d'amore form a perfect common chord, it is very easy to produce rather rapid arpeggios of its basic chord, D, in the higher octave:

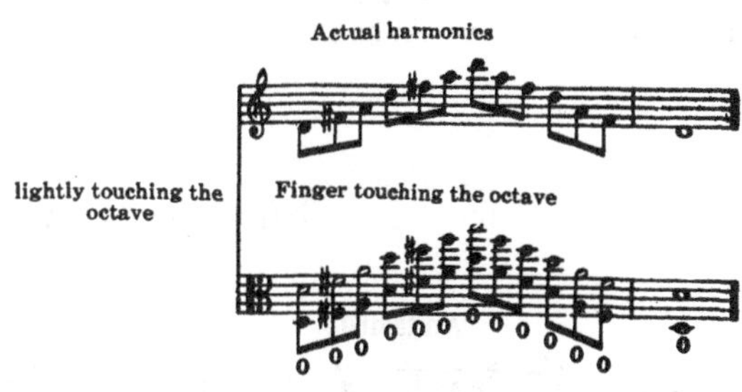

and in the double octave:

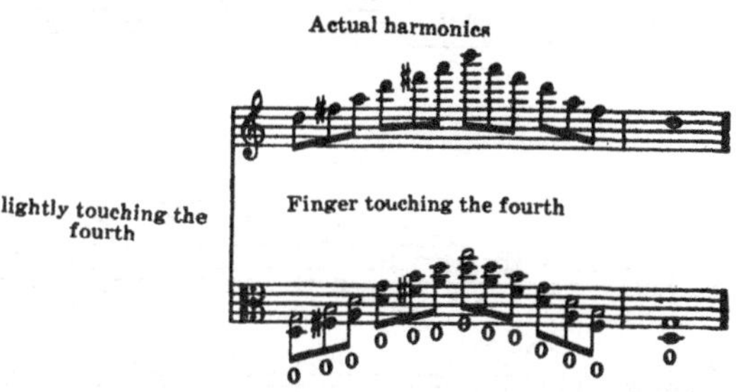

as well as of the A-major chord in the higher twelfth:

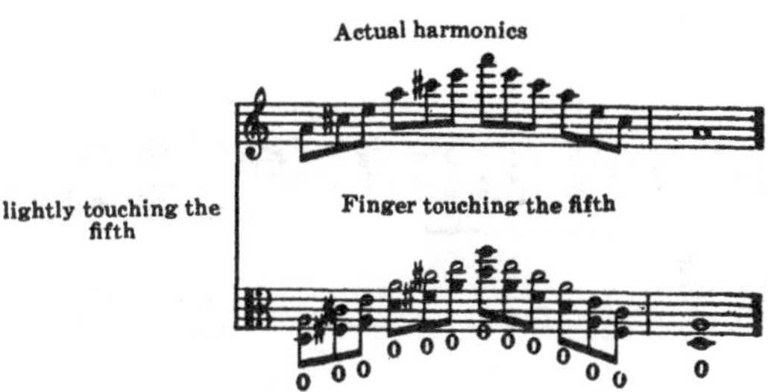

and of the F♯-major chord in the higher seventeenth:

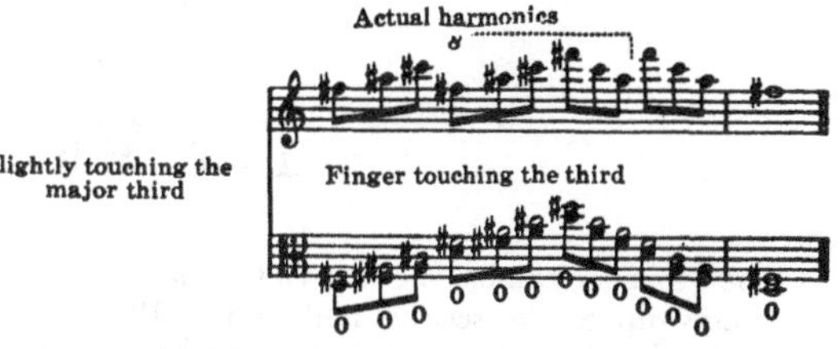

These examples show that, if one wants to use these charming arpeggios on the viola d'amore, the keys of D, G, A, F♯ and B offer the best opportunities. But as those three chords (D, A, F♯) are obviously not adequate in accompanying a modulating melody without interruption, this could easily be remedied by using several differently tuned violas d'amore, for instance in C or D♭, according to the chords required by the composer for his piece. The extraordinary charm of these harmonics on open strings would well justify all possible devices to take full advantage of them. The viola d'amore has a weak and soft tone; it has something seraphic, similar both to the viola and to the harmonics of the violin. It is particularly suitable to the legato style, to dreamy melodies, to the expression of ecstatic or religious sentiments. Meyerbeer used it to advantage in Raoul's Romance, in the first act of "Les Huguenots" (Example 30). But here it serves only as a solo instrument. How beautiful would be the effect of a mass of violas d'amore in an Andante, executing a beautiful prayer in several voices, or accompanying in sustained harmonies a melody of the viola, violoncello, the English or French horn, or the flute in the middle of its range—combined, perhaps, with harp arpeggios! It would truly be a pity if this wonderful instrument were lost for practical use, especially since any violinist can learn to play it within a few weeks.

No. 30. Les Huguenots, Act I

The Viola da gamba

The viola da gamba (i.e. leg-viol) was in use in Germany up to the second half of the 18th century. At first it had five strings, then six; at the end of the 17th century a low string (A) was added. This formerly popular instrument has a beautiful, sonorous tone. It was tuned in fourths, with one exception, and had the following range:

Its finger-board, like that of the lute, was furnished with frets marking the divisions between the tones.

The viola da gamba is the ancestor of the modern violoncello. It was somewhat smaller than the violoncello, and was written, according to the pitch, in the bass-clef, the tenor-clef, the alto-clef or the soprano-clef

The Violoncello

Its four strings are tuned in fifths, exactly an octave lower than the four strings of the viola:

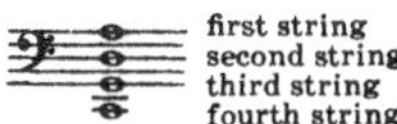

Its range may be three and a half octaves, even in the orchestra:

Great virtuosos go still higher. However, these extremely high notes are attractive only at the end of slow phrases; they are usually employed not as natural tones but as harmonics, which are produced more easily and sound much better.

Before we proceed further, it is necessary to acquaint the reader with the double meaning of the G-clef in violoncello notation. If this clef occurs at the very beginning of a piece or directly after a bass-clef, the notes indicate the octave above the actual sounds:

The G-clef has its proper meaning only if it follows a tenor-clef (C-clef on the fourth line); only then does it indicate the actual tones, and not their higher octave:

There is nothing to justify this practice; it frequently leads to errors, since many violoncellists ignore it and always play the G-clef according to its usual meaning. To avoid misconceptions, we shall use it here only after the tenor-clef, when the continued use of that clef would lead us too far beyond the stave. The G-clef will thus always represent the actual pitch—as in the preceding example.

What was said concerning double stops, arpeggios, trills and bowing on the violin, applies equally to the violoncello. But one must never forget that the violoncello strings, being longer than those of the violin, require wider stretches between the fingers of the left hand. Consequently, double-stop passages in tenths, possible on the violin and viola, cannot be executed on the violoncello. One can write tenths only if the lower note is on an open string:

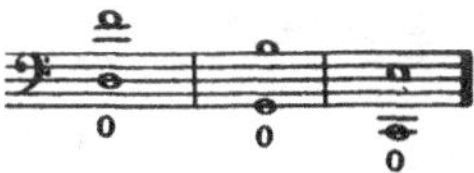

The following tenths would, therefore, be impossible:

Neither is the violoncello capable of the extreme agility of the violin and viola—because of the depth of its tone and the thickness of its strings. The natural and artificial harmonics, frequently employed on the violoncello in solos, are produced in the same fashion as on the violin and viola. The length of the violoncello strings makes even the very high natural harmonics, produced near the bridge, much more easy and beautiful than on the violin. Here is a list of those harmonics which sound best on each string:

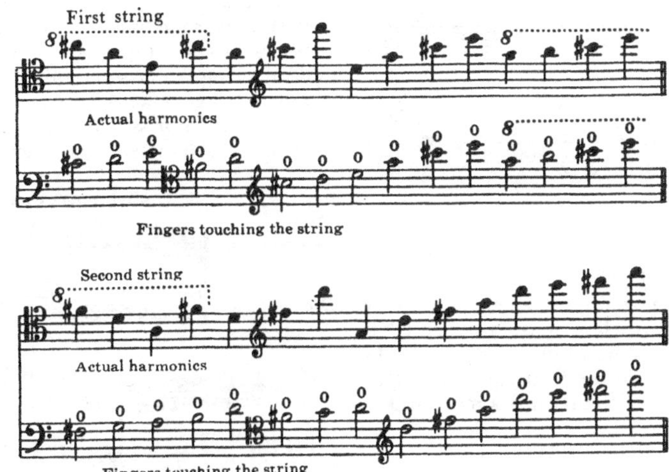

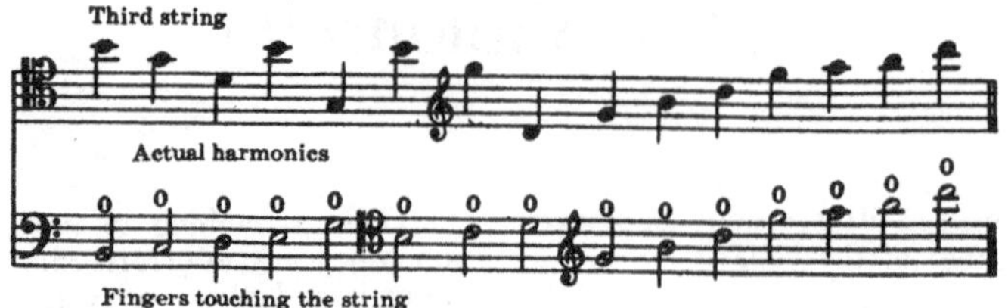

The best way of producing artificial harmonics is by pressing down the first finger as an artificial, movable nut and then lightly touching the fourth:

This fingering is almost the only one practicable on the violoncello. The position of the touched fifth can be used only near the bridge where the distances and proportions are much smaller than on the lower part of the string, and the stretches of the left hand diminish similarly. In this case the fourth finger touches the interval of the fifth while the thumb serves as the nut:

The sign O indicates the thumb

Scales in natural and artificial harmonics:

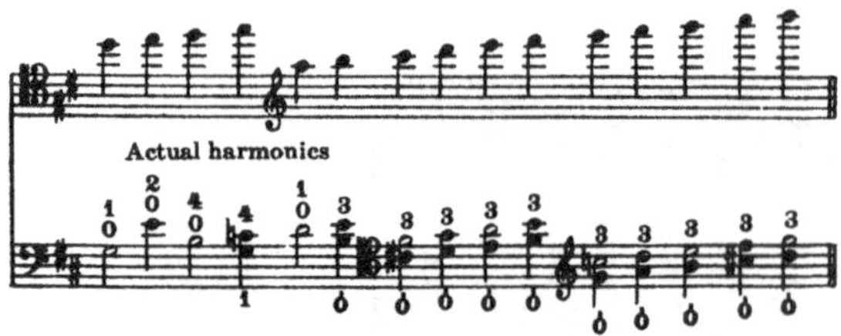

On the violoncello chords in harmonics would doubtless have a charming orchestral effect in slow and tender pieces. Nevertheless, it is easier and less dangerous to obtain the same result by means of divided violins playing high on the E-strings with mutes. The two sounds are so similar that it is almost impossible to distinguish them.

The following passage, written in harmonics for the violoncello,

can be precisely and much more easily executed by natural tones on the violins:

In the orchestra the violoncellos usually take the part of the double-basses, doubling it in the higher octave or in unison. But it is frequently advisable to separate the violoncellos from the double-basses. In such cases the violoncellos may play a melody or a melodious phrase on the high strings. The violoncello part may sometimes be written below the double-basses to take advantage of the peculiar sound of an open string or for some other special harmonic effect. Finally, the violoncello part may be similar to that of the double-basses, but in more rapid motion—such as the double-basses could not execute well:

Here the violoncello part has a more excited and restless motion, but nevertheless plays approximately the same notes as the double-basses and follows their lead almost throughout.

Immediately after this passage, however, the violoncellos separate completely from the double-basses and go below them. This results in the tremendous collision of the minor second below, and at the same time the rough vibration of the C, the lowest open string of the violoncello — while the double-basses drone a B with full power on their first string against the higher octave of the C in the violoncellos. (Example 31.)

No. 31. Requiem, Rex tremendae

Otherwise one should never separate the violoncellos from the double-basses without sufficient reason, that is, without being sure of producing a distinct effect thereby; nor should the violoncellos be written two octaves above the double-basses, as some composers have done. This procedure can only result in weakening the sonority of the fundamental tones of the harmony. The bass part, thus forsaken by the violoncellos, becomes dull, rough and extremely heavy, and combines very poorly with the upper parts because the double-basses are too far removed from them by their low pitch.

This chapter has undergone great changes. The use of low horns, the introduction of the bass clarinet, the frequent employment of the tuba as a melodic element—all these are supplementing the double-bass to a great extent. Bassoons are also used for doubling the basses; I personally prefer them for inner parts. They should take the bass part of a wood-wind group only if supported by the double bassoon.

The string quartet, when it is not weighted down by wind instruments, gains in clarity by using only the violoncellos as the bass, reinforced occasionally by a pizzicato in the double-basses, unless one prefers to omit the double-basses altogether for long stretches, as Wagner deliberately did in "Meistersinger" for the first time.

A melody in the violoncellos and double-basses is greatly intensified if the violoncellos are written an octave lower than the double-basses so that they play in unison; also if a number of violoncellos are supported by only one desk of double-basses.

When a very soft harmony is to be produced by string instruments, it is frequently better to give the bass part to the violoncellos alone and to let the double-basses rest. Weber did so in the accompaniment to the Adagio of Agathe's wonderful aria in the second act of "Freischuetz". In this example it is notable that in the beginning the violas alone supply the bass below a four-part harmony in the violins; the violoncellos enter a little later, doubling the violas. (Example 32.)

No. 32. Freischuetz, Act II

I.
Viol.
II.
Viola.
Ag.
auf zum Sternen-krei-se! Lied er-schalle, fei-ernd wal-le mein Ge-bet zur Himmelshal-le!
Vlc.
K. B.
Recit.
Recit. (hinausschauend)
O wie hell die gold'nen Sterne, mit wie rei-nem Glanz sie glühn! nur dort in der Berge Ferne scheint ein
Fl.
Klar. in A.
Adagio.
Wet-ter auf-zu-ziehn, dort am Wald auch schwebt ein Heer dunkler Wolken dumpf und schwer.
Zu dir etc.

Violoncellos, in a group of eight or ten, are essentially melodic instruments; their tone on the upper strings is one of the most expressive in the entire orchestra. Nothing is so melancholy, nothing so suitable to rendering tender, languishing melodies, as a mass of violoncellos playing unisono on the highest string. They are equally excellent for melodious passages of a religious character. Composers ought to select the appropriate strings on which such passages should be played. The lower strings, C and G, have a particularly suitable timbre, full of dignity and seriousness, especially in keys permitting the use of open strings; but their depth of pitch limits them to more or less melodic basses, actual melodies being reserved for the upper strings (as mentioned above). In his Overture to "Oberon", Weber, with rare felicity, lets the violoncellos sing high notes while two A-clarinets play unisono below them. The effect is both novel and touching. (Example 33.)

No. 33. Oberon, Overture

The versatility of this instrument is shown by the following excerpts from Wagner's works: in "Meistersinger" the violoncellos, unisono with the violins, intensify the noble ardor of the Prize Song (Example 34); in the introduction to the third act of "Tannhaeuser" they express profound contrition (Example 35).

No. 35. Tannhaeuser, Act III (Introduction)

The violoncellos interpret with equal eloquence the ecstasy of the dying Tristan (Example 36) and the mature wisdom of Hans Sachs (Example 37).

2 Fl.
Ob.
Klar. in A.
Hrnr. in E.
Fag.
Pke.
Viol. I.
Viol. II.
Violen.
Trist.
Vlc.
K. B.
p dolce
cresc.
f dim.
(weich)
più p
pp
(ohne Dämpfer)
(noch mit Dämpfer)
führt mir letz - te La - bung zu.
p (weich)
(ohne Dämpfer)
Fl.
Ob.
Klar. in A.
Hrnr. in E.
Fag.
Pke.
Viol.
Violen.
Trist.
Vlc.
K. B.
Ach, I sol - - - de!

Immer breiter.
Breit.
zu 2.
Lebhafter.
Fl.
Ob.
Klar. in A.
Hrnr in E.
I.
Fag.
II.III.
Baßklar. in A.
Pke.
Harfe.
I.
Viol.
II.
Violen.
Trist.
Vlc.
K. B.
dim.
p dolce
piu p
pp
p stacc.
pizz.
I - sol - de!
wie schön
bist
du!

No. 37. Meistersinger, conclusion

scherzando
Fl.
Ob.
Klar. in B.
Hrnr. in F.
Fag.
Trp. in F.
Viol.
Viola.
Sachs.
Vlc.
K.B.
p stacc.
p dolce
p marc.
p stacc. scherz.
p marcato
Mei - ster! Dann bannt ihr gu - te Gei - - ster;
und gebt ihr ih-rem Wir - - - - ken Gunst,

Violoncellos are able to express a complete gamut of moods, both in man and in nature. See the beginning of "Walkuere"—storm (cf. Example 3, p. 11); in the first act of the same work the violoncello solo (quoted by Gevaert)—first stirring of love; the Prelude to "Tristan"—yearning (Example 38); Kurwenal's derisive song in the first act of "Tristan" where the violoncellos are combined with violas and French horns—roughness (Example 39).

No. 38. Tristan, Prelude

2 Fl.
2 Ob.
Klar. in A.
Engl. H.
in F.
Hrnr.
in E.
Fag.
Baßklar. in A.
I.
Viol.
II.
Viola.
Vlc.
K.B.
a 2.
cresc.
sfz
più f
ff
p
pp
pizz.
Bog.
dim.
f
poco rall.
riten.
a tempo
Hrnr. in E.
(auf dem G)
zart

No. 39. Tristan, Act I

Ob.
Hrnr. in F.
Fag.
1.u.2.
Trp. in F.
unis.
Viola.
Bog.
cresc.
Kurw.
Welt, Tris - tan der Held! Ich ruf's: du sag's und groll-ten mir tausend Frau I - sol -
unis.
Vlc.
(geteilt)
K.B.
Schneller.
Ob.
Hrnr. in F.
Fag.
Pke.
I.
Viol.
II.
Viola.
(Da Tristan durch Gebärden ihm zu wehren sucht, und Brangäne entrüstet sich zum Weggehen wendet, singt Kurwenal der zögernd sich Entfernenden mit höchster Stärke nach:)
Kurw.
den! Herr Morold zog zu Mee-re her, in Kornwall Zins zu
Vlc.
K.B.

Hrnr. in F.
Fag.
Baßklar. in B.
Viol. II.
Viola.
Kurw.
Vlc.
K.B.
cresc.
pizz.
Bog.
ha - ben; ein Eiland schwimmt auf ö-dem Meer, da liegt er nun be-gra - - ben! Sein Haupt doch hängt im
I - renland, als Zins gezahlt von En-ge - land: heil unser Held Tris-tan, wie der Zins zah-len kann!"

Although our present violoncellists are very skillful and can master all kinds of difficulties without trouble, fast passages on low notes seldom fail to produce some confusion. As for notes in high positions requiring the use of the thumb, there even less is to be expected; they are not very sonorous and are always of doubtful precision. Violas or second violins are obviously more appropriate for passages in these high ranges. In modern, well-staffed orchestras, containing a great number of violoncellos, these are frequently divided into two groups. The first violoncellos execute a separate melodic or harmonic part, the second ones double the basses in the octave or in unison.

For accompaniments of a melancholy, veiled and mysterious character, two different violoncello parts are sometimes placed above the double-basses, leaving the bass part to them alone; this, together with the violas, produces a quartet of low harmonies. This arrangement is seldom well-contrived. One should guard against misusing it. (Example 40.)

No. 40. Roméo et Juliette, Part III (Scène d'amour)

The tremolo on two strings as well as arpeggios in forte are well suited for the violoncello. They add greatly to the richness of harmony and increase the general sonority of the orchestra.

In the introduction of the overture to "Guillaume Tell", Rossini wrote a quintet for five solo violoncellos, which is accompanied pizzicato by the rest of the violoncellos, divided into two groups. The deep tones of uniform character are very effective here; they enhance the brilliance of the orchestration in the ensuing Allegro.

The pizzicato on the violoncello cannot have much rapidity. The method proposed for the pizzicato on the violins would not be suitable on the violoncello—because of the thickness and tension of its strings and their too great distance from the finger-board. According to the procedure generally in use for pizzicato, one should not exceed the speed of eight eighths in an alla-breve (Allegro non troppo) or of twelve sixteenths in 6-8 time (Andantino).

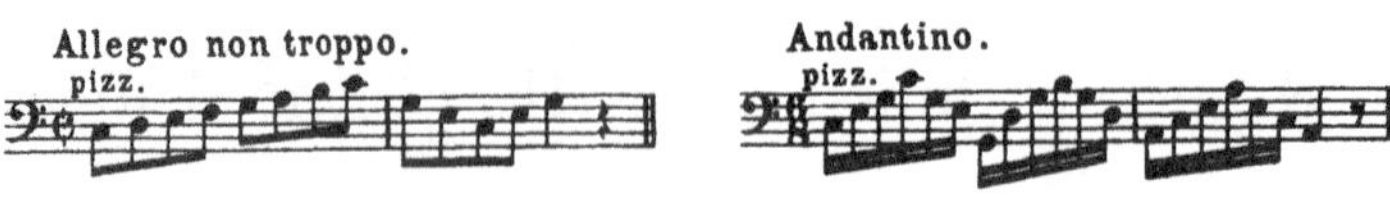

The Double-bass

There are two kinds of double-basses: those with three, and those with four strings. Those with three strings are tuned in fifths:

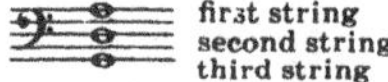

those with four strings are tuned in fourths:

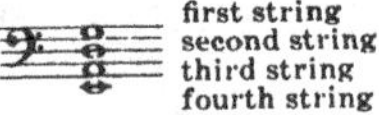

The actual sound of both is an octave below the written notes. Their range in the orchestra is two octaves and a fourth; but the double-bass with three strings has three tones less in the low range.

Double-bass with four strings

Double-bass with three strings

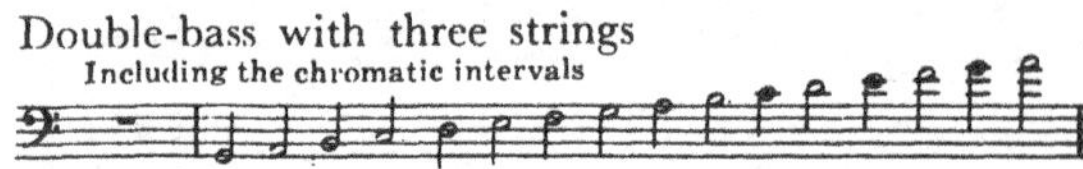

The four-stringed double-bass appears preferable to me; tuning in fourths makes for greater facility of execution because the player is not compelled to shift on the finger-board when playing scales. Furthermore, the three low notes E, F and F♯, missing on the three-stringed double-bass, are extremely useful; their absence frequently spoils the form of the best-designed bass part by requiring unpleasant and difficult transposition to the higher octave. This deficiency is still more apparent in the English double-basses, which, although tuned in fourths, have only three strings—A, D, G: . A good orchestra should have several four-string double-basses, some of them tuned in fifths and thirds: Together with the other double-basses tuned in fourths, a combination of open strings would be available which would greatly increase the sonority of the orchestra:

Double-bass tuned in a third and fifths

Double-bass tuned in fourths

In order to extend their lower range, double-basses with five strings have already been used for many years, i.e. a new string was added to the old four-string double-bass. The addition of this low range is doubtless a gain in sonority; but this is counter-balanced by the increased difficulty in pressing down the strings, since with five strings the middle ones are placed very high above the finger-board. Therefore, a four-stringed double-bass with a lever device which easily changes the low E to C is definitely preferable to the five-stringed one.

The device invented by Max Poike and produced by Ludwig Glaesel in Markneukirchen is most satisfactory. It sufficiently extends the E-string and part of the fingerboard to produce the low C. To make the tones below E easily playable, a mechanism of four little brass tubes with keys for E, E♭, D and D♭ is attached to the side of the finger-board. When E♭, D, D♭ and C are not used, the E-key is locked by pushing a lever with the thumb; this key is padded and replaces the nut for the E-string. It is noiselessly released by holding the E-key and pressing the E♭-key.

I recommend using double-basses of different systems wherever possible; among them, in any case, also the three-stringed one, which is far better suited to cantilena than the German double-bass.

To this day, two kinds of bows are used for the double-bass: those with a curved stick, which are not good in cantilena and produce a harsh and brittle tone; and the enlarged violoncello bow, which permits all the styles of bowing possible on the other stringed instruments.

The double-basses in the orchestra take the lowest tones of the harmony. It has been shown above in which cases they may be separated from the violoncellos. The resulting impairment of the bass part can be remedied (to a certain degree) by doubling them, in unison or in the octave, with bassoons, basset-horns, bass clarinets or the lowest tones of ordinary clarinets.* But I detest the practice of some musicians to use in such cases also trombones and ophicleides, whose timbre has neither sympathy nor similarity with that of the double-bass and combines with it very poorly.

Particularly the employment of trombones for reinforcing the bass is to be rejected. Concerning this problem, everything depends on the tasteful manner of using the instruments suitable for doubling the bass. I may be permitted to refer the reader to the application of the various bass tubas in the scores of my "Zarathustra" and "Heldenleben".

In large tutti important bass themes of the three trombones are frequently reinforced by bassoons, violoncellos and double-basses; I myself have made this mistake. This is quite useless: the hard, piercing tone of the three weighty trombones in unison is softened rather than strengthened by this support. Unless one wants to give the bassoons and low string instruments complementary parts or figurations, it is better to omit them in such marcato passages for the trombones, except, of course, when one intends to soften their power.

There are occasions when the harmonics of the double-basses may be used successfully. The tension of their strings, their length and distance from the finger-board prevent the use of artificial harmonics. Natural harmonics, however, sound very well, especially those from the middle of the string (which give the higher octave) upward. They are the same harmonics as those on the violoncello, except that they are one octave lower.

Chords and arpeggios may be used on the double-bass if unavoidable; however, only chords of two are at most three notes can be used, of which only one may be fingered:

Double-basses tuned in fourths:

Double-basses tuned in fifths:

The *intermittent tremolo* can be produced easily, thanks to the elasticity of the bow, which rebounds several times on the strings after a single rather vigorous attack:

Allegro moderato.

This does not hold good in the following passage:

Allegro moderato.

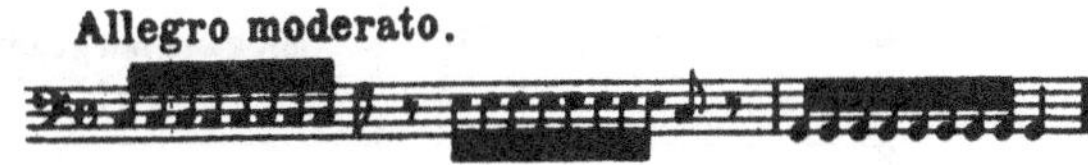

*Preferably with the double-bassoon.

This can be played only at the point of the bow as a *continuous tremolo,* and not without some difficulty; it lacks force and elicits but little tone.

The continuous tremolo, however, somewhat less close than in the preceding example, is of excellent dramatic effect;—

Compare the expression of sublime awe in the Prelude to "Parsifal". A unique application of the lowest instruments in the orchestra is to be found in the second act of "Walkuere", during Wotan's narration. (Example 41.)

No. 41. Walkuere, Act II

Wot.
Wü-ten gejagt, gewann ich mir die Welt. Un-wissend trugvoll Untreu-e übt' ich, band durch Ver-
Vlc.
(nur die 6 zweiten Vlc.)
pp
K.B.
(nur die 4 zweiten K.B.)
pp
2 Baß-Tuben in B.
pp
K.B.-Tuba
pp
Wot.
trä-ge was Un-heil barg: li-stig verlock-te mich Lo-ge, der schweifend nun verschwand.
Vlc. (geteilt)
(6 Erste)
p
(ten.)
pp
pizz.
K.B. (4)
(ten.)
pp
pizz.
2 Baß-Tub. in B.
(ten.)
K.B.-Tuba
(ten.)
Wot.
p
Von der Lie-be doch mocht ich nicht lassen, in der Macht verlangt ich nach Min-ne.
(6) Vlc. (6)
pp
Bog.
pp
K.B. (4)
Bog.
pp
3 Pos.
pp
p
K.B.-Pos.
pp
p
K.B.-Tuba
pp
p
Wot.
pp
p
Den Nacht gebar, der ban-ge Ni-be-lung, Al-berich brach ih-ren Bund; er fluch-te der Lieb' und ge-
(6) Vlc. (6)
p
p
K.B. (4)
p

2 Fag.
3 Pos.
K.B.-Pos.
Wot.
wann durch den Fluch des Rhei - nes glän - zen - des Gold, und mit ihm maß - lo - se Macht.
Vlc.
K.B. (geteilt)
Den Ring, den er schuf, ent - riß ich ihm li - stig; doch nicht dem Rhein gab ich ihn zu - rück; mit ihm be-
Baß-Trp. in Es.
Ten. Tuba I u. II in Es.
Baß Tub. I in B.
Baß Tub. II in B.
K.B.-Tuba.
zahlt' ich Wal - halls Zin - nen, der Burg, die Rie - sen mir bau - ten, aus der ich der
(Alle)

2 Klar. in A.
Baß-Trp. in Es.
3 Pos.
K.B.-Pos.
Ten. Tuba I u. II in Es.
Baß Tub. I in B.
Baß Tub. II in B.
K.B.-Tuba.
Violen. (geteilt)
(6)
(6)
Wot.
Welt nun ge-bot.
Die al-les weiß, was einsten war, Er-da, die weihlich wei-se-ste Wa-la,
Baßklar. in A.
3 Pos.
K.B.-Pos.
K.B.-Tuba.
Wot.
(etwas heftiger)
riet mir ab von dem Ring, warn-te vor e-wi-gem En-de.
Von dem En-de wollt' ich mehr noch
Vlc.
(nur die 6 zweiten Vlc.)
K.B.
(nur die 4 zweiten K.B.)

Fag.
Baßkl.in A.
Wot.
(zurückhaltend)
(belebend)
wis-sen; doch schweigend ver-schwand mir das Weib. Da ver - lor ich den leich-ten Mut; zu
pizz.
Bog.
Vlc. (get.)
K.B. (get.)
Klar. in A.
Violen. (get.)
wissen begehrt' es den Gott: in den Schoß der Welt schwang ich mich hinab, mit Liebeszauber zwang ich die Wa-la,
Vlc.
K.B.

1. allein
Klar. in A.
1.2.
Fag.
3.
Baßkl. in A.
3 Pos.
Violen. (get.)
Wot.
stört ih-res Wissens Stolz, daß sie Re-de nun mir stand. Kun-de empfing ich von ihr; von
Vlc.
(zus.)
K.B.
(zus.)
Pos. I.
Pos. II u. III.
K.B.-Pos.
K.B.-Tuba.
Horn II. in E.
Wot.
mir doch empfing sie ein Pfand: der Welt wei-se-stes Weib ge-bar mir, Brünnhil-de, dich.
Vlc. 1.2.3. Pult.
(geteilt)
Vlc. 4.5.6. Pult.
(geteilt)
K.B.
p dolce

Ein wenig bewegter.
Horn II. in E.
Fag.
3 Pos.
K.B.-Pos.
E u. H
Pke.
Wot.
Mit acht Schwestern zog ich dich auf; durch euch Wal - kü-ren wollt ich wenden, was mir die
Vlc. 1.2.3. Pult.
(get.)
Vlc. 4.5.6. Pult.
(get.)
pizz.
K.B.
Horn II. IV. in E.
Klar. I. in A.
Baßkl. in A.
Fag.
3 Pos.
K.B.-Pos.
Pke.
Wot.
Wa - la zu fürchten schuf: ein schmähliches En - de der Ew'gen. Daß stark zum Streit uns
Vlc. 1.2.3. Pult.
(get.)
Vlc. 4.5.6. Pult.
(get.)
pizz.
K.B.

Horn II. IV. in E.
Fag.
Baßkl. in A.
3 Pos.
K.B.-Pos.
Violen.
(get.)
Wot.
fän-de der Feind, hieß ich euch Hel - den mir schaffen: die herrisch wir sonst in Ge-
(6)
Vlc.
(6)
K.B.
Fag.
Violen.
cresc.
Wot.
se-tzen hiel-ten, die Män - ner, de - nen den Mut wir ge-wehrt, die durch
Vlc.
cresc.
cresc.
K.B.
cresc.
Violen.
Wot.
trü-ber Ver-trä-ge trü-gen-de Ban-de zu blin-den Ge-hor-sam wir uns ge-
Vlc.
K.B.

Horn II.IV. in E.
Baßtromp. in D.
3 Pos.
K.B.-Pos.
K.B.-Tuba.
Pke. II.
Violen.
Wot.
Vlc.
K.B.
(zu 2.)
(zu 3.)
I.
A.
pizz.
(immer belebter, doch mit gemäßigter Stärke)
bun - den, die solltet zu Sturm und Strei-te ihr stacheln, ih-re Kraft rei - zen zu
(Alle Vlc.)
pizz.
I. u. III.
Hrnr. in E.
II. u. IV.
poco cresc.
Baßtrp. in D
1. u. 2.
3.
più p
rau-hem Krieg, daß kühner Käm - pfer Scharen ich sammle in Walhalls Saal.
pizz.

I. u. III.
Hrnr. in E.
II. u. IV.
3 Trp. in E.
1.
pp
2. u. 3.
pp
Baßtrp. in D.
pp
3 Pos.
K.B.- Pos.
K.B.- Tuba.
pp
Pke. II.
Brünnhilde.
Deinen Saal
füll-ten wir weid - lich:
Vie - le schon führt ich dir
zu.
Wieder etwas langsamer.
2 Klar. in A.
p
più p
Fag. II. u. III.
p
più p
Trp. II. u. III. in E.
più p
Baßtrp. in D.
più p
3 Pos.
più p
più p
K.B.- Pos.
più p
K.B.- Tuba.
più p
Violen.
(get.)
p
più p
Brünnhilde.
Was macht dir nun Sorge, da nie wir ge - säumt?
Wotan.
(wieder gedämpfter)
Andres ist's: ach - te es
Vlc.
p
più p
pp
K.B.
arco
p
più p
pp

2 Klar. in A.
3 Fag.
Baßkl. in A.
3 Pos.
K.B.-Pos.
Pke. II.
Violen.
Wot.
Vlc.
K.B.
wohl, weß' mich die Wa-la ge - warnt. Durch Alberichs Heer droht uns das En - - de: mit nei - - dischem
belebend
(belebend)
Grimm grollt mir der Niblung; doch scheu' ich nun nicht seine nächtigen Scharen, meine Hel-den schüfen mir
più p
pizz.
Bog.
ten.
cresc.
poco cresc.

Ten.Tub. I in Es.
Baß Tub. I in B.
3 Pos.
K.B.-Pos.
Violen.
Wot.
Vlc.
K.B.
pizz.
(Bog.)
(gedämpfter)
(noch gedämpfter)
Sieg.
Nur wenn je den Ring zurück er gewänne,
dann wä-re Wal-hall ver-
lo-ren: der der Lie-be fluch-te, er al-lein nütz-te nei-disch des Rin-ges Ru-nen zu al-ler
(nur die 6 zweiten)
(6) trem.
(4 erste)
poco cresc.
Edlen end-loser Schmach; der Helden Mut entwendet er mir, die Kühnen selber zwäng' er zum Kampf, mit ihrer
(belebend)
cresc.

I. rallent.
2 Klar. in A.
2 Fag.
1. u. 2.
Baßklin A.
3 Pos.
K.B.-Pos.
2 Ten.-Tuben in Es.
2 Baß-Tuben in B.
K.B.-Tub.
Pke I.
Violen.
pizz.
Wot.
(gedämpft)
Kraft bekriegte er mich.
Sorgend sann ich nun selbst, den Ring dem Feind zu entreißen.
Der Riesen
Vlc.
K.B.
dim.
cresc.
Pke.
ei-ner, de-nen ich einst mit verfluchtem Gold den Fleiß vergalt,
Fafner hü-tet den Hort, um den er den

2 Ten.-Tub. in Es.
I. 2 Baß-Tub. in B. II.
K.B.-Tub.
Pke.
Wot.
Bruder gefällt. Ihm müßt ich den Reif ent-ringen, den selbst als Zoll ich ihm zahl-te. Doch mit wem ich ver-
Vlc.
K.B.
(Bog.)
3 Pos.
K.B.-Pos.
(bitter)
trug, ihn darf ich nicht treffen; macht-los vor ihm er-lä-ge mein Mut; das sind die Bande die mich
stacc.
poco cresc.
Etwas belebter.
pstacc.
Viol. II.
Violen.
bin-den: Der durch Ver-trä - - ge ich Herr, den Ver-trä-gen bin ich nun Knecht.

With all its simplicity, this scene is for me the inconceivable miracle of a genius who was able, better than anyone else, to transform all emotions and passions into orchestral sounds which overpower and irresistibly convince all listeners.

—Nothing gives the orchestra a more menacing expression. But it should not last too long; otherwise it exhausts those players who really endeavor to execute it well, and soon becomes impracticable. When it is thus necessary to stir the depths of the orchestra during a longer passage, it is better to divide the double-basses into two parts. These are given, not a real tremolo, but quick strokes of different rhythm, while the violoncellos execute the real tremolo:

The sixteenths of one part coincide with the triplet eighths of the other only at the beginning of each beat. Thus they produce a vague murmur which comes very close to a tremolo and is a tolerably good substitute for it. I believe that in many cases these different rhythms, simultaneously played, are even preferable to the tremolo proper.

Rapid diatonic runs of four or five notes often have an admirable effect and are easy to play if they contain at least one open string:

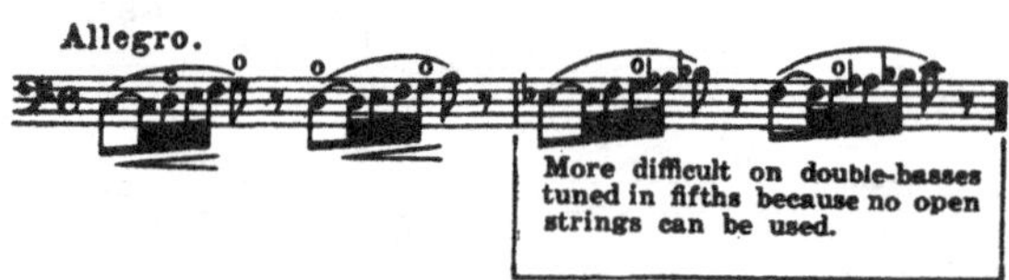

More difficult, on account of the descending notes:

If it is necessary to use more extended rapid runs in the double-basses, it is best to divide them in the fashion indicated above for the violins; but special care should be taken to avoid keeping the first double-basses too far removed from the second.

It is a current mistake to write for the heaviest of all instruments passages of such rapidity that even the violoncellos would have trouble executing them well. Hence there result serious disadvantages: some double-bass players, too lazy or in fact incapable of tackling such difficulties, give up at once and try to simplify the passage. But each one simplifies it in a different manner, since they do not all have the same ideas regarding the harmonic importance of the different notes; this causes a horrible disorder and confusion. This buzzing chaos of strange sounds and ugly snarls is still further increased by the vain efforts of more zealous or more confident players to master the passage just as it is written.

Composers should therefore take care to ask of double-bass players no more than is practicable. Only in this way can they be sure of an accurate execution; and only this will do away with the old system of simplification by the double-bass players, a system generally adopted in the old instrumental school, and whose danger has just been demonstrated. If the composer writes only that which is compatible with the nature of the instrument, the player must execute it literally. But if the composer errs, then he as well as the audience must bear the consequences; the performers are no longer to blame.

The double-basses are particularly suitable to express gloom, awe, meditation and preoccupation. Out of many examples only the following are quoted: the solo in Verdi's "Otello"; the old woman's song in Marschner's "Hans Heiling"; Tristan's awakening (third act). (Examples 42, 43, 44.) Also to be mentioned here is the fugue from my tone-poem "Thus spake Zarathustra".

No. 42. Otello, Act IV

2 Fl.
Picc.
2 Ob.
2 Klar. in B.
4 Fag.
I. II. in F.
4 Hrnr.
III. IV. in C.
2 Kornetts in C.
2 Tromp. in C.
3 Ten. Pos.
1 Baßpos.
Pke.
I.
Viol.
II.
Viola.
Otello.
(er nähert sich dem Bette.)
Vlc.
(ohne Sord.)
K.B.
staccato
un poco marcato
cresc.
cresc.
a 2.

No. 43. Hans Heiling, Act II

Marschner.

Klar. in A.
Fag.
Hrnr. in E.
Viola.
Gertr.
Vlc.
K.B.
cresc.
dim.
wie er gräbt, da steigt empor ein blei - ches To-ten-gerippl.–
„Still, raschelt es nicht an der
Tür? (sie horcht)
Sie ist es noch nicht!"–
Auf der Hei - de, da brennt ein Flämmchen blau.–
Du

Klar. in A.
Fag.
Hrnr. in E.
Viola.
Gertr.
hörst nicht auf der Ar - men Not, drum würge ich dich jetzt zu Tod. Des Nachts wohl auf der Hei -
Vlc.
K.B.
de, da brennt ein Flämm - chen. _
Wer kommt da? (steht auf, wendet sich nach der Tür; Konrad trägt Anna herein.)
All' ihr Heil'gen, was ist geschehn?
Konrad: Erschreckt nicht, Mutter Gertrude.

No. 44. Tristan, Act III

Slides of short notes, preceding longer ones,

are executed by sliding rapidly with the finger on the string, without paying too much attention to the precision of the intervals; this can be extremely effective. The passage in the Hades scene of "Orfeo" is well known, where the double-basses deal furious blows to the orchestra by running up to F with the four short notes B, C, D, E (with the words "at the terrible howling of foaming Cerberus"). This rough barking, one of Gluck's finest inspirations, becomes all the more terrible as the composer uses the third inversion of the diminished seventh chord (F-G♯-B-D). Furthermore, to give his idea all the weight and vehemence possible, he doubles the basses not only with the violoncellos but also the violas and the whole mass of violins in the octave. (Example 45.)

No. 45. Orfeo, Act II

Beethoven has also availed himself of these not too clearly articulated notes; but—contrary to the previous example—he accents the first note of each group. These bass passages are to be found in the storm scene of the Pastoral Symphony; they depict in striking fashion the wind driving the rain violently, and the hollow rumbling of the storm. It is interesting to note that Beethoven here, as in many other pieces, gave the double-basses notes which they cannot execute. One might conclude from this that the orchestra for which he wrote possessed double-basses descending as low as the C an octave below the violoncello C. Such instruments are no longer to be found today. (Example 46.)

No. 46. Pastoral Symphony, 3rd movement. (Thunderstorm)

Fl.
Ob.
Klar. in B.
Fag.
Hrr.r. in F.
Trp. in Es.
Pkn.
I.
Viol.
II.
Viola.
Vlc.
K. B.
f
più f
sf
fp
p
pp
Fl.
Ob.
Klar. in B.
Fag.
Hrnr. in F.
Trp. in Es.
I.
Viol.
II.
Viola.
Vlc.
K. B.

Fl.
Ob.
Klar. in B.
Fag.
Hrnr. in F.
Trp. in Es.
I.
Viol.
II.
Viola.
Vlc.
K.B.
pp
Fl.
Ob.
Klar. in B.
Fag.
Hrnr. in F.
I.
Viol.
II.
Viola.
Vlc.
K.B.
pp

In passages for wind instruments only it is excellent to double the lowest part of the bassoons, bass clarinets, low horns, or even of the trombones or bass tubas, with one or, if necessary, several desks of double-basses; unless one prefers to let the double bassoon or the double-bass clarinet play the lower octave.

The cemetery scene in "Don Giovanni" is frequently executed by wind instruments alone; however, just the double-basses which the divine Mozart added to the trombones give the scene a peculiar, ghostlike color (especially if placed backstage). (Example 47.)

47. Don Giovanni, Act II

A fine and dramatic effect can sometimes be obtained by giving the real bass to the violoncellos, or at least the notes which determine the chords and fall on the accented beats, while the double-basses, below the violoncellos, play an independent part whose design, interrupted by rests, permits the harmony to rest on the violoncellos. In the admirable scene of "Fidelio" where Leonore and the jailer dig Florestan's grave, Beethoven has displayed all the solemn dignity and gloomy sadness of this kind of instrumentation. However, he gave the real bass to the double-basses. (Example 48.)

No. 48. Fidelio, Act II

Fl.
Ob.
Klar. in C.
Fag.
Hrnr. in C.
Pos.
I.
Viol.
II.
Viola.
Leon.
Roc.
Vlc.
K.B.
fp
sfp
decresc.
pp
(mit halblauter Stimme)
Nur hur-tig fort, nur frisch ge - gra - ben,
p
(ebenfalls arbeitend)
Ihr sollt ja
es währt nicht lang, er kommt her - ein, es währt nicht lang, es währt nicht lang er kommt her - ein.
pizz.
ohne Kontrafag.

Fl.
Ob.
Klar. in C.
Fag.
Hrnr. in C.
Pos.
I.
Viol.
II.
Viola.
Leon.
nicht zu kla - gen ha - ben, Ihr sollt ge - wiß zu-frie - den sein.
Roc.
Nur hur-tig fort, nur frisch ge-
Vlc.
arco
K.B.
arco
mit Kontrafag.
cresc.
sf p
gra - ben, es währt nicht lang, er kommt her-ein.
Ihr sollt ja nicht zu kla - gen ha - ben, Ihr sollt ge -
pizz.
ohne Kontraf.

Fl.
Ob.
Klar. in C.
Fag.
Hrnr. in C.
Pos.
pp
I.
Viol.
II.
Viola.
Leon.
wiß zu-frie-den sein.
(einen großen Stein hebend)
Roc.
Komm hilf, komm hilf doch diesen Stein mir
arco
Vlc.
arco
K.B.
mit Kontrafag.
Fl.
Ob.
cresc.
fp
Klar. in C.
Fag.
cresc.
fp
Hrnr. in C.
cresc.
fp
Pos.
cresc.
fp
I.
Viol.
cresc.
fp
II.
cresc.
fp
Viola.
cresc.
fp
(hilft heben)
Leon.
Ich
Roc.
he-ben, hab acht! hab acht! er hat Ge-wicht!
Vlc.
cresc.
fp
K.B.
cresc.
fp

Fl.
Ob.
Klar. in C.
Fag.
Hrnr. in C.
Pos.
I.
Viol.
II.
Viola.
Leon.
Roc.
Vlc.
K.B.
cresc.
fpp
a2
p
sfp
hel - fe schon, sorgt Euch nicht, ich will mir al - le Mü - he ge - ben. Ge - duld!
Ein we - nig noch! Er
weicht! es ist nicht leicht! es ist nicht leicht!
nur et - was noch! nur et - was noch! nur et - was noch!

To indicate a mournful silence, I have divided the double-basses into four parts in a cantata; they play sustained pianissimo chords beneath a decrescendo of the rest of the orchestra. (Example 49.)

Fl.
a 2.
poco sf p
Klar. in C.
sf p
Fag.
in Es.
Hrnr.
in C.
Gr. Tr.
I.
Viol.
II.
pp
Viola.
Baß.
Au-tour de moi, au-tour de moi pleu-rent ses en-ne-mis.
Rings um mich her, rings um mich her weint sei-ner Fein-de Schar.
Chor.
Vlc.
K.B.
ppp
dimin. sempre
sotto voce
Loin de ce roc nous fuy-ons en si-len-ce, l'as-tre du jour a-ban-don-ne les
Von die-sem Fels laßt weit hinweg uns flie-hen, des Tags Ge-stirn... be-reits weicht es der

Fl.
Klar. in C.
Viol. I.
Viol. II.
Viola.
Baß.
Chor.
Vlc.
K.B.
ppp
Man nehme den Dämpfer.
Man nehme den Dämpfer.
(Doppelgriff.)
Man nehme den Dämpfer.
Cieux, l'as-tre du jour a-ban-don-ne les Cieux.
Nacht, des Tags Ge-stirn... be-reits weicht es der Nacht.
Diese Töne müssen mehr geseufzt als gesungen werden, so sanft wie möglich.
sotto voce
Ah!
Hä!
(Doppelgriff.)
Man nehme den Dämpfer.
pp
pppp
p

The pizzicato of the double-basses, in forte as well as in piano, is of good sonority unless it is employed on very high tones; but it changes its character according to the harmonies which it supports. Thus, the famous pizzicato A in the overture to "Freischuetz" derives its threatening and infernal effect only from the echo of the diminished seventh chord (F♯-A-C-E♭), which thereby is transformed into its first inversion on a weak beat. The same A, written as a major tonic or dominant, and played mezzoforte similarly to the passage in question, would no longer have anything strange about it.

Also compare:

No. 50. Tristan, Act I

In this passage the pizzicato G of the double-basses together with the ninth-chord always gives me a sensation of color. — — — — — — — — — — — — —

I should like to offer a few suggestions for the treatment of the string group, always so difficult, and a strangely refractory instrument in the hand of bunglers. The best models for study are to be found in Mozart's string quartets with their impeccable style and technique, and particularly in the polyphony of the string quintet in Wagner's scores. The "Siegfried Idyll" with its wonderful melodic contours, as well as "Tristan" and "Meistersinger" with their almost total avoidance of tremolos, offer on almost every page a complete compendium of the art of developing the full sonority of the strings. The whole Prize Song is an outstanding model for polyphonic line and the employment of open harmony, permitting a rich resonance of overtones; see particularly the bars from Walther's "Dort unter einem Wunderbaum" to "das schoenste Weib" (Example 51).

No. 51. Meistersinger, Act III (Prize Song)

Ein wenig zurückhaltend.
Klar. in B.
Horn III IV in C.
Fag.
Harfe.
Viol. I.
II.
Viola.
er und die Übrigen hören nur teilnahmsvoll zu.)
(wie entrückt)
Walther.
ein, dort unter einem Wunderbaum, von Früchten reich be - han - gen, zu schau'n in sel'gem Liebestraum, was höchstem Lust - ver -
Vlc.
K. B.
dolce
pp
poco cresc.
p sehr zart
sehr zart
p zart
cresc.
Allmählich wieder in etwas bewegterem früheren Zeitmaß.
Ob.
Klar. in B.
I.II. in F.
Hrnr.
III.IV. in C.
Fag.
Harfe.
Viol. I.
II.
Viola.
Walther.
lan - gen Er - fül - lung kühn ver - hieß, das schönste Weib, E - va, im Pa - ra - dies.
(zart)
Vlc.
K.B.
cresc.
dim.
p dolce
p dolcissimo
più p

What other group of instruments could improve upon the effect of the string quintet in the passage, unique in its sublime inspiration, after Tristan's words, "Siehst du sie, siehst du sie noch nicht"? Entering in low position, with infinite softness, seemingly motionless and yet vibrating mysteriously, it leads the dying Tristan to a beautiful world of dreams. (Example 52.)

No. 52. Tristan, Act III.

Wagner.

Ob.
I.
II.
dim.
p
più p
p dolce
Klar. in A.
(zart)
p dolce
Horn I in E.
(sehr zart)
pp
Fag. I.
Baßklar. in A.
sempre più p
Solo-Viol. I.
Viol.
Viola.
Tristan.
hold mir Süh - - ne trinkt:
siehst du sie?
siehst du sie noch nicht?
Vlc.
K.B.
(mit Dämpfer)
Sehr ruhig und nicht schleppend.
III.
Hrnr. in E.
IV.
ppp
Wie sie se - lig, hehr und mil - de wan - delt durch des Meers Ge - fil - de?

Mutes are employed on double-basses, as on other bowed instruments; but their effect is not very characteristic; they diminish the tone of the double-basses very little and make it sound more gloomy and vague.

A Piedmontese artist, M. Langlois, who played in Paris about fifteen years ago, produced very peculiar high tones of incredible power on the double-bass (with the bow) by pinching the highest string between the thumb and forefinger of the left hand, thus moving almost to the bridge. If there were need to render in the orchestra the violent outcry of a female voice, no other instrument could produce it better than the double-basses treated in this fashion. I doubt whether our artists are familiar with M. Langlois' method; but they could easily learn it within a short time.

Instruments With Plucked Strings

The Harp

This instrument is essentially anti-chromatic; that is to say, successions of semitones are, basically, not possible on it. The reason for this will be discussed presently. Formerly the range of the harp was only five octaves and a sixth.

As one sees, this scale is in the key of Eb. All harps were tuned in this key, until the skillful manufacturer Erard invented a mechanism which eliminated the disadvantages of this system. He proposed tuning the harp in Cb, a method adopted by almost all modern harp players.

The chromatic intervals can be obtained on the old harp only by means of seven pedals, successively set into position by the player's foot. Each of these raises the note to which its mechanism applies by a semitone over the entire range of the instrument—not individually. Thus the F♯-pedal cannot sharp one F without raising at the same time all the other Fs on the instrument. Hence, the following combinations are all impossible (except in very slow tempo): chromatic scales; sequences of chords with chromatic progressions, or belonging to non-related keys; most embellishments consisting of appoggiaturas with accidentals or several such short notes. All these are impracticable or, at best, extremely difficult and very ugly. Completely impossible on the Eb-harp are the following three seventh and three ninth chords, which must therefore be banned forever from the composer's store of harmonies:

It is evident that all chords containing Cb and Bb simultaneously are not possible. As the harp is tuned in Eb and the pedals raise each string only a semitone, Cb can be produced only with the B♮-pedal, which immediately eliminates all the Bbs of the scale. The situation is the same with Db, which is attained by raising the C♮, as well as with Gb, produced by raising the F.

The pedals of the Eb-harp can restore to their natural state only the three flatted tones (Bb, Eb, Ab) and can sharp only four other tones (F, C, G, D); therefore, this harp is playable only in eight keys: Eb, Bb, F, C, G, D, A, E. The other four keys (Ab, Db, Gb, Cb) can be obtained only by enharmonic changes, and by quickly taking and releasing one or more pedals. In Ab major, for instance, the Db is nothing but an enharmonic C♯. The player must therefore quit the C♯-pedal immediately after taking it to keep the C♮ open, the major third of the key in which he is playing; furthermore, he must skip the D♮-string when ascending diatonically. This is so awkward that such scales may be considered almost impracticable:

These inconveniences and difficulties are still greater in Db major and Gb major, both keys being almost inaccessible, with the exception of a few chords. Furthermore, the keys of Gb major and Cb major present new difficulties by compelling the player to transpose several notes of their scales: he must strike the F♯-string when the written note is Gb, the B♮-string for Cb, and the C♯-string for Db. The key of Cb becomes somewhat easier if it is written in its other form—B♮. But since this key (like that of Ab) requires all the pedals, there still remains the frightful difficulty of skipping one string and then releasing and at once retaking a pedal because the leading-tone (enharmonic) and the tonic are played on the same string.

The following example illustrates the fact that the execution of a chromatic scale of two octaves, e.g.

necessitates the use of five pedals, which have to be put into action very quickly—in succession—for the first octave alone; then they have to be released just as quickly to restore the raised notes to their original position so that they are available for the second octave; finally the pedals have to be retaken as in the first octave. Such a scale is therefore impossible on *any harp,* even in very moderate tempo.

In the case of a succession of chords in several non-related keys, the impossibility of execution becomes still more evident. Here several pedals would have to be taken and released simultaneously:

Certain appoggiaturas and ornaments containing chromatic successions may, in fact, be executed after a fashion; but most of them are, as I have already mentioned, scarcely practicable. Those which may be admitted as exceptions are of rather poor quality, since the taking and the instantaneous release of the pedal impairs the vibration of the strings:

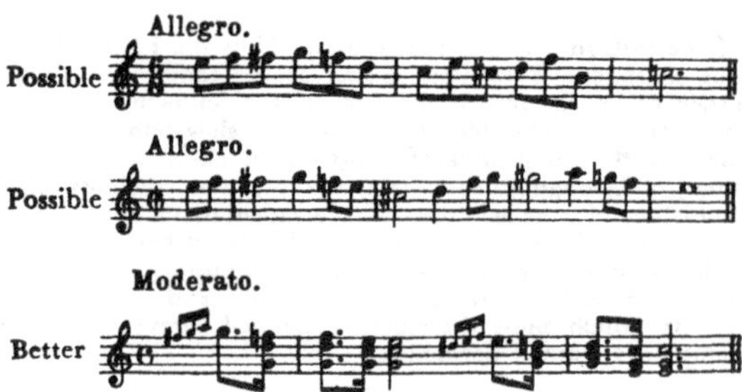

Figurations like the following, however, and similar passages containing several semitones in a brief tonal gamut and at a lively pace, are next to impossible:

Since the harp is played with both hands, it is also written on two staves. The lower stave usually has the F-clef, the upper one the G-clef; but if the high range of the bass notes or the low range of the treble notes demands it, either clef may be used on both staves simultaneously.

This arrangement increases the number of passages impracticable on the Eb-harp still further. A passage that may be easy for the right hand becomes impossible if the accompaniment in the left hand contains notes which are chromatically altered by a pedal while the harmony uses them in their natural form:

The two chords marked * are not played since they contain an F♮ which is sharped in the melody. In these cases the note appearing in two different forms must be omitted in one of the two parts. In the preceding example it is better to leave the chord in the left hand incomplete and to eliminate the F♮.

When a melody previously played by other instruments is to be repeated by the harp, and if it contains impossible or dangerous chromatic passages, it must be skillfully modified by substituting notes belonging to the same harmony for one or more of the altered notes. Thus, instead of giving the following melody to the harp in the form previously played by the violins:

the author considered it better to write it for the harp as follows:

The nature of the harp mechanism requires the sacrifice of the four consecutive semitones in the third bar.

Impressed by all these grave disadvantages, M. Erard some years ago invented a different mechanism, after which the new harps are called *double-action* harps. In the following I am going to explain this mechanism; I shall show how it permits the harpist to play in all keys and to produce all chords, solidly or in arpeggio-form—even though he may not be able to execute chromatic sequences.

The double-action harp is tuned in Cb. Its range is six octaves and a fourth:

Its seven pedals are so arranged that the player, by means of each of them, can raise each string at his option either a *whole tone* or a *semitone.* By using the seven pedals successively for the semitones, the Cb-harp is altered to the keys of Gb, Db, Ab, Eb, Bb, F and C, and is set for these keys. If each string is then raised another semitone by means of the second notch for the pedal, the seven tones of the natural scale are altered to F♯, C♯, G♯, D♯, A♯, E♯ and B♯, whereby the harp is tuned in G, D, A, E, B, F♯ and C♯.

Thus, all keys are available to the harp. The minor keys can be set only if they are played the same way ascending as descending, without observing the usual modifications of the sixth and seventh steps; otherwise two more pedals would have to be taken and released.

If the augmented second between the sixth and seventh steps is used in both directions of the minor scale, this scale can be set too, and the accidental use of the pedal is not necessary, an advantage considerable enough to justify the use of this scale:

As for the six chords impracticable on the E♭-harp, it will be seen that the double action makes them possible. The chord is very easy to execute, its four notes being part of the scale of the C♭-harp. The chord merely requires the use of the two semitone pedals D♮ and F♮; also requires two, F♮ and C♮. Three pedals, C♮, E♮ and G♮, are needed for the chord ; requires but one, F♮; and the last chord again three (F♮, A♮ and C♮). All this is done without difficulty. Even the chord which seems to contain at once C♮ and C♭ is practicable: . The D♭♭ (or C♮) is attained by means of the pedal raising C♭ a semitone, and C♭ is produced with the pedal raising B♭ a semitone; A♭♭ comes from the G♭ raised a semitone; F♭ requires no pedal, being a normal tone in the scale of the C♭-harp. This chord, as it is written above, will therefore be executed in this strange form: ; hence it is better to write it in C major in this form: . If the double-action harps are to be employed in an orchestral piece set in B major for the other instruments, it is better to write the harp part, for the sake of sonority and convenience, in its normal key of C♭:

Composers should take care, in writing harp parts, to forewarn the player a little in advance of the changes in pedaling, for instance by placing a few bars before the occurrence of the modulation such words as, *Prepare G♯, Take pedal for C♮,* etc.

The nature of the harp having been sufficiently explained, we now proceed to the fingering. Many composers confound it with that of the piano, which it does not resemble at all.

Chords of four notes can be struck with each hand if the two extreme notes are within an octave:

Thanks to the great stretch between the thumb and little finger, intervals of a tenth can also be played; consequently, chords such as these are possible:

However, this position is less convenient and less natural, and therefore also less sonorous because none of the fingers can attack the string with as much force as in the normal position.

Incidentally, chords in the extreme low range of the instrument have no sonority and produce confused harmonies; they should be avoided:

These low tones are only fit for doubling a bass passage an octave lower:

To produce the tones of a chord successively, either ascending or descending, is in the very nature of the harp; these chord figurations have been named *arpeggios* from the Italian, *arpa.* They should, generally, also not exceed an octave, especially in a fast movement; otherwise the hand would have to change its position, which causes considerable difficulties.

Only the note at the conclusion of a passage may exceed the octave:

The following example is also very easy to execute because the change in the position of the hand occurs in the upward direction, and the third finger, which could scarcely be used here, is not needed at all; nor does it demand two consecutive notes with the third finger:

Generally care must be taken not to place the two hands too close together; they should be an octave or at least a sixth apart; otherwise they interfere with each other. If the two hands play an arpeggio chord in thirds with each other, the same string will be taken by one hand as soon as the other has left it. Consequently the string has no time to vibrate, and the tone is stifled the moment it is produced.

All passages which require the skipping of a finger from one string to another can be written only in very moderate tempo.

When a rapid series of diatonic octaves or sixths is desired, they should generally be written for two hands. The sixths, as well as scales in thirds, can also be played by one hand, but only in descending. In this case the thumb slides from one upper note to the next while the other three fingers play the lower notes. This passage:

is difficult because of the distance between the thumb and the other fingers; the following two are easier:

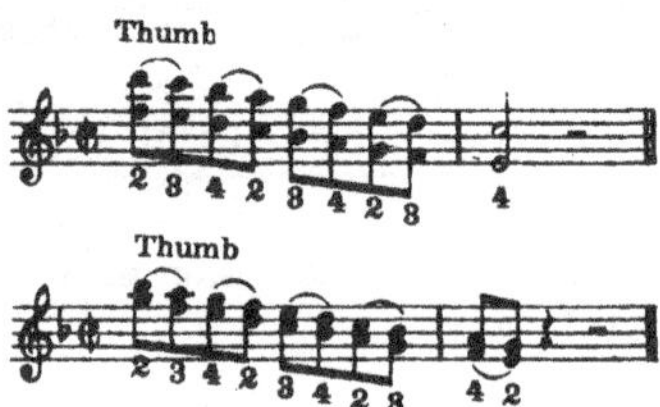

These scales in thirds form an exception to what has been said about keeping the hands apart; they can be executed with both hands. The disadvantage of one string being taken by two hands in quick succession is much smaller in diatonic progressions because the intermediate note allows a little more time for vibration. Nevertheless, it is better to write these series of thirds for two harps, giving the higher part to one and the lower part to another; or, if only one harp is available and a full tone is desired, to separate the two parts by an octave, writing series of tenths:

If one wants to employ a rapid arpeggio of more than an octave, it must be written in one part distributed between both hands, instead of two parts. One hand plays a fragment while the other changes its position and prepares for the next fragment, and so on, reciprocally:

This arpeggio would be impossible if doubled in the octave. The following example is impracticable in quick movement, but quite possible in slow time:

In the second act of "Tannhaeuser", with Tannhaeuser's words "Zu Gottes Preis, in hoch erhab'ne Fernen, etc." occurs a harp passage which it is practically impossible to execute:

The *trill* can be executed on the harp, but its effect is only tolerable in the high notes. The *repetition* of one note was difficult and unpleasant on the old harps on account of the grating noise caused by the first finger striking the string immediately after the thumb, thus interrupting its vibration:

On the new harps the repetition is easy and pleasant: the double action of the pedals makes it possible to raise the adjoining string by a whole tone so that the repetition is produced on two strings in unison:

Repetition in two or four voices (occasionally very useful in the orchestra) can be obtained by using two or more harps and giving them chord figures which cross each other. These offer no difficulty and produce exactly the desired effect:

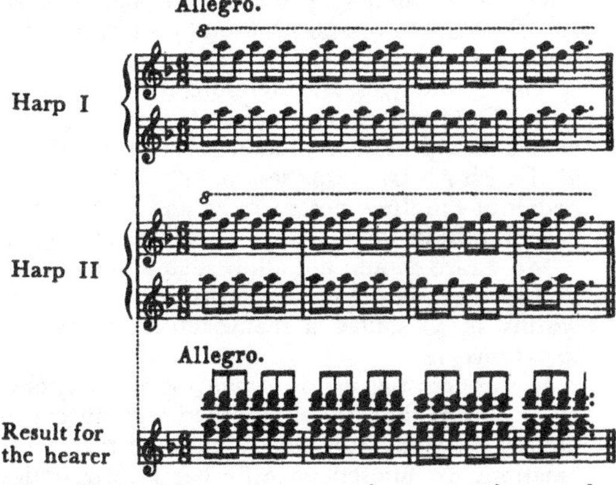

The effect of harps increases in proportion to the number employed (except where music is intended for execution in a small circle and close to the listeners). The tones, chords and arpeggios of a mass of harps can be heard with extraordinary brilliance above a whole orchestra and chorus.

Nothing can be more in keeping with ideas of supernatural splendor or of religious rites than the tones of a great number of harps, ingeniously employed. Employed singly or in groups of two, three or four, they also have a very felicitous effect, either in combination with the orchestra or as an accompaniment to voices or solo instruments. It is remarkable that of all known timbres those of horns, trombones, and brass instruments generally blend best with the harp. Unfortunately, the lower strings, whose tones (with the exception of the soft and dull strings of the extreme low range) are veiled, mysterious and beautiful, have scarcely ever been used for anything other than bass accompaniments of the left hand. It is true that the players have no special liking for pieces moving within the lower octaves. These strings are far from the performer's body, forcing him to bend forward, stretch his arms and to stay for longer or shorter periods of time in this uncomfortable position. But this reason can have had little weight with composers. The fact is, they simply have not thought of utilizing this peculiar timbre.

An example of the beautiful and soft sound of the low strings:

Andantino.

The strings of the highest octave have a lovely crystalline tone of voluptuous freshness, able to paint pictures of fairy-like delicacy and to whisper delicate secrets with lovely melodies. It is necessary, however, that they are not attacked with force by the player, lest their tone become dry and hard, similar to that of a broken glass.

The *harmonics* of the harp—particularly of many harps in unison—are still more magical. Solo players employ them frequently in the cadenzas of their fantasias, variations and concertos. But nothing can match the beauty of these mysterious sounds when they are combined with the medium tones of flutes and clarinets. It is strange that the affinity of these timbres and the poetry of their combination should have been recognized and actually used only once—very recently. (See example 8, p. 30, quoted in reference to harmonics on the violin, where harmonics on the harp are also employed.)

The best and almost the only harmonics on the harp are produced by touching the center of the string lightly with the lower, fleshy part of the hand while playing with the thumb and the first two fingers of the same hand; this produces the upper octave of the normal sound. Harmonics can be played by both hands simultaneously.

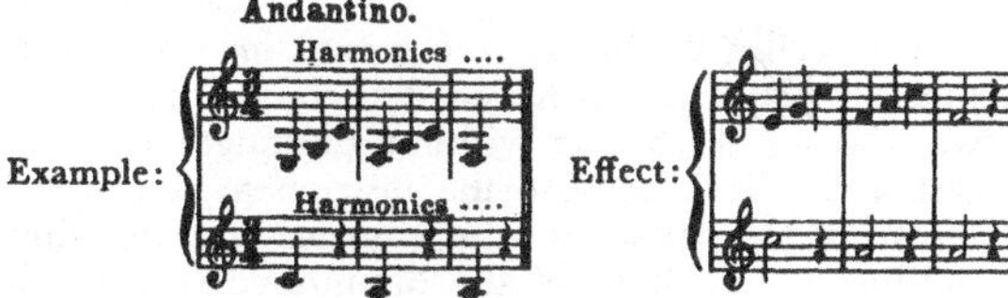

It is even possible to produce two or three harmonics at a time with one hand; but then it is advisable to let the other hand play only one:

Not all strings of the harp are fit for harmonics. Only the two octaves above the lowest should be used; they alone are long enough to be divided by touching in the center and have sufficient tension to produce clear harmonics.

If the course of a piece or the character of its instrumentation require the sudden transition of the harp part from one key into another very remote one (e.g. from E♭ to E♮), this cannot be effected on the same instrument. A second harp must be kept ready, tuned in the sharped key, which immediately continues the part of the harp in the flatted key. If the transition is not so sudden and only one instrument is available, the composer must give the player a sufficient number of rests to set all pedals necessary for the modulation. When the harps are numerous and are treated as an integral part of the orchestra (not merely as an accompaniment for an instrumental or vocal solo), they are usually divided into first and second harps and are given two separate parts; this adds greatly to the richness of their effect. Even a greater number of different harp parts may be well justified. This becomes indispensable, as we have seen, when a sudden transition into distant keys is intended.

The Theban bas-reliefs, where an exact representation of ancient harps is to be found, prove that these had no pedals and consequently could not modulate. The no less ancient harps used to this day by Welsh and Irish bards have several rows of strings. This arrangement doubtless places the chromatic style and modulation more or less within their power.

In speaking of repeated notes I have pointed out above the advantage offered by modern harps in tuning two strings in unison by means of the double action, e.g. one of these C♭s being produced by the C♭-string, the other by the B♭-string raised a semitone; or where one E♭ is played on the E♭-string, the other on the D♭-string raised two semitones. It is hardly believable what effects great harpists are now able to derive from these double strings, which they call *synonyms.* M. Parish-Alvars, perhaps the most extraordinary virtuoso ever to be heard on this instrument, executes runs and arpeggios which at first sight seem utterly impossible. Yet their whole difficulty consists only in an ingenious application of the pedals. He plays, for instance, the following passage with astonishing rapidity:

Allegro assai.

etc.

The facility of this passage is explained by the fact that the player simply has to slide three fingers downward across the strings without any fingering and as fast as he likes, because the instrument is tuned by means of the synonyms in a sequence of minor thirds producing the chord of the dinimished seventh. Instead of the scale

the strings are tuned in this sequence of intervals:

The A♮, it must be remarked, cannot be doubled and hence cannot be played twice in succession. In fact, it is not possible to have four synonyms at a time, simply because there are only seven tones in the scale, whereas four synonyms would require eight strings. Furthermore, the tone A♮ can be produced only on one string, A♭, and not on G♭, which can be raised only two semitones by the double action, that is to A♭. The same limitation is found on two other strings, C♭ and F♭.

Three synonyms are therefore still wanting on the harp: D, G and A. This defect (for such it is indeed) would disappear if the manufacturers would provide, as Parish-Alvars proposes, a triple action for the pedals of the three notes C♭, F♭ and G♭, which would permit raising these strings by three semitones.

Mr. Erard should not allow such a defect to remain in the mechanism of this instrument. It would be worthy of so skilled a manufacturer to be the first to remove it.

If one does not use all synonyms at once, obviously other chords than the diminished seventh can be obtained. Anybody can work out these manifold combinations for himself once he has clearly understood the effect of the pedals upon the strings. There will be even more combinations available after the three synonyms lacking at present are gained by a triple action of the pedals C♭, F♭ and G♭.

A brilliant example for the above mentioned method of glissando (on the diminished seventh chords) is to be found in Liszt's Dante-Symphony; here it symbolizes the spirits of the unfortunate Francesca da Rimini and her lover as they rise from the inferno. (Example 53.)

No. 53. Dante-Symphony, 1st movement

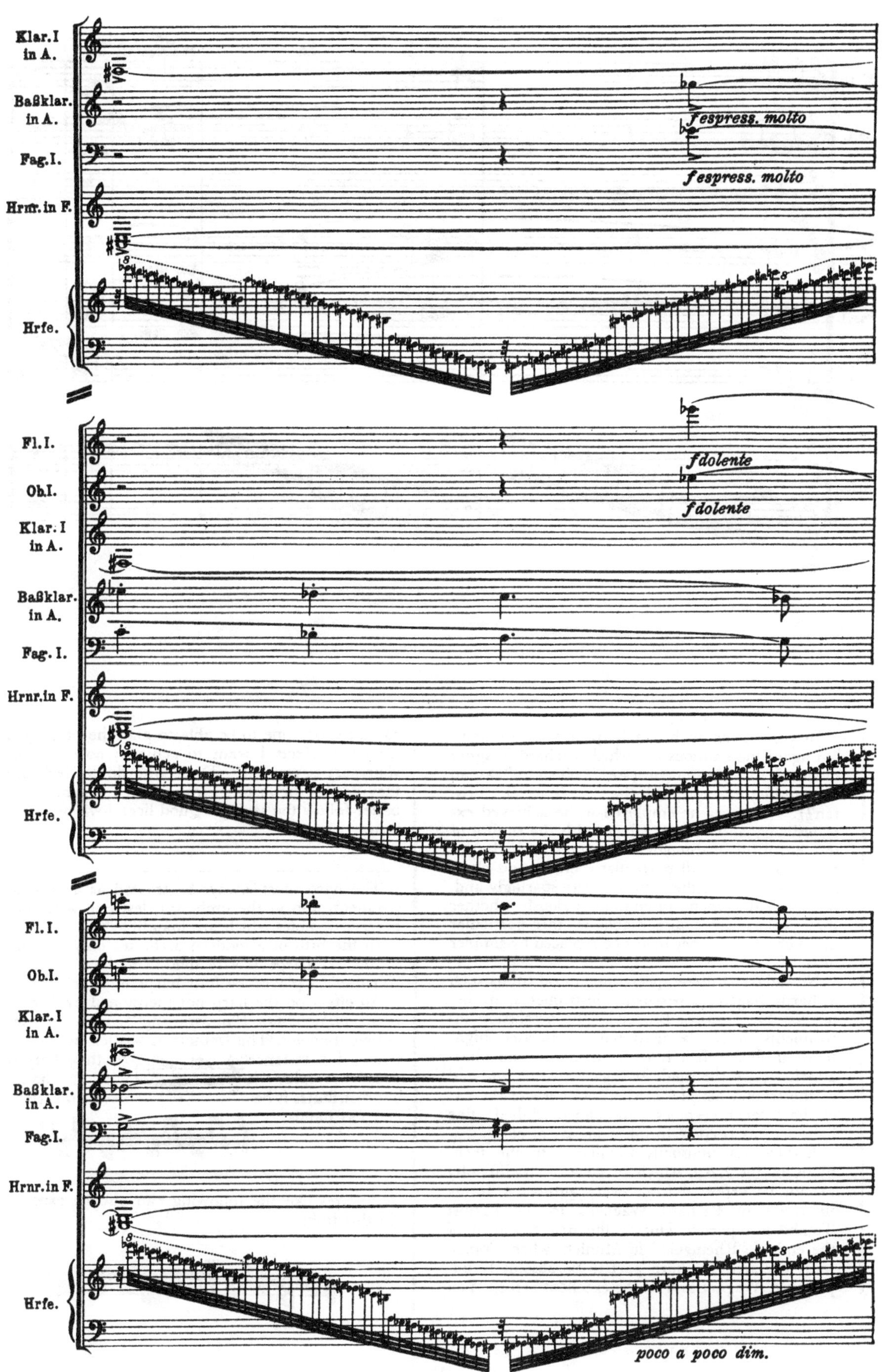
Klar. I in A.
Baßklar. in A.
f espress. molto
Fag. I.
f espress. molto
Hrnr. in F.
Hrfe.
Fl. I.
f dolente
Ob. I.
f dolente
Klar. I in A.
Baßklar. in A.
Fag. I.
Hrnr. in F.
Hrfe.
Fl. I.
Ob. I.
Klar. I in A.
Baßklar. in A.
Fag. I.
Hrnr. in F.
Hrfe.
poco a poco dim.

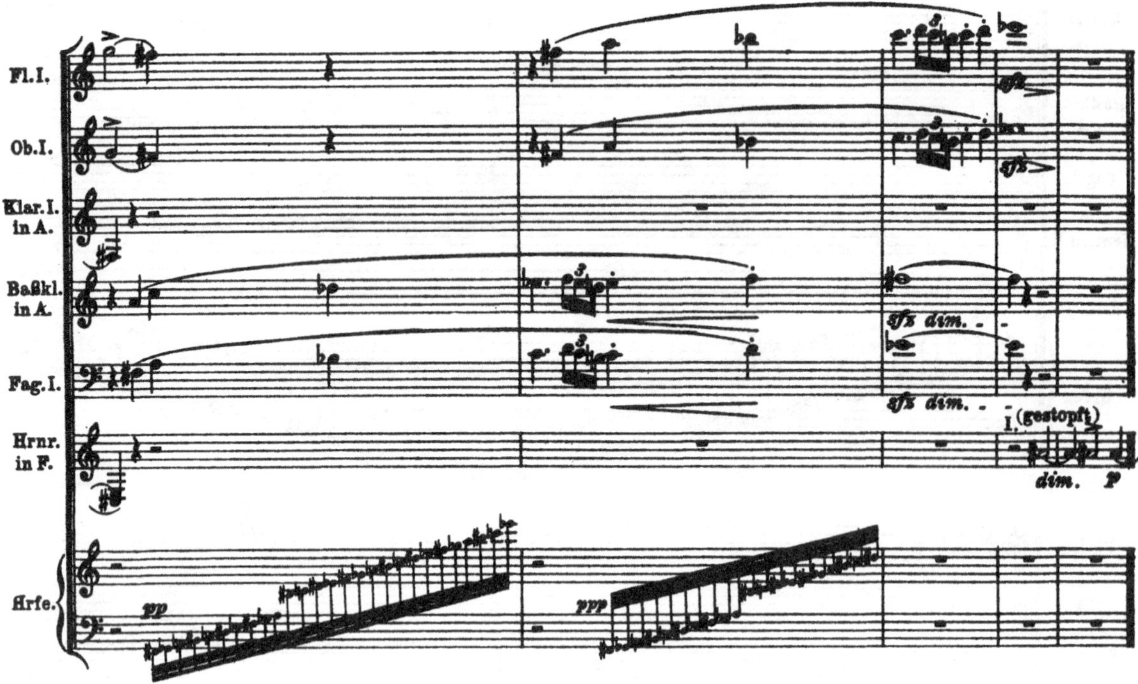

In connection with the harp, I wish to point out again the cautious use which Richard Wagner made of this instrument (see "Lohengrin" as an outstanding example, also the second act of "Tristan"). Whenever he employed it, he achieved extraordinary and striking effects with the timbre of this beautiful instrument. I can only warn beginners again to use all particularly bright and characteristic colors of the orchestra very sparingly and, before writing them, to consider seriously whether these colors are indispensable in this particular place or whether they might be replaced by simpler ones.

Nowadays all these special orchestral titbits such as harps, flageolets, percussion instruments, are being terribly misused. Especially the percussion instruments should be used only as isolated highlights if their effect is to be felicitous and characteristic; see the single triangle stroke at the end of the second act of "Tristan". Otherwise the ear of the listener becomes unnecessarily dulled: fine light-accents become formless smears of color.

Berlioz was unusually familiar with the technique of the harp, which in view of its difficulty cannot be expected from every author. A funny utterance of Richard Wagner's to the harpist Tombo is reported. During the first rehearsal of the end of "Rheingold" in Munich, when Tombo sadly declared the harp part to be absolutely unplayable, Wagner said to the excellent artist, "You cannot expect me to be able to play the harp; you see what effects I want to achieve; now arrange your part as you like". Those who do not feel sure they possess the inspired instinct of a Wagner, had better follow the saying: Quod licet Jovi, non licet bovi.

The harp must always be treated as a solo instrument, also in the orchestra, lest one write unnecessarily notes which are inaudible.

In the tutti of a modern orchestra only a group of several harps is effective. The harp part of "Tristan" is played by four harps in Bayreuth!

An effect on the harp not mentioned by Berlioz is the *bisbigliando* ("murmuring"), used for executing tremolos. The tremolo is written as for the piano, for instance ; the harpist does not play it with one hand, but distributes it between the right and left hands:

Figures like the following can also be executed in this fashion:

The Guitar

The guitar is an instrument suitable for accompanying the voice and for taking part in instrumental compositions of intimate character; it is equally appropriate for solo performance of more or less complicated compositions in several voices, which possess true charm when performed by real virtuosos.

It has six strings, tuned in fourths and thirds as follows:

Sometimes it is tuned in the following manner, especially for pieces in the key of E:

The three lower strings are made of silk covered with silver wire; the other three of catgut. The guitar is a transposing instrument with a range of three octaves and a fifth, written in the G-clef, an octave higher than the actual sound:

Notation:

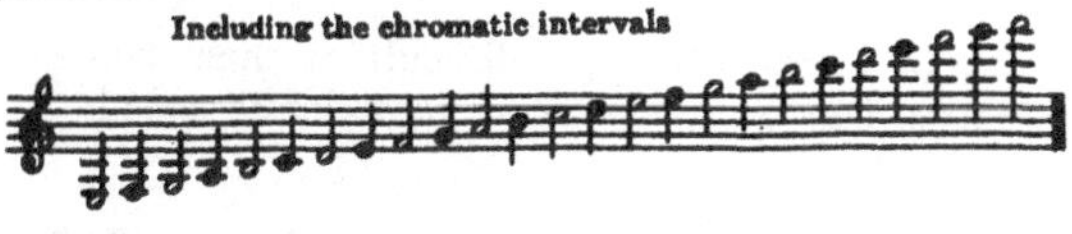

Sound:

Major and minor trills can be played throughout the range of this scale.

It is almost impossible to write well for the guitar without being able to play the instrument. However, the majority of composers who employ it do not possess an accurate knowledge of it. They write things of excessive difficulty, weak sonority and small effect for the instrument. We shall at least try to indicate here how simple accompaniments should be written for it.

In the usual position of the right hand the little finger rests on the body of the instrument; the thumb is used for plucking the three lower strings:

the forefinger plays on the G-string ; the middle finger, on the B-string ; and the third finger, on the high E-string

Consequently, for chords of more than four notes the thumb has to slide across one or two of the lower strings while the other three fingers strike the three high strings directly. In chords of four notes each finger strikes only its own string; the fingers change strings only to play chords in low positions, for instance:

Since the guitar is mainly a harmonic instrument, it is important to become familiar with the chords and hence also the arpeggios which it can execute. We start with the easiest—those which can be played without the *barrage,* a procedure whereby the forefinger of the left hand is placed across the neck of the instrument over two, three or four strings, and thus serves as an artificial fret. (The fret is the little ledge across the neck, on which the strings rest and which limits their vibrating length.)

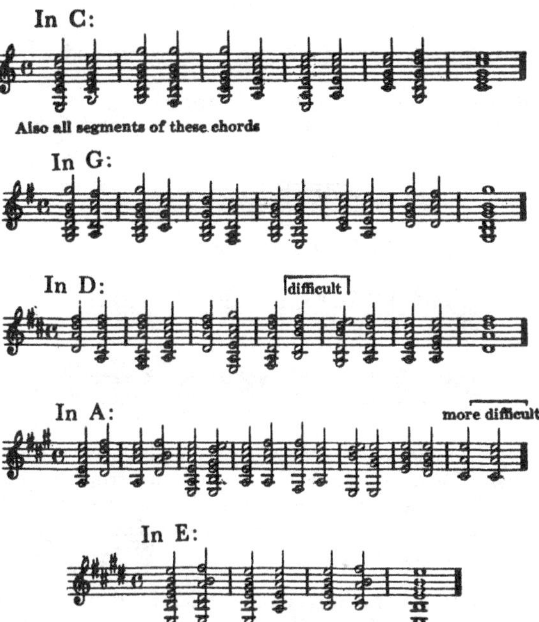

The flat keys are incomparably more difficult than the preceding; all of them require the barrage. The following chords are the easiest:

In all chords one must avoid using the first and third strings *without the second* because the thumb would be forced to skip over the second string to go from the first to the third. It is impossible to play the following chords:

But if the second string is added, they become easy:

Dominant seventh chords should not be written in the usual position of three thirds one above the other, as:

They are next to impossible. The following, though difficult, is possible: because G is an open string; only is very easy and sonorous on account of the open E-string.

The following three chords are easy and link together well in all keys:

Likewise in F#, G, Ab, etc.:

Of course, these chords may sometimes have more than four notes, namely in keys which permit the addition of a low open string, as in A, E, G, F—in short, wherever one of these three notes can serve as bass.

The following succession of chords, requiring the barrage across four strings, is practicable on the lower two thirds of the neck of the guitar:

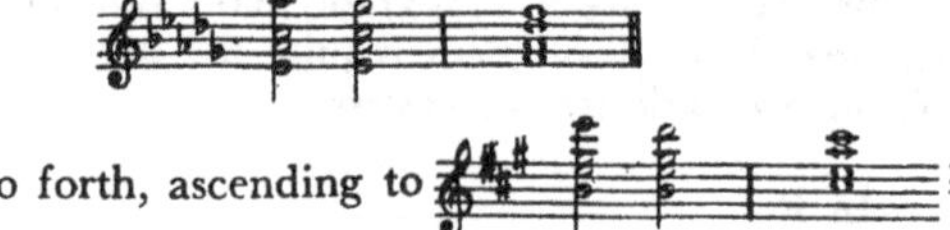

and so forth, ascending to ; this is the highest point where this fingering can be used.

The following arpeggios on the guitar are of excellent effect:

The two slurred high notes in the last example are played by plucking the E-string with the little finger of the left hand.

Descending arpeggios are rather awkward but feasible:

In the opposite direction they are very easy. The following are much more difficult and less advantageous on account of the retrograde movement of the thumb on the low two notes:

Scales in groups of two slurred notes with the repetition of one note are elegant and sound well, especially in the brilliant keys of the instrument:

Allegro.

Scales in thirds, although difficult at their two extremities, can be executed at a moderate speed:

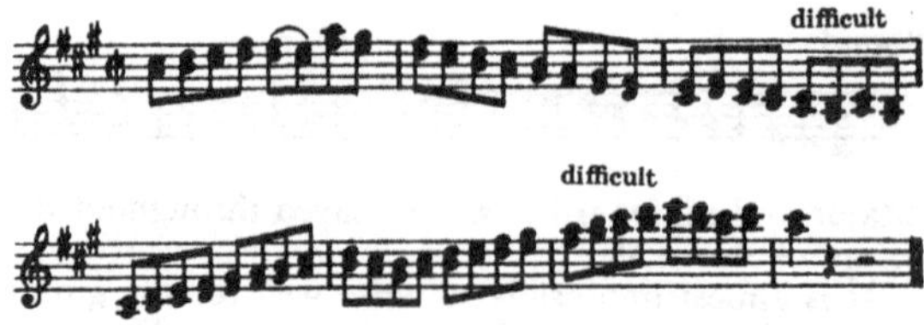

This applies equally to series of sixths and octaves.

Repeating the same tone two, three, four and even six or eight times is easy; prolonged repetitions (rolls), however, are appropriate only on the highest string or possibly on the three high strings:

The tones marked T are played with the thumb, the others alternatingly with the first and second fingers.

In rolls the thumb alternates with the first and second fingers on the same string:

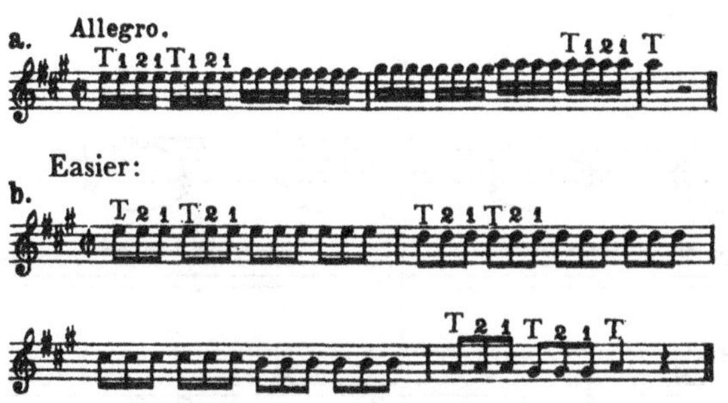

Harmonics are easily produced on the guitar and may be excellently employed in many cases. The best are those produced on open strings—by lightly touching the octave, fifth, fourth or major third.

As we have explained in the chapters on the stringed instruments, the octave, lightly touched, produces that same octave:

The minor third produces the higher octave of the twelfth:

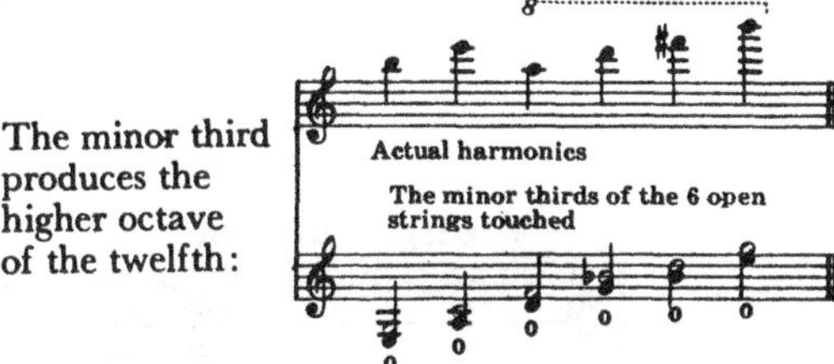

The last-mentioned harmonics are the least sonorous and are difficult to produce. It should be understood that the expression *actual harmonics* in the preceding list refers only to the pitch of the guitar, not to absolute pitch; for in absolute pitch these harmonics, like all other tones on the guitar, are an octave lower than the written notes.

Chromatic and diatonic scales in artificial harmonics can also be produced on each string. For this purpose the fingers of the left hand are pressed on the tones whose higher octave is to be produced; the forefinger of the right hand then touches the center of the vibrating part of the string, and the thumb of the same hand plucks the string behind the forefinger.

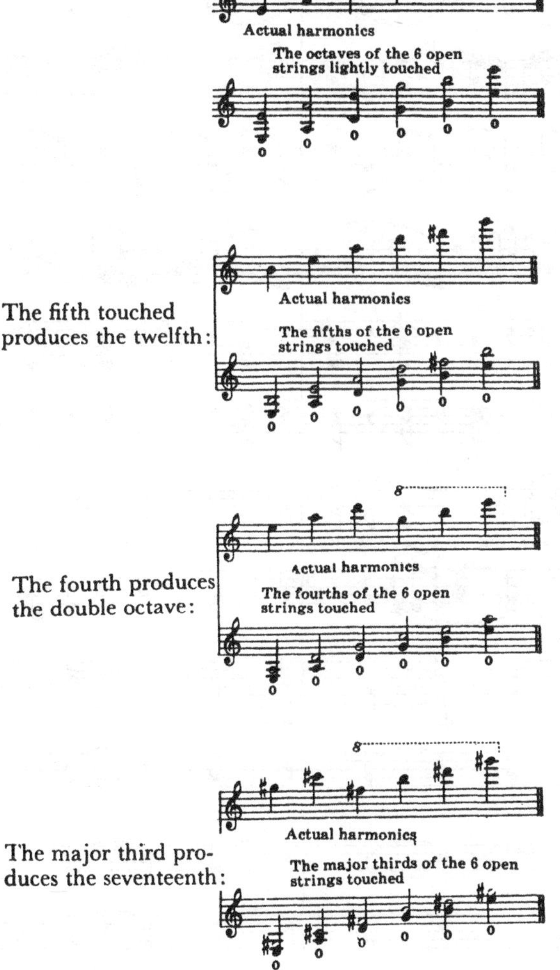

Unless one can play the guitar oneself, I repeat, it is impossible to write for it pieces in several voices, containing passages that require all the resources of the instrument. If one wants to get an idea what virtuosos are able to achieve in this respect, the compositions of such famous guitar players as Zanni de Ferranti, Huerta, Sor, etc. should be studied.

Since the introduction of the piano into all homes where there is any interest in music the guitar has been gradually disappearing, except in Spain and Italy. Some virtuosos have cultivated and are still cultivating it as a solo instrument; they are able to create pleasant and original effects on it. Otherwise composers employ the guitar neither in the church nor in the theater or the concert hall. Its weak tone, which prevents its combination with other instruments or with several singing voices of normal tone volume, is doubtless the cause of this. Its melancholy, dreamy character might nevertheless be used more frequently. Its charm is undeniable, and it is not impossible to write for it so as to make this manifest. The guitar —in contrast to other instruments—loses when reinforced in number. The sound of twelve guitars playing unisono is almost ridiculous.

In Verdi's "Otello" the guitar is employed very felicitously in combination with a mandolin and bagpipe as an accompaniment of the chorus:

No. 54. Otello, Act II

Fl.
più p
Ob.
Klar. in A.
Fag.
p
Hrnr. in E.
pp
pp
Dud.
Mand.
Git.
I.
Viol.
II.
arco
più p
Viola.
arco
più p
scen-do-no nu- vo-le di fio-ri. Qui tra gi-gli e ro-se co-me a un ca-sto al-ta--re, padri,
Chor.
rag- gi, av-vam-pan cuo-ri, do-ve pas- si scen- do- no nuo-vo-
Vlc.
K.B.

Fl.
Ob.
Klar. in A.
Fag.
Hrnr. in E.
Dud.
Mand.
Git.
I.
Viol.
II.
Viola.
Kinder.
Chor.
Vlc.
K.B.
morendo
cantabile
pp
pp legato
T'of- fria - mo il gi- glio so-
bim-bi, spo-se ven-go-no a can- tar.
Men-tre al-l'au-ra vo-la, vo - la
le di fio - - ri.
a - ve stel- che in man de - gl'an-ge- li fu as- sun - to in ciel che ab-
lie-ta la can- zon, men-tre al l'au-ra vo-la lie- ta, vo - la lie- ta la can- zon, la can-zon.

The Mandolin

This instrument is almost forgotten nowadays, which is a pity. Despite its thin and nasal quality, its tone has something piquant and original about it and might be frequently used with good effect.

There are several kinds of mandolins. The one best known has four double strings—i.e., four times two strings in unison, tuned in fifths like those of the violin. It is written in the G-clef:

The two E-strings are of catgut; the A-strings, of steel; the D-strings, of brass; finally the G-strings, of catgut covered with silver wire.

The range of the mandolin is almost three octaves:

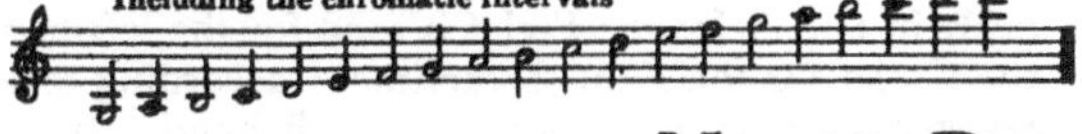

Including the chromatic intervals

It is an instrument better suited for melody than for harmony. Its strings are vibrated with a quill or plectrum held in the right hand of the player. They can produce four-part chords such as these:

if the plectrum is passed quickly across the four double strings; however, the effect of such groups of simultaneous tones is rather poor.

The mandolin shows its real character and effect only in such melodious accompaniments as Mozart wrote in the second act of "Don Giovanni" (Example 55).

No. 55. Don Giovanni, Act II

Allegretto. Mozart.

Mandoline. Viol. I. II. Viola. Don Juan. Bassi. (Vlc. u. K. B.)

pizz. *p*

Deh vieni alla finestra, o mio tesoro! Deh vieni a consolar il pianto mio!

Er klinge, liebe Zither, das Liebchen lauschet. Er klinge bis sie Seel' um Seele lauschet.

At present the mandolin is so completely neglected that in theaters where "Don Giovanni" is performed the execution of this serenade always presents difficulties. Although a guitar player or even a violinist could familiarize himself with the mandolin in a few days, so little respect is entertained for the ideas of the great masters whenever some old habit would have to be sacrificed, that people almost everywhere and even at the Opéra (the last place in the world where such liberties should be taken) venture to execute the mandolin part pizzicato on violins or on guitars. The tone of these instruments has by no means the peculiar delicacy of the mandolin; and Mozart knew what he was doing when he chose this particular instrument to accompany the amorous song of his hero.

Stringed Instruments With Keyboard

The Pianoforte

The pianoforte is an instrument with a keyboard and metal strings set in vibration by hammers. Its present range is six octaves and a fourth, frequently even seven octaves.* Its music is written simultaneously in two clefs: the F-clef is used for the left hand, the G-clef for the right. Sometimes—according to the registers of passages assigned to both hands—two F-clefs or two G-clefs are used.

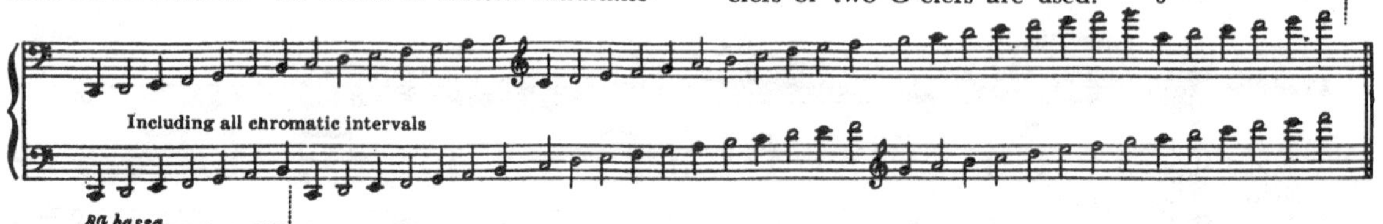

The trill is possible on all degrees of the scale. Chords of four and even five notes can be played simultaneously or arpeggiated in any manner and with both hands; but the harmony should be as close as possible:

Chords embracing an interval of a tenth are possible, too; but then the third and even the octave are omitted for the sake of greater ease of execution:

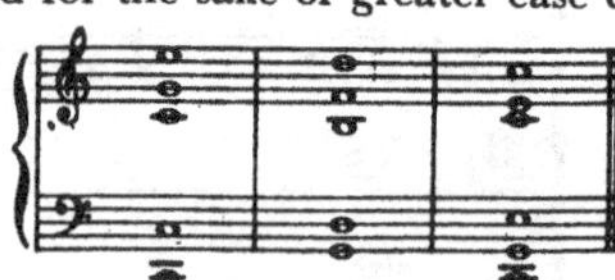

Four and even five real voices may be written for the pianoforte if care is taken to keep the outer parts in each hand within the space of an octave or at most a ninth. Otherwise the pedal has to be used. This raises the dampers and permits the player to prolong the tones without keeping the fingers on the keys, in which case one is free to place the voices even further apart.

Example in four parts without pedal:

Example with pedal:

*Now 7¼ octaves (i.e. 88 notes)

The sign * (or similar) in the second example indicates that the pedal is to be released in order to restore the function of the dampers. Whenever possible, it is used when the harmony changes in order to prevent the continuation of the previous chord during the ensuing one. On account of this long prolongation of each tone, appoggiaturas with accidentals and passing notes should be avoided as much as possible in the middle of the instrument while the pedal is being used; for these notes, sustained like all the others and thereby mixed with a harmony to which they do not belong, produce excessive dissonances. Such melodic ornaments are possible only in the highest octaves of the keyboard, where the strings are very short and have relatively little resonance.

Modern Steinway Grand Pianos have a third pedal, which serves to prolong a single tone at will. This is very effective and may occasionally help the player in passages of several voice-parts.

Sometimes the hands are made to cross, the left hand passing over the right or vice versa:

The number of such combinations among the manifold groups of tones playable on the pianoforte is very considerable. In fact, it would be impossible to mention them all here. Only by studying the compositions of great virtuosos, especially Liszt's, can one form a clear idea of the progress made in the art of piano playing. The student will then perceive that the limits of what is attainable on this instrument are still quite unknown, and that they are extended continuously through astonishing new exploits by performers.

For the pianoforte, as for the harp, it is better in certain cases (for instance in arpeggios) not to place the two hands too near each other. A passage like the following would be rather inconvenient:

It would be much better to write as follows:

Diatonic and chromatic scales in thirds for both hands are, however, quite easy:

Such scales in thirds can also be executed by one hand alone, but they are difficult in a fast tempo. Moreover, in keys with few sharps or flats one may write for both hands consecutive sixth-chords consisting of three notes:

Thanks to the high degree of perfection attained by our skilled manufacturers, the pianoforte may now be considered from two viewpoints: either as an orchestral instrument or as a small orchestra complete in itself. Only once * has it been employed in the same fashion as the other instruments, so as to add its peculiar resources to the ensemble of the orchestra and to create effects which could not be attained in any other way.

*Cf. "Lélio" by Berlioz, p. 157

Certain passages in Beethoven's concertos ought to have drawn the composers' attention to this point long ago. They have surely admired the wonderful effect in Beethoven's Concerto in E♭, produced by the slow chord figurations of both hands in the high region of the piano, while the flute, clarinet and bassoon play the melody over eighth-notes of the strings in contretemps. In such combination, the tone of the pianoforte has an alluring charm, it is full of calm of freshness—the very image of grace. (Example 56.)

No. 56. Concerto in E♭, Adagio

Fl.
Klar. in A.
Fag.
Pfte.
I.
Viol.
II.
Viola.
Bassi.
cresc.
dim.
pp
p

Fl.
Klar. in A.
Fag.
sempre più dim.
Pfte.
Ped.
morendo
I.
Viol.
II.
Viola.
Bassi.
Fl.
Klar. in A.
Fag.
pp
Hrnr. in Es.
pp
pp
Pfte.
Ped.
pizz.
p
Viol.
II.
pizz.
p
Viola.
pizz.
p
Bassi.
pizz.
p

The employment of the pianoforte in the singular case mentioned above is entirely different. In a chorus of airy spirits, the author lets two pianos for four hands accompany the voices. The lower pair of hands executes a rapid, ascending arpeggio passage in triplets, which is answered by a descending three-part arpeggio of flutes and clarinets; the latter passage is illuminated by a double-trill in thirds, executed by the other pair of hands on the higher piano. No other instrument could produce such a harmonious glimmering of tones, which the piano renders without difficulty, and which the sylph-like character of the piece requires. (Example 57.)

No. 57. Lélio, Monodrame Lyrique, Finale (Fantaisie sur la tempête)

Pfte. I.
Pfte. II.
Picc.
Gr. Fl.
Klar. in C.
Viol. I.
Viol. II.
Chor.
ppp
ran - - - - da, Mi - ran - - - - - da, Mi-
Mi - ran - - - - - da,
Mi - ran - - - - - da,
Mi - ran - - - - - da,
Mi - ran - - - - - da,

Pfte. I.
Pfte. II.
Picc.
Gr. Fl.
Klar. in C.
Viol. I.
Viol. II.
Chor.
ran - - - - da, Mi-ran - - - - - - da,
Mi-ran - - - - - - da,
Mi-ran - - - - - - da,
Mi-ran - - - - - - da,
Mi-ran - - - - - - da,

Pfte. I.
Pfte. II.
Picc.
Gr. Fl.
Klar. in C.
Viol. I.
Viol. II.
Chor.
vien' chi t'è de - sti - na - to spo - - - - - so.
sieh' den Ver - lob - ten sich dir na - - - - - hen.
vien' chi t'è de - sti - na - to spo - - - - - so.
sieh' den Ver - lob - ten sich dir na - - - - - hen.
vien' chi t'è de - sti - na - to spo - - - - - so.

Whenever the piano is forced to go beyond its own tender effects and to compete with the power of the orchestra, it disappears completely. It must accompany or be accompanied, unless, like harps, it is employed in large numbers. I would not be inclined to scorn such an arrangement; however, in view of the large space required, it would be difficult to place a dozen pianofortes in a moderately large orchestra.

Regarded as a small independent orchestra in itself, the pianoforte must have its own appropriate instrumentation, which is closely connected with the performing pianist's art. On many occasions it is left to the player to bring out certain voices or to keep others in the background; to play a passage in the middle register with emphasis while giving lightness to the ornamental passages above and reducing the sonority of the basses. It is for him to decide where a change of fingers is indicated or where only the thumb should be used for a particular melody. In writing for his instrument, he knows when to employ close or open harmony; he understands the various degrees of distance between tones in arpeggios and the different kinds of sound resulting from them. Especially important is the judicious use of the pedals. Outstanding composers of pianoforte music have always indicated with the utmost care where the damper pedal is to be taken and released. Unfortunately, many virtuosos — and some of the most brilliant among them — wantonly disregard these pedaling marks and play almost continuously with raised dampers. They pay no attention to the prolongation of unrelated harmonies into one another and to the ugly discords caused thereby. This bad habit is really a deplorable abuse of an excellent device; the result is noise and confusion instead of harmony! This is only the natural consequence of that intolerable tendency of virtuosos—great and small, singers and instrumentalists—to put interest in their own personality in the foreground.

This reproach can now also be extended to a great number of conductors.

They have little regard for the indispensable respect which the performer owes the composer, and for the tacit but absolute obligation to transmit the composer's ideas faithfully to the audience—whether the performer honors a mediocre author by interpreting him, or is honored himself in rendering the immortal ideas of a genius. In either case, the performer who, catering to a momentary whim, works contrary to the composer's intentions, ought to contemplate the fact that the author of the work, whatever it may be, has probably devoted considerably more attention to the place and duration of certain effects, to the design of his melody and rhythm, to the choice of chords and instruments, than the performer has in taking his own peculiar liberties. One cannot protest enough against this senseless privilege too often claimed by instrumentalists, singers and conductors. Such presumption is not only ridiculous; if it develops further, it must produce unspeakable confusion and cause serious harm to the art. Composers and critics must fight against this at all times.

(These are golden words! The Editor)

The soft pedal is used much less frequently than the damper pedal; but Beethoven and several other composers have employed it very felicitously. It is of excellent effect when contrasted with the ordinary sound of the pianoforte or with the splendid sonority produced by the damper pedal. It is equally useful in accompanying singers, especially if their voices are weak, and in the more frequent instances where the entire performance is to have a soft and tender character. Its use is indicated by "una corda" or "mit Verschiebung". Its action consists in shifting the whole keyboard so that the hammers hit only two of the three unisono strings which are now provided in all good instruments for each tone (excepting the lower ranges). Since only two strings vibrate instead of three, the sound is reduced and the timbre is changed considerably.

Wind Instruments

Before studying individually each member of this large family, we shall establish as clearly as possible a musical vocabulary indicating the different degrees of high or low pitch of certain instruments, the transpositions causing these differences, as well as the customary notation and denomination of these instruments.

We begin by making a line of demarcation between instruments sounding as they are written and instruments whose tones sound higher or lower than the written notes. The following two categories result from this division:

NON-TRANSPOSING INSTRUMENTS whose tones sound as written	TRANSPOSING INSTRUMENTS whose tones are different from the written notes
Violin	
Viola	
Viola d'amore, Viola da gamba	
Violoncello	Double-bass
Ordinary flute	All other flutes
Oboe	Oboe d'amore, English horn
Clarinet in C	All other clarinets
Bassoon	Tenoroon, Double bassoon
Russian bassoon	
French horn in high C	All other French horns
Cornet in C	All other cornets
Trumpet in C	All other trumpets
Alto trombone	Valve alto trombone
Tenor trombone	
Bass trombone	
Ophicleide in C	All other ophicleides
Bombardon	Serpent
Bass tuba	All other tubas
Harp, Mandolin	Guitar
Pianoforte	
Organ	
Voices (if written in their individual clefs and not, without any distinction, in the G-clef).	Tenors and Basses (if written in the G-clef, their sound being an octave below the written notes).
Kettledrums	
Bells	
Ancient cymbals	
Chime	
Glockenspiel	
Keyboard harmonica	Harmonica with steel tongues

Viola alta	
Violotta	
Cellone	
	Heckel-Clarina
	Heckelphon
Saxophone in C	All other saxophones, saxhorns, saxotrombas and saxtubas
Celesta	

It will be seen from this table that all non-transposing instruments marked "in C", whose tones sound as they are written, belong to the same category as those without any designation of key (like the violin, oboe, flute, etc.); the latter are completely equivalent to the instruments in C from the composer's point of view. However, the designation of some wind instruments in accordance with the natural sound of their tubes has led to the most singular and absurd consequences; it has made the notation of transposing instruments very complicated and the musical vocabulary very illogical. It is, therefore, necessary to discuss this practice thoroughly and to re-establish order where it is generally conspicuous by its absence.

Performers sometimes call the tenor trombone, "the trombone in B♭"; the alto trombone, "the trombone in E♭"; and still more frequently, the ordinary flute, "the flute in D".

These designations are correct in the sense that the tube of the two trombones with the slide closed produces the tones of the B♭ chord on the first trombone, and those of the E♭ chord on the second trombone; likewise, the ordinary flute with all holes stopped and all keys closed plays the tone D. Yet performers need not pay any attention to the natural sound of the tube; they simply play the written notes. Thus, the C of a tenor trombone is a C and not a B♭, the C of an alto trombone is also C and not E♭, that of the flute is again a C and not a D. The evident conclusion is that these instruments belong not to the transposing, but to the non-transposing instruments. One may consider them to be in C just as well as the oboes, clarinets, horns, cornets and trumpets in C. They require no designation of key, unless they be called "in C". This shows at once how important it is *not* to call the ordinary flute, "flute in D"; for it has become the fashion to name the higher-pitched flutes according to the difference between their pitch and that of the ordinary flute. Thus, the flute in the third (i.e., "third-flute") is called "flute in F"; the flute in the ninth (i.e., "ninth-flute") is called "flute in E♭". The designation of the instruments by interval rather than by key would at least have avoided the confusion of terms. The following illustrates what this terminology can lead to. In a score the small clarinet in E♭, whose C really produces E♭, can execute the same part as a third-flute, so-called "in F". The two instruments bearing the names of different keys nevertheless produce the identical tone. One of the two designations must be false. Is it not absurd to adopt a nomenclature for the keys of the flute completely at variance with that used for the other instruments?

Hence I propose the following principle, which makes any misunderstanding impossible: the tone C is the only point of comparison upon which the designation of the key of transposing instruments is to be based. The natural sound of the tube of non-transposing wind instruments is to be disregarded completely. All non-transposing instruments and those transposed only in the octave (i.e., in which the written C produces C) are considered as being *in C*.

If an instrument of the same family is tuned below or above the pitch of the basic instrument, this difference is designated according to the relation to C. Consequently, the violin, the flute, the oboe, playing unisono with the clarinet in C, the trumpet in C, the horn in C, *are in C;* whereas a violin, a flute, an oboe which are tuned a tone higher than the usual instruments of the same name, are called *in D,* because they play unisono with the clarinet in D and the trumpet in D.

Hence it follows that the old designations for the flutes should be abandoned: the third-flute should no longer be called flute in F, but rather flute in E♭, since its C produces E♭; likewise, flutes in the minor ninth or second should not be called flutes in E♭, but rather large or small flute in D♭, since their C produces D♭; and so on for all keys.

Reed Instruments

The family of double-reed instruments is to be distinguished from that of single-reed instruments. The former is composed of five members: the oboe, the English horn, the bassoon, the tenoroon, and the double-bassoon; the latter comprises clarinets, basset-horns, saxophones, etc.

The Oboe

This instrument has a range of two octaves and a fifth and is written in the G-clef:

The two highest notes should be used with caution; the F in particular is risky when it enters abruptly.* Some oboes have the low B♭ ; but this tone, not generally available on the instrument, should better be avoided. With the application of Boehm's system the present difficulties of fingering will disappear, as for instance in rapid passages from the middle C♯ (D♭) to the note above:

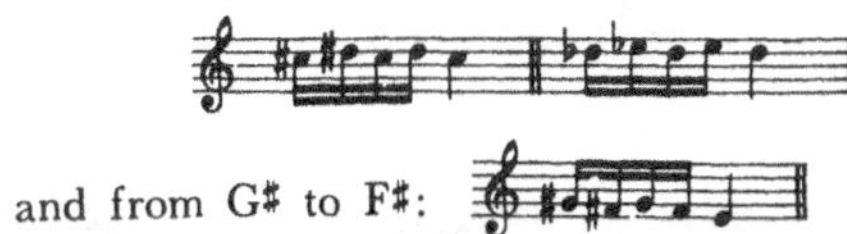

and from G♯ to F♯:

On these tones and also on certain others, major trills are therefore impossible or very difficult and of poor effect, as the following table shows:

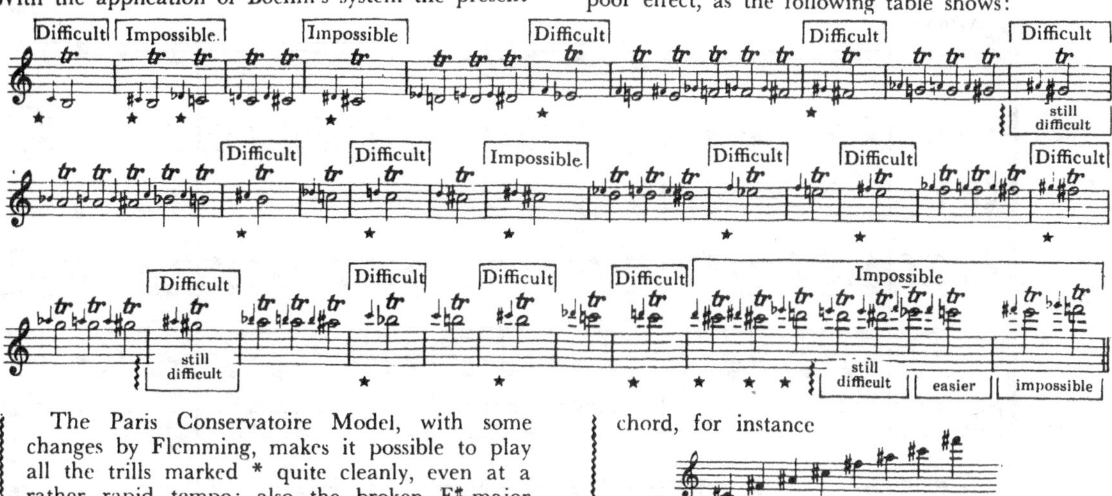

The Paris Conservatoire Model, with some changes by Flemming, makes it possible to play all the trills marked * quite cleanly, even at a rather rapid tempo; also the broken F♯-major chord, for instance

* This no longer applies to the modern French oboes;

they can play piano up to ; they even produce and , but only legato.

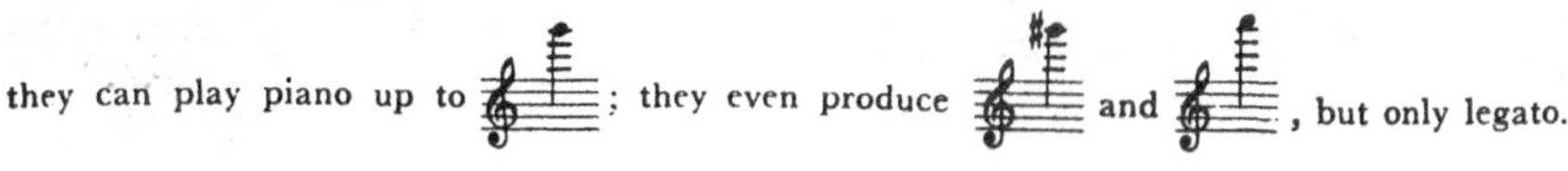

Oboes, similarly to all other instruments, play with greater ease in keys with few flats and sharps.

Scales in B are difficult, in A♭ easier, in D♭ again more difficult. The following passages are easy, even at the most rapid tempo:

In melodious passages the following range should not be exceeded:

The tones above or below this range sound weak or thin, hard or shrill and are all of poor quality. Rapid chromatic or diatonic runs have an unpleasant, almost ridiculous effect, even though they can be executed quite easily on the oboe; the same is true of arpeggios. There should hardly ever be any need of writing such passages; in fact, we have never come across any. The use that virtuosos make of them in their fantasias and variations does not disprove their impracticability. The oboe is above all a melodic instrument; it has a pastoral character, full of tenderness—I might even say, of shyness.

In the tutti of the orchestra the oboe is used, however, without consideration of its timbre; for here it is lost in the ensemble, and its peculiar expression cannot be identified. We may mention here in advance that this applies also to most of the other wind instruments. Only those of extremely strong volume or with very distinctive peculiarities of tone offer an exception. They cannot be treated for purposes of general harmony like other instruments without offending both art and common sense. Among these we can put the trombones, ophicleides, double-bassoons, and in many instances also the trumpets and cornets.

Artless grace, pure innocence, mellow joy, the pain of a tender soul—all these the oboe can render admirably with its cantabile. A certain degree of excitement is also within its power; but one must guard against increasing it to the cry of passion, the stormy outburst of fury, menace or heroism; for then its small voice, sweet and somewhat tart at the same time, becomes ineffectual and completely grotesque. Even some of the great masters—Mozart among them—did not avoid this error entirely. In their scores we find passages whose passionate contents and martial accents contrast strangely with the sound of the oboes executing them. This causes not only thwarted effects, but also startling disparities between stage and orchestra, between melody and instrumentation. The theme of a march, however vigorous, beautiful and noble it may be, loses its nobility, vigor and beauty when played by oboes. It may possibly preserve its character if given to the flutes; played by clarinets, it almost invariably retains its full power.

Only in pp have martial rhythms been employed successfully—to imitate trumpets played in the distance (especially by Mozart). Cf. Figaro's aria (Example 58).

No. 58. Le Nozze di Figaro, Act I

Ob.
Fag.
Hrnr. in C.
I. Viol. II.
Viola.
Figaro.
Vlc. u. K.B.
a 2.
ten.
mfp
bel-le turban-do il ri- po-so, Nar-ci- set-to, A-don-ci-no d'a-mor, del-le bel-le tur-ban-do il ri-
Fl.
Tromp. in C.
Pke.
p
po-so, Nar-ci- set-to, A-don-ci-no d'a- mor. Che-ru-bi-no al-la vit- to-ria,

Fl.
Ob.
Fag.
Hrnr. in C.
Trp. in C.
Pke.
Figaro.
al-la glo-ria mi-li- tar, Che-ru- bi-no al-la vit- to-ria, al-la glo- ria mi- li-
a 2.
I.
Viol.
II.
Viola.
tar, al-la glo- ria mi- li- tar, al-la glo- ria mi- li- tar!
Vlc. u. K. B.

Occasionally, however, oboes have to be used in pieces of a martial nature in order to give more weight to the harmony and to reinforce the other wind instruments. Since its sound is not suitable for this style, the oboe part should be written so that it is completely covered by the other instruments. It should blend with the ensemble so as not to be recognizable as an individual instrument. The lower tones of the oboe, unpleasant when used prominently, may be combined very effectively in certain strange and lamenting harmonies with the low tones of the clarinet and the low D, E, F, G of the flutes and English horns.

Gluck and Beethoven showed admirable understanding for the use of this valuable instrument; the profound effect of several of their finest pages is due to the oboe. Concerning Gluck, I need only mention the oboe solo in Agamemnon's aria in "Iphigénie en Aulide" ("Peuvent-ils ordonner"). What other instrument could so poignantly express these laments of an innocent voice, this prolonged and ever more urgent supplication? (Example 59.)

No. 59. Iphigénie en Aulide, Act I

Fl.u.Ob.
I.
Viol.
II.
Viola.
Ag.
chè-re, peu-vent-ils l'or-don - ner? Je n'o-bé-i-rai point a cet ordre in-hu-main, je
Lie-be: welch ein grau-sam Ge - bot! Nein, ich be-geh' sie nicht, die unmenschli-che Tat, nein,
Bassi.
Oboe Solo.
n'o-bé-i-rai point a cet ordre in-hu-main!
ich be-geh' sie nicht, die unmensch-li-che Tat!
J'en-tends re-ten-tir dans mon
Das Kla - ge-ge-schrei der Na-
Fag.
pizz.
Ob.
sein le cri plain-tif de la na - tu-re, el-le parle à mon coeur,
tur in mei-nem Bu-sen hallt es wie-der! ach! sie spricht zu mei-nem Her-zen,
pp

Ob.
I.
Viol.
II.
Viola.
Ag.
et sa voix est plus su - re que les o - ra - cles du des - tin, que les o - ra - cles
und ihr Wort faßt mich mächt'ger als des O - ra - kels Don - ner - wort, als des O - ra - kels
Bassi.
Fl. u. Ob.
du des - tin! Je n'o - bé - i - rai point à cet ordre in - hu - main, je n'o - bé - i - rai point à cet
Don - ner - wort! Nein, ich be - geh'sie nicht, die unmenschli - che Tat, nein, ich be - geh'sie nicht, die un-
arco
Fl. u. Ob.
ordre in - hu - main!
mensch - li - che Tat!

Consider, too, the famous ritornelle in the aria from "Iphigénie en Tauride": "O malheureuse Iphigénie!" (Act II, Scene 4). Again, the childlike cry of the orchestra when Alceste, in the enthusiasm of her heroic self-sacrifice, is struck by the recollection of her two little sons and suddenly interrupts the theme "Eh, pourrai-je vivre sans toi?" to respond to the touching appeal of the instruments with her heart-rending cry, "O mes enfants!" (Act I, Scene 5). Finally, let us mention the discord of the minor second in Armida's aria, with the words "Sauvez-moi de l'amour" (Example 60). All this is sublime—not only in its dramatic idea, its profound expression and in its melodic grandeur and beauty, but also in its instrumentation and the admirable choice of the oboe as the instrument most adequate and appropriate for creating such impressions.

No. 60. Armide, Act III

Fag.
Hrn. in F.
I.
Viol.
II.
Viola.
Arm.
gner une é - ter - nelle hor - reur! Ve - nez, ve - nez, haine im - pla -
Nacht, wo Schre - cken nur re - giert, her - auf, her - auf, Haß un - ver -
Bassi.
Ob.
ca - ble, sor - tez du gouffre é - pou - van - ta - ble, sauvez - moi de l'a -
söh - net, her - auf aus grau - en - vol - ler Tie - fe! Ret - te mich, ret - te
mour, sau - vez - moi de l'a - mour! Rien n'est si re - dou - ta - ble,
mich vor der Lie - be Glut! Kei - ne Qual ist so furcht - bar!

Ob.
Fag.
Hrn. in F.
I.
Viol.
II.
Viola.
Arm.
contre un en - ne - mi trop ai - ma - ble, ren - dez - moi mon cour - roux, r'al - lu - mez
Ge - gen einen Feind, den ich lie - be, waffne mich, gib mir Haß und ent - flamm'
Bassi.
f
p
— ma fu - reur! Venez, ve - nez, haine im - pla - ca - ble, sor - tez du
— meinen Zorn! Herauf, her - auf, Haß, un - ver - söh - net! her - auf aus
gouffre é - pou - van - ta - ble, où vous fai - tes ré - gner une é - ternelle hor - reur!
grau - en - vol - ler Tie - fe! Dort, wo e - wi - ge Nacht, wo Schreckennurre - giert!

Examples of extended oboe melodies, invented with the peculiar character of the instrument in mind, are to be found in Berlioz' works, such as the overtures to "King Lear" and "Cellini", and in the "Symphonie Fantastique". (Examples 61 and 62.).

No. 61. King Lear, Overture

No. 62. King Lear, Overture

a tempo
Ob.
I.
Viol.
II.
Viola.
Vlc.
K. B.
rit.
a tempo
poco a poco
Fag.
animato
a tempo
Fl.
Klar. in C.
Hrn. in C.
Vcl.

No other instrument could reveal the sweet secret of love's innocence in such affecting tones as the oboe in "Tannhaeuser". (Example 63.)

No. 63. Tannhaeuser, Act II

Wagner.

Andante. ♩= 76.

Violen. (geteilt)

Landgraf.

Vcelli. (geteilt)

Noch blei-be denn un-aus-ge-spro-chen dein süß Ge-heimnis kur - ze

Klar. in B.

Fag.

Violen.

Lndgrf.

Vlc.

Frist; der Zau - ber blei-be un - ge-bro - chen, bis du der Lö-sung mäch-tig bist, bis

dimin. pp

Fl.

Ob.

Klar. in B.

Ventilhorn in F.

Fag.

Violen.

Lndgrf.

Vlc.

— du der Lö-sung, der Lö - sung mäch - tig bist.

(alle Violoncelli)

As a rule, however, Wagner rarely gives extended melodies to one instrument alone. He prefers the method of distributing melodies among intricate combinations of several instruments. A classical example of this is to be found in the second act of "Walkuere" (Example 64).

No. 64. Walkuere, Act II

The oboe with its thick and impudent low tones and its thin and bleating high tones, especially if they are exaggerated, is very suitable for humorous effects and for caricature. The oboe can rattle, bleat, scream just as well as it can sing and lament nobly and innocently, or play and warble cheerfully.

Beethoven used predominantly the gay expression of the oboes. Examples of this are to be found in the solo in the Scherzo of the Pastoral Symphony (Example 65), in the Scherzo of the Ninth Symphony, in the first movement of the B♭-major Symphony, etc. But he was no less successful in assigning tones of sadness or despair to the oboe. This is illustrated by the solo in minor, in the recapitulation of the first movement of the A-major Symphony, in the episodic Andante of the "Eroica" finale, and particularly in the aria in "Fidelio" where the starving Florestan imagines seeing his weeping wife in his delirious agony and mingles his anguished cries with the sobs of the oboe. (Examples 66, 67, 68.)

No. 65. Pastoral Symphony, 3rd movement

Beethoven.

Allegro.

Oboe I.
p

Klar. in B.

Fag.
I.
p

Viol. I.
dimin. - - - - - pp

Viol. II.
dimin. - - - - - pp

Ob.
cresc.
dolce

Klar. in B.

Fag.

Viol. I.

Viol. II.

Ob.
cresc.

Klar. in B.

Fag.

Viol. I.
pp

Viol. II.
pp

Ob.
dolce

Klar. in B.
I.
dolce

Fag.

Viol. I.

Viol. II.

No. 66. Symphony in A major, 1st movement

Beethoven.

No. 67. Sinfonia Eroica, Finale

Fl.
Ob.
Klar. in B.
Fag.
I. II.
Hrnr. in Es.
III.
Pke.
I.
Viol.
II.
Viola.
Vlc. u. K. B.
sf
p
cresc.
pp
pizz.
I.

No. 68. Fidelio, Act II

Ob.
Hrnr. in F.
I. Viol. II.
Viola.
Flor.
Engel im ro - si-gen Duft sich tröstend zur Sei-te, zur Sei-te mir stellet, ein Engel, Le-o-
Vlc.
K. B.
cresc. poco a poco - - f dolce
no-ren, Le-o-noren, der Gat-tin, so gleich, der, der führt mich zur Freiheit ins himm-lische Reich.

The French instruments are of finer workmanship, their registers are more even, they respond more easily in the treble and allow a softer pp on low tones. Correspondingly, the style of playing and the tone of French oboists is by far preferable to that of the German players. Some German "methods" try to produce a tone as thick and trumpet-like as possible, which does not blend in at all with the flutes and clarinets and is often unpleasantly prominent.

The French tone, though thinner and frequently tremulant, is much more flexible and adaptable; yet, when it is necessary, its forte can be penetrating and also much more resonant.

This applies particularly to the English horn. Observe its admirable application and combination with flutes, oboes, clarinets, bassoons in the first and second acts of "Lohengrin." Their effect would be completely changed, against the author's intentions, if the English horn were to stand out as an independent part, as it often happens when the German method is used, instead of acting as a discrete mediator between the timbres of the wood-wind instruments.

The Oboe d'amore

It is a minor third lower than the oboe and has the following range:

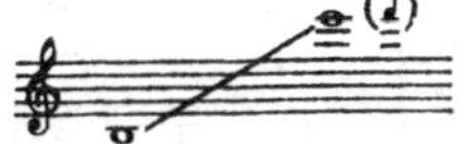

Actual sound:

Its timbre is milder and of a more subdued character; its agility in the sharp keys is greater than that of the oboe.

It was frequently employed by J. S. Bach and his contemporaries, mostly as a concertante instrument, preferably two oboes d'amore together.

At the beginning of the second part of his Christmas Oratorio, Bach introduces two of them in combination with English horns—a delightful representation of the peaceful pastoral music.

As an example of the employment of this instrument in modern times, I should like to mention my "Sinfonia Domestica", where the oboe serves as a symbol of the child, dreaming innocently as well as playing gaily. (Full score, p. 13—"III. Thema", and p. 15—Scherzo.)

The English Horn

This instrument is, so to speak, the alto of the oboe. It has almost the same range; some English horns also have the low B♭. It is written in the G-clef like an oboe in low F; consequently, its real sound is a fifth lower than written. Its scale

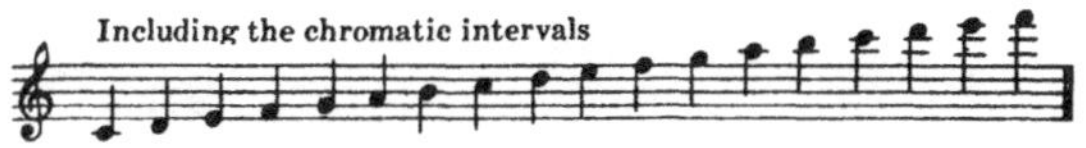

sounds as follows to the listener:

If the orchestra plays in C, the English horn must be written in G; if it plays in D, the English horn is written in A, etc.

Everything that has been said in connection with the oboe concerning difficulties in the fingering for certain groups of sharped or flatted tones applies equally to the English horn*; rapid passages have an even poorer effect on the latter instrument. Its tone, less piercing, more veiled and heavy than that of the oboe, does not lend itself so well to the gaiety of rustic melodies. Nor can it express passionate laments; tones of keen grief are scarcely within its range. Its tones are melancholy, dreamy, noble, somewhat veiled—as if played in the distance. It has no equal among the instruments for reviving images and sentiments of the past if the composer intends to touch the hidden chords of tender memories.

Thus, Halévy has very felicitously employed two English horns in the ritornelle of Eleazar's aria in the fourth act of "La Juive" (Example 69).

A most marvellous example is the sad strain of the shepherd in the third act of Wagner's "Tristan" (Example 13, p. 39).

No. 69. La Juive, Act IV

*Similarly to the oboe, this is no longer true today, the present technical qualities of the English horn being about equal to those of the oboe.

In the Adagio of one of my symphonies the English horn repeats the phrases of the oboe in the lower octave, like the voice of a youth replying to a girl in a pastoral dialogue. Then, at the end of the piece, it reiterates fragments of these phrases with a hollow accompaniment of four kettledrums, while the rest of the orchestra remains silent. The mood of absence and oblivion, of sorrowful loneliness, which arises in the soul of many a listener at the recurrence of this melancholy tune, would be far less poignant if it were played by another instrument. (Example 70.)

No. 70. Symphonie Fantastique, Scène aux Champs

The combination of the low tones of the English horn with those of the clarinets and French horns during a tremolo of the double-basses produces an effect as characteristic as it is novel; it is particularly well suited to cast a menacing color upon musical ideas in which fear and anguish predominate. This effect was known neither to Mozart nor to Weber or Beethoven. A magnificent example is to be found in the duet in the fourth act of "Les Huguenots"; I think Meyerbeer was the first to have used it in the theater. (Example 71.)

No. 71. Les Huguenots, Act IV

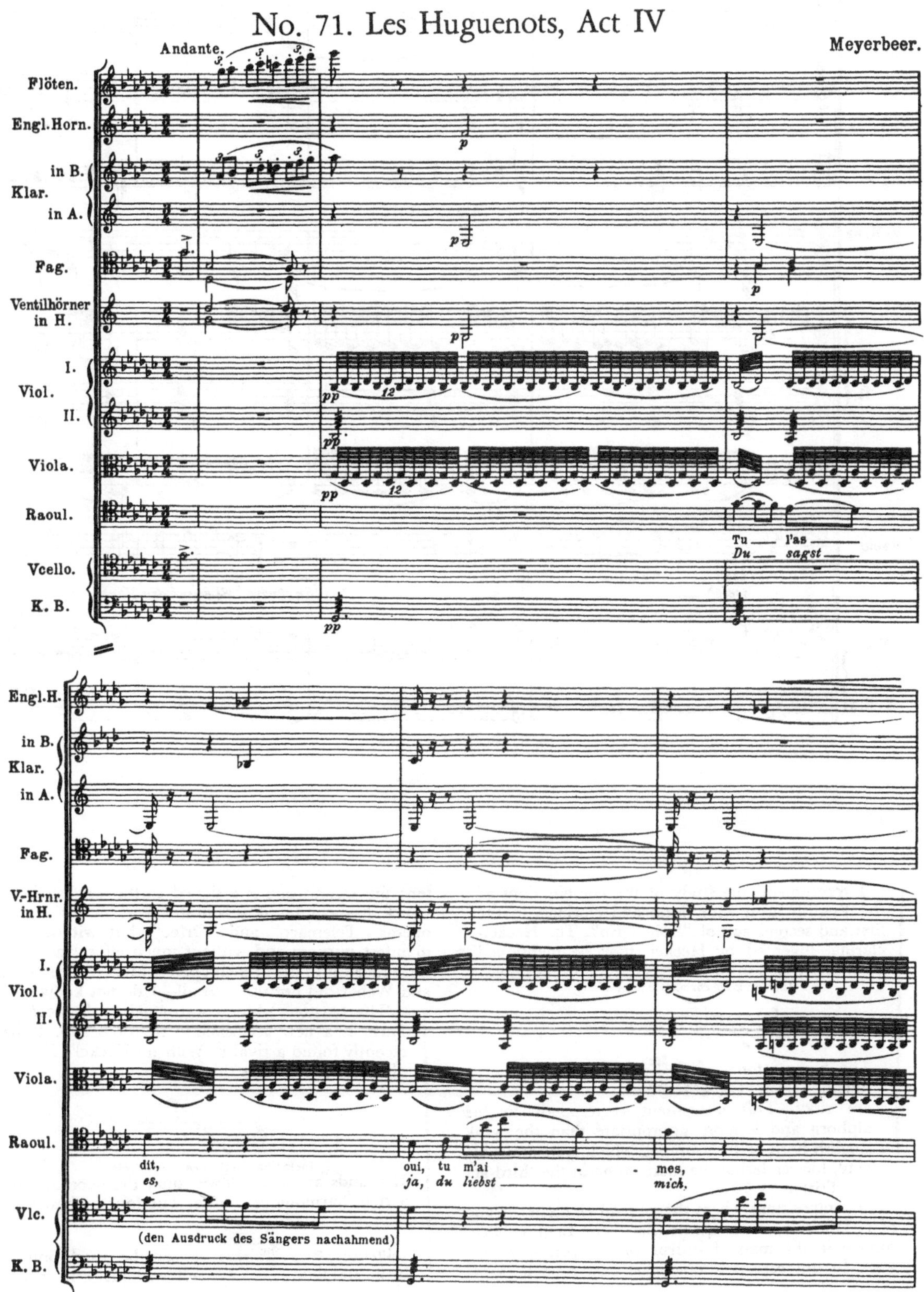

Engl. H.
in B. Klar.
in A.
Fag.
V.-Hrnr. in H.
Viol. I.
II.
Viola.
Raoul.
dans — ma — nuit quelle é-toi-le a bril - lé!
welch — ein — Stern glänzt mir hell durch die Nacht!
Vlc.
K. B.

I recommend the study of the combinations of the English horn with flutes and clarinets in the first and second acts of "Lohengrin". The Heckel-clarina, invented by Heckel, may be mentioned here. It is tuned in B♭ and has the following range:

Including the chromatic intervals

The highest tones starting from C♯ 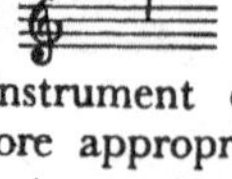 are risky. This instrument corresponds to the alphorn and is more appropriate than the weak English horn or the trumpet, which is inadmissible here, for rendering the merry tune in the third act of "Tristan".

In compositions where the general character is one of melancholy, the frequent use of the English horn, hidden in the mass of instruments, is perfectly suitable. In this case only one oboe part need be written; the second one is assigned to the English horn. Gluck has employed this instrument in his Italian operas "Telemaco" and "Orfeo", but without any manifest purpose and without much effect; he never introduced it in his French operas. Mozart, Beethoven and Weber did not use it at all—I do not know why.

The baritone oboe, constructed by F. Lorée in Paris, is a new accession to the orchestra. It has recently found a rival in Wilhelm Heckel's Heckelphon. The latter has this range:

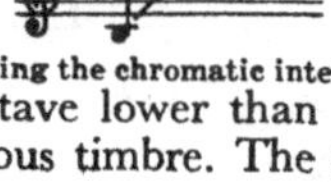

Including the chromatic intervals

It sounds an octave lower than the oboe and has a rich, harmonious timbre. The four highest tones (starting from) can be used only in forte, and then not without some risk.

The Bassoon

The bassoon is the bass of the oboe*; it has a range of more than three octaves and is written in two clefs, the F-clef and tenor-clef:

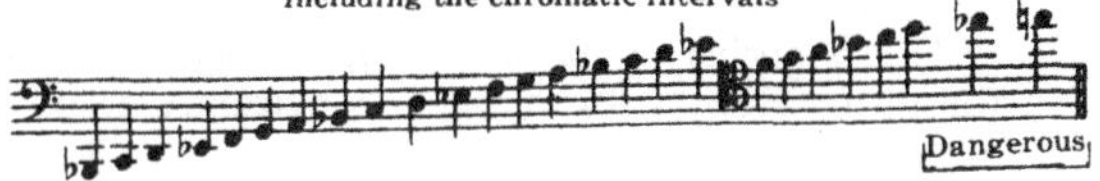

It is not advisable to go above the last Bb.

Wagner carries the bassoon up to the high C in his "Meistersinger" where he depicts the pitiable condition of Beckmesser after his thrashing. (Example 72.)

The high Eb can now be quite easily produced, but its production is harmful to the embouchure of the player.

No. 72. Meistersinger, Act III

---

*Through the courtesy of M. Gevaert, I heard in the Brussels Conservatory a double-bass oboe, whose tone had not the slightest similarity with the low tones of the bassoon. It was, down to the extreme depth, the typical shawm timbre of the oboe. If, in the near future, our ears should demand even finer differentiations of sound and a still greater wealth of tonal colors, we might reintroduce this instrument into the orchestra; thus, each individual timbre would be represented by a whole family group instead of the one or two members we have at present.

What wealth of contrasts is to be found in a combination of :

2 small flutes
4 large flutes
1 or 2 alto flutes
} flute family

4 oboes
2 oboes d'amore
2 English horns
1 Heckelphon
1 double-bass oboe
} oboe family

1 clarinet in Ab
2 clarinets in F
2 clarinets in Eb
4 or 6 clarinets in Bb
2 basset-horns
1 bass clarinet
1 double-bass clarinet
} clarinet family

It first occurred to me to develop this idea when one of the professors at the Brussels Conservatory had Mozart's G-minor Symphony played to me in an arrangement for 22 clarinets, namely:

1 clarinet in Ab
2 clarinets in Eb
12 clarinets in Bb
4 basset-horns
2 bass clarinets
1 double-bass clarinet

The wealth of tone colors emanating from the various combinations of the clarinet family drew my attention to the many treasures still hidden in the orchestra, waiting to be raised by a dramatist and tone-poet able to interpret them as the sensitive expression of new color symbols and as the characterization of new and subtler emotions and nervous vibrations.

The keys with which the bassoon is now furnished permit the production of the two low notes which were formerly out of its reach.

For the low A in "Tristan" the bassoon players have to attach a so-called double-bell with an A-key. The low tones 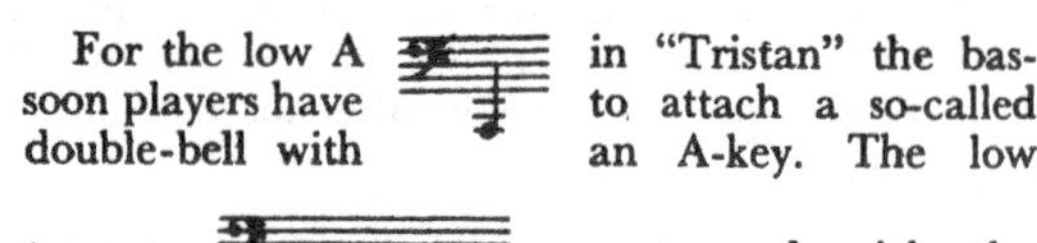 are stopped with the thumb of the left hand, only 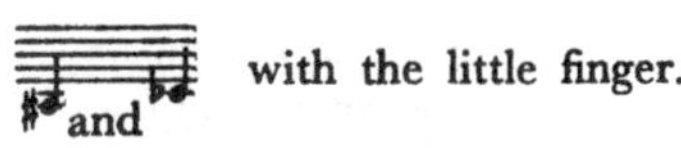 and with the little finger.

The fingering of the bassoon is the same as that of the flute. Many trills at the two extremes of its scale are impossible:

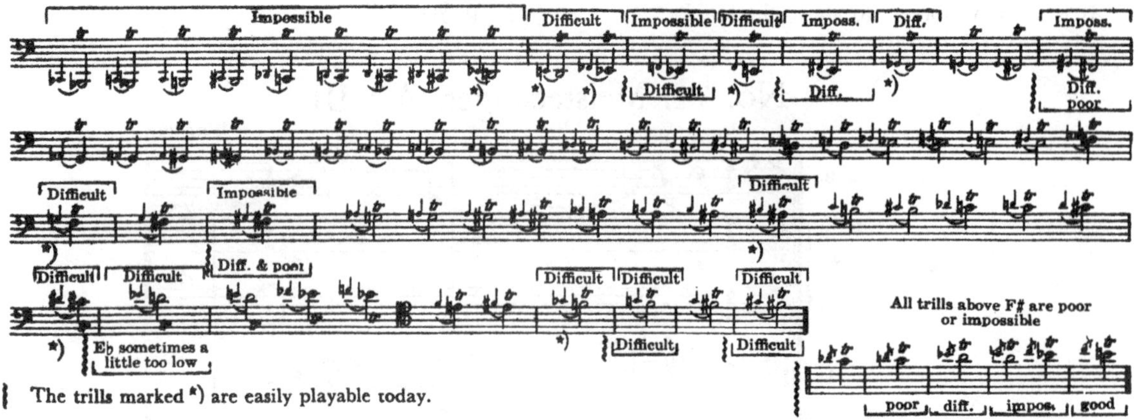

The trills marked *) are easily playable today.

This instrument leaves much to be desired in the matter of purity of intonation. It would probably gain more than any other wind instrument if it were constructed according to Boehm's system.

The bassoon is of great value in the orchestra on numerous occasions. Its tone is not very strong and, being devoid of brilliance or nobility, has a tendency toward the grotesque. This should always be kept in mind when the instrument is used prominently. Its low tones furnish an excellent bass to the whole group of wood-wind instruments. The bassoon is ordinarily written in two voices, but large orchestras being always provided with four bassoons, four real parts may be written or, still better, three, because the lowest part can then be doubled an octave below to reinforce the bass. The character of its high tones has something painful and suffering about it, I might even say, something miserable, which may be used occasionally with surprising effect in a slow melody or in an accompaniment. Thus the odd little clucking sounds heard in the Scherzo of Beethoven's C-minor Symphony toward the end of the decrescendo are produced solely by the somewhat forced sound of the high tones (A♭ and G) of the bassoons. (Example 73.)

No. 73. Symphony in C minor, 3rd movement

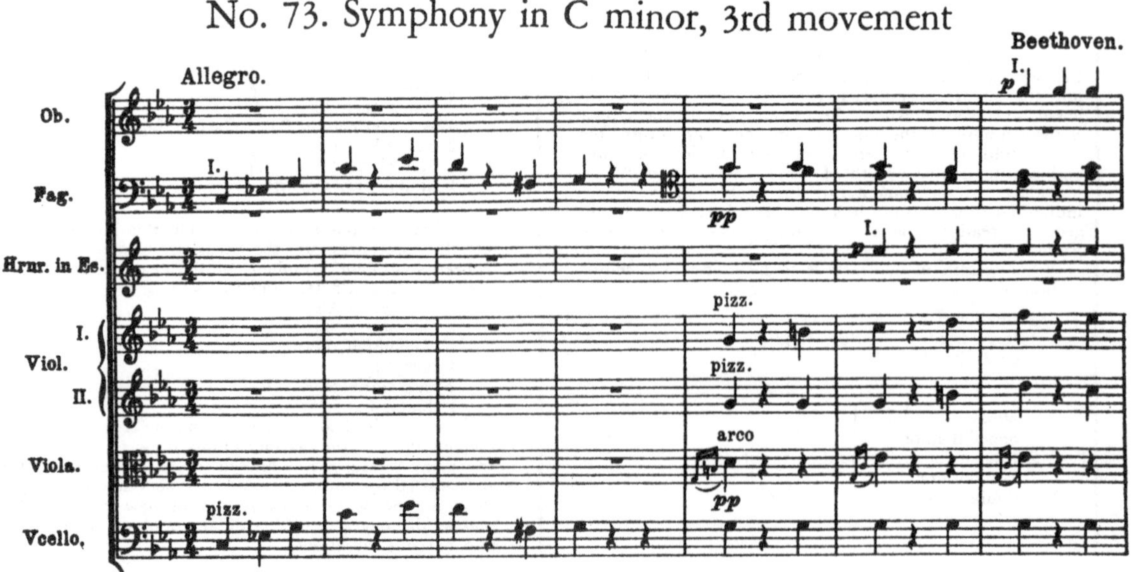

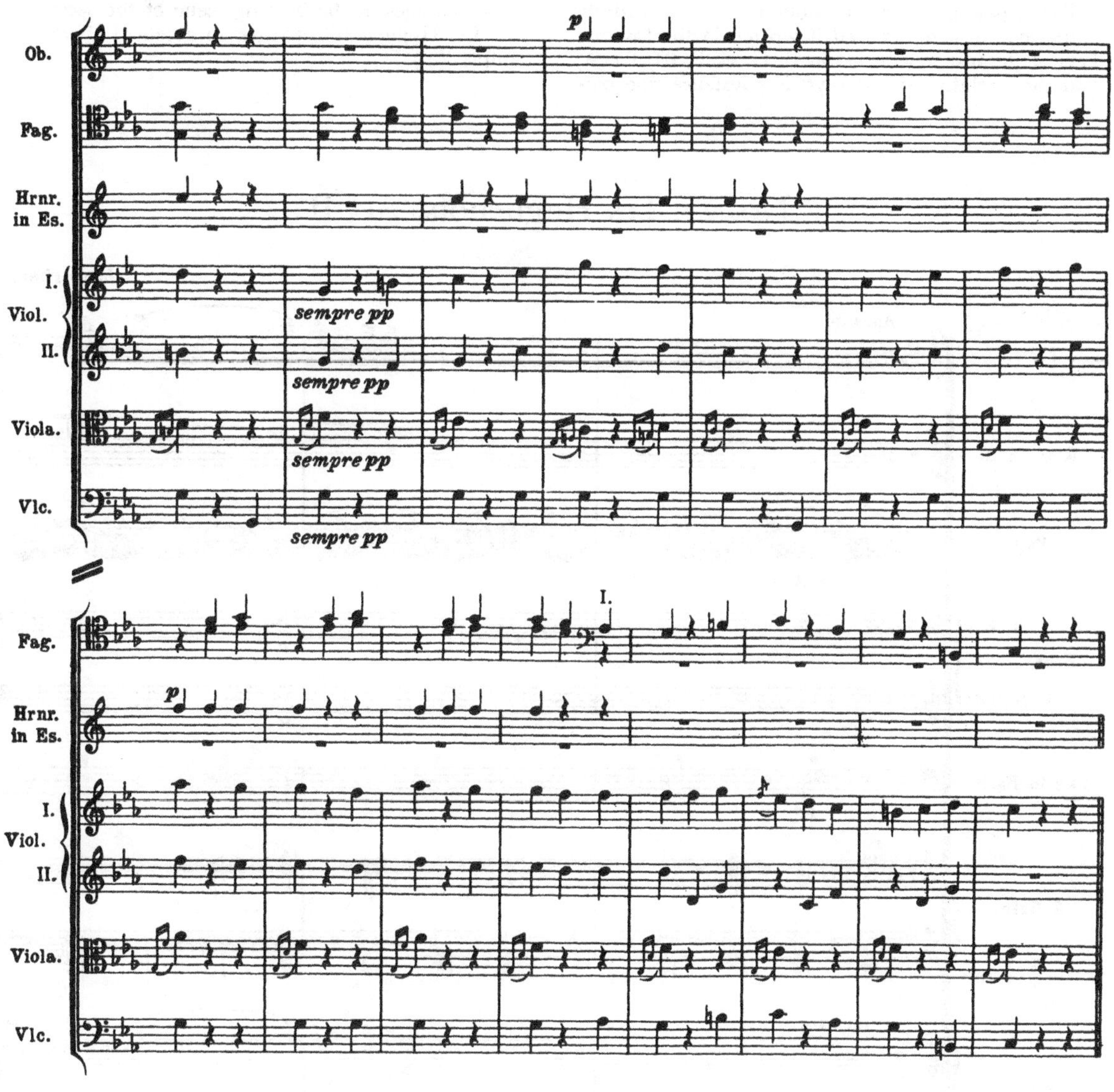

Ob.
Fag.
Hrnr. in Es.
I. Viol. II.
Viola.
Vlc.
sempre pp

Fag.
Hrnr. in Es.
I. Viol. II.
Viola.
Vlc.

Meyerbeer, on the other hand, attained the pale, cold, cadaverous color desired for the resurrection of the nuns in "Robert le Diable" through the flaccid tones in the medium range of the bassoon. (Ex. 74.)

No. 74. Robert le Diable, Act III

Rapid passages of slurred notes may be successfully employed; they sound well if written in the favorite keys of the instrument, i.e. in D, G, C, F, B♭, E♭, A, and their relative minor keys. For instance, the bassoon passages in the bathing scene of the second **act** of "Les Huguenots" produce an excellent effect. (Example 75.)

No. 75. Les Huguenots, Act II

Meyerbeer.

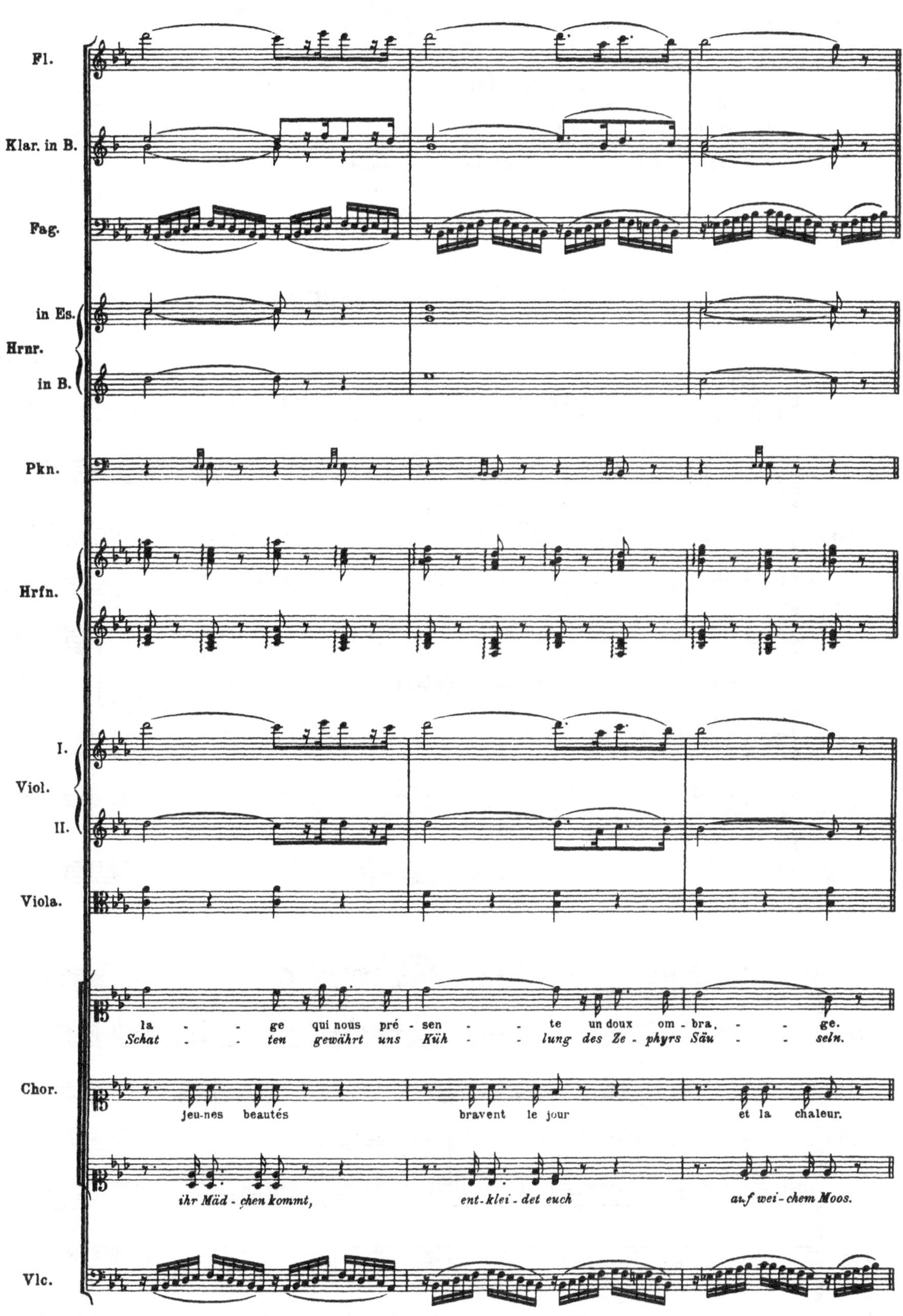
Fl.
Klar. in B.
Fag.
in Es.
Hrnr.
in B.
Pkn.
Hrfn.
I.
Viol.
II.
Viola.
la - - ge qui nous pré - sen - - te un doux om - bra, - - ge.
Schat - - ten gewährt uns Küh - - lung des Ze - phyrs Säu - - seln.
Chor.
jeu-nes beautés bravent le jour et la chaleur.
ihr Mäd - chen kommt, ent-klei - det euch auf wei - chem Moos.
Vlc.

Mozart has expressed wonderfully the character of tender shyness, so peculiar to the upper and medium range of the bassoon in piano, in the duet in "Don Giovanni", "Là ci darem la mano", at Zerlina's words, "Vorrei e non vorrei". A peculiarity in the scores of Haydn, Mozart and Beethoven is the bassoons' joining in the melody of the treble in one or two octaves. They frequently sound like the voice of an old man humming the favorite melodies of his youth—for instance in "Le Nozze di Figaro".

Another example by Mozart is to be mentioned where he employs the bassoon with the oboe, two octaves below the latter, to express an affected coyness: in the scene in "Così fan tutte" where Fiordiligi tries to hide her weakness in high-sounding retorts to the wooings of her disguised suitors. (Example 76.)

No. 76. Così fan tutte

See also the expression of embarrassed slyness in Mime's deliberative thirds in the first act of Wagner's "Siegfried" (Example 77)

Klar. in A.
Baßklar. in A.
Hrn. IV. in F.
3 Pos.
K. B.-Pos.
Viola.
Mime.
Wanderer.
Vlc. (geteilt)
cresc.
pizz.
Bog.
III.
(sammelt sich zum Nachdenken)
stell ich nur frei.
Dreimal muß ichs treffen.
più p
Klar. III. in A.
Bßkl. in A.
Fag.
Vlc.
K. B.
(nur 2) pizz.
Du rührtest dich viel auf der Er - de Rücken, die Welt durchwanderttest
I. II.
in C.
Pke.
(nur 6)
(nur 3)
weit; nun sa - ge mir schlau: wel - ches Geschlecht tagt in der Er - de Tie - fe?

Weber draws from the bassoon heart-rending tones of suffering innocence — in the cavatina (third act) of Euryanthe languishing alone in the forest. The overtones of the bassoon are particularly strong. It once occurred to me that in the A♭-minor chord in my tone-poem "Death and Transfiguration" (played by trombones, the English horn, bassoon and double-bassoon) a C♮ was frequently audible, apparently as an overtone of the bassoon or double-bassoon. (Example 78.)

No. 78. Death and Transfiguration

The Tenoroon (Basson Quinte)

The tenoroon is a diminutive of the bassoon; its pitch is a fifth higher. It has about the same range and is also written in two clefs, but it is a transposing instrument. Its B♭-scale:

actually produces an F-scale:

The tenoroon occupies the same position above the bassoon as the English horn below the oboe. The English horn is written a fifth above the real sound, the tenoroon a fifth below. The tenoroon therefore plays in F when the bassoons play in C, and in G when they are in D, etc. This instrument is missing in most orchestras; but it is successfully replaced in its upper two octaves by the English horn. Its tone has less feeling but more power than that of the English horn. It would be of excellent effect in military bands. It is a great pity, and of great detriment to wind-instrument bands, that bassoons should be entirely excluded from them, whereas the rough and harsh sound of these orchestras could be considerably softened by an appropriate number of large and small bassoons.

The Double-bassoon

The double-bassoon is to the bassoon what the double-bass is to the violoncello; that is, its sound is also an octave lower than the written notes. It is assigned a range of not more than two octaves and a fifth:

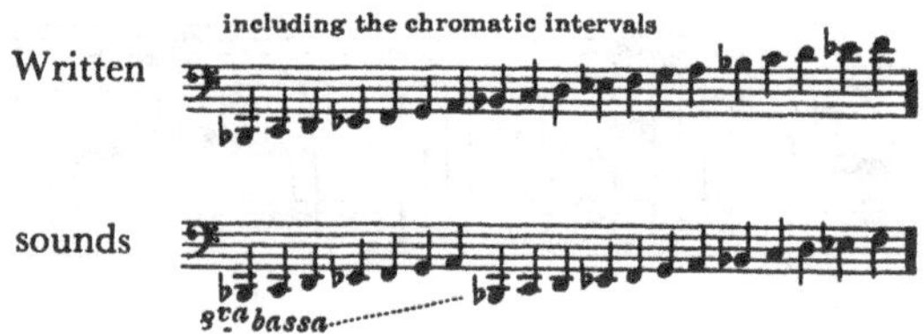

The first two notes of this scale are produced with difficulty and can hardly be distinguished on account of their extreme depth.

It is obvious that this instrument, because of its extreme ponderousness, is only suitable for grand harmonic effects and for bass movements of moderate speed. Beethoven used it in the finale of his C-minor Symphony and in that of his Ninth Symphony.

He also used it in the dungeon scene of his "Fidelio" (cf. Example 48, p. 124). As stated above in connection with the violoncellos, the lowest tones of the bassoons have also, in my opinion, no bass character—unless they are doubled by the low horns. In the modern orchestra, where even the smallest string quartet is weighted down by at least six double-basses, the wood-wind section requires a bass foundation of at least one double-bassoon—the natural bass of the wood-wind instruments, one bass clarinet, and perhaps one double-bass oboe if the composer wants to give the whole wood-wind group an independence matching approximately that of the string quintet. (Even the plain bass clarinet can serve as the bass for the three bassoons; cf. the chapter on the bass clarinet.) The double-bassoon has recently been much improved by Wilhelm Heckel, and its use is urgently recommended.

The double-bassoon is very valuable in large bands, but only few players care to use it. Occasionally it is replaced by the ophicleide, whose tone, however, has not the same depth, since it is in unison with the ordinary bassoon, and not in the octave below; besides, the character of its timbre is entirely different from that of the double-bassoon. I think, therefore, that in the majority of cases it is better to do without the double-bassoon part than to replace it in such fashion.

Clarinets*

The instruments with a *single reed,* such as the clarinets and the basset-horns, constitute a family whose relationship with the oboe is by no means as close as might be supposed. It is the nature of their tone, above all, which distinguishes them. The medium range of the clarinets has a clearer, fuller, purer sound than the double-reed instruments, whose tone never lacks a certain tartness or harshness—though this is more or less concealed by the player's skill. Only the high tones of the last octave of the clarinet, starting from , have something of the tartness possessed by the loud tones of the oboe; the lowest tones, because of their rough sound, resemble certain tones of the bassoon.

The clarinet is written in the G-clef; its range is three and a half octaves or more:

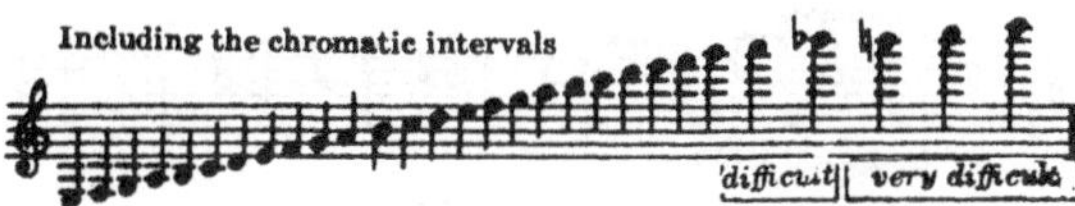

Four registers are distinguished on the clarinet: the low, the chalumeau, the medium and the high. The first comprises this part of the scale:

(The low tones do not sound well; they are rather hollow.)

The second:

(These tones are generally dull.)

The third register comprises the following tones:

Finally, the fourth register covers the rest of the scale up to the highest D:

A considerable number of diatonic progressions, arpeggios and trills, formerly impracticable on the clarinet, are no longer so thanks to the ingenious mechanism of keys attached to the instrument. They will become even easier as soon as the system of Sax is generally adopted.

Sharp keys are easier on Sax clarinets, those with flats on the German ones (by Iwan Mueller, improved by Baermann).

It is advisable to avoid, for the time being, passages like the following—or to write them only in moderate tempo:

*The French clarinets have a flat, nasal tone, while the German ones approximate the human singing voice.

The following passages are easy, too:

but very difficult from:

Passages like these are still easier:

Clar. in B♭

The number of major and minor trills practicable on the clarinet is considerable; those whose execution is not easy are indicated in the following table.

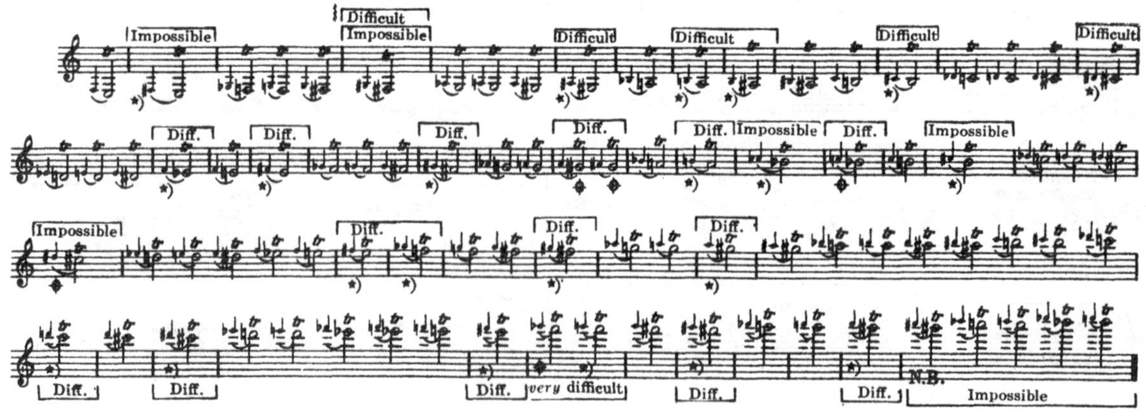

All trills marked *) are practicable today. For those marked ⌽ there are auxiliary keys.
N.B. The five highest trills are practicable with auxiliary keys if much pressure is used.

The trill [music example] is very bright and good.

The favorite keys of the clarinet are mainly the keys of C, F, G; furthermore—B♭, E♭, A♭, D, and their relative minors.

This view is now out of date. My clarinetist in Berlin tells me that with the modern, improved keys he actually prefers playing in B♮ major to playing in B♭ major on the clarinet in B♭.

Since there are clarinets in different keys, their appropriate use makes it unnecessary for the performer to play in keys with many sharps or flats, such as A, E, B, D♭, G♭, and their relative minors.

There are four clarinets in general use today:

The *small clarinet in E♭*, which should be assigned a range of not more than three octaves and two notes:

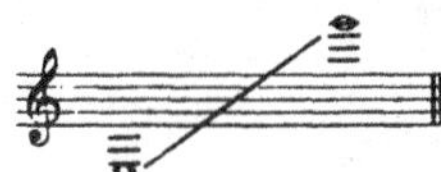

are to be used only with caution, or ff in a tutti!

It is a minor third above the clarinet in C and is written transposed; thus, to produce the following passage

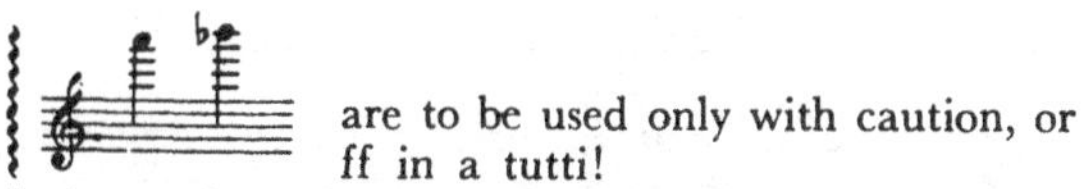

one must write

The *clarinet in C*, the *clarinet in B♭*, and that *in A*. The two latter instruments have the same range as the clarinet in C; but as the one sounds a major second and the other a minor third lower than the clarinet in C, their parts must be written a major second and a minor third higher, respectively.

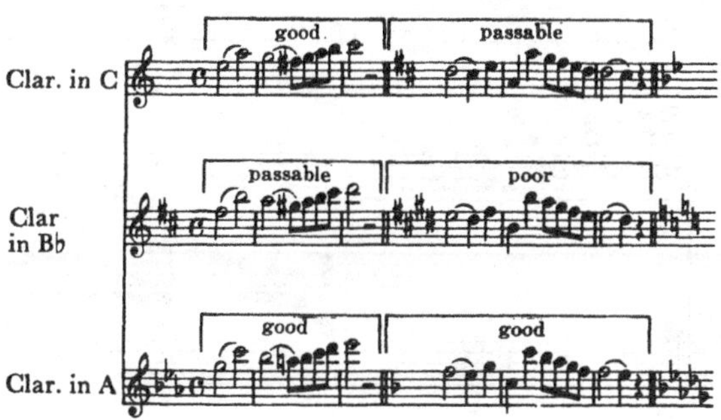

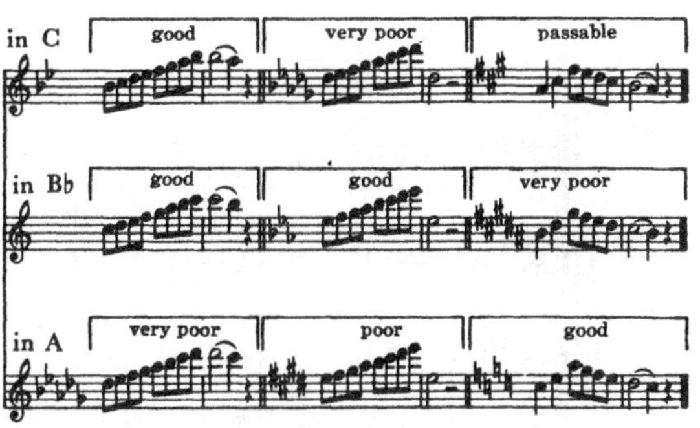

The expressions "good", "poor", "passable" do not refer here to the difficulty of executing the phrases used as examples, but merely to the difficulty of the keys in which they are written. However, the more difficult keys, such as A and E, need not be entirely avoided in simple and slow passages.

The clarinet in C is indispensable for certain pieces of brilliant character. Cf. the Entr'acte in Méhul's "Joseph" (Example 79) and the ballet in Auber's "La Muette de Portici" (Example 80). It is also preferable for passages demanding brighter colors.

No. 79. Joseph, Act II (Entr'acte)

Fl.
Ob.
I.
Klar.in C.
a 2.
Fag.
Hrnr.in G.
Fl.
Ob.
Klar.in C.
Fag.
Hrnr.in G.
I.
Viol.
II.
Viola.
Vlc.
Fl.
Ob.
Klar.in C.
Fag.
Hrnr.in G.
I.
Viol.
II.
Viola.
Vlc.
K.B.

No. 80. La Muette de Portici, Act I

Allegretto. **Auber.**

Viol. I. II.

Viola.

Vcello u. K.B.

Klar. in C. I.

Hrnr. in C.

Fag.

Viol. I. II.

Viola.

Vlc. u. K.B.

Klar. in C.

Hrnr. in C.

Fag.

Viol. I. II.

Viola.

Vlc. u. K.B.

The clarinet in D is used infrequently, though undeservedly so. Its tone is pure and possesses considerable power of penetration. It could be used advantageously in many instances.

Unfortunately, it is even today usually replaced by the clarinet in E♭, in spite of the important role given to it in Liszt's "Mazeppa" and Wagner's "Ride of the Valkyries". I have used it for roguish and droll humor in my "Till Eulenspiegel" (Example 81).

No. 81 a and b. Till Eulenspiegel

Independently of the particular character of their timbre—of which I shall speak presently—it will be seen that these different clarinets are very useful insofar as facility of execution is concerned.

(This is no longer necessary.)

It is to be regretted that there are not still more clarinets available. Those in the keys of B and D, for instance, are rarely found; yet they would be of great value to composers on numerous occasions.

The high clarinet in F is the one to be most highly recommended; it has now been introduced into all military bands. There are also clarinets in A♭. High clarinets in F and E♭ should be used in greater numbers in the modern orchestra. They are the only instruments capable of counter-balancing a strong body of stringed instruments and the massive effect of the brass (especially in polyphonic pieces); for the oboes are quite useless in the high register, and the flutes are without character in forte. Compare, for instance, the symphonies of Gustav Mahler.—It may be mentioned here that an improvement of the piccolo would also be highly desirable, as its tone and technique are still in a rather primitive stage.

The small clarinet in high F, formerly much used in military music, has been displaced almost completely by the clarinet in E♭. This is justified by the fact that the latter is less screamy, and is quite adequate for the keys ordinarily used in compositions for band. Clarinets lose proportionally in purity, sweetness and nobility as their key is raised higher and higher above that of B♭; this key is one of the finest on the instrument.

The tone of the clarinet in C is harder than that of the one in B♭ and has much less charm. The small clarinet in E♭ has penetrating tones, which tend to become rather commonplace beginning from the A above the stave. It has been used in a modern symphony to parody and degrade a melody; the dramatic meaning of the piece requires this rather strange transformation. The small clarinet in F has a still more marked tendency in this direction. Conversely, the lower the instrument becomes, the more veiled and melancholy are the tones it produces.

Generally, performers should use only the instruments indicated by the composer. Since each of these instruments has its own peculiar character, it may be assumed that the composer has preferred one or the other instrument for the sake of a definite timbre and not out of mere whim. To persist—as certain virtuosos do—in playing everything on the clarinet in B♭ by transposition, is an act of disloyalty toward the composer in most instances. This disloyalty becomes even more obvious and culpable when, for example, the clarinet in A is prescribed by the composer just in order to reach the low E (producing C♯). This occurs frequently.

Clarinet in A:

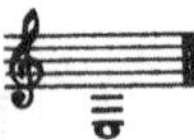

Real sound:

What would the player of the clarinet in B♭ do in such a case, since its low E only reaches the D?

Clarinet in B♭:

Real sound:

He would transpose the note to the higher octave and thus destroy the effect intended by the author. This is intolerable!

The new clarinets in B♭ and bass clarinets have a C♯-key. Bass clarinets in A are now used very rarely; one frequently has to transcribe them in B♭.

It has been mentioned above that the clarinet has four registers. Each of these has its own distinct quality of tone. The high register has something piercing, which can be used only in the fortissimo of the orchestra or in the bold runs of a brilliant solo. (Some of the very high notes can, however, be sustained *piano* if the tone has been properly prepared.) The medium and chalumeau registers are suited to cantabile melodies, arpeggios and runs. The low register, especially in sustained notes, produces those coldly threatening effects, those dark accents of quiet rage which Weber so ingeniously invented.

Wagner utilized cleverly the change of registers in the third act of his "Meistersinger", with David's words, "Nur gestern, weil der Junker versungen". (Example 82.)

No. 82. Meistersinger, Act III

Wagner.

Ob.I.
Klar.I in A.
Hrn. I in E.
Fag.I.
Viol. I. II.
Viola.
Dav.
Vlc.
dolce
dim.
pizz.
Bog.
lich; muß ich ca - ri - ren, füt - tert sie mich, und ist in al-lem gar lie - be-
Ob.I.
Klar.I in A.
Hrnr. I.II. in E. III.IV. in D.
Fag.I.
Viol. I. II.
Viola.
Dav.
Vlc.
cresc.
zu 2
sfz
lich! Nur gestern, weil der Jun-ker ver - sungen, hab ich den Korb ihr nicht ab - ge - run-gen.

When one desires to use the penetrating sound of the highest notes prominently, but if it is feared that the sudden attack of these difficult tones would be too risky for the performer, the entry of the clarinet should be hidden under a strong chord of the entire orchestra until the tone has become firm and clear.

Opportunities for using these high sustained tones appropriately are, however, very rare.

The character of the tones of the medium register is imbued with loftiness tempered by a noble tenderness, appropriate for the expression of the most poetic feelings and ideas. Only the expression of frivolous gaiety and even of artless joy seems to be denied to the instrument. The character of the clarinet is *epic* rather than idyllic—like that of the horns, trumpets and trombones. Its voice is that of heroic love; and if the mass of brass instruments in grand military symphonies suggests the idea of warriors covered with glittering armor, marching to glory or to death, so do numerous clarinets playing in unison seem to represent loving women who, with proud glances and deep affection, exalted by the sound of arms, sing during the battle, crowning the victors or dying with the vanquished.

Compare Bruennhilde's exit in the second act of "Walkuere" (Example 83).

No. 83. Walkuere, Act II

I have never been able to hear military music from afar without being profoundly moved by that feminine quality of tone present in the clarinets; it has always left me with impressions similar to those received when reading ancient epic poems. This beautiful instrumental soprano, so resonant, so rich in penetrating accents when employed in masses, gains as a solo instrument in delicacy what it loses in power and brilliance. Nothing is so virginal and pure as the tinge given to certain melodies by the tone of a clarinet in the medium register, if played by a master of the instrument.

This is beautifully felt, but it is somewhat one-sided. In my opinion, the clarinet can express all gradations of feeling if the registers are properly employed, the melodic lines skillfully formed and the instrument appropriately blended with other groups. Thus the same clarinet which has so much sweetness and innocence in Weber's works has become the embodiment of demonic sensuality in Wagner's "Parsifal" and proclaims in Kundry's scenes the dreadful and haunting voices of seduction—unforgettable to anyone who has ever heard them. Of course, one must not overlook the fact that each particular character is determined not only by the timbre of the instrument, but also by the form of the theme and by the rhythm, harmony and melody.

There is no other wind instrument which can produce a tone, let it swell, decrease and die away as beautifully as the clarinet. Hence its invaluable ability to render distant sounds, an echo, the reverberation of an echo, or the charm of the twilight. I know no more admirable example of such shading than the dreamy melody of the clarinet, accompanied by the tremolo of the strings, in the Allegro of the "Freischuetz" overture. Is this not the lonely maiden, the blond betrothed of the huntsman, with her eyes raised to heaven uttering her tender plaint, amidst the rustling noise of the deep forest shaken by the storm?—O Weber!

No. 84. Freischuetz, Overture

Klar. in B.
Hrnr. in Es.
Viol.
I.
II.
Viola.
Vcello.
K.B.
II.
Ob.
Fag.
I.
pizz.
Vlc.
arco
dolce

The clarinet, more capable than any other wood-wind instrument to produce all dynamic shadings from a whispered pp to a crying ff, can therefore reproduce the finest nervous impulses of a melody entrusted to it within the well-balanced framework of the modern orchestra. Its enormous range of almost four and a half octaves makes it more flexible than any other wood-wind instrument. In the octave the character of its tones is indifferent in piano; in forte it has something commonplace. Since the arrangement of the modern orchestral score always places the clarinets on the stave under the oboe, the carelessness of composers and the ignorance of beginners frequently cause them to place the clarinet in chords below the oboes. In four-part chords the two lower parts should best be given to the oboes, whose strong, deep tones form a much better foundation for the high register of the clarinets than the slack and dull medium register of the latter for the oboes placed above them. An example of this is found in the march from "Tannhaeuser" (Example 85).

No. 85. Tannhaeuser, Act II (March)

I take the liberty of quoting from my Monodrama "Lélio" another analogous—if not similar—effect of a clarinet melody whose fragments, interrupted by rests, are also accompanied by a tremolo of a section of the stringed instruments while the double-basses play an occasional low note pizzicato, thus giving the harmony a heavy pulsation, with the harp introducing fragments of scarcely audible arpeggios. However, in order to make the sound of the clarinet as vague and remote as possible in this instance, I had the instrument enveloped in a leather bag serving as a mute. The sadly murmuring and half-blurred sound of this solo, repeating a melody previously heard, has always made a deep impression upon the listeners. This shadow-like music creates a somber sadness and tends to provoke tears—beyond the power of the most dolorous tones; it has a melancholy similar to the trembling harmonies of the aeolian harp. (Example 86.)

No. 86. Lélio, Monodrame Lyrique, Le Retour à la Vie

Klar. in A.
ten.
rall.
mf>pp
ppp
f
Harfe.
ppp (fast wie nichts)
Viol.
I.
II.
div.
pp
Viola.
Vlc.
K.B.
pizz.
mf p
geteilt zu 4.
poco sf
sf
pppp
(geteilt)
(auf zwei Saiten so sanft als möglich)
arco
(fast wie nichts)

Beethoven assigned the A-major melody in the immortal Andante of his Seventh Symphony to the medium range of the clarinet on account of its melancholy, noble character and in order to bring out all its inherent painful plaintiveness. Gluck first wrote the ritornelle of Alceste's aria, "Ah, malgré moi" for the flute; but then, doubtless perceiving that the tone of this instrument is too weak and not sufficiently noble to render a theme of such desolation and mournful grandeur, he gave it to the clarinet. It is the clarinets again which sing, together with the human voice, that other aria of Alceste, "Ah, divinités implacables" with its expression of sorrowful resignation. An effect of an entirely different kind results from the three slow notes of the clarinets in thirds in an aria from Sacchini's opera "Œdipe", "Votre cour devint mon asile". These two clarinets in thirds, softly descending previous to the entry of the singing voice while the two lovers exchange a tender glance, have an excellent dramatic meaning and produce a fine musical effect. The two instrumental parts serve here as a symbol of love and purity. Listening to them, one almost sees Eryphile modestly casting down her eyes. It is truly admirable!

If one substitutes two oboes for the clarinets, then the effect is destroyed. This wonderful orchestral effect is missing, however, in the printed score of Sacchini's masterwork; but I have been moved by it too often during performances not to feel sure of my memory.

Neither Sacchini nor Gluck nor any other great master of the period availed himself of the low range of the instrument. I do not know the reason for this. Mozart appears to be the first who used it for accompaniments of a somber character as, for instance, in the trio of masks in "Don Giovanni". It was reserved for Weber to discover all that is awful in the timbre of these low tones when employed in sustaining somber harmonies. In such cases it is better to write them in two voices than to combine the clarinets in the unison or in octaves. The more numerous the notes in the harmony, the more striking will be the effect. If, for example, three clarinets are available for the chord C♯-E-B♭, this diminished seventh, if well motivated, well introduced and scored in this fashion, would have an awesome aspect, whose gloom might be increased even further by the addition of the low G on a bass clarinet:

The anxiety of Bruennhilde, thinking longingly of Siegfried, and the presentiment of the approaching disaster could not be expressed more magnificently than has been achieved in the incomparable solo passage of the two clarinets in the entr'acte music before the last scene of the first act of "Goetterdaemmerung" (Example 87).

No. 87. Goetterdaemmerung, Act I

Klar. in B.
Viol. II.
Viola.
(sehr ausdrucksvoll)
Ob I.
Klar. in B.
Viol. II.
Viola.
Ob.
dim.
cresc.
Klar. in B.
Horn I. II. in F.
(offen)
(ohne Dämpfer)
(sehr ausdrucksvoll)
Viol.
I.
II.
Viola.
Vlc.
(ohne Dämpfer)
K.B.

Etwas zurückhaltend
Ob.
Klar. in B.
I. II. in F.
4 Hrnr.
III. IV. in C.
(offen)
cresc.
p cresc.
Pke
Harfe.
(breit)
Viol.
dim.
Viola.
Vlc.
pizz.
Bog.
K.B.
poco rall.
3 Fl.
2 Ob.
Engl. Hrn.
Klar. in B.
più p
p (zart)
Fag.
Viol.
Viola.
Dritte Szene. – Der Vorhang wird wieder aufgezogen. Die Felsenhöhe wie im Vorspiel. – (Brünnhilde sitzt am Eingange des Steingemaches in stummem Sinnen Siegfrieds Ring betrachtend.)
(Von wonnigen Erinnerungen ergriffen, bedeckt sie den Ring mit ihren Küssen.)
Vlc.

Ever since Wagner's wonderful blackbird call ("Meistersinger", second act, before the setting in of the night) the clarinet has frequently been used for the imitation of bird calls. (Example 88.)

No. 88. Meistersinger Act II

The clarinet can also execute accompaniment figurations of a serious or humorous character better than any other wood-wind instrument. Recently, during an examination of clarinetists, I heard the passage quoted above, p. 200, at the end of the examples; it makes an excellent effect and is very easy to play.

Cf. also Ferrando's aria in B♭ in Mozart's "Così fan tutte" (Example 89).

No. 89. Così fan tutte

The Alto Clarinet

This is simply a clarinet in low F or E♭, and consequently a fifth below the clarinets in C and B♭; it has their full range. It is written transposed; the first one is a fifth, and the second one a major sixth above the real sound.

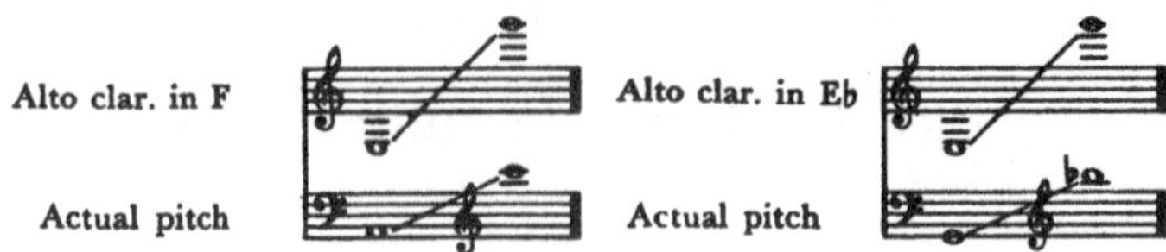

It is a very beautiful instrument, but unfortunately is not to be found in all well-constituted orchestras.

The Bass Clarinet

Still lower in range than the preceding, it is a full octave below the clarinet in B♭. There is also a bass clarinet in C (an octave below the clarinet in C), but the one in B♭ is much more common. Since it is exactly the same instrument as the ordinary clarinet built in larger dimensions, its range is also much the same. The reed of the bass clarinet is somewhat weaker and more covered than that of the other clarinets. The bass clarinet is not intended to replace the high clarinets with its upper notes, but to extend their range downward. Yet the effect of doubling the high tones of the clarinet in B♭ in the lower octave by the bass clarinet is very beautiful. It is written, like the other clarinents, in the G-clef.

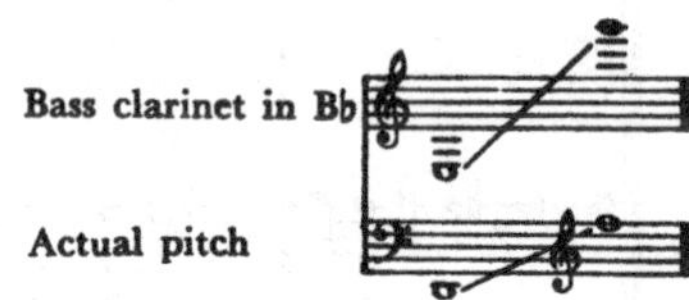

Its lowest notes are the best; but because of the slowness of their vibrations they should not follow one another too rapidly. Meyerbeer gave the bass clarinet an eloquent monologue in the trio of the fifth act of "Les Huguenots" (Example 90).

No. 90. Les Huguenots, Act V

According to the style of its music and the skill of the performer, the bass clarinet can assume in its low register the wild character of the low tones of the ordinary clarinet or the calm, solemn expression of certain organ registers. It may therefore be used frequently and advantageously. Moreover, if four or five are employed in unison, it imparts an excellent devotional sonority to the basses of the wind instruments.

Wagner always used the bass clarinet in the character of solemn resignation; see Elisabeth's prayer in "Tannhaeuser" and King Marke's great scene at the end of the second act of "Tristan" (Example 91).

No. 91. Tristan, Act II

Baßklar. in A.
Violen.
Marke.
dort, den treu'sten aller Treuen; blick auf ihn, den freundlichsten der Freunde: seiner
(alle)
Vlc. (get.)
(alle)
pizz.
K.B.
Baßklar. in A.
poco cresc.
più cresc.
dim.
Violen.
Marke.
Treue frei'ste Tat traf mein Herz mit feindlichstem Ver-rat! Trog mich Tristan,
Vlc.
arco
K.B.
cresc.
poco riten. Lebhaft.
Ob.
Klar. in A.
Baßklar. in A.
Viol. II.
Violen.
più p
Marke.
sollt ich hoffen, was sein Trügen mir ge-trof-fen, sei durch Melot's Rat redlich mir be-wahrt?
Vlc.
poco cresc.
1. Hälfte
pizz.
K.B.

As the low tones of the bassoon are still devoid of any flexibility, the bass clarinet is the finest and softest bass for the wood-wind instruments, especially as the lowest voice in combination with three bassoons—cf. Isolde's Love Death (Example 92).

No. 92. Tristan, Isolde's Love Death

THE BASSET - HORN

The basset-horn differs from the alto clarinet in low F only by having the added little brass bell extending its lower end, and by its faculty to descend chromatically to C, a third lower than the lowest note of the clarinet.

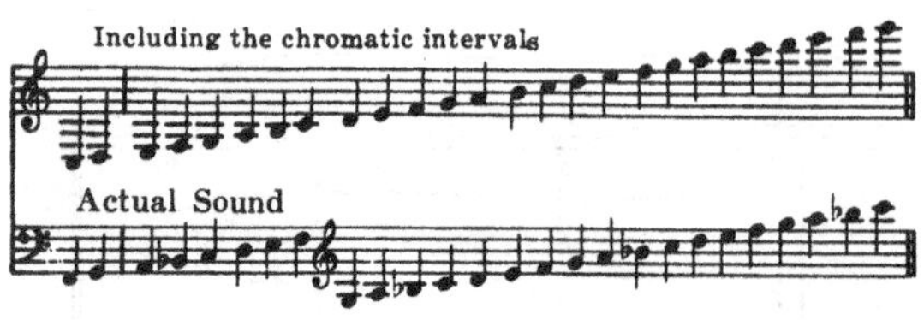

The tones above this range are very risky; besides, there is no good reason for employing them, since the clarinets can produce them without any difficulty and with much more purity.

On the basset-horn, as on the bass clarinet, the low tones are the finest and the most characteristic. It should be observed, however, that those below E  can only be played slowly and detached from each other. A passage like the following would not be practicable:

Mozart used this beautiful instrument in two voices to darken the color of the harmony in his Requiem; he also assigned to it some important solos in his opera "La Clemenza di Tito"—

and employed it in wonderful combinations in his "Entfuehrung aus dem Serail" and especially in the solemn arias of Sarastro in "Die Zauberfloete."

The basset-horns are suitable as soft middle voices and for filling in the harmony, particularly when one wants to avoid the more distinct timbres of violas and bassoons or the characteristic low clarinet tones. However, as filling-in voices they can be replaced just as well by the French horns, which adapt themselves to any timbre; this is why Richard Wagner made the most extensive use of the latter. The Adagio from Mozart's Serenade for 13 wind instruments (K. 361) offers a wonderful example of the above described application of the basset-horn.

THE DOUBLE - BASS CLARINET*

Its range is that of the double bassoon, with the timbre of the clarinet. It provides the lower octave to the bass clarinet (corresponding to the double-bass oboe.)

IMPROVEMENTS IN THE CLARINETS

The manufacture of these instruments, which remained almost in its infancy for so long a time, has now progressed to a point where excellent results may be expected. Great advances have already been made by M. Adolphe Sax, an inventive and skilled manufacturer in Paris. By slightly lengthening the tube of the clarinet toward the bell, an additional semitone was gained at the lower end of its range; the new instrument can now produce the E♭ or D#. The medium B♭, of poor quality on the old clarinet, is one of the best tones on the new one.

The following trills: , the arpeggios between F and F and many other passages, formerly impracticable, have now become both easy and effective. The tones of the high register were once dreaded by composers and performers; only rarely and with extreme caution did they dare to use them. By means of a little key close to the mouthpiece of the clarinet, M. Sax has rendered these tones just as pure and mellow, and almost as easy, as those of the medium register. Even the highest B♭ which one hardly ever ventured to write, responds on the Sax clarinets without any preparation or effort on the part of the performer. He can play it pianissimo without the slightest risk, and it is at least as soft as that of the flute. To remedy the disadvantages of the wooden mouthpiece (i.e. dryness when used infrequently, moisture in the opposite case), M. Sax has given the clarinet a mouthpiece of gilded metal, which increases the brilliance of its tone** without being subject to the changes affecting the wooden mouthpiece. This clarinet has a

*Manufactured by F. Besson & Co., New York, and W. Heckel, Biebrich.

**It makes it brighter, but also harder.—
My first clarinetist at the Berlin orchestra, Herr Schubert, after experimenting with mouthpieces of marble, glass, porcelain, hard rubber and gold, has gone back to the wooden mouthpiece because of the beauty of its tone.

Clarinets in E♭, made of metal, are said to be still in use in some military bands. They might perhaps serve as substitutes for the very high trumpets required by Bach in one of his Brandenburg Concertos.

greater range, greater evenness, facility and purity than the old one; yet, the fingering remains unchanged or is in some cases even simplified.

M. Adolphe Sax's new bass clarinet is still further improved. It has 22 keys. It surpasses the old instrument above all by its perfect purity of intonation, also by its equal temperament throughout the chromatic scale, and by its greater volume of sound. Its tube is very long, and the bell almost touches the ground when the player stands upright. This could have caused a considerable weakening of the tone; but the skillful manufacturer remedied it by attaching a concave metal reflector under the bell. The reflector not only prevents any loss of sound, but also permits the player to emit the tone in any direction and thereby even increases its sonority. The bass clarinets of M. Sax are tuned in B♭.

INSTRUMENTS WITHOUT REEDS

THE FLUTE

The Ordinary, Large Flute

This instrument, for a long time so imperfect in many respects, has now achieved such perfection and evenness of tone that no further improvement remains to be desired. We owe this to the skill of some manufacturers and to Boehm's method, following Gordon's discovery.

The same will soon happen with the other wood-wind instruments. The purity of their tones remained far from perfect as long as the holes were placed according to the natural distance of the fingers instead of the rational division of the sound-tube, i.e. a division based on the laws of acoustics and determined by the nodal points of vibrations. Gordon and subsequently Boehm* started by boring the holes of their wind instruments at the points fixed by acoustical laws without considering whether the fingers could reach these holes with ease, with difficulty, or perhaps not at all. They felt sure that the difficulties thus created would be resolved in the course of time through some new contrivances.

After the instruments had been bored in this fashion and thus tuned to correct pitch, they invented a mechanism of keys and rings which could easily be reached by the fingers of the player. This device opened or closed the holes which otherwise would not be accessible to the fingers. This necessitated a complete change in fingering; but the difficulty was soon conquered. In view of the compensations offered by the new instruments built according to Gordon's and Boehm's system, we have no doubt that they will displace the old wood-wind instruments within a few years.

Unfortunately, this is still not so in Germany.

Some of Boehm's flutes as well as the old flutes have the B [music], but flutes without this low B are said to have a better intonation. The B♭ and B can still be produced in piano, the C only with caution. In forte C# and D [music] can also be played.

Wooden flutes have a finer tone than metal ones (silver or gold), but the latter respond more easily.

Just a few years ago the flute had a range of only two octaves and a fifth:

Two semitones below and three above were gradually added to this scale; this increased the range to three complete octaves:

However, not all flutists having instruments with the device necessary for producing the lowest C and C#, it is usually better not to use these tones in the orchestra.

This restriction is no longer valid. I must not fail to warn the composer against using the high C as in my "Heldenleben."

The end of Act 2 of "Meistersinger" is also extremely difficult for the flutes, especially in staccato; in legato the figure [music] is easier. Compare also the end of "Goetterdaemmerung", which is very difficult for the flute. The trill [music] etc. in the "Ride of the Valkyries" (full score, p. 305) is very difficult to execute on the old flute.

The two highest tones, B and C, are rather difficult to produce and sound somewhat shrill; they should not be employed in pianissimo. High B♭ [music], however, can be sounded easily and sustained in the softest piano without any danger.

The number of tones permitting trills was rather limited on the old flute. Thanks to the keys added to the new flute, major and minor trills are practicable over the greater portion of its range:

*In France, there are also Boehm clarinets, bassoons and oboes in use.

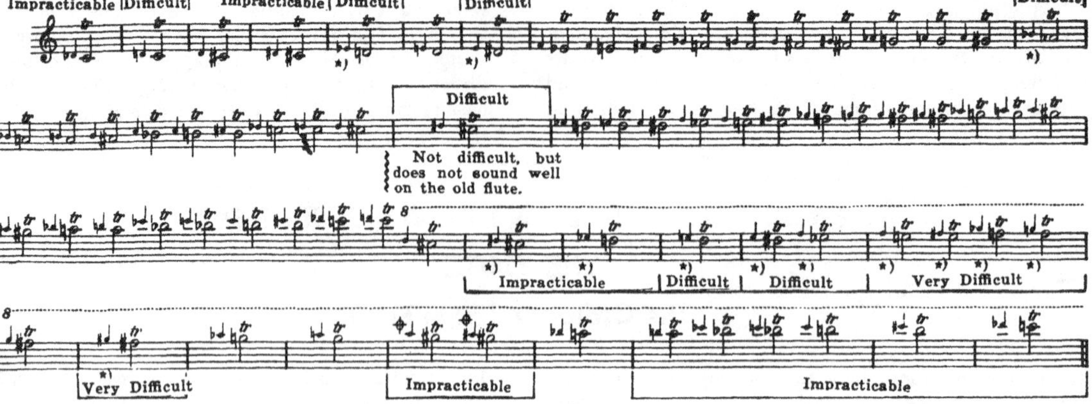

The trills marked ★ are all practicable today; the two marked ⊕ are impracticable on the old flute unless a special key is provided for them.

Up to the trill 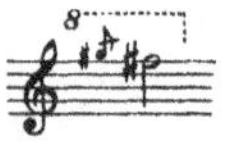 the modern mechanism also permits the execution in piano.

On the flute built according to Boehm's system all trills are practicable up to the extreme high range (i.e. from low D^b to the highest C); moreover, their intonation is much purer.

The flute is the most agile of all wind instruments. It is just as suitable for fast diatonic or chromatic passages —slurred or detached—as for arpeggios and figures with wide jumps, e.g.

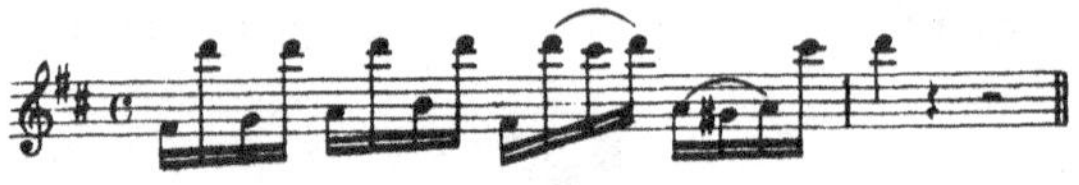

Even repeated notes, like those played staccato on the violin, can be played by means of *double-tonguing*:

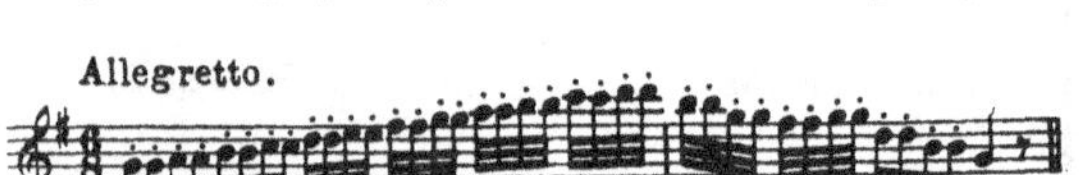

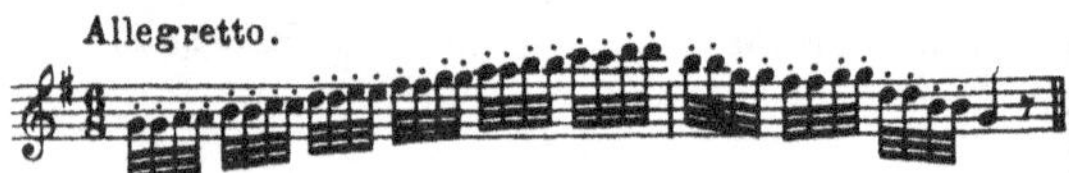

A special effect on the flute is the *Flatterzunge* (flutter-tonguing). (Cf. my "Don Quixote"). It is applicable to the oboe and clarinet. The player pronounces "drrrrr" during a moderately fast chromatic scale. The effect is something like the sound of birds fluttering through the air, or — in pp — like the soft chuckling of frolicsome girls in the distance.

The keys of D, G, C, F, A, E, B^b, E^b and their relative minors are the favorite keys on the flute; the others are much more difficult.

On the contrary, keys with flats are easier.

However, on Boehm flutes the key of D^b is almost as easy as D.

The sound of the flute is soft in its medium range, rather piercing in its high notes, and very characteristic in its low register. The medium and high tones have no especially characteristic expression They are suitable for the most varied melodies and accents; however, they do not possess the artless gaiety of the oboe or the noble tenderness of the clarinet. One might, therefore, assume that the flute is an instrument almost devoid of expression, and that it may be used anywhere and for any purpose because of the facility with which it executes rapid passages or sustains the high tones so useful in the orchestra for filling out the high harmonies.

Generally speaking, this is true; yet a closer scrutiny will show that the flute is endowed with a character peculiarly its own and with a special aptitude for expressing certain feelings, in which it is matched by no other instrument. For instance, if one desires to give an expression of desolation to a sad melody, combined with a feeling of humility and resignation, the weak medium tones of the flute, especially in C# minor and D minor, will certainly produce the intended effect. As far as I know, only one master knew how to avail himself of this pale tone-color—Gluck. When listening to the D-minor melody of the pantomime in the Elysian-Fields scene in "Orfeo", one is immediately convinced that only a flute could play this melody appropriately. An oboe would be too child-like, and its tone not sufficiently clear. The English horn is too low. A clarinet would doubtless have been more suitable, but it would have been too strong for some of the passages; for even its softest tones cannot be reduced to the weak and veiled sound of the medium F and of the B^b above the stave, which imparts so much sadness to the flute in the key of D minor where these notes frequently occur. Finally, neither the violin, nor the viola, nor the violoncello—solo or in groups—could express this sublime lament of a suffering and despairing spirit. It required precisely the instrument selected by the composer. Moreover, Gluck's melody is conceived in such a way that the flute can follow every impulse of this eternal grief, still imbued with the passions of earthly life. The voice starts almost inaudible, seemingly afraid to be overheard; then its sighs softly and rises to the expression of reproach, of deep pain, to the cry of a heart torn by incurable wounds; gradually it sinks back into a plaint, a sigh and the sorrowful murmur of a resigned soul. Gluck was, indeed, a great poet! (Example 93.)

No. 93. ORFEO, ACT II

Gluck.

An effect remarkable for its tenderness can be achieved by two flutes playing successions of thirds in the medium range in the keys of E^b and A^b, which are so favorable to the soft timbre of this instrument. A beautiful example of this can be found in the cavatina of the duet in "La Vestale": "Les Dieux prendront pitié". The tones B^b, A^b, G, F and E^b, linked together in the flutes in this fashion, have something of the sound of a harmonica. Thirds in the oboes, English horns or clarinets could not produce a similar effect.

Very few composers know how to employ the low tones of the flute advantageously. However, Gluck in the religious march in "Alceste" and later Weber in numerous passages of "Freischuetz" have shown how effective they are in harmonies of a serious or dreamy character. As mentioned above, these low tones blend very well with the low tones of the English horns and clarinets, providing the more subdued shade of a dark color.

No. 94. ALCESTE, ACT I

Gluck.

Cf. the passage in the second act of "Lohengrin" in Ortrud's scene, where three flutes sustain an E unisono as the bass for the oboes and English horns (Example 95).

No. 95. LOHENGRIN, ACT II

In his later works Wagner employed the flute very rarely, but always very characteristically, as, for instance, in the third act of "Tristan"—the fluttering of the flag on Isolde's boat (Example 96); in the second act of "Walkuere"—the expression of frivolous voluptuousness with Fricka's words, "wie des Wechsels Lust du gewaennest" (Example 97); in the third act of "Tannhæuser"—the expression of holiness.

No. 96. TRISTAN, ACT III

No. 97. WALKUERE, ACT II

One can see from these brief examples how varied are the expressive possibilities of even so soft and relatively neutral an instrument as the flute—in the hands of a great musical poet utilizing it for his symbolic language.

Compare also the previously quoted example from Weber's "Freischuetz" (Example 32, p. 80). There is something wonderfully dreamy in the low, sustained tones of the two flutes as Agathe, during her prayer, beholds the tree tops in the silvery light of the moon.

The modern masters generally keep the flutes too persistently in the higher ranges. They always seem afraid that they will not be sufficiently clear amidst the mass of the orchestra. Consequently the flutes predominate in the ensemble instead of blending with it; the instrumentation thus becomes hard and sharp rather than sonorous and harmonious.

(very true indeed!)

The flutes constitute a family just as numerous as that of the oboes and clarinets. The large flute—with which this chapter deals—is the one most frequently used. In normal orchestras it is generally used in two parts, although soft chords sustained by three flutes would frequently produce wonderful effects. The combination of one high flute with four violins in a high, sustained five-part harmony sounds very charming. Although it is natural to assign the highest tones of the harmony to the first flute, there are many occasions where an inverse arrangement would be equally satisfactory.

THE SMALL FLUTE
(The Piccolo)

It is an octave higher than the large flute. The following notes, for example, [music notation] actually sound like this: [music notation]

It has the same range as the large flute, with the exception of the highest C [music notation], which is difficult to produce;
(also the high B)
this tone is almost intolerably harsh and should therefore be avoided.

Even B [music notation] is very harsh and can be employed only in a fortissimo of the entire orchestra. On the other hand, it is practically useless to write the notes in the lowest octave since they are scarcely audible. However, if one wants to use precisely this weakness of sound for a special effect, it is better to employ the corresponding tones in the second octave of the large flute.

Piccolos, like all instruments with a loud and penetrating sound, are frequently misused nowadays. In pieces of a joyful character, the tones of the second octave [music notation] may be used in varied dynamics. The higher tones [music notation] are excellent in fortissimo for violent and incisive effects—for example, in a thunderstorm or in a scene of fierce or infernal character. Thus, the piccolo is used very felicitously in the fourth movement of Beethoven's Pastoral Symphony—sometimes alone, freely suspended over the low tremolo of violas and basses, imitating the whistling of a storm not yet fully unchained; sometimes its highest notes combined with the entire mass of the orchestra. Gluck, in the storm scene of his "Iphigénie en Tauride", enhanced the shrillness of two piccolo flutes in unison by writing them, in a succession of chords, always a fourth above the first violins. The piccolos, sounding an octave higher, and the first violins thus form a series of elevenths, whose roughness and sharpness achieve precisely the appropriate effect. (Examples 98 and 99.)

No. 98. PASTORAL SYMPHONY, 3rd MOVEMENT

Kl.Fl.
Gr.Fl.
Ob.
Klar. in B.
Fag.
Hrnr. in F.
Viol.
I.
II.
Viola.
Vlc.
K.B.
p cresc.
cresc.
sempre più f
fp
sf
Trp. in Es.
Pke.
Pos.
Alt u. Ten.
ff

No. 99. IPHIGENIE EN TAURIDE, ACT I

Gluck.

In the chorus of Scythians in the same opera by Gluck the two piccolos double the turns of the violins an octave higher; these whistling tones, mingled with the ravings of the savage crowd and the rhythmic, incessant din of cymbals and tambourins are truly awe-inspiring. (See Example 148, p.392)

The diabolical sneer produced by two piccolo flutes in thirds, in the drinking song of "Freischuetz", is well known. It is one of Weber's happiest orchestral effects:

Spontini, in his magnificent Bacchanal of the Danaïdes (later used as a drinking chorus in "Nurmahal"), first conceived the idea of combining a short, piercing cry of the piccolos with a stroke of the cymbal. Nobody before him had discovered the strange sympathy between these two instruments of such contrasting quality. The resulting sound is like the stab of a dagger. The effect is very characteristic, even if only these two instruments are employed; but it is further increased by a dry stroke of the kettledrums combined with a short chord in the other instruments:

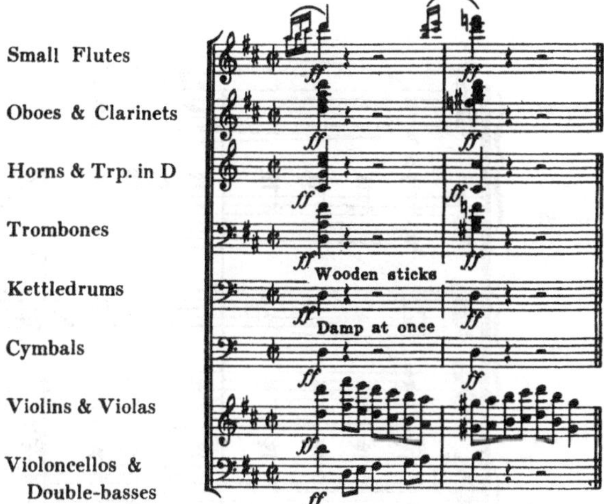

These examples, as well as others which I might cite, are admirable in every respect. Beethoven, Gluck, Weber and Spontini used the piccolo in a fashion as ingenious and logical as it was original.

The following quotation from "Tristan", third act, owes its profoundly moving effect to the impressive tones of the small flute:

No. 100. TRISTAN, ACT III

Kl. Fl.
Gr. Fl.
Ob.
Klar. in B.
I. in F.
II. in F.
Hrnr.
III. in E.
Fag.
Baßklar. in B.
Viol. I.
Viol. II. geteilt.
trem.
Violen geteilt.
Trist.
Schat - - tens küh - lend Um - nach - - ten! Für die - ser Schmer - zen schreck - li - che
Vlc. u. K.B.

Kl. Fl.
Gr. Fl.
Ob.
Klar. in B.
I. in F.
II. in F.
Hrnr.
III. in E.
IV. in E.
Fag.
Baßklar. in B.
I.
Pos.
II. III.
Viol. I.
Viol. II.
Violen.
Trist.
Vlc. u. K. B.
p molto cresc.
più f
Pein, welcher Bal-sam soll-te mir Lind'rung ver-leih'n? Den furcht-baren Trank,
der der

But when I hear this instrument doubling, in the triple octave, the melody of a baritone voice, or casting its screaming tones into a religious harmony, or reinforcing and sharpening the upper voice of an opera orchestra, out of the sheer love of noise, then this kind of instrumentation appears to me to be just as shallow and stupid as is the melodic style to which it is usually applied.

The piccolo may also be of excellent effect in soft passages; it is mere prejudice to think it can be used only in forte. Sometimes it serves the purpose of continuing high-pitched scales transgressing the range of the large flute; in such cases the piccolo enters at the extremity of the flute's high range. In this instance it is easy for the composer to conceal the transition from one instrument to the other in such a way that only one flute of extraordinary range seems to be playing. For instance:

In military music use is made of three other flutes, which might also be employed advantageously in ordinary orchestras:

1. The *flute in the third* (the so-called flute in F), whose C produces E^b; this belongs to the transposing instruments in E^b, as stated above. It is a minor third higher than the ordinary flute; besides, its timbre is more crystalline.

Actual Pitch

2. The *piccolo flute in the minor ninth* (the so-called small flute in E^b), whose C produces D^b. It is a semitone higher than the piccolo, and should be treated similarly.

Actual Pitch

3. The *piccolo flute in the tenth* (the so-called small flute in F), whose C produces E^b, and which we shall name the piccolo tenth-flute in E^b. It is an octave higher than the third-flute and a tenth higher than the ordinary flute.

Actual Pitch

It should never go beyond high A: ; even this excessively shrill tone is obtained with difficulty.

Some orchestras also possess a large flute in the minor second, whose C produces D^b, and which must therefore be called, flute in D^b. It is tuned only a semitone higher than the ordinary flute:

Actual Pitch

All these flutes serve to increase the upper range of the instrument. Their timbres have different characteristics. They also facilitate the execution and preserve the sonorousness of the flute by permitting it to play in one of its favorable keys when the piece is written in a difficult key. For instance, in a piece in E^b it is obviously preferable to use, instead of the piccolo flute in the octave, the one in the minor ninth (D^b); for the latter then plays in D, which is much easier and more sonorous.

It is a pity that the *flûte d'amour* has been allowed to fall into disuse. It was tuned in A, a minor third below the ordinary flute:

It would complete the lower range of this family of instruments (which, incidentally, might be made as numerous as the clarinet family, if necessary), and its soft and mellow timbre would produce excellent effects, either as a contrast to the high flutes and oboes, or to lend more sonority and color to the very peculiar harmonies produced by combining the low notes of flutes, English horns and clarinets.

The most effective manner of employing the piccolo flute is to use two piccolos unisono as is shown by Siegfried's scene at the forge in the first act of "Siegfried". In "Der fliegende Hollaender" Wagner even requires three piccolos to depict, most effectively, the howling and whistling of the hurricane.

THE ALTO FLUTE

Theobald Boehm, to whom the flute owes so many of its improvements, constructed a flute in low G, in response to the need for lower-pitched and at the same time more sonorous and powerful flute tones. The notation as well as the fingering is the same as on the flute in C (from low C to high A); but the "alto flute in G" sounds a fourth lower. Its tone production is easier and more secure than that on the ordinary large flute; its tone is richer in shadings and can be increased to an astonishing power. All these advantages make it highly desirable that Felix Weingartner's recent initiative in reintroducing the instrument (in his "Gefilde der Seligen") will be followed by others.

WIND INSTRUMENTS WITH KEYBOARDS

THE ORGAN

The organ is a keyboard instrument with pipes of wood and metal, which are made to sound by the wind sent through them by bellows. The greater or smaller number of series of pipes, differing in character of sound and in size, give the organ a corresponding number of *stops,* by means of which the organist can freely change the timbre, the volume of sound and the range of the instrument. The voices are selected by a mechanism of small draw-knobs, called *registers.*

The old tracker action (a mechanism of wooden strips and wire, which opened the tone-valves and admitted the wind) was put in motion by draw-stops with knobs. Organs with the now generally accepted pneumatic action, where air pressure discharges those mechanical functions, have to the right and left of the keyboard small register-plates, just large enough to carry the name of the stop. To be put in operation, they are slightly pressed down by a finger.

The present *keyboard range* of the instrument is usually from C_1 to f′ on the pedal keyboard, and from C to G‴ or a‴ on the manual. Older instruments have a range on the pedal from C to c′ or d′, on the manual from C to f‴.

The actual *tonal range* of large organs, however, surpasses that of the entire orchestra. An organ becomes larger as it has more registers (stops. ranks); this in turn causes an increase in the number of hand keyboards, or manuals. Up to five manuals may be arranged one above the other—each operating a number of registers. Since the pneumatic action has furnished an almost unlimited number of mechanical devices for operating single and combined registers, the number of manuals has been somewhat reduced. Whereas one formerly spoke of the Great Organ, the Choir Organ, Positive, Echo Organ, etc., today this simply means, Manuals I (Principal), II, III and IV, which represent a decrescendo in the number of stops as well as in their power. The hand keyboard is based on the 8′ tone; its largest pipe (that for C) is 8 feet long and it sounds the tone which we call great C. The great number of 8′ stops is supplemented by 4′, 2′, 16′, and even 1′ stops The 4′ stop is an octave higher than the 8′; the 2′ stop—two octaves; the 1′ stop—three octaves. Consequently, if the a‴-key of a 1′ stop is pressed down, a′′′′′′ is sounded. A 16′ stop is an octave lower, a 32′ stop (provided in the manual of only the largest organs) is two octaves lower than the 8′; their C-keys produce C_1 and C_2, respectively.

The 16′ tone is the basis of the foot keyboard or

pedal, supplemented below by the 32′ tone, above by the 8′, 4′ etc. As a rule, the 8′ tone forms the core of the manual, the 16′ tone of the pedal.

In addition there are stops named $1\frac{1}{3}'$, $2\frac{2}{3}'$, $5\frac{1}{3}'$, $10\frac{2}{3}'$. They produce, instead of the normal tone of a key, its fifth in different octaves, or—as the $3^{1/5}{}'$—its third. Some stops, the so-called mixtures, are 2 rank, 3, 4, 5 rank etc., in addition to the foundation stop. This means that each key of these stops is connected with two, three, four or five different pipes, and that consequently the C-key produces also c, its fifth, octave, tenth, etc. Playing a C-major triad in this stop causes, therefore, the most awful nonsense. It is obvious that all these mixed stops may be used only—to reinforce, as it were, the harmonic partials—if the 8′, 4′, 2′ and 16′ are properly emphasized.

Hence, one distinguishes between *foundation* and *mutation* stops. The foundation stops include the basic stops (8′) and octave stops (16′, 4′, 2′, 1′); the mutation stops are those mentioned in the preceding paragraph. Some stops reinforce a particular range (e.g. the treble) and cover, therefore, only a part of the keyboard (in this case the upper part). They are called half-stops.

Organ stops are either *flue-stops* or *reed-stops*. In the flue-stops pipes have "lips" forming the tone; in the reed-stops a brass reed is vibrated. Pipes are *open* or *stopped* (gedackt). The pitch of stopped pipes is an octave lower than that of open pipes of the same size. Stopped 8′ has, therefore, a largest pipe of only 4′; the largest stopped pipe of the 16′ sub-bass is 8′.

Besides these stopped pipes, the basis of the organ tone proper is formed by an open stop, the *diapason*, probably the oldest organ stop. It appears as 32′, 16′, 8′ diapason in various scales (widths of pipes) and in various timbres, e.g. as Violin Diapason, Sanftprinzipal etc., furthermore as 4′ octave, 2′ octave and super-octave. In addition, there are the above mentioned mixtures, likewise components of the typical organ tone.

On the other hand, the organ has a great number of stops imitating orchestral instruments, such as the numerous family of flute stops, the Viola da Gamba, etc. The reed-stops belong to this class, for instance the Trombone, the Bombard, the Trumpet, the Clairon, the Clarinet, Oboe, English Horn, etc. Even the imitation of the human voice is attempted in a reed-stop (Vox humana). Far more successful is the imitation of the celestial voice (Vox coelestis). In this stop each key is provided with two soft pipes of slightly different pitch, which results in a peculiarly tremulant (beating) tone. Similarly, in the "Unda maris" beats are produced between the same tone in different octaves.

It is not advisable to list here the names of all the organ stops; they can be found in any textbook on organ construction. The sensitive conductor should consider it his duty to examine closely the registers of the particular organ to be used; he should try them out and not rely on mere names. Different organ builders frequently give the same stop a different construction or at least different voicing. Besides, some names of stops are ambiguous, and others defy any attempt at etymological explanation.

The fingering on the organ is the same as on the pianoforte. A strict legato should be the basis of an appropriate performance on the organ. *Staccatissimo* should be avoided in forte and, particularly, when reed-stops are used. *Staccato* is better on flute stops than on the diapason, and better in the lower ranges than in the high ones where it often gives the impression of mechanical orchestrion playing. All this (as well as the choice of a more robust or more delicate style of phrasing, and of a slower or faster tempo) depends not only on the character of the stops, but also on the acoustics of the room. Presto runs are impossible on a viola da gamba stop, while certain flute stops admit a beautiful, close arpeggio. A fugue by Bach has to played more slowly in an empty Gothic church, where each tone reverberates for a long time, than in a completely filled concert hall.

Organ music is preferably written on three staves, the lowest of these pertaining to the pedal. The organ —like the pianoforte—may be considered from two different viewpoints in reference to its position within the family of instruments: first, as an orchestral instrument joining the rest of the orchestra; secondly, as an independent and complete orchestra in itself. Berlioz' remarks concerning this point reveal his keen observation in reference to the organ:

> It is doubtless possible to blend the organ with the various elements constituting the orchestra; this has been done many times. Nevertheless, assigning such an inferior function to the organ is actually a degradation of this instrument. Moreover, it is obvious that the even and uniform tones of the organ can never fuse completely with the extremely variable sounds of the orchestra; there is a secret antipathy between these two musical powers. Both the organ and the orchestra are kings; or rather, one is the emperor and the other the pope. Their tasks are different; their interests are too vast and too divergent to be mixed together. Every time this strange combination has been attempted, either the organ predominates, or the orchestra—raised to excessive power—almost completely eclipses its adversary.
>
> Only the softest stops on the organ seem suitable for accompanying the voice. In general, the nature of the organ is to be the absolute ruler; it is a jealous and intolerant instrument. It seems to me that in one case only can the organ combine with a chorus and orchestra on an equal basis, and even then only if it remains in solemn isolation. This is the instance where a great mass of voices placed in the choir of a church at a considerable distance from the organ interrupts its chant from time to time to let the organ repeat it in part or in its entirety; perhaps also in a ceremony of a mournful character where the chorus is accompanied by alternating laments of the organ and of the orchestra, placed in two extreme points of the temple, so that the organ sounds like a mysterious echo of the orchestra. Such a manner of instrumentation could certainly produce magnificent and sublime effects. But even in this case the organ would not actually blend with the other instruments; it would reply to them or question them. An alliance between the two contending powers is possible only inasmuch as neither of them would lose anything in dignity. Whenever I have heard the organ together with the orchestra, the effect seemed to be negative—diminishing rather than increasing the power of the orchestra.

What Berlioz has in mind here probably corresponds with what we have found in certain orchestral scores, e.g. Rubinstein's. The clumsy and continuous employment of the wood-wind together with the brass results in a kind of dim and muddy color; the brilliance of the orchestra is lost, its power seems to be paralyzed. The organ, with its many wood-winds, has a similar effect. The reed-stops, too, frequently impair the brilliance of the orchestral brass. Moreover, small differences of pitch—never entirely avoidable—add to the deleterious effect.

We must remember, however, that the organ provided the accompaniment for concertante orchestral instruments during long periods (cf. Bach's church music). The tone of some of the organ stops as well as an unlimited number of possible combinations (for which our organists frequently have no ear) blends far better with the tone of orchestral instruments than does the pianoforte. Yet we hear the latter instrument in our chamber music year after year in a frequently unhappy marriage with violins and even with wind instruments. There can be no doubt that many characteristics of the organ style have been taken over by the orchestra.

Moreover, all this has been changed by recent progress in the construction and mechanism of organs. The former absolutism of the organ has given way to a constitutional understanding with the orchestra. The organ has actually enriched the orchestra with many new colors and color combinations. Basically the organ is really nothing but a wind instrument—perhaps not a soulful individual like the oboe, but still a soulful mechanism, comparable with the attitude of some instrumentalists toward the dynamics of a particular piece.

We are not thinking now of the *Rollschweller* (crescendo pedal), already mentioned by Berlioz. This is a pedal by means of which all voices from the softest pp to the loudest ff can be made to enter on a tone or chord in rapid or slow succession, thus producing a kind of crescendo effect. For instance, a sustained C-major chord appears at first pp (Aeolina); more and more voices join it, first the pp stops, then p, mp, mf, f and ff stops, up to perhaps a 6-rank mixture and finally a trumpet stop. Then we return similarly in a decrescendo from the fff to the ppp of the Aeolina. The crescendo pedal can certainly produce powerful effects if combined with a great apparatus of orchestra and chorus. These effects can also be dynamically pleasing if the sequence of stops is arranged with sensitivity.

However, this "jerky" crescendo and decrescendo is of little use in accompanying, for example, instrumental and vocal solos, where frequently only one stop or a small number of stops can be employed. The organ tone of these few stops remains rigid and stiff in contrast to the dynamic flexibility of the voice or the violin. The warmth radiated by an organ voice when it is first heard (similar to a low chord of the horns in p) is gradually transformed into tonal "coldness".

This is remedied by the *Venetian swell.* It consists of a wooden box surrounding the organ pipes, with shutters in front and sometimes also on the sides, which can be opened and closed by means of a pedal. With the shutters open, the tone is clear, bright, f; if they are closed, it sounds distant, muted, pp; gradually opening and closing them provides the intermediate shadings. In large organs this device is usually found only on the swell or solo manual—the softest and weakest keyboard of the organ, which contains from one-sixth to one-eighth of the stops, and only very soft ones. Here the Venetian swell has a very negligible effect. It is advisable to build all organ registers, i. e. all pipes, into this box and to furnish them with Venetian swells. Then a single stop as well as the entire organ sound could be increased and decreased at will.

The dynamics of the organ—such as crescendos—become even more perfect if the crescendo pedal is combined with the Venetian swell—by employing, for example, first the crescendo pedal with closed shutters, and then opening them.

Some organists are satisfied with a crescendo produced by the rigid addition of voices through the crescendo pedal (for it always lets the voices or registers enter in the same order). Even if this increasing and decreasing is done musically, i.e. in accordance with the musical phrases (which, unfortunately, is rarely the case), it becomes monotonous after a while. Frequently the composer requires a sequence of stops different from that provided by the crescendo pedal; or the conductor considers this kind of crescendo harmful to the ensemble tone of the orchestra. In these cases the organist will have to forego his Rollschweller-"virtuosity" and arrange with a "stop-drawer" (and page-turner at the same time), who will be indispensable in any case, to take care of the increasing and decreasing of the tone by adding or taking off accurately predetermined stops. Registration is also greatly facilitated in pneumatic, electro-pneumatic and the impending purely electrical organs by the great number of *mechanical* draw-stops supplementing the *sounding* stops. They are little plates, pushbuttons or pedals, which make it possible to alter very quickly any number of combinations of registers. There are combination stops, fixed and free combinations, which are arranged before the performance and put into action by a slight touch. One can also couple the different manuals with each other and transfer one manual to another, or even make the pedal voice playable on the manual.

Unfortunately, too little care is given to this matter of "instrumentation" of pieces on the organ; the orchestral effect is thus frequently impaired. The manifold sound effects planned by modern composers through the combination of orchestra and organ cannot be indicated precisely because of the diversity of organs; they have to be left to the intelligence of organists and are frequently distorted. In the future the conscientious conductor will have to pay more attention to this heretofore rather timidly treated instrument and to its unapproachable master, who usually combines the dignity of a monarch with the rudeness of a bellows-blower; in works of the past, such as a Handel oratorio, this was much less necessary. The clarity of Bach's melody and polyphony, its "unfolding" as it were, also depends upon careful shading on the organ. Bach's great organ works—the Preludes, Fugues, Toccatas, etc.—should be "orchestrated" like a symphony, utilizing all the resources of the instrument: combination of colors, dynamics, the simultaneous use of different manuals and stops, and of the pedal. Only thus can the listener be brought to a full appreciation of Bach's immensely rich and intricate melodic language.

Finally I should like to mention an innovation which deserves the conductor's special attention because the German organ builders in particular are none too enterprising or fond of innovations. It was not so long ago that the organ action was constructed out of little pieces of wood and wire, just like in the middle ages, while everywhere else steam, pneumatic power and electricity had taken over the mechanical work.

In the performance of large works for chorus, soli, orchestra and organ, the great distance of the organ console frequently makes the participation of the organ illusory if not impossible. At a music festival, how are the singer, the obbligato violin and the string quintet to stay in contact with an organist separated from them by the entire orchestra, a large chorus, frequently also by the audience—an organist who sits high up in the corner of a gallery and frequently canot even see the conductor? He relies upon his ear as well as he can—and his ear deceives him; for the great distance from the participating soloists causes various acoustical illusions. The composer, whom the audience does not "understand", is the victim of all this.

The only remedy for this consists in movable consoles, connected with the body of the organ by electric cables. The organist sits wherever the conductor deems it best—perhaps behind the soloists, near the first violins or the conductor, or anywhere else. This arrangement, generally instituted and approved for the past ten years in France, England and America (in churches the organist is placed near the officiating clergyman) has recently also been introduced in Germany. Thanks to the rapidity of the electric current, it makes a precise ensemble of orchestra and organ possible, a beneficial cooperation, as it were, between "state" and "church". Here, at a distance from the organ, the organist can also judge much better the musical effect of his registration, the volume of sound, etc.; whereas, when he sits near or practically in the organ, he cannot see the forest because of the trees.

This is not the place to explain in detail the treatment of the organ as an individual instrument, constituting an orchestra in itself. Our purpose is not to write a textbook on the performance of various instruments, but a study of their musical effect when combined in ensemble. A knowledge of the organ, skill in selecting and combining the different stops constitutes the art of the organist, inasmuch as he is—according to custom—an extempore player. In the opposite case—where the organist is simply a performer executing a written work—he should strictly follow the indications of the composer, who, therefore, must be thoroughly familiar with the resources of the instrument and their application. But these resources are so numerous and diverse that no composer. in our opinion, can understand them adequately unless he himself is an accomplished organist.

If the organ is to be combined with voices and with other instruments in a particular composition, it should not be forgotten that it is tuned one tone lower than the present pitch of the orchestra. It must therefore be treated as a transposing instrument in B♭.

This applies only to ancient organs. Modern organ builders tune their organs to the pitch of the orchestra. But unfortunately they frequently fail to tune them at the correct temperature by means of a warmed-up oboe. Tuned in a cold church according to the Paris tuning fork, the organ is useless for ensemble playing with an orchestra.

The organ of the church of St. Thomas in Leipzig, on the other hand, is a tone higher than the orchestra.

This is no longer the case.

The organ has soft, brilliant, but also awful sound effects; however, it is not within its nature to deliver them in rapid succession. It cannot, like the orchestra, pass suddenly from piano to forte, or vice versa.

The organ can produce all effects, the softest and the loudest chords, in *immediate* succession; by means of the crescendo pedal, it can pass from ppp to fff. (Here Berlioz' opinions are entirely out of date.)

Recently devised improvements make it possible to produce a kind of crescendo by the gradual addition of stops, as well as a decrescendo by gradually withdrawing them in similar fashion. But the increasing and decreasing of the tone obtained by this ingenious method still lacks those intermediate shadings which lend so much color and life to the orchestra. One cannot help feeling the inanimate mechanism. Only Erard's instrument, known under the name "expressive organ", has the possibility of really swelling and diminishing the tone; but it has not yet been adopted in churches. Serious people, otherwise generally intelligent, condemn its use as contrary to the religious character and purpose of the organ.

We shall not examine here the frequently discussed question whether or not *expression* is admissable in sacred music—a question which could be solved in a moment by unprejudiced, plain commonsense. Yet we take the liberty of pointing out to the champions of unembellished music, of plainsong, of the expressionless organ (as if the loud and soft stops of different timbre did not lend variety and expression to the organ) that they are the first to burst out in exclamations of delight when the performance of a choir in a sacred work enchants them by the delicacy of nuance, by shadings of crescendo and decrescendo, by chiaroscuro, by tones which swell, are sustained and fade out—in short, by all those qualities wanting in the organ, and with which Erard wants to enrich it by means of his invention. These people are obviously inconsistent, unless they should claim (as they are quite capable of doing) that nuances in expression which are perfectly appropriate, religious and catholic in vocal music suddenly become irreligious, heretical and blasphemous on the organ. Is it not strange (the reader will pardon this digression) that these same critics who are so conservative in all matters of sacred music and rightly demand that it should be inspired by truly religious feelings (banning, of course, all nuances that would express these feelings)—that these critics have never thought of prohibiting the use of quick fugues, which for ages have formed the basis of organ music in all schools? Is it that the themes of these fugues—some of which are quite trivial, others even almost grotesque—become religious and dignified merely by being treated in fugal style, that is, in the form permitting their most frequent repetition and continuous display? Is it that these innumerable entries of different voices, these canonic imitations, these fragments of twisted and tangled phrases pursuing and fleeing each other, even falling over each other, this confusion that excludes all true melody, where the chords succeed one another so rapidly that their character can scarcely be discerned, this continuous commotion of the entire system, this appearance of disorder, these sudden interruptions of one voice by another, all these detestable harmonic absurdities appropriate in depicting an orgy of savages or a dance of demons—is it that they are all transformed in the pipes of an organ and assume the solemn, grandiose, calm, devout or meditative expression of a sacred prayer, of quiet contemplation or even of terror and religious awe?

Although I share Berlioz' opinion regarding organ fugues, nevertheless, this whole paragraph seems to me to be inspired by his purely personal hatred of the polyphonic style in general—a hatred not generally shared even by the admirers of Berlioz' genius. In this respect, the German and the Latin are antipodes.

There may be some queerly constituted beings who believe all this to be true. At any rate, these critics do not consider quick organ fugues inappropriate even though they do not claim them to be imbued with religious spirit. Their opinion is based on the fact that these fugues have been in long-established use, that they have been written in great number by the most accomplished masters, following long-accepted custom. This is understandable when one considers the fact that writers on religious music are usually dogmatic and consider anything tending towards a change of ideas consecrated by time as dangerous and incompatible with faith. To return to our subject—it is my conviction that Erard's invention would be a great improvement, entirely to the benefit of a true religious style, even if it were applied to the old organ merely as one new stop, so that the organist would be free to employ the expressive tones if he chose to do so, or at least to swell and diminish certain tones independently of others.

BRASS INSTRUMENTS WITH MOUTHPIECE

THE FRENCH HORN*

Since this instrument is adapted for numerous changes of key by which its pitch can be raised or lowered, it is impossible to indicate its precise range without also naming the particular key of the horn in question. In fact, it is easier to produce high tones than low ones on horns of a low key—with the exception of the horns in low A, B♭ and C, the extreme length of whose tubes makes the execution of high tones difficult. On the other hand, it is easier to produce low tones than high ones on horns of a higher key. Besides, some horn players who use a wide mouthpiece and are mainly experienced in playing the lower tones cannot produce the higher ones; others who use a narrow mouthpiece are only accustomed to playing the higher tones. Each key of the instrument has its own specific range; moreover, there is the difference between the ranges of the players of the high (first) and the low (second) horn.

The horn is written in the G and F-clefs; but the G-clef is to be read an octave lower than written. The examples below will make this clear.

All the horns except the one in high C are transposing instruments. Their notation does not correspond with the actual sound.

Horns are capable of producing two very different types of tone. The *open* tones, almost all of which give the sound of the harmonic divisions of the tube, are produced by the player's lips and breath alone. The *stopped* tones are produced by more or less closing the *bell* (the lower orifice of the horn) with the hand.

The following table gives the open tones in the different keys and ranges of the first and second horns.

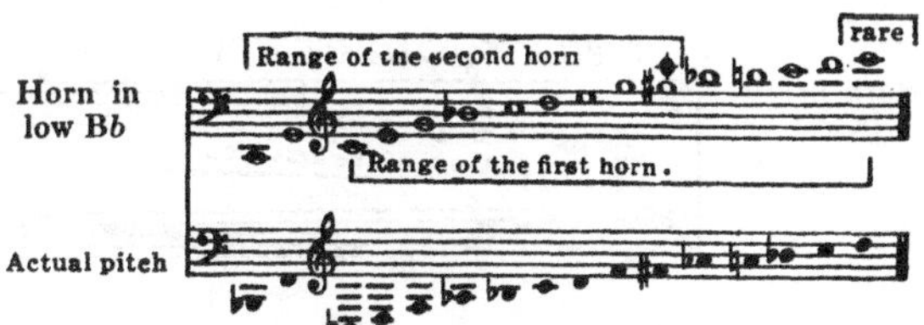

♦ This open G♯ is not so easy to produce as the G but it becomes easy if prepared by a neighboring tone, i.e. G, F♯ or A. It is a little too high.

*Most of Berlioz' statements in this chapter are out of date. See note on p. 257

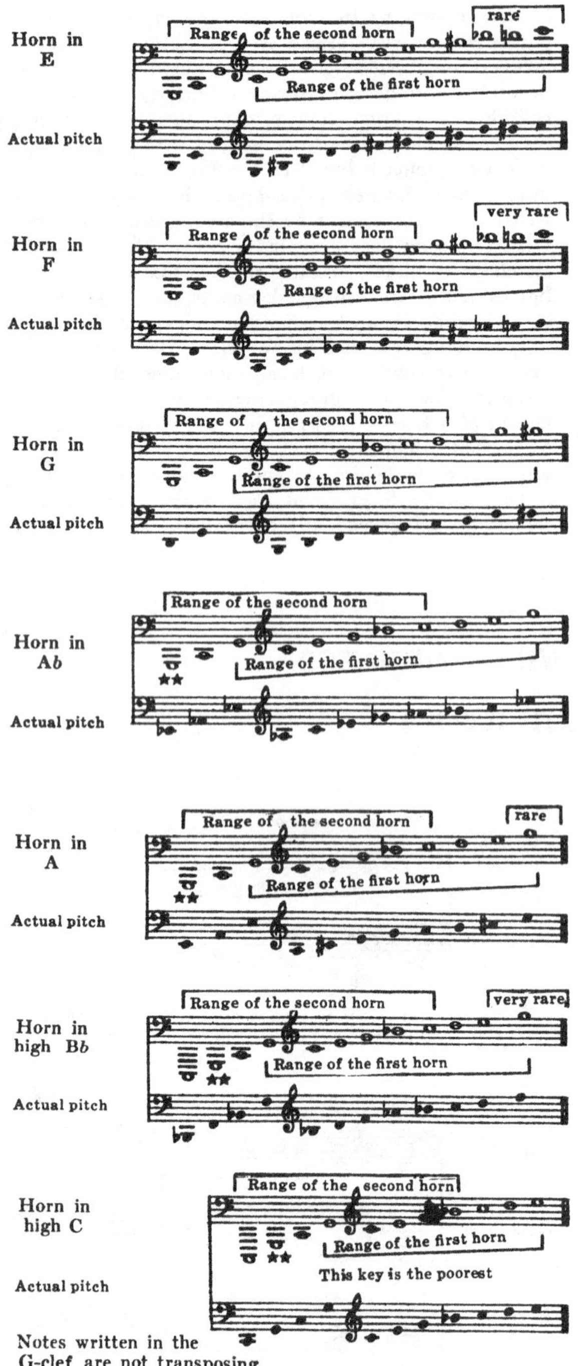

Notes written in the G-clef are not transposing.

The family of horns is complete. There are horns in *all keys,* although this is not generally known. The keys which seem to be missing in the chromatic scale are obtained by means of a lengthening piece which lowers the instrument by a semitone. Thus, only the horns in low B♭, C, D, E♭, E, F, G, A♭, high B♭ and high C are made in one piece; but by adding the lengthening piece to the horns in low B♭ and low C, one obtains low A and B. In the same fashion, D is changed into D♭ (or C#), G into G♭ (or F#) and high C into high B (or C♭). The last key can also be obtained by pulling out the slide of the horn in high C.

The *stopped* tones show marked differences of character and sonority, not only in comparison with the open tones, but also among themselves. These differences are caused by the greater or smaller opening left in the bell by the performer's hand. For certain notes the bell must be closed a quarter, a third or one-half, for others almost completely. The more the bell is closed, the duller and rougher becomes the tone and the more difficult is its secure and clean production. The stopped tones are therefore very different from each other. We shall use the sign ½ to indicate those tones for which the bell is only half closed, and which are therefore better in quality. In the following example, white (whole) notes indicate the above listed open tones, black (quarter) notes represent stopped tones.

In order to be able to list the complete range of the horn we must first mention several additional open tones which are less well known than the others, but which may be used to good advantage. These are: the high G♭, which is always a little too low and seems in tune only when used between two Fs: (therefore it can never be used as F#); then the low A♭, which is obtained by forcing the G and compressing the lips; the low F, which, on the contrary, is produced with relaxed lips. These last two notes are of great value; the A♭ in particular frequently produces excellent effects in all keys higher than the key of D. However, the playing of the F is a little more risky; it is more difficult to sustain it safely and cleanly. These low tones can be produced without any preparation if they are not preceded by very high ones; but it is usually best to place them after a G—for example:

Passing from A♭ to F is possible in moderate tempo:

**This low G is easier in the higher keys, but it is generally poor and uncertain in all the keys.

Below these notes some horn players can produce the

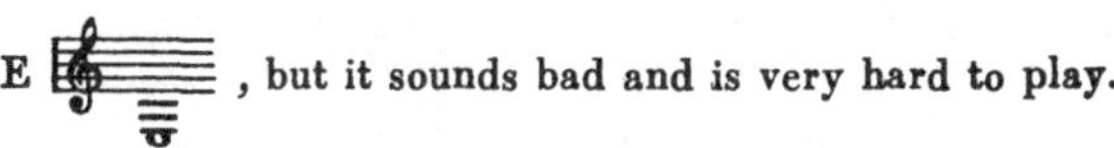

E , but it sounds bad and is very hard to play.

I advise composers against employing it, as well as the following five notes beneath the low C; they are seldom in tune and can be sustained only with difficulty. If used at all, they should be written only for medium horns such as those in D, E and F, and then only in a descending progression:

By combining the range of the first horn with that of the second horn, and by adding to the natural open tones the artificial open tones and the stopped tones, we obtain the following immense chromatic scale, progressing upwards:

COMPLETE RANGE OF THE HORN

The lower the key, the more difficult are rapid successions on the horn; in this case the tube is longer and cannot be put into vibration instantaneously. Low tones, even the natural ones, can succeed each other in all keys only in moderate tempo. Incidentally, this is a general law which has to be observed with all instruments. Since the low tones result from a smaller number of vibrations, the sonorous body requires more time to produce them. Hence, a passage like the following would be impracticable or of poor effect on a low horn (in B^b, C or D):

Also the following would be very bad on a horn in low C or B^b, even though practicable on a horn in F and in higher keys:

When using stopped tones, especially in the orchestra, one should try to intersperse them as much as possible with open ones, and not to pass from one stopped tone to another stopped one, particularly from one poor stopped tone to another equally poor one.

Thus it would be senseless to write:

A passage like the following, however,

would not lack sonority and would be easy to execute because it contains but one poor stopped tone (the first A^b); whereas the same passage transposed to its lower octave or fifth would be ridiculous as well as exceedingly difficult:

(Bad examples)

These three examples show that the best stopped tones are to be found above the medium A^b—with the exception of the following four:

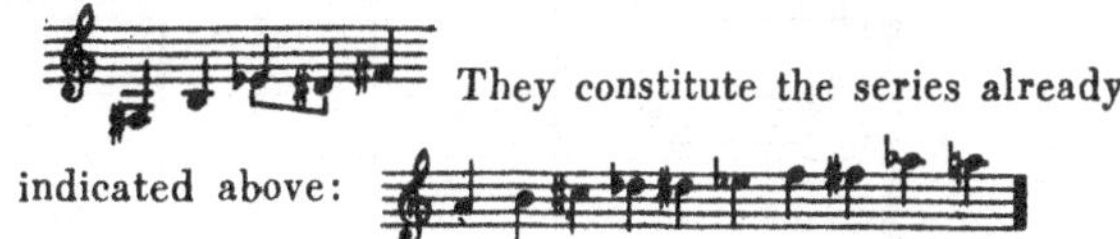

They constitute the series already indicated above:

Hence, the above cited example in A^b, although good in one octave, is very bad in the lower one—where it consists almost completely of the poorest stopped tones:

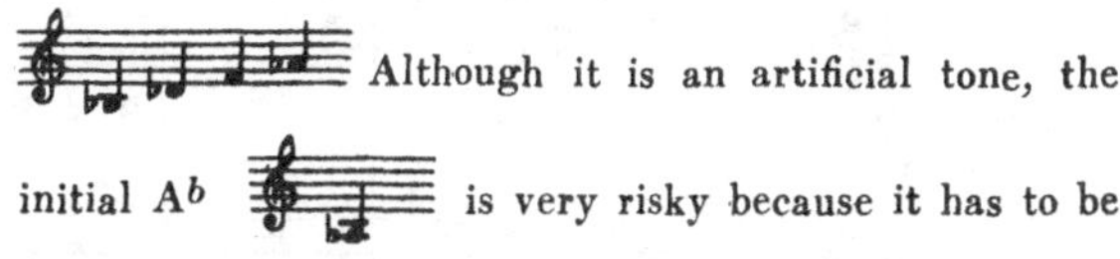

Although it is an artificial tone, the initial A^b is very risky because it has to be taken quickly and without preparation.

In general the old masters limited themselves to the use of open tones; to be frank, they employed them quite clumsily. Even Beethoven is very reluctant to use stopped tones, exеcpt in a solo passage. His scores offer very few examples of them; whenever he has recourse to them, it is usually for some striking effect. For example, see the stopped tones of the three horns in E^b in the Scherzo of the Eroica, and the low F# of the second horn in D in the Scherzo of the A-major Symphony (Examples 101 and 102).

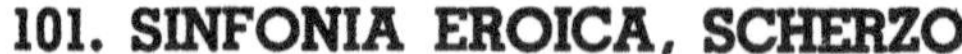

101. SINFONIA EROICA, SCHERZO

Beethoven.

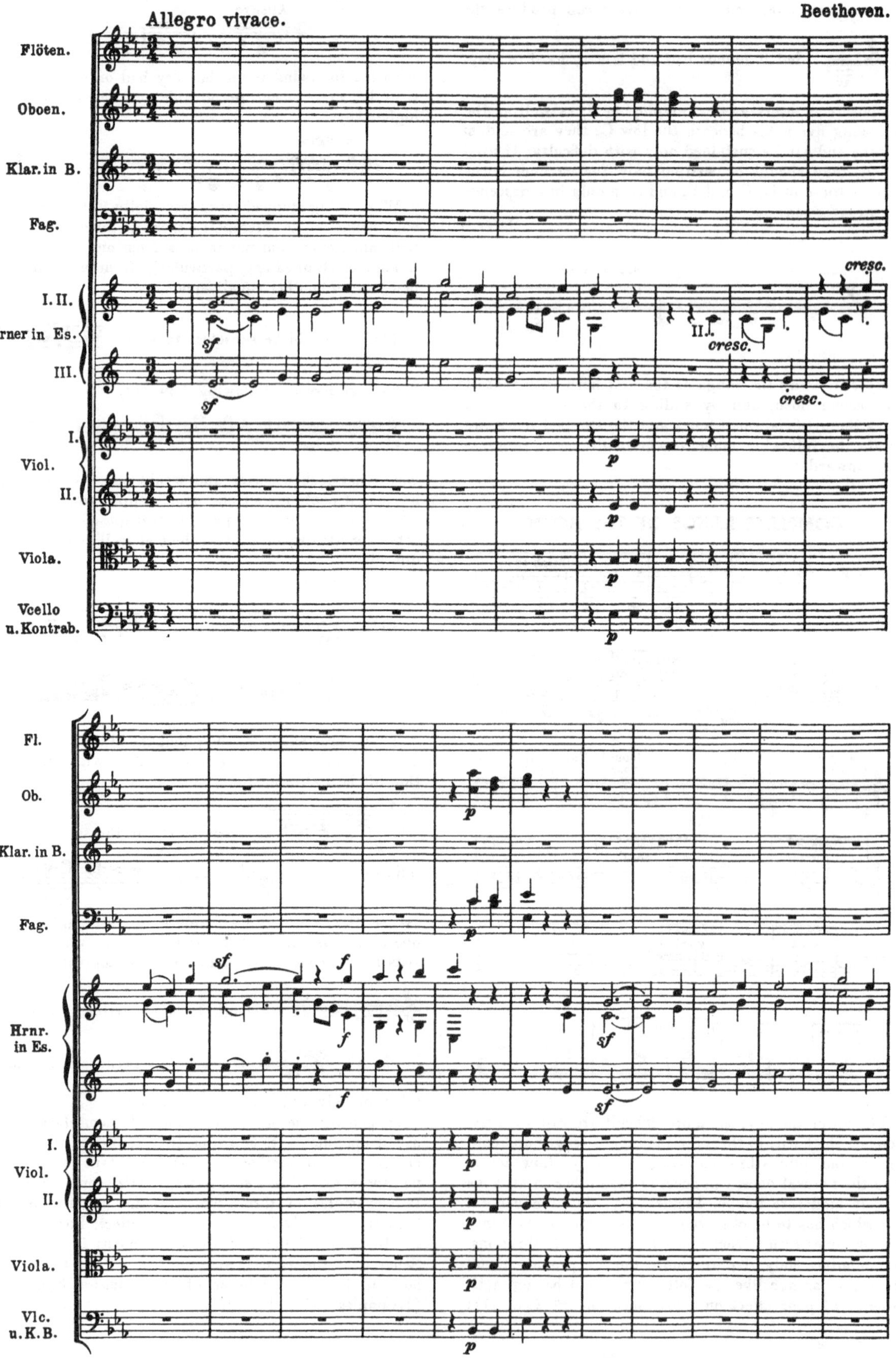

Allegro vivace.
Flöten.
Oboen.
Klar. in B.
Fag.
I. II.
Hörner in Es.
III.
I.
Viol.
II.
Viola.
Vcello
u. Kontrab.
cresc.
sf
p
Fl.
Ob.
Klar. in B.
Fag.
Hrnr.
in Es.
I.
Viol.
II.
Viola.
Vlc.
u. K. B.
f

Fl.
Ob.
Klar. in B.
Fag.
Hrnr. in Es.
cresc.
Viol. I.
Viol. II.
Viola.
Vlc. u. K. B.
p dolce, sempre legato

Fl.
Ob.
Klar. in B.
Fag.
Hrnr. in Es.
I.
Viol.
II.
Viola.
Vlc. u. K. B.
p
cresc.

Fl.
Ob.
Klar. in B.
Fag.
Hrnr. in Es.
I.
Viol.
II.
Viola.
Vlc. u. K. B.
p
sf
f
cresc.

Fl.
Ob.
Klar. in B.
Fag.
Hrnr. in Es.
I.
Viol.
II.
Viola.
Vlc. u. K. B.
p
sf
pp
f
Fl.
Ob.
Klar. in B.
Fag.
Hrnr. in Es.
I.
Viol.
II.
Viola.
Vlc. u. K. B.

102. SYMPHONY IN A, 3rd MOVEMENT

This method is doubtless better than the opposite one, adopted nowadays by the majority of French and Italian composers. They treat the horns very much like bassoons or clarinets, without taking into account the enormous difference between stopped and open tones as well as the differences among the stopped tones. They pay no attention to the difficulties encountered by the player in taking a particular note after another one which does not naturally lead up to it; nor are they concerned with the dubious intonation, the weak tone or the rough and strange character of sound caused by the fact that the bell remains two-thirds or three-quarters closed. In short, they have not the slightest idea that a thorough knowledge of the instrument together with good taste and commonsense may have something to do with the application of these tones, which these schoolboy-masters fling at random into the orchestra. Even the parsimony of the old composers is preferable to this ignorant and odious prodigality.

Unless stopped tones are wanted for some particular effect, one should at least avoid those whose sound is too weak and too unlike the other tones of the horn. These are: D and D^b under the stave  ; the low A and B^b  ; the medium A^b  . They should never be used as mere filling notes, but only for the sake of an effect which corresponds with their hollow, rough and wild sound. I would except only the medium A^b, if it is indispensable for the completion of a melody, such as:

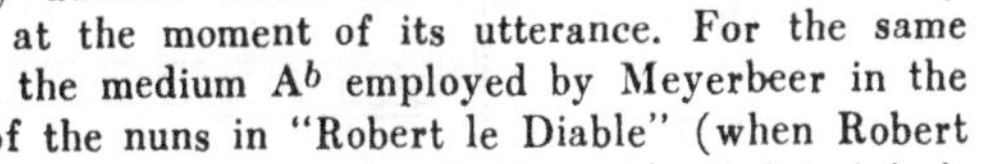

The low B^b  has been used by Weber in one instance with excellent dramatic purpose—in the scene in "Freischuetz" where Kaspar conjures Samiel; but this tone is so closed and hence so hollow that it is scarcely audible unless the entire orchestra suddenly pauses at the moment of its utterance. For the same reason, the medium A^b employed by Meyerbeer in the scene of the nuns in "Robert le Diable" (when Robert approaches the tomb to break the enchanted twig) is noticeable only because almost all the other instruments are silent; and yet this note is much more sonorous than the low B^b. In scenes of secret horror these stopped tones, employed in several voices, may produce great effects. Méhul, I believe, is the only composer who made use of them, in his opera "Phrosine et Mélidore". (Example 103).

103. PHROSINE ET MELIDORE

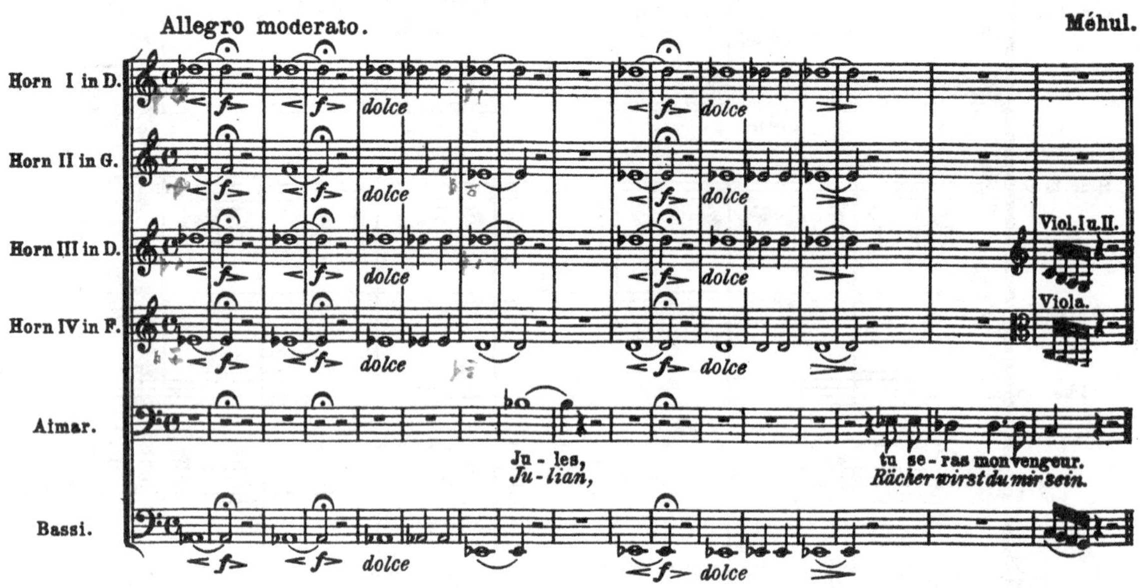

Major and minor trills are practicable on the horn, but only over a small portion of its scale. The following are the best:

Horns are usually written without signature—regardless of their key or that of the orchestra. However, when the melody is in the horn and the instrument is not in the same key as the orchestra, it is better to indicate the signature required by the key of the piece; but one should always endeavor to use as few accidentals as possible. Thus, the horn in F, for instance, is very suitable for a solo when the orchestra plays in E♭: first, because it is one of the best keys on the instrument, and secondly, because this combination requires only two flats for the horn (i.e. B♭ and E♭), of which one, the B♭, is an open tone in the medium and high range of the scale and does not impair the sonority of the part of the scale which would chiefly be used; for instance:

To be sure, a horn in E^b would have been just as suitable for this passage:

but if the melody should contain frequently the fourth and sixth steps of this scale (A^b and C), then the horn in F would be preferable, since its two notes E^b and G

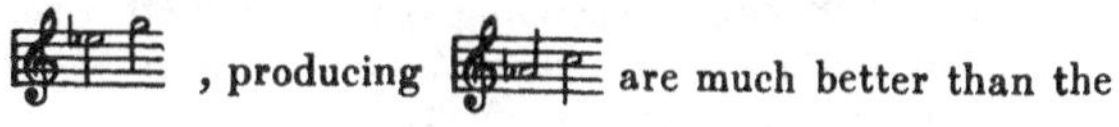

, producing … are much better than the corresponding notes of the horn in E^b,

Orchestras formerly included only two horns; at present there are always four. With two horns—even if the stopped tones are fully utilized—the use of the instrument would be greatly limited in the case of modulation into distant keys. With four horns, however, it is easy to manage this by using horns in various keys. The use of four horns in the same key would almost inevitably betray a flagrant lack of skill. It is incomparably better to use two horns in one key and two horns in another; or the first and second horns in one key, the third horn in another, and the fourth horn in a third key—which would be still more useful; or, finally, four horns in four different keys—which would be particularly advantageous if many open tones are required.

For example, if the orchestra plays in A^b, the first horn may be in A^b, the second in E (on account of its E, which produces G# or, enharmonically, A^b), the third in F, the fourth in C. Or else, the first horn could be in A^b, the second in D^b, the third in E, and the fourth in low B (on account of its E, producing D# or, enharmonically, E^b). The four keys can be combined in many different ways according to the contents of the work. It is the composer's task to calculate the combination most suitable to his harmonies, and to select his horns accordingly. In this fashion one can arrange to have only very few chords not containing four, three, or at least two open tones—as the following examples show:

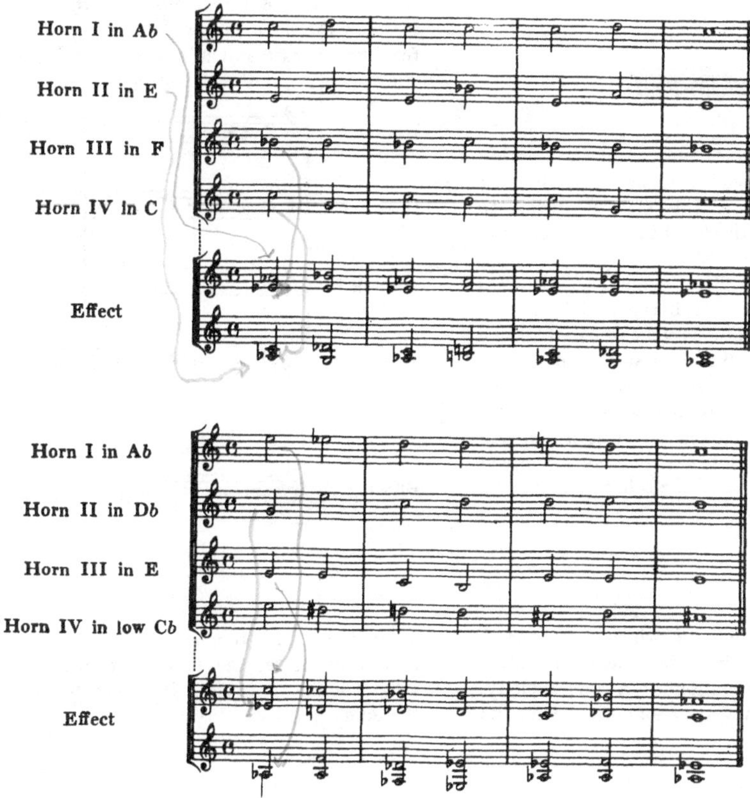

If several different keys are used, it is better to assign the higher keys to the first horns and the lower keys to the second horns. Another precaution, frequently disregarded by many composers, is the avoidance of changing from a very high to a very low key (or vice versa) during a piece. For example, the sudden transition from high A to low B^b is very difficult for the player. With four horns now available in all orchestras, such awkward skips are easily avoidable.

Up to this point, Berlioz' text is obsolete and is only of historical value. (See the appendix at the end of this chapter.)

The horn is a noble and melancholy instrument; but the expression and the character of its tone is such that the instrument is not limited to any particular type of composition. It blends well with the general harmony. Even a composer of limited skill can employ it as he sees fit—either prominently or in a more unobtrusive though useful role. In my opinion, no composer has used the horn in a more original, poetic and accomplished fashion than Weber. In his three masterworks, "Oberon", "Euryanthe" and "Freischuetz", he has endowed the horn with a new and wonderful language—a language which, before him, only Méhul and Beethoven understood, and whose purity has been preserved by Meyerbeer better than by anybody else. Of all the orchestral instruments, the horn is the one for which Gluck wrote least felicitously. A simple scrutiny of one of his works will suffice to prove his want of skill in this respect. However, we must cite as a stroke of genius the three horn tones imitating Charon's conch in the aria "Caron t'appelle" in his opera "Alceste". The medium C is repeated three times by two horns in D in unison. The composer requires the bells of the two horns to be placed one against the other, so that they serve mutually as "sordines". The tones bounding against each other sound as if emanating from a distant cave. This produces a very strange and dramatic effect:

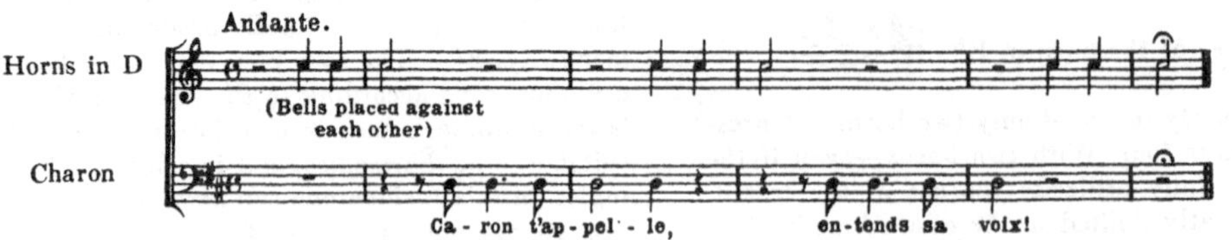

I believe, however, that Gluck would have obtained approximately the same result with the stopped medium A♭ of two horns in G♭:

But it is possible that the horn players of that period were not sufficiently sure of such attacks; in that event the composer did well in using this strange device to damp the most open tone of the horn in D and to make it sound distant.

In the hunting scene of his "Guillaume Tell" Rossini conceived the idea of having four horns in E♭ execute a diatonic passage in unison. This is very original. When four horns are thus to be combined in a sustained melody or in rapid passages containing open as well as stopped tones, it is far better to use horns in four different keys (unless the idea is based just on the variety and unevenness of these tones). The open tones of one horn compensate for the weak stopped tones of the others, preserving the balance and giving evenness to the whole scale of the four combined horns. If the horn in C plays a stopped E♭, the horn in E♭ an open C, the horn in F an open B♭, and the horn in low B♭ a stopped F, these four different timbres result in a quadruple E♭ of great sonority. The same applies to the other tones.

A very advantageous method—of which, however, I know only one example—is to have four horns in different keys alternate in the execution of a solo melody. Each of them takes the notes corresponding with its open tones. If the melodic fragments are skillfully linked together, the melody seems to be played by a single horn, almost all of whose tones are open and of the same quality.

As I have said above, the horn is a noble and melancholy instrument—notwithstanding the frequently quoted hunting fanfares. In fact, the gaiety of these flourishes arises rather from the melodies themselves than from the timbre of the horn. Hunting fanfares lose much of their gaiety if they are not played on real hunting horns—instruments of little musical value,whose strident and obtrusive tone differs greatly from the chaste and reserved voice of the French horn. However, by forcing the flow of air in the tube of the horn in a particular manner, its tone can be made to resemble that of the hunting horn. This is called making the tone *brassy.*

This may occasionally produce excellent effects even with stopped tones. When open tones are to be forced, composers generally require the performers to turn the bells upward so as to give the sound the greatest possible sharpness. This position of the instrument is indicated by : *Bell turned upward.* A magnificent example of this method is found in the violent outburst at the end of the duet "Gardez-vous de la jalousie" in Méhul's "Euphrosine et Coradin". Grétry, still under the impression produced by this terrible outcry of horns, one day answered someone who asked him for his opinion of this crushing piece: "It is as if one wanted to split the roof of the theater with the skulls of the audience."

THE VALVE HORN

(Horn with three pistons or cylinder valves)

This instrument can render all its tones open by means of a special mechanism which makes it possible to change the key of the instrument instantaneously. By using the different pistons one can transform the horn in F into a horn in E, E♭ or D, etc.; and by combining the open tones of one key with those of the other key, the complete chromatic scale can be played in open tones. Moreover, the use of the three pistons adds six semitones to the scale of the instrument below its lowest natural tone.

C being the lowest natural tone of the horn, the pistons would give it the following additional tones:

This applies to all brass instruments which have this mechanism—i.e. trumpets, cornets, bugles and trombones.

The range of the horn with three pistons in a mixed key such as that of E♭ would therefore be as follows:

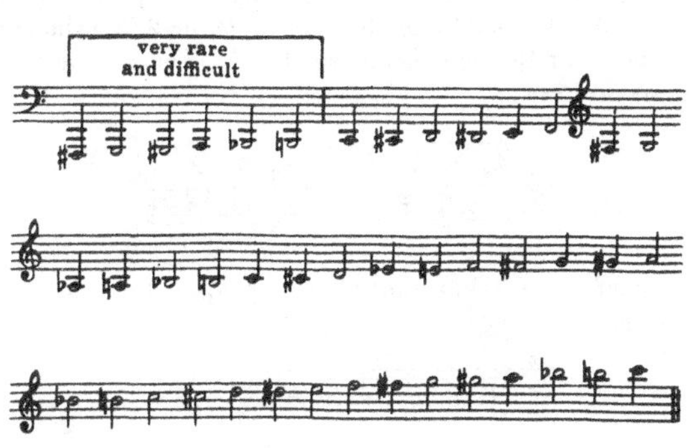

This system offers great advantages, especially for the second horns, by filling the great gaps between their low natural tones from the lowest C upward. But the timbre of the horn with pistons differs a little from that of the ordinary horn; therefore, it cannot replace it altogether. I think it should be treated almost as a separate instrument, particularly suitable in furnishing good, sonorous and energetic basses, similar to the low tones of the tenor trombone, although without their strength. It can also render melodies quite well, especially those moving mainly in the medium range.

The medium keys are the best on the piston horn—in fact, they are the only ones leaving nothing to be desired as to purity of intonation. The horns in E, F, G and A♭ are therefore far preferable to any of the others.

Since their introduction into orchestras, many composers have shown a certain hostility toward these new instruments because some horn players have used them in cases where an ordinary horn is indicated. By means of the new mechanism they find it easier to play open tones instead of the stopped ones actually desired by the composer. This is, of course, a dangerous abuse; but it can easily be checked by the conductor. One must not forget that the piston horn, in the hands of a skilled player, can produce all the stopped tones of the ordinary horn as well as some additional ones; for it can play the whole scale without using a single open tone. Since the pistons, by changing the key of the instrument, add to the open tones of the principal key those of the changed keys, it is obvious that the stopped tones of all keys can be combined in the same fashion. The horn in F, for instance, plays this open C, which sounds F, as a natural tone, and by means of the pistons also the open D, which sounds G. By placing the hand into the bell and thus lowering these notes a tone, the first becomes B♭, sounding the stopped E♭, and the second becomes C, sounding the stopped F.

Hence, to indicate those tones which he does not want executed as open tones, the composer simply has to add the word "stopped" and the figures ½ or 2/3 (showing how much of the bell should be closed). For a scale written as follows:

the performer takes the pistons proper for the open scale of C:

By inserting the hand, which closes the bell two-thirds during each note, this scale is transformed into one in B♭, whose tones are the most hollow and most stopped obtainable on the horn. In this fashion a passage previously heard in open tones can be repeated by the piston horn in stopped tones—like a distant echo.

The horn with cylinder valves differs from the preceding only in the nature of its mechanism. The difference is entirely in its favor as far as facility of tone production is concerned. The tones of the cylinder horn can scarcely be distinguished from those of the ordinary horn. The instrument is already in general use in Germany and will doubtless soon be adopted everywhere.

Of all the instruments the horn is probably the one that blends best with all instrumental groups. To demonstrate this fact in its full measure I should have to insert here the entire score of "Meistersinger"; for I think I am not exaggerating in saying that this score, differing from the ensemble of Beethoven's C-minor Symphony only by the addition of the third trumpet, harp and tuba, has become so entirely different, new and unheard-of principally because of the enormous versatility and highly developed technique of the valve horn.

Mozart's two flutes, two oboes, two clarinets and two bassoons are certainly utilized here to the full virtuosic extent of their expressive potentialities; they are combined by a stupendous application of all the secrets of their registers. The string quintet, with most intricate divisions, creates ever new miracles of sound, enriched by the harp and exalted to an unheard-of warmth of feeling by the most wonderful polyphony. Trumpets and trombones are made to reveal all solemn and comic features of the work. But the most essential of all is the faithful horn functioning untiringly in carrying the melody or as a medium filling-in voice, or as the bass. The "Meistersinger" score is the finest eulogy for the horn. The introduction and improvement of the valve horn has undoubtedly inaugurated the greatest advance in the technique of the modern orchestra since Berlioz.

To demonstrate exhaustively the truly protean nature of this instrument I should have to go through the scores of the great magician bar after bar, beginning with "Rheingold".

The horn, whether it calls ringingly Siegfried's exuberant vitality into the virgin forest;
whether it fades away in Liszt's "Mazeppa" as the last, hoarse cry of the dying Cossack prince in the endless steppe (Example 104);
whether it seeks to conjure the picture of the unknown mother to Siegfried, who is pining for her like a child (Example 105);
whether it brings Isolde's shining image over the gentle waves to the dying Tristan;
whether it indicates Hans Sachs' thanks to his faithful apprentice (Example 106);
whether in Erik's dream ("Fliegender Hollaender", second act) it lets with a few hollow accents the surf of the northern sea hit the nocturnal shore (Example 107);
whether it is the symbol of Freya's youth-giving apples (Example 108);
whether it pokes fun at the henpecked husband ("Meistersinger", third act)—(Examples 109 and 110);
whether it thrashes Beckmesser with the jealous apprentice David and actually functions as leader of the brawl ("Meistersinger", second act);
whether it sings in muted sounds of the miracles of the Tarnhelm (Example 111)—it always serves its task fully and entirely, it is unique in its versatility, and its effect is always conspicuous.

104. MAZEPPA

Liszt.

Kl.Fl.
Gr.Fl.
Ob.
Engl.Hrn.
Klar. I. in D.
Klar. II. in A.
Baßklar. in C.
Fag.
Hrnr. in F.
Trp. in D.
Ten.Pos.
Baß-Pos. u. Tuba.
Pke.
Triangel.
Becken u.Gr.Tr.
I.
Viol.
II.
Viola.
Vlc.
K. B.

poco ritenuto
Kl. Fl.
Gr. Fl.
Ob.
Engl. Hrn.
Klar. I. in D.
Klar. II. in A.
Baßklar. in C.
Fag.
a 3.
Hrnr. in F.
Trp. in D.
Ten. Pos.
Baß-Pos. u. Tuba.
Pke.
Triangel.
Becken u. Gr. Tr.
poco ritenuto
I.
Viol.
II.
Viola.
Vlc.
K. B.

a2.
poco a poco rallentando
Andante.
Gr.Fl.
Ob.
Engl. Hrn.
Klar. I. in D.
Klar. II. in A.
Baßklar. in C.
a3.
Fag.
Hrnr. in F.
in D.
Trp.
in E.
Ten.Pos.
Baß-Pos. u.Tuba.
Pke.
Triangel.
Becken u.Gr.Tr.
poco a poco rallentando
Andante.
I.
Viol.
II.
Viola.
Vlc.
Solo.
K. B.

Gr. Fl.
Engl.Hrn.
Klar. in A.
Baßklar. in C.
Fag.
Viol. I. II.
Viola.
Vlc.
K. B.
a2.
sehr lang
I.Solo
a 3. sehr lang
cresc.
pizz.
arco
I. Solo
Hrnr. in F.
con sord
3 Vcelli
Tutti pizz.
Tutti arco
pizz.
Hrn. in F.
Viol. II.
dim.
poco ritenuto

105. SIEGFRIED, ACT II

Wagner.

I.II. in E.
Hrnr. III.IV. in C.
(mit Dämpfer.)
V.VI. in F.
pp
p zart
Viol. I.
p
(mit Dämpfer)
(1. Pult)
(2. Pult)
Viol. II.
Violen.
Vlc.
Siegfr.
K. B.

Fl. I.
p
Ob. I.
p
Hrnr. in E.
pp
Eine allein.
2. P.
pp
più p
3. 4. P.
6. 7. 8. P.
(ohne D.)
Viol. I.
1. 2. P.
Viol. II.
6. 7. 8. P.
1. P.
Violen.
5. u. 6. P.
(ohne D.)
1. 2. P.
3. 4. P.
Vlc.
5. 6. P.
(ohne D.)
(Wachsendes Waldweben. — Siegfrieds Aufmerksamkeit wird endlich durch den Gesang der Waldvögel gefesselt.
Siegfr.
(Die 4 ersten)(ohne Dampfer)
K. B.
(Die 4 letzten)(ohne Dämpfer)

Fl.
Klar. I. in A.
Viol. I.
Viol. II.
Violen.
Vlc.
K.B.
1. 2. 3. u. 4. P.
6. 7. u. 8. P.
1. 2. u. 3. P.
5. u. 6. P.
+)Das 5. Pult tritt hinzu.
+)Das 4. Pult tritt hinzu.
(ohne Dämpfer.)
marc.
f dim.
Ob.
Siegfr.
1. 2. 3. P. (ohne Dämpfer.)
(Siegfried lauscht mit wachsender Teilnahme einem Waldvogel in den Zweigen über ihm.)

Ob. I.
Klar. I. in A.
Viol. I.
Viol. II.
Violen.
Vlc.
K. B.
Klar. I. in A.
I. II.
Hrnr. in E. III. IV.
V. VI.
(ohne D.)
(ohne Dämpfer.)
(ohne Dämpfer.)
pp cresc.
dim.
più p
molto cresc.
Siegfr.
Du hol- des Vög- lein, dich hört ich noch nie: bist du im Wald hier da-heim? Ver-
dolce
più f
cresc.

Hrn. I. in E.
Viol. I.
Viol. II.
Violen.
Siegfr.
stünd ich sein süßes Stammeln! Ge-wiß sagt' es mir was, vielleicht von der lie-ben Mut-ter?
Vlc.
I. in E.
dolce
più p
II. in E.
Hrnr.
(mit Dämpfer)
III.IV. in F.
(mit Dämpfer)
V.VI. in C.
p
pp

106. MEISTERSINGER, ACT III

Wagner.

107. DER FLIEGENDE HOLLAENDER, ACT II

Fag.
V-Hrn. in F.
Hrnr. in F.
Viola.
Erik.
träu-mend, sah un-ter mir des Mee-res Flut; — die Bran-dung hört' ich, wie sich schäumend am U-fer
Vlc.
K.B.
Klar. in B.
pp
II. Solo.
trem.
Viol. I. II.
brach der Wo-gen Wut! Ein fremdes Schiff am na-hen Stran-de erblickt' ich, selt-sam, wun-der-
pizz.
geteilt zu 3.
cresc.
dim.
Senta.
Der andre?...
bar. Zwei Män-ner nah-ten sich dem Lan-de, der ein' — ich sah's — dein Va-ter war's.

108. RHEINGOLD, SCENE II

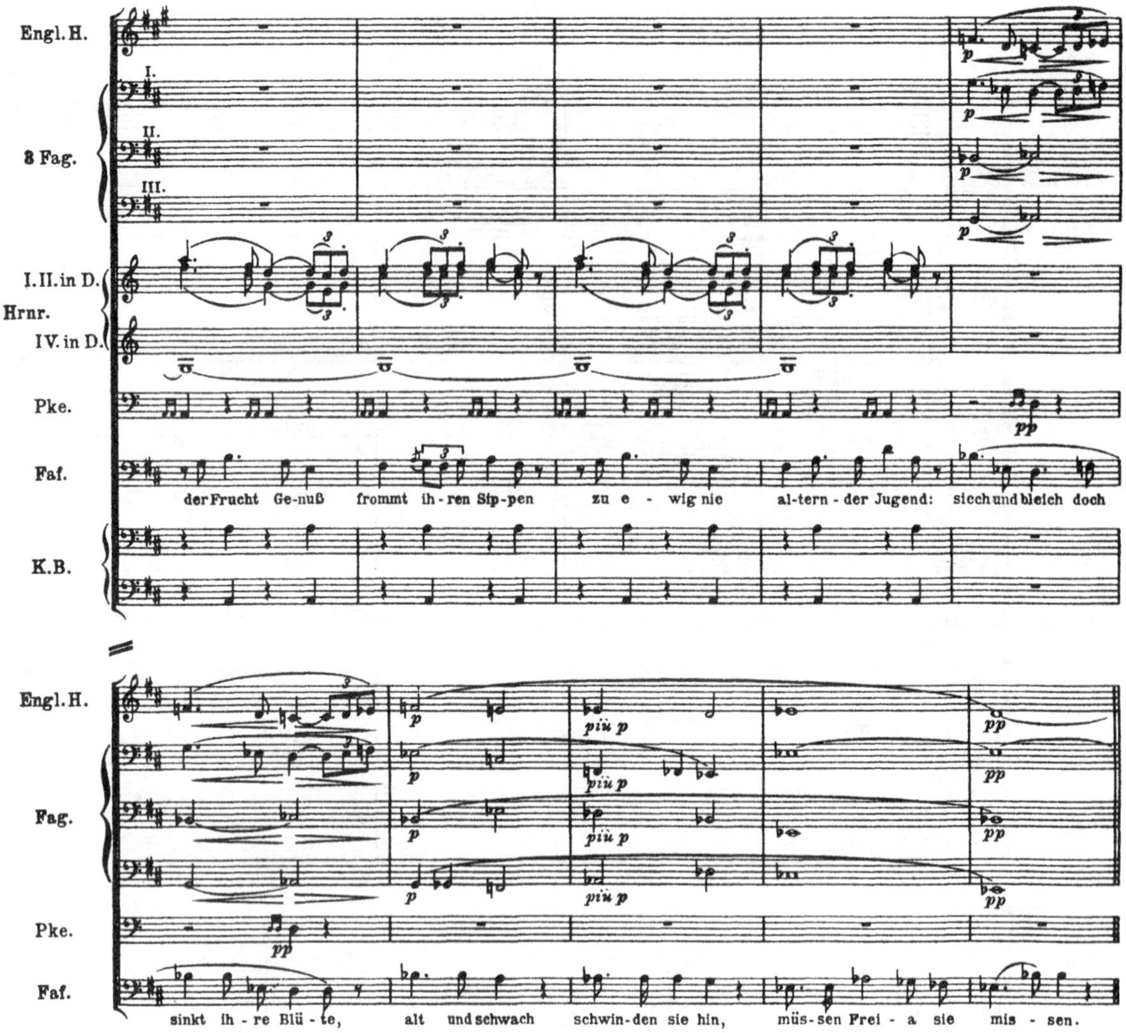

Engl. H.
I. II. III. 3 Fag.
I. II. in D. Hrnr. IV. in D.
Pke.
Faf.
K.B.

der Frucht Ge-nuß frommt ih-ren Sip-pen zu e - wig nie al-tern - der Jugend: siech und bleich doch

Engl. H.
Fag.
Pke.
Faf.

più p

pp

sinkt ih - re Blü - te, alt und schwach schwin-den sie hin, müs - sen Frei - a sie mis - sen.

109. MEISTERSINGER, ACT III

Wagner.

110. MEISTERSINGER, ACT III

Ob.
Klar. in B.
Hrnr. in F.
Fag.
Viol.
I.
II.
Viola.
Sachs.
Vlc.
K.B.
ohne Dämpfer
Bog.
ausdrucksvoll
pizz.
stacc.
dim.
cresc.
dann noch will ge-lin - gen ein schö-nes Lied zu sin - gen, seht:
Trp. I in F.
Pos. I.
Harfe.
a 2.
marc.
Mei- - - - - - ster nennt man die!
ausdrucksvoll

111. RHEINGOLD, SCENE III

Although horn players now use almost exclusively the horns in E, F, high A and high B♭ (incidentally, it requires practice to change the bright and sharp tone of the horn in B♭ into the soft and noble timbre of the horn in F), it is nevertheless advisable to retain Richard Wagner's method of indicating the key of the horn according to the changes of key in the music. It is true that horn players do not observe these different keys any more; but they are accustomed to transpose any key instantly into the key of the horn they are using, and they much prefer this method to being forced to read all the time the horn in F, for instance, with a great number of accidentals (sharps, double sharps, etc.). Hence, composers should continue to indicate: horn in E♭, D, D♭ as they see fit. In my opinion, this has the advantage of a cleaner. appearance of the score. Personally I prefer to read the horns in the different keys and to transpose them (habit may have something to do with this, too). The score is much clearer on first sight, since the staves of the horns and trumpets at once stand out plastically in contrast to the staves of the wood-winds and strings with their transpositions and numerous accidentals.

Except for the above stated difference in softness between the horns in F and high B♭, all the other differences in timbre between the various valve horns are merely illusory. This is why many horns in different keys are no longer used. Generally, the players of the first and third horns use the horn in high B^b for almost all pieces in flat keys and the horn in high A for all pieces in sharp keys. The players of the second and fourth horns use horns in E and F.

High keys are less strenuous and permit greater sureness. For instance, Siegfried's solo (Example 112) is executed with surprising ease by all horn players in spite of its seeming difficulty; likewise the following passage ("Meistersinger", Act III, Scene 3).

Horns in high F and high C are now said to be in the process of construction. This would be of very particular interest in reference to the rendition of Bach's first Brandenburg Concerto.

112. SIEGFRIED, ACT II

Mäßig bewegt.

Wagner.

Siegfried nimmt das silberne Hüfthorn und bläst darauf.

Die Fermaten sehr lang und bedeutungsvoll.

Ein Horn in F auf dem Theater.

f sehr kräftig *(sehr stark ausgehalten)* *(weich gestoßen)*

(Bei den langgehaltenen Tönen blickt Siegfried immer erwartungsvoll auf den Vogel.)

p *cresc.* *accel.* *f dim.* *p* Mäßig. *p (zart)*

p *p* *poco cresc.* *f dim.*

Lustig, und immer schneller und schmetternder.

più p *pp* *p* *cresc.*

immer stärker *(sehr schnell und schmetternd)*

Baßtuba.

K.B.- Tuba.

Hrn. in F auf d. Theater.

p *p* *ff* *ff* *ff*

(Im Hintergrunde regt es sich. Fafner in der Gestalt eines ungeheuren, eidechsenartigen Schlangenwurmes, hat sich in der Höhle von seinem Lager erhoben; er bricht durch das Gesträuch, und wälzt sich aus der Tiefe nach der höheren Stelle vor, so daß er mit dem Vorderleibe bereits auf ihr angelangt ist, als er jetzt einen starken, gähnenden Laut ausstößt.)

Allmählich immer gedehnter.

Baßtuba.

K.B.- Tuba.

Hrn. in F auf d. Theater.

p *p* *cresc.* *ff*

THE TRUMPET

Its range is approximately the same as that of the French horn; it has the same natural open tones, one octave higher. It is written in the G-clef.

Some performers succeed to a degree in producing stopped tones on the trumpet by introducing the hand into the bell, as on the horn. But the effect of these tones is so bad and their intonation is so uncertain that the great majority of composers have wisely abstained and are continuing to abstain from using them. The high F, however, should be excepted from this proscription and may be considered an open tone. It is produced by the lips only; but since it is always a little too high in pitch, it can be used only as a passing note between G and E, and one must refrain from employing it as an unprepared note or from sustaining it. The medium B♭, on the other hand, is always a little flat. The low C should be avoided on trumpets in keys lower than F. It sounds weak and rough and is not suitable for characteristic effects. It can be easily replaced by a horn tone, which is better in every respect.

The three highest notes, very hazardous on the trumpets in low A, B♭ and C, are impracticable in higher keys. However, the high C can be produced with some effort even on trumpets in E♭ if it is introduced similarly to the following example:

Such a passage, which most German and English players would attack without hesitation, would be considered very risky in France, where one generally has to overcome great difficulties in employing the brass.

There are trumpets (made in one piece) in B♭, C, D, E♭, E, F, G and—very rarely—in high A♭. By means of the lengthening piece previously mentioned in connection with the horn, which lowers the pitch of the instrument by a semitone, one obtains trumpets in A, B, D♭ (or C#) and G♭ (or F#). By using a double lengthening piece, which lowers the pitch a whole tone, even a trumpet in low A♭ can be produced; but this key sounds worst of all. The trumpet in D♭ has the most beautiful tone; it is very brilliant and of pure intonation. But this instrument is hardly ever used because most composers do not know of its existence.

What has been said above of the notes at the two extremes of its scale shows that the range of the trumpet is not the same in all keys. Low trumpets, similarly to all other instruments of this type, must avoid the lowest notes, and high trumpets cannot reach the highest notes.

The range of the trumpet in the different keys is as follows:

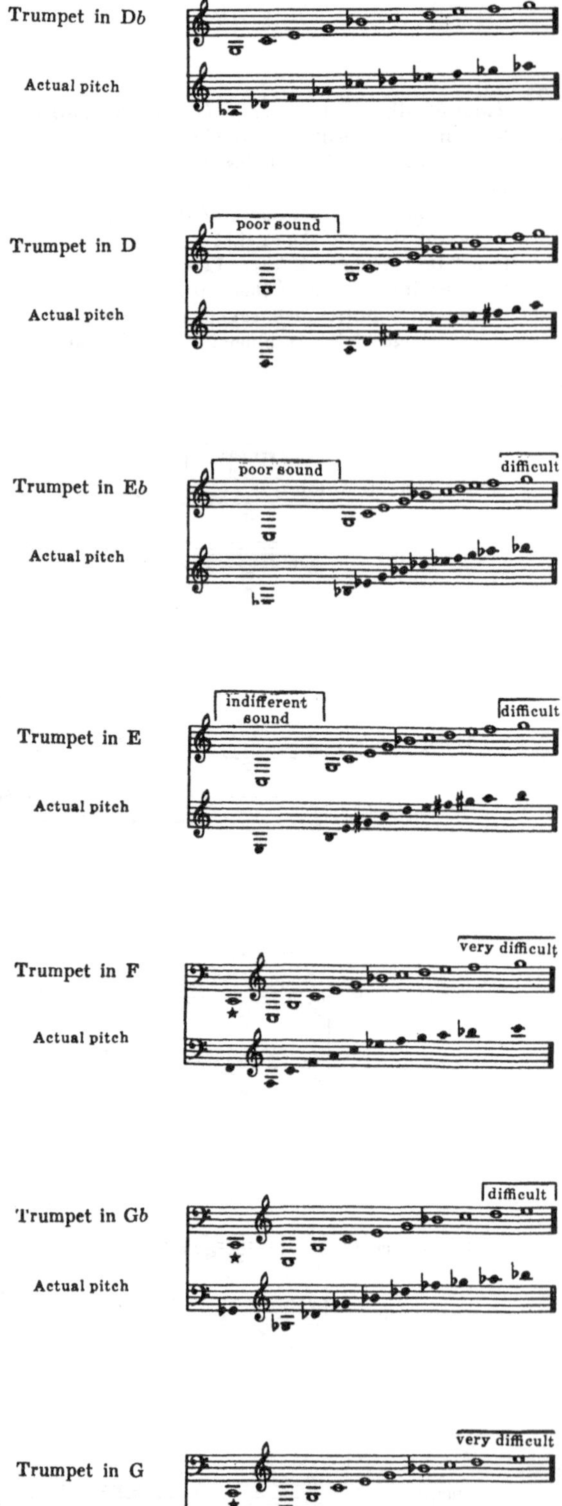

The low C (marked *), which is written in the F-clef, is of excellent sonority in the three high keys (F, G^b, G). It can be used very effectively on many occasions.

Trumpets in high A^b are found only in some military bands. Their tone is very brilliant, but their range is still smaller than that of the trumpet in G, since they cannot go above the fourth C.

Adolphe Sax now makes small octave and tenth trumpets (in high C and high E^b) of excellent tone. They should be employed in all orchestras and military bands.

Trills are generally impracticable on the trumpet; in my opinion, they should not be used in the orchestra. The following three trills, however, sound quite well:

All that has been said above concerning the different keys of the horns and about the method of taking advantage of them in combination applies equally to the trumpets. It should be added, however, that there is rarely an opportunity for using them in different keys. Most of our orchestras provide the composer with only two trumpets and two cornets, instead of four trumpets. It is therefore better to have two trumpets in the same key since the cornets can complete the harmony; the latter can play all intervals, and their timbre is not so dissimilar from that of the trumpets that they could not blend with them sufficiently in the ensemble.

This chapter is now also obsolete. All the composer needs is orchestral technique and tonal imagination; the key in which he writes the trumpet is unimportant. It is best to apply here, too, Wagner's method of writing in all keys so as to leave the trumpet part in C major as much as possible. One can then leave the choice of the most suitable key to the individual trumpet player.

To the best of my knowledge, trumpet players now prefer the following keys: first trumpets—high A, B^b C; second trumpets—F, D, E^b.

Only in minor keys is it necessary to use trumpets in two different keys, if there are passages containing the third and fifth steps of the scale. In G# minor, for instance, if one trumpet is to play G# and B while the other one plays B and D# a third higher (or a sixth lower), it is necessary to employ one trumpet in E (whose E and G produce G# and B) and another one in B (whose C and E produce B and D#). This is what Meyerbeer did in the great scene of the fourth act of "Les Huguenots":

Trumpet in E
Trumpet in B
Effect

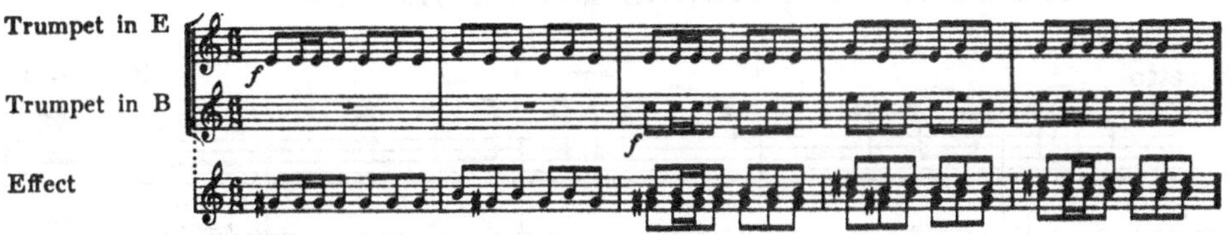

Contrary to traditional usage, the piano tone of the trumpets can be employed with charming effect. Gluck was one of the first to give a convincing example of this in the long sustained note of the two trumpets, united pianissimo on the dominant, in the Andante of the introduction to "Iphigénie en Tauride." Beethoven (particularly in the Andante of his A-major Symphony) and Weber both used the piano possibilities of the trumpets very felicitously. (Examples 113 and 114).

113. IPHIGENIE EN TAURIDE, ACT I.

Gluck.

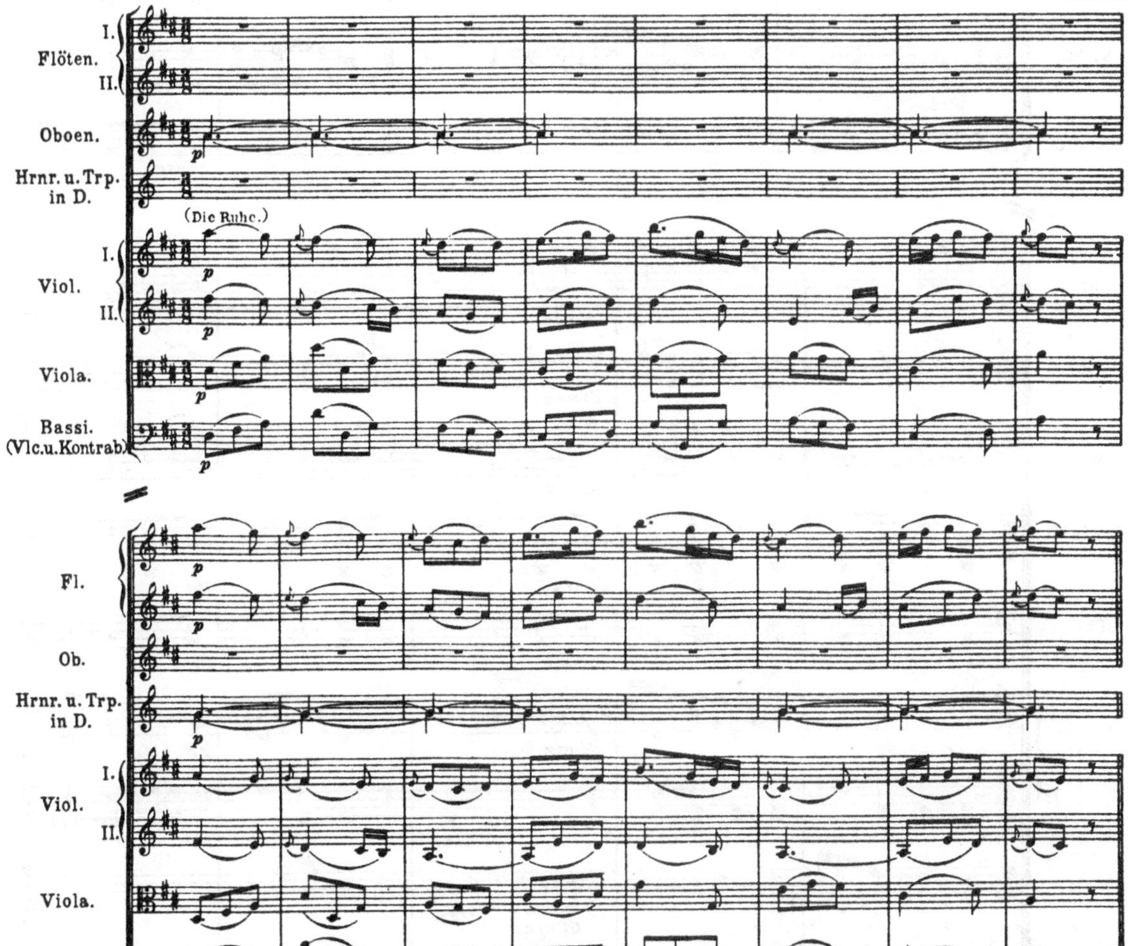
Flöten.
I.
II.
Oboen.
Hrnr. u. Trp. in D.
(Die Ruhe.)
Viol.
I.
II.
Viola.
Bassi. (Vlc.u.Kontrab.)
Fl.
Ob.
Hrnr. u. Trp. in D.
Viol.
I.
II.
Viola.
Bassi.

114. SYMPHONY IN A MAJOR, 2nd MOVEMENT

These soft tones should generally be in the medium range and should not succeed one another too rapidly, so that they can be produced with certainty. The following five tones can be played and sustained in pianissimo:

The medium B^b is a little flat; this must be remedied by a strong attack. Therefore, it cannot be included among the soft tones. The C above  does not offer the same risk. It can be taken and sustained softly, at least in the low keys of A, B^b, B and C. I think that even in the key of D a skillful player can sustain this C very softly; but it is better to conceal its entry by a forte of the rest of the orchestra.

(All this has been improved by the new mechanism.)

The tone of the trumpet is noble and brilliant. It is suitable in expressing martial splendor, cries of fury and vengeance as well as chants of triumph; it can render vigorous, violent and lofty feelings as well as most tragic accents.

Cf. the demonic call of the low trumpets in Bizet's "Carmen" (Example 115).

115. CARMEN, ACT I, PRELUDE

Andante moderato (♩=58.)

Bizet.

Klar. in A.
Fag.
Hrnr. in D.
Trp. in A.
Pos.
Pke.
Harfe.
Viol. I.
Viol. II.
Viola.
Vlc.
K.B.

Klar. in A.
Fag.
Hrnr. in F.
in F.
Trp. in A.
a 3.
Pos.
Pke.
Harfe.
Viol.
I.
II.
Viola.
Vlc.
K.B.
ff
p
f
dim.
meno

Fl.
Ob.
Klar. in A.
Fag.
in F.
Hrnr.
in Es.
Trp. in A.
Pos.
Pke.
Gr.Trom. u. Becken.
I.
Viol.
II.
Viola.
Vlc.
K.B.
cre - scen - do molto
ff

The trumpet can be employed even in pieces of gay character, provided that this mood is characterized in a spirited or brilliant manner.

In spite of its proud and distinguished timbre, the trumpet has been degraded as few other instruments. Up to the time of Beethoven and Weber, all composers—not even excepting Mozart—limited its use to the low sphere of mere filling-in voices or to a few commonplace rhythmic formulas, as vapid as they are ridiculous, and usually contrary to the character of the piece in which they occur. This trivial practice has at last been abandoned. All composers possessing style strive to give to their melodic passages, accompaniments and figurations all the latitude, variety and independence which nature has accorded to the trumpet. It took almost a century to attain this!

Verdi used the trumpet (as well as the trombone) in his later works ("Falstaff", "Otello") very individually, but without real feeling for its soul and true character. This application of the heavy brass, resulting from the use of the key trombones with their vulgar tone, is not to be recommended, although it belongs to the peculiarities of the old master.

In view of the incisive effect which the trumpet always has it is not necessary to quote the innumerable examples from Richard Wagner's works: Siegmund's sword motif, Bruennhilde's fighting call at the beginning of the second act of "Walkuere", the trumpet octaves, as painful as sword thrusts, at the end of the second act of "Tristan"—all these are unforgettable to anyone who has ever heard them.

The *valve trumpets* (with pistons or cylinders) have the advantage of being able to produce all the intervals of the chromatic scale, similarly to the valve horns. They have lost nothing of the peculiar timbre of the ordinary trumpet through the addition of this mechanism; and their intonation is satisfactory. Trumpets with cylinders are best of all; they will soon come into general use.

Key trumpets (still in use in some Italian orchestras) cannot match them in this respect.

The general range of the valve trumpet (with pistons or cylinders) is as follows:

The high cylinder trumpets, such as those in F and G, can descend chromatically as far as F# ; but these extremely low notes are of rather poor quality.

Major and minor trills practicable on the cylinder trumpet are the same as those on the cornet with three pistons. (See the table of trills on this instrument, p.299)

Slide trumpets (so called on account of the attached slide, which is moved by the right hand, similarly to that of the trombone) produce the purest intervals because of this mechanism. Their tone is exactly the same as that of the ordinary trumpets; their range is as follows:

Muted trumpets frequently produce enchanting effects. In forte they are suitable for caricature and for the presentation of fantastic apparitions. The piano of muted trumpets has a magical, silvery sound (Example 116).

The muted trumpet is much easier to play than the muted horn. The latter still offers difficulties in regard to purity of intonation, which can be overcome only by diligent practice.

116. NOCTURNES—LES FETES*

Debussy

*This piece replaces two excerpts from "Feuersnot" quoted by Strauss.

TROMP.
1re HARPE
2e HARPE
TIMB.
Div.

un peu rapproché
TROMP.
1re HARPE
2e HARPE
TIMB.

THE CORNET

(Cornet with three pistons or with cylinders)

Its range is approximately two octaves and two or three tones. The valve mechanism with which it is furnished enables it to play all chromatic steps down to the low F# ; however, this tone and the two or three preceding ones (A, A♭, and G) are practicable only on high cornets. On these high cornets it is even possible to produce the low C , the first natural tone of the cornet (as will be presently seen); but its production is very risky; moreover, its sound is poor and of very questionable usefulness.

There are cornets in C, B♭, A, A♭, G, F, E, E♭ and D. By means of the lengthening pieces mentioned above in the chapters on the horn and the trumpet, the pitch of the instrument is lowered a semitone, and the keys of B, F# and even D♭ can thus be obtained. But the facility of modulating as a result of the valves makes these changes of key almost useless. Besides, the low keys—such as G, F, E and D—are generally of poor tone quality and lack purity of intonation. The cornets in A♭, A and B♭ are the best; I think they should be used almost exclusively. The highest cornet—the one in C—is rather difficult to play.

The following table shows the range which may be assigned to the various cornets. Some performers can produce a few additional tones above and below this range; but these are very risky, and we are disregarding them. The cornet is written in the G-clef. The following are the natural tones of its tube, which is shorter than that of the trumpet:

Range of the Cornet in different keys:

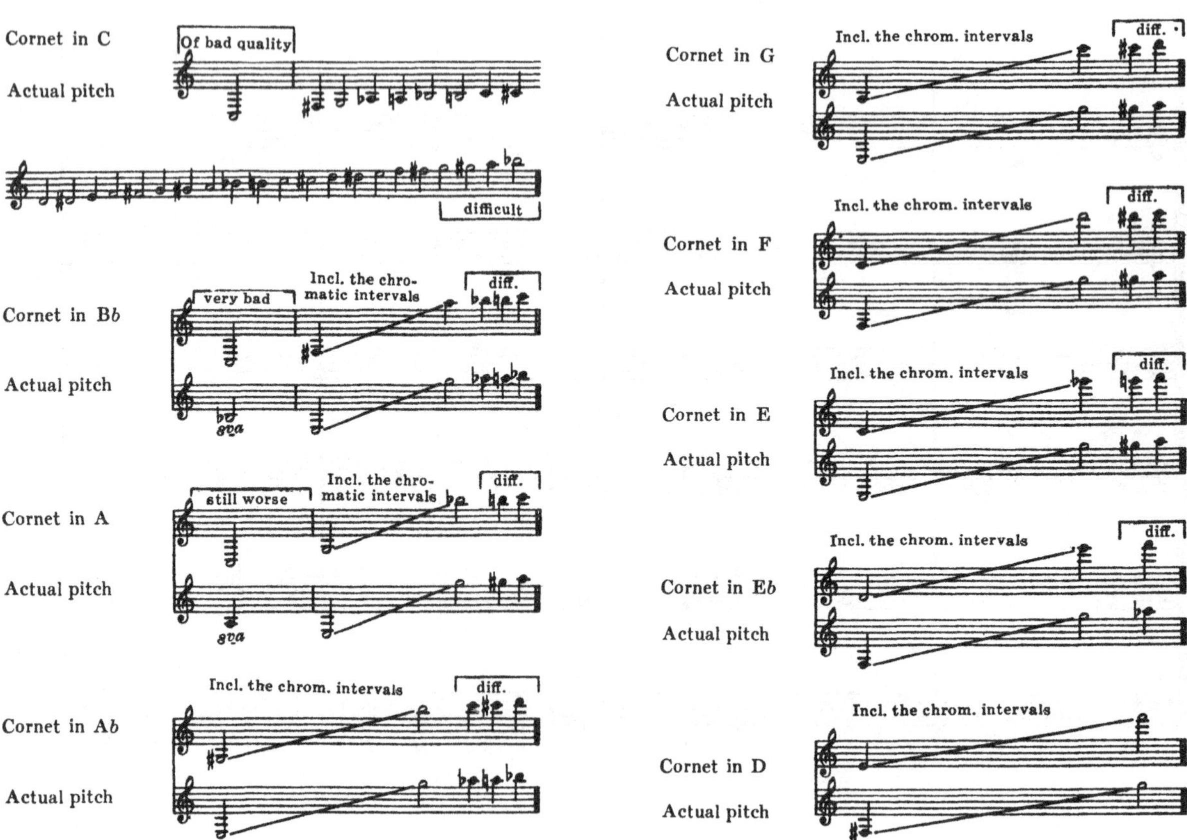

The highest notes of these examples, all of which sound the same G, are less risky and of better quality in the higher keys. Thus, the high B♭ of the cornet in A, the high A of the cornet in B♭ and the high G of the cornet in C are incomparably better and easier than the high F of the cornet in D or the high E of the cornet in E♭.

All these notes sound the same G. Moreover, this observation applies to all brass instruments.

Most major and minor trills are practicable and of good effect on high cornets—for instance those in A, B♭ and D—but only on the following part of the scale:

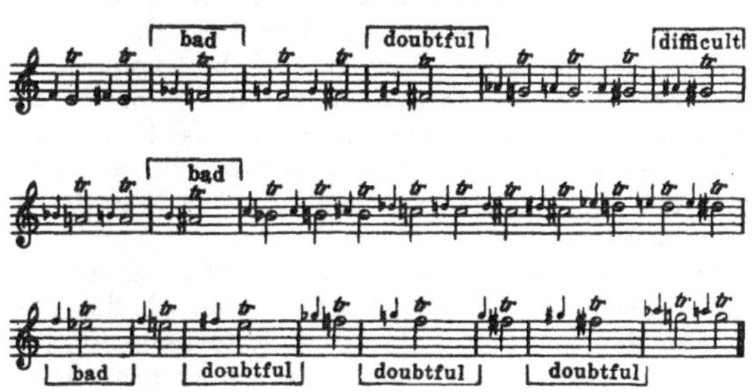

The following list shows the relation between the horns, trumpets and cornets in their various keys. The first low tone of the cornet in C is, as stated above, the higher octave of that of the trumpet in C; just as the first low tone of the trumpet in C is in turn the higher octave of that of the horn in C. The natural tones of the horns (those which result from the resonance of the tube) are thus reproduced by the trumpet in the same order, but in the higher octave. Those of the trumpet would be reproduced in the same fashion by the cornet if the lips of the player were strong enough to produce the highest tones, which, however, is not the case.

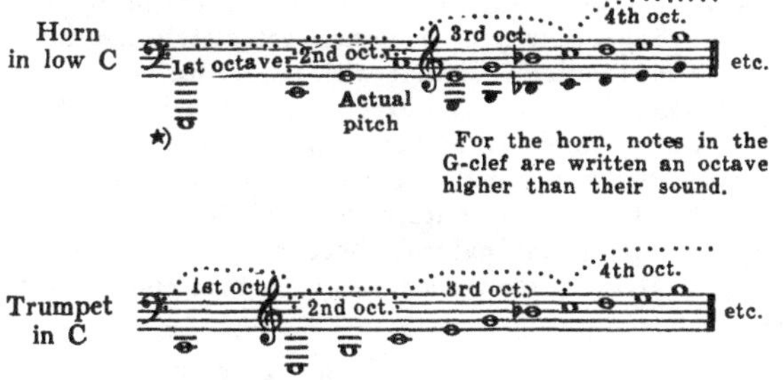

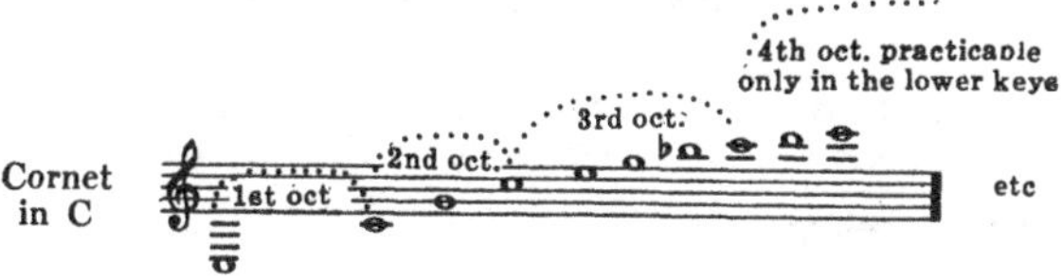

One sees—and it is important to remember this—that the part of the range of a brass instrument on which only the following three natural tones can be produced (without valves)

is always its *second octave,* i.e. proceeding from low to high.

The cornets have their best tones mainly in the second octave. Considering the cornets in A, B♭ and C as high trumpets (an octave higher than the trumpets in A, B♭ and C), one could have written them accordingly. This has been purposely avoided, and cornets are written according to their place on the general musical scale, their lowest tone an octave above that of the trumpet. The best tones of the cornets are in or near their second octave:

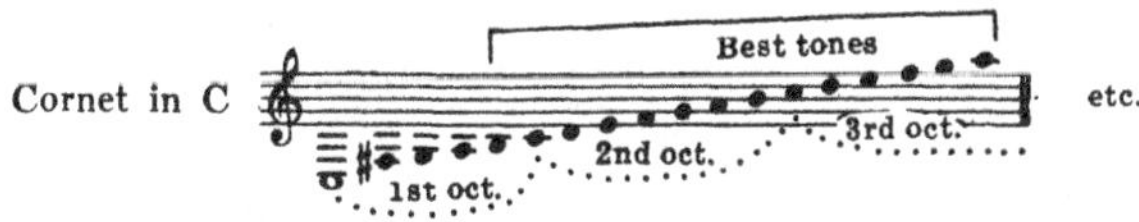

If the cornets were written like the trumpets, these notes would always be below the stave and would necessitate the constant use of ledger lines:

This inconvenient method of notation has nevertheless been preserved in Prussian military music; one should be aware of this.

In the following table the key of C has been taken as the point of departure for the various kinds of horns, trumpets and cornets. As for the cornets, the lower their key, the longer becomes their scale; this is why the listing of cornets starts with the highest keys. On the other hand, the scale of trumpets and horns becomes shorter as they rise in key (with the exception of the three keys below C—low B, B♭ and A).

***This tone exists; it is really the first low tone on the horn; but its sound is so poor and indistinct in low keys that I have omitted it from the scale of the horn in low C and B♭.**

COMPARISON OF THE DIFFERENT KEYS

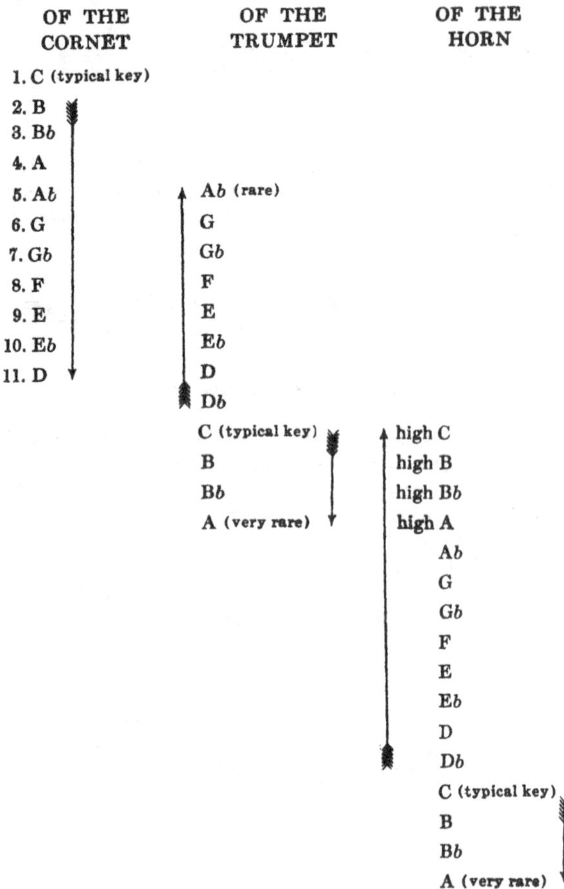

This will clarify the relations between horns, trumpets and cornets and their respective positions in the scale of tones.

I should like to add that the best tones of the valve trumpets (with pistons or cylinders) are near their third octave, *which is identical with the second octave of the cornets.* Therefore, passages for the cornets in A, B and C, written within the following range:

can also be executed on trumpets in A, B and C, without any change. This makes it possible to replace them with trumpets without any disadvantage—in orchestras lacking cornets (as the German ones).

The cornets in A, B♭ and C have a smaller range than the trumpets in A, B♭ and C; they can scarcely go above the sounding A : Cornet in A

Cornet in B♭ Cornet in C

On the other hand, the trumpets not only have several additional tones at the low end of their range—even though they may be poor—but they also produce more easily than the cornets the same A in the keys of D and F:

Trumpet in D . Trumpet in F

Some players with a particularly strong embouchure can even produce the E on the trumpet in G, whose sound is B ; and the G on the trumpet in F, whose sound is C ; but only in passing, and only if they are skillfully prepared. In any case, performers capable of reaching these extreme notes are rare; in composing it is better not to write them.

Trumpets, having a narrow tube, a small mouthpiece and a not very wide bell, play high tones with greater facility. The cornets, on the contrary, have a rather wide and almost conical tube, their bell and mouthpiece are somewhat larger, which makes their low notes easier than the high ones and gives their tone the peculiar quality distinguishing it from that of the trumpets.

Before proceeding to examine the timbre of the cornet, it may be useful to repeat here what has been said in connection with the valve horn about the function of the three cylinder or piston valves attached to brass instruments in general.

These three valves give to these instruments the chromatic scale (from the second octave upward), filling al the gaps between their natural tones; furthermore, they add six chromatic notes below the two lowest sounds:

But this first low C is already so indistinct and so difficult to sustain that the lower notes added by the valves become, as may be imagined, completely impracticable. The situation is similar with the horns.

Although the cornet can execute all steps of the chromatic scale, the choice of key is not unimportant. It is always better to select that key which permits the use of the greatest number of natural tones (it is hardly necessary to repeat that natural tones are those produced without valves by the resonance of the tube alone), such as

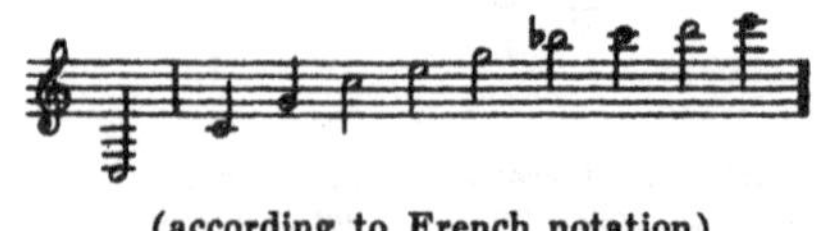

(according to French notation)

—and which requires but few flats or sharps in the signature. For instance, if the orchestra plays in E, the cornet in A should be used, which would then play in G (the cornet in E being one of the least satisfactory ones):

With an orchestra playing in D, it would also be better to use the same cornet, this time playing in F:

If the orchestra plays in E♭, the cornet in B♭ is used which plays in F—with one flat in its signature; and similarly in other cases.

I refer the reader again to the explanations regarding the various keys of horns and trumpets. The immense progress in orchestral technique (though unfortunately not in the art of phrasing) since Berlioz' time should always be kept in mind.

In France the cornet is very much in fashion at present, especially in certain musical circles where elevation and purity of style are not considered essential qualities. It has become the indispensable solo instrument in quadrilles, galops, variations and other second-rate compositions. The prevailing custom in dance orchestras of assigning melodies more or less devoid of originality and distinction to the cornet, as well as the essential character of its tone—which has neither the nobility of the horn nor the dignity of the trumpet—make the introduction of the cornet into the higher melodic style very difficult. Nevertheless, it might be used here with advantage; but only in rare instances, and provided that it is given only slow and dignified passages. Thus, the cornet is very suitable for the ritornelle of the trio in "Robert le Diable"—"O mon fils" (Example 117).

117. ROBERT LE DIABLE, ACT V

I must admit that I have a violent aversion against the manner of using the trumpet as melody-carrying instrument (that is, the trumpet alone with just a simple accompaniment). The kind of polyphonic style which Bach developed to its highest point and which was to find a wonderful rebirth in Beethoven's last quartets and later in "Tristan" and "Meistersinger"—this style was completely alien to Berlioz Hence, the finer combinations of the trumpet tone with wood-winds and horns were really created only by Richard Wagner's tonal imagination.

Example 118 ("Walkuere", first act) gives a wonderful illustration of this kind of tone combination.

118. WALKUERE, ACT I

Gay melodies played on this instrument will always run the risk of losing some of their nobility, if they possess any. If they lack it, their triviality is greatly increased. A commonplace phrase which might appear tolerable when played by the violins or wood-winds would become trite and vulgar if rendered by the blaring, obtrusive and coarse tone of the cornet. This danger is obviated if the passage is played by one or several trombones at the same time; their powerful voice would cover and ennoble that of the cornet. Employed in harmonies, the cornet blends very well with the mass of brass instruments. It serves to complete the chords of the trumpets, and it can contribute to the orchestra those diatonic or chromatic groups of notes which, because of their rapidity, suit neither the trombone nor the horns. Cornets are generally written in two voices, and frequently in different keys.

THE TROMBONES

There are four kinds of trombones, each of which bears the name of the human voice which it resembles most in character and range. The *soprano trombone*, the smallest and highest of them, exists in Germany; it is unknown in France. It has hardly ever been used in the works of the great masters. This is no reason why it should not be employed sooner or later, especially since it is by no means certain as yet whether it can be successfully replaced by the valve trumpets—even by those highest in range. Only Gluck has used the soprano trombone under the name of cornetto in the Italian score of "Orfeo". Here it serves to double the soprano voices of the chorus, while the other three trombones (alto, tenor and bass) double the other voices.

These three last-named trombones are the only ones in general use. It must be mentioned, however, that the alto trombone is not found in all French orchestras and that the bass trombone is almost unknown there. The latter is almost always confused with the third tenor trombone, which executes the lowest voice and is therefore quite incorrectly called the bass trombone, although differing from it essentialy.

Trombones are instruments with slides; their double tube can be lengthened or shortened instantly by a simple movement of the player's arm. It is obvious that these changes in the length of the tube must completely change the key of the instrument. Thus the trombones, possessing all the notes which result from the natural resonance of the tube in all positions, like the other brass instruments, attain a complete chromatic scale with just one gap at the bottom of the scale, as we shall presently see.

THE ALTO TROMBONE

It has a range of more than two and a half octaves. It is written in the C-clef on the third line (alto-clef):

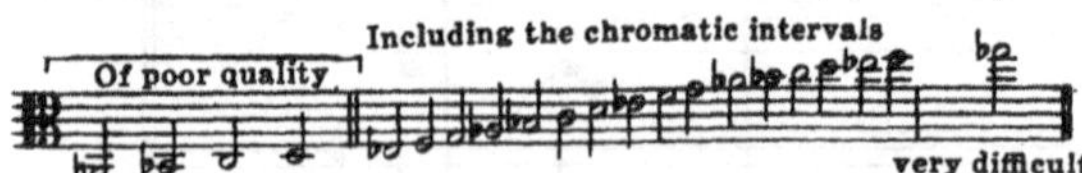

Its timbre is somewhat shrill in comparison with that of the lower trombones, and its low tones are rather poor. It is generally advisable not to use them, particularly since their quality is excellent on the tenor trombone; the latter is almost always to be found in orchestras together with the alto trombone. However, the high tones such as B, C, D, E, F may be very useful. For their sake it is regrettable that the alto trombone is at present banished from almost all French orchestras. When its slide is closed, the lips alone produce the following tones, in the same order as the natural tones of the horns, trumpets, cornets and all other brass instruments in E♭:

Hence the name Small Trombone or Alto Trombone in E♭, given to it by players. The latter name would be useless in scores, since the instrument emits the tones as they are written and does, therefore, not belong to the transposing instruments. As we have explained above, only transposing instruments require such indications of key.

THE TENOR TROMBONE

This is undoubtedly the best of all the trombones. Its strong and full tone remains of good quality over the whole extent of its scale. It can execute passages of a rapidity unobtainable on the bass trombone. It is usually written in the tenor-clef (the C-clef on the fourth line). But since in many orchestras the three trombone parts, although differently named, are played on three tenor trombones, it follows that the first tenor trombone is written in the alto-clef, the second in the tenor-clef, and the third in the F-clef. With its slide closed, it produces the following tones, which are the natural tones of all brass tubes in B♭, i.e. of those tubes which produce B♭ as their first low tone, if the entire mass of air in them is put into vibration.

For this reason it has been called trombone in B♭. It is a fourth below the alto trombone and has the following range:

One perceives that the low E♭ is missing on the tenor trombone. This causes innumerable errors even in the most learned scores. Thus, one of our contemporary composers, whose skill in the art of instrumentation is outstanding and uncontested, starts one of his operas with several low E♭s of the third tenor trombone. Actually the ophicleide plays them, while the trombone only doubles them in the higher octave. The composer has perhaps never noticed that the low E♭ is not played by the instrument for which it was written.

THE BASS TROMBONE

The only cause of its infrequent use is the great fatigue experienced even by the most robust players. It is the largest and consequently the lowest of all trombones. When it is employed, there should be adequate pauses to give the players sufficient rest. Altogether sparing and well-founded use should be made of this instrument. With its slide closed, it sounds the following tones:

whence it is also called the Large Trombone or Bass Trombone in E♭. It is an octave lower than the alto trombone and a fifth lower than the tenor trombone. It is written in the F-clef; its range is as follows:

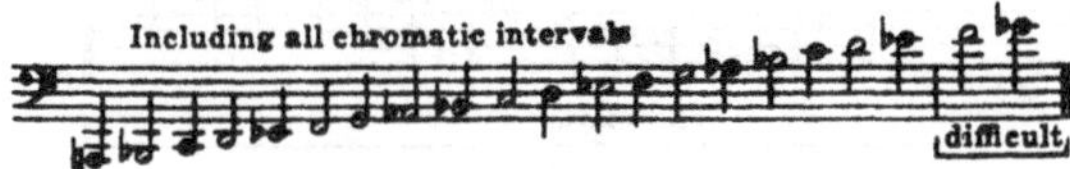

The tone of the bass trombone is majestic, awe-inspiring and formidable. The bass trombone deservedly takes the lowest voice in the brass family. Unfortunately, it is entirely lacking in Paris; it is not taught at the Conservatoire, and thus far no trombone player has been willing to study it. Consequently, most of the modern German works and even the old French and Italian works scored for orchestras with bass trombones are more or less distorted when performed in Paris. For instance, in Weber's "Freischuetz" the low D occurs several times in the accompaniment of the hunters' chorus, and the low E♭ is found when the hermit enters. These notes have to be transposed an octave higher, because the three trombone players of the Opéra orchestra use tenor trombones exclusively, on which these low tones cannot be played. The situation is the same with the sustained low C in the chorus in Gluck's "Alceste"—"Pleure, o patrie". Here the effect of the low C is extremely important and its transposition is, therefore, all the more deplorable. The bass trombone is not so well suited to rapid movements as the other instruments of this family. Because of the length and width of its tube, it needs more time for vibrating; besides, the slide of this trombone is operated by means of a special handle (because the length of the arm is not sufficient for certain positions). Thus it is easily understandable why the bass trombone does not possess greater agility. It is, therefore, simply impossible for the German performers using the bass trombone to execute many passages in modern French scores, which French players can execute on the tenor trombone after a fashion. The imperfection in the performance of these passages—in spite of the talent of some of our artists—proves moreover that they are too fast even for the tenor trombone, and that trombones are altogether unsuited for passages of this kind. At any rate, this shows that the performers—as long as the composers do not impose too great difficulties upon them—should always use the instruments indicated by them, and no others. Unfortunately, many composers obstinately insist on indicating in their scores alto trombones, tenor trombones and bass trombones instead of tenor trombones I, II, III, although they know quite well that most of our orchestras have only tenor trombones. Consequently, in order to perform these works elsewhere exactly as in Paris, it would be necessary to disregard the composer's indications and to use the same instruments as in Paris. But can such interpretation of the composer's intentions be permitted at all? Would this not open the door to all sorts of distortion and abuse? Is it not more just to let those composers who are so negligent in marking their works suffer a little, rather than let others who write theirs carefully and with an exact knowledge of instrumental resources run the risk of seeing their scores disfigured?

All trombones have the same range, starting from their different lowest tones. This range, as we have seen, is two octaves and a sixth. But that is not all. Besides this extensive scale they possess at the extreme low end and starting from the first natural tone downward four additional tones, tremendous and magnificent on the tenor trombone, indifferent on the alto trombone, and terrible on the bass trombone—if they can be produced at all. They are called *pedal tones,* doubtless because of the similarity of their sound with the lowest tones of the organ, which have the same name. It is rather difficult to use them well and they are even unknown to many trombone players. These tones are:

on the alto trombone

on the tenor trombone

and on the bass trombones they would be *8va bassa*

if all players had the power to produce them. Even if the bass trombone had only the first of these pedal tones, E♭, this one tone could be of great value for certain effects which are unattainable without it, since no other instrument of the orchestra, with the exception of the tuba and the double-bassoon, reaches this extraordinary depth. These tones are separated from the others on all trombones by a gap of an augmented fourth between the first natural note and the lowest note produced by means of the slide; e.g. on the trombone in B♭:

gap

On account of this gap it is sometimes indispensable to designate the keys of the trombones to be employed. For this gap changes its place on the scale according to the length of the tube and the key of the instrument, so that one or more or even all pedal tones available on a trombone in one key may be wanting on one in another key. For instance, if a composer fails to indicate that he requires a trombone in B♭ when writing these pedal tones, the orchestra which is to play his work may have a real bass trombone in E♭, which lacks the low A♭ and G; or a bass trombone in F, which lacks the four notes B♭, A, A♭, G (these two trombones are very popular in Germany); or, finally, a bass trombone in G (frequently found in England), which also lacks B♭, A, A♭. This will become clearer by the following list:

Pedal tones of the tenor trombone in B♭:

Pedal tones of the bass trombone in F (it has none of those of the trombone in B♭):

Pedal tones of the bass trombone in G (only one of these exists on the trombone in B♭):

Pedal tones of the bass trombone in E♭ (it lacks the A♭ and G of the trombone in B♭):

General range of the three trombones

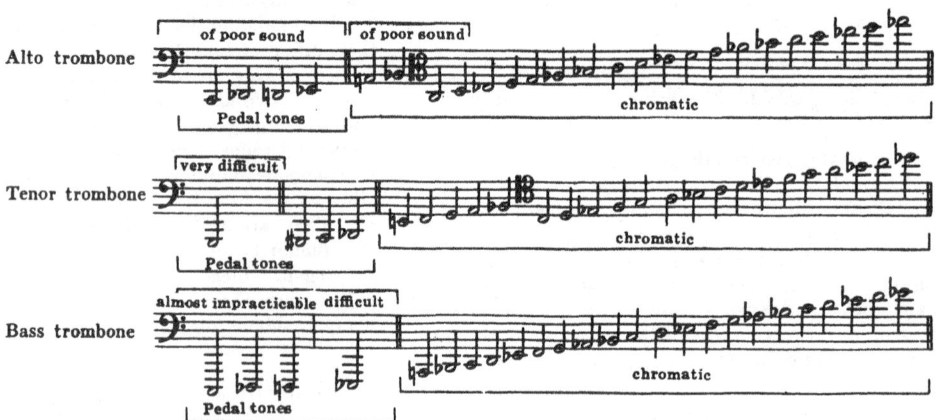

If the pedal tones of the alto trombone were not of such poor quality, they might be used in the orchestras that have no bass trombone to fill the gap between the E of the tenor trombone and its first pedal tone, B♭ Unfortunately, they are so thin and dull that they can by no means replace the beautiful low tones of the tenor trombone. Only the bass trombone with the powerful tones of the extreme low range of its scale can supply this need.

The ingenious manufacturer Sax, of Paris, has fortunately surmounted this difficulty by means of a single valve attached to the body of the tenor trombone. This valve is controlled by the player's left-hand thumb while his right hand remains completely free to move the slide. By filling the gap, the valve gives the tenor trombone in B♭ the following tremendous range:

Including the chromatic intervals

with the thumb-valve | pedal tones

(It is now generally used by the third trombone.) All orchestras should have at least one of these fine instruments!

The vibrations of the pedal tones are slow and demand much breath To make them come out well, one must give them sufficiently long duration. They should follow one another slowly and be interspersed with rests to give the player time for breathing. Care should also be taken to keep the part in which they occur generally rather low so as to allow the lips of the trombone player to become gradually accustomed to the production of these very low tones. The best manner of writing pedal tones for the tenor trombone, for instance, is to approach the first pedal tone by a downward leap of a fifth or octave from the F or B♭ above and, after a rest for breathing, to proceed chromatically downward to A and G# (the G is more difficult, very rough and rather risky). The composer of a Requiem (BERLIOZ) has recently introduced these three tones in this fashion. Although at the first rehearsal of this work five or six of the eight trombone players exclaimed with indignation that this was impossible, nevertheless the eight B♭s, the eight As and the eight G#s came out quite full and pure—played by artists who did not believe in the existence of these tones because they had never tried to produce them. The sound of the three pedal tones appeared even more beautiful than that of the higher and more frequently used tones F# and F.

This effect is used in the work just mentioned below a three-part harmony of flutes, without any voices or other instruments. The sound of the flutes, separated from that of the trombones by an immense interval, seems to be the realization of the extremely high resonance of the pedal tones, whose slow movement and profound voice enhance the solemn impression of the Hostias during the rests interrupting the choir. (Example 119.)

119. REQUIEM, HOSTIAS

I have used the pedal tones of the tenor trombone in yet another place, but for an entirely different purpose. The intention was to produce low harmonies of extreme roughness and of unusual timbre. I believe I have attained this by means of the fifth on two tenor trombones and furthermore through a diminished seventh between the G♭ of an ophicleide and the pedal-A of a tenor trombone:

A special difficulty, sometimes even impossibility, unknown to most composers despite its importance, exists for the trombones if they are to play the following tones in rapid succession:

The transition from one of these notes to the other requires an enormous change in the position of the trombone slide and consequently a considerable stretch of the performer's arm; this is why it can be executed only in very moderate tempo. A famous master wrote the rapid succession of B, A#, B, several times repeated. The trombone players of the Théâtre Italien carried this out like the players of the Russian horns—each playing a single note: one took the B, the other one A#, to the great amusement of their colleagues; they laughed particularly at the efforts of the second trombone player to edge in his A# on the weak beat. For the same reason it is also rather difficult to play the following passage rapidly on the tenor trombone:

It is better to write this reversed, because the figure requires no change in the position of the slide.

The trill is practicable on the trombone—but only on the tones of its highest octave. I believe that one should not write it for the bass trombone, where it is too difficult. In the hands of skilled players the tenor and alto trombones can execute the following trills:

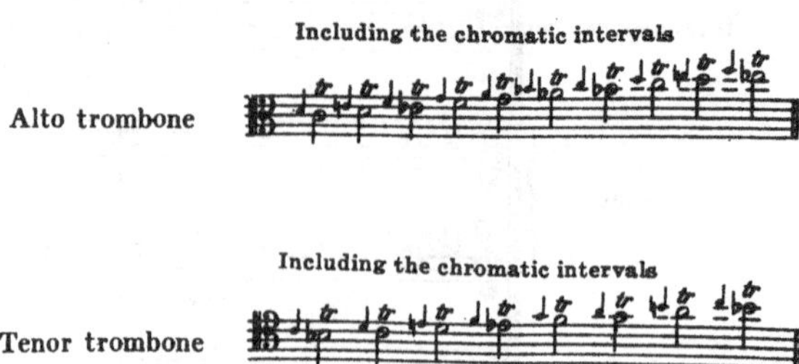

One sees that all these are *major* trills; *minor* trills are impossible.

In my opinion the trombone is the true head of that family of wind instruments which I have named the *epic* one. It possesses nobility and grandeur to the highest degree; it has all the serious and powerful tones of sublime musical poetry, from religious, calm and imposing accents to savage, orgiastic outbursts. Directed by the will of a master, the trombones can chant like a choir of priests, threaten, utter gloomy sighs, a mournful lament or a bright hymn of glory, they can break forth into awe-inspiring cries and awaken the dead or doom the living with their fearful voices.

Nevertheless, ways were found some thirty years ago to degrade this instrument by limiting its use to the worthless and ridiculous doubling of the double-bass part. Fortunately, this method has now been almost completely abandoned; but in many otherwise beautiful scores one can still find the basses almost continuously doubled in unison by a single trombone. I know nothing less harmonious or more vulgar than this manner of instrumentation. The tone of the trombone is so characteristic that it should never be used except for special effects. It cannot be its function merely to reinforce the double-basses, with whose timbre, moreover, it has no sympathy whatever—

—whereas the softer bass tuba or, still better, the low horns are excellently suited to support the basso cantante.

Besides, it must be admitted that one single trombone always seems more or less out of place in the orchestra. This instrument needs harmony or at least unison with other members of its family to display its true qualities.

Some very interesting examples which contradict this statement are to be found in the third act of Wagner's "Meistersinger", where the two first trombones together and the third trombone alone play two themes with sharply contrasting rhythms; this is extremely effective. The passages in question may serve here as examples of the polyphonic treatment of the brass. (Examples 120 and 121.)

120. MEISTERSINGER, ACT III

121. MEISTERSINGER, ACT III

Beethoven sometimes employed the trombones in pairs, like the trumpets; but the accepted custom of writing them in three parts appears preferable to me.

It is difficult to determine with precision the degree of speed obtainable on the trombone in certain passages. Nevertheless, the following may be stated: in 4-4 time of an Allegro moderato, a passage in simple eighths (i.e. eight notes to a bar) is practicable on the brass trombone:

The tenor and alto trombones, being a little more agile, can execute passages in triplet eighths (twelve to a bar) without too much trouble:

But these are the natural limits of their agility; to go beyond them means to venture into unsafe regions, to cause confusion—if not to attempt the impossible.

The character of the timbre of the trombones varies with the degree of loudness. In fortissimo is is menacing and terrifying, especially if the three trombones are in unison, or if at least two are in unison and the third takes the octave of the same tone. Such is the thunderous D-minor scale which forms the basis of the chorus of Furies in the second act of Gluck's "Iphigénie en Tauride". (Example 122.) Such also—but still more sublime—is the immense outcry of the three trombones in unison answering, like the angry voices of the gods of the underworld, Alceste's cries, "Ombre! larve! compagne di morte!", in that wonderful aria whose original main idea Gluck allowed to be perverted by the French translator, but which has nevertheless remained in everybody's memory with its unfortunate first verse, "Divinités du Styx! ministres de la mort!" There is another remarkable passage in this piece toward the end of its first section where the trombones, divided into three parts, answer the phrase of the aria, "Je n'invoquerai point votre pitié cruelle", imitating its rhythm: by the very effect of this division the sound of the trombones immediately assumes something at once ironic, rough, frightful and jocose, which differs markedly from the sublime rage of the preceding unisons. (Example 123.)

122. IPHIGENIE EN AULIDE, ACT II

Ob.u. Klar. in C.
Fag.
Pos.
I.
Viol.
II.
Viola.
Chor.
Bassi.
Dieux en cour - roux, et les Dieux en cour - roux! In - ven - tons des tour - mens, in - ven -
rächt der Göt - ter Zorn, auf, und rächt der Göt - ter Zorn!
ture et les Dieux, et les Dieux en cour - roux!
Ta - ten und rächt, auf, und rächt der Göt - ter Zorn! Schaf - fet Mar - tern und Qual, schaffet
geons et la na - ture et les Dieux en cour - roux! In - ven - tons des tour - mens, in - ven -
straft des Frevlers Ta - ten und rächt der Göt - ter Zorn!
geons et la na - ture et les Dieux en cour - roux!
rächt der Göt - ter Zorn, auf, und rächt der Göt - ter Zorn! Schaf - fet Mar - tern und Qual, schaffet
tons des tour - mens! il a tu - é sa mè - re!
Mar - tern und Qual dem Mör - der sei - ner Mut - ter!
tons des tour - mens! il a tu - é sa mè - re!
Mar - tern und Qual dem Mör - der sei - ner Mut - ter!

123. ALCESTE, ACT I

Adagio.
Tempo primo.
Ob.u. Klar. in C.
Hrnr. in B.
Pos.
I.
Viol.
II.
Viola.
Alc.
Styx,
Nacht,
mi - ni - stres de la mort! Je n'in - vo-que-rai point
des Or - kus Die - nerschar! Nimmer ruf'ich euch an,
Fag.
Bassi.
vo-tre pi-tié cru-el-le,
daß eu-er Grimm ver-zei-he,
je n'in-vo-que-rai point,
nimmer ruf'ich euch an,
je n'in-
nimmer

Ob. u. Klar. in C.
Hrnr. in B.
Pos.
I.
Viol.
II.
Viola.
Alo.
vo-querai point votre pi-tié cru-el - - - le, votre pi-tié cru-
ruf' ich euch an, daß eu-er Grimm verzei - - - he, daß euer Grimm ver-
Bassi.
Andante un poco.
el - le!
zei - he!
J'en-
Ich
p

Ob.u.
Klar. in C.
Hrnr. in B.
Pos.
I.
Viol.
II.
Viola.
Alc.
lè-ve un tendre é-poux à son fu-ne-ste sort, mais je vous abandonne une é-pouse, mais je
raub' euch den Ge-mahl, der eu-er O-pfer war, doch für ihn bietet sich ei-ne Gattin, bietet
Bassi.
Ob.u.
Klar. in C.
Hrnr. in B.
Pos.
Animato.
I.
Viol.
II.
Viola.
Alc.
Animato.
vous a-bandonne une é-pou-se fi-dè-le. Di-vi-ni-tés du Styx,
sich ei-ne Gattin, ei-ne Gat-tin voll Treue. Ihr Götter ew'-ger Nacht,
Fag.
Bassi.

Ob. u. Klar. in C.
Hrnr. in B.
Pos.
Viol. I. II.
Viola.
Alc.
Bassi.
Lento.
Tempo primo.
Fag.
di-vi-ni-tés du Styx, mi-ni-stres de la mort! Mou-rir pour ce qu'on
ihr Götter ew'ger Nacht, des Or-kus Die-nerschar! Dem O-pfertod aus
ai-me, pour ce qu'on ai-me, est un trop doux ef-fort, u-ne ver-tu si na-tu-
Lie-be weih' ich mich freudvoll; ich wähl' ihn oh-ne Furcht, ich wähl' ihn oh-ne Furcht und

Ob.u. Klar. in C.
Hrnr. in B.
Pos.
I.
Viol.
II.
Viola.
Alc.
rel-le, si na-tu-rel-le, mon coeur est a-ni-mé du plus no-ble, plus no-ble trans-
Reu-e, und oh-ne Reu-e! Dies Herz durchlodert Mut, den die Lie-be, die Lie-be ge-
Bassi.
Prestissimo.
Ob. u. Klar. in C.
Hrnr. in B.
Pos.
I.
Viol.
II.
Viola.
Prestissimo.
Alc.
port! Je sens u-ne for-ce nou-vel-le, je vais où mon a-mour m'ap-
biert. Ich fühl' ih-re Allmacht aufs neue, sie ist's, der sterbend ich mich
Bassi.

Ob. u. Klar. in C.
Hrnr. in B.
Pos.
I.
Viol.
II.
Viola.
Alc.
pel - le, je sens u - ne for - ce nou - vel - le, je vais où mon a -
wei - he, ich fühl' ih - re Allmacht aufs neue, sie ist's, der sterbend
Bassi.
Ob. u. Klar. in C.
Hrnr. in B.
Pos.
I.
Viol.
II.
Viola.
Alc.
mour m'ap - pel - le, mon coeur est a - ni - mé du plus no - ble transport!
ich mich weihe; dies Herz durchlodert Mut, den die Lie - be ge - biert!
Bassi.

In three-part harmony and particularly in their medium range, the trombones have in forte an expression of heroic splendor, full of majesty and pride, which could be weakened and destroyed only by the prose of a vulgar melody. In such cases they assume the expression of the trumpets—but with far more nobility. They no longer threaten—they admonish; instead of roaring they sing.

Wagner lets them accompany Wotan as an almost continuous symbol of proud power. Compare also: "Tannhaeuser," third act, (Wolfram), as a symbol of solemn resignation (Example 124); "Tristan", first act, death potion (Example 125); Isolde's threat to Kurwenal (Example 126); "Tristan", third act ("goettlich ewiges Urvergessen"—divine, unending all-oblivion)—(Example 127).

124. TANNHAEUSER, ACT III

125. TRISTAN, ACT I

Ob.
2 Klar. in B.
Engl. H.
Hrnr. in F.
Bßkl. in B.
Fag.
Pos.
Bßtuba.
Pke.
Viol.
I.
II.
Violen.
Isolde.
Brang.
Vlc.
K. B.
pp
p
cresc.
p cresc.
I. II.
cresc. poco a poco
Du irrst, ich kenn' ihn besser; ein star-kes Zeichen schnitt ich ihm ein.
(sie ergreift ein Fläschchen und zeigt es.)

Schnell.
zu 2.
Ob.
cresc.
ff
2 Klar. in B.
più f
Engl. H.
(4 Hörner in F.)
Hrnr. in F.
Bßkl. in B.
Fag.
zu 3.
Pos.
II. III.
Bßtuba.
Pke.
tr
I.
Viol.
II.
pizz.
arco
Violen.
Isolde.
Der Trank ist's, der mir taugt!
Brang.
Der To - destrank!
Vlc.
K. B.
p
f

126. TRISTAN, ACT I

Wagner.

Engl. H.
Fag.
Pos.
II.
III.
I.
Viol.
II.
Viola.
Isolde.
meld' ihm was ich sa - ge. Sollt' ich zur Seit' ihm ge - hen, vor Kö - nig Mar - ke zu
Vlc. u. K.B.
dim.
ste - hen, nicht möcht' es nach Zucht und Fug geschehn, em - pfing' ich Süh - ne nicht zu - vor für un - ge - sühn - te
trem.
f dim.

127. TRISTAN, ACT III

Wagner.

Hrn. II in F.
II.
3 Fag.
Baßklar. in B.
Pos.
Baßtuba.
I. Viol. II.
Viola.
Tristan.
Vlc.
K. B.
(mit Dämpfer.)
pp
geh': im wei - ten Reich der Wel - - ten - nacht.
Nur ein Wis - sen dort uns
Sehr langsam.
più p
ppp
riten.
ei - gen:
gött - lich ew' - ges Ur - - ver - ges - - sen!

As a magnificent contrast to these examples I should like to mention the ringing laughter after Hagen's words "Ruestig gezecht bis der Rausch euch zaehmt. Alles den Goettern zu Ehren, dass gute Ehe sie geben." (Example 128.)

Ob.
Klar. in B.
in F.
in C.
8 Hrnr.
in F.
in C.
Fag.
Tromp. in C.
I.
Pos.
II.
III.
K.B.-Pos.
Pke.
I.
Viol.
II.
Viola.
Vlc.
K. B.

In the entire "Ring" Wagner generally wrote for four trombones, adding a double-bass trombone in order to separate the sound of the bass tuba completely from the trombones and to combine it with the kindred timbre of tubas and horns. When using three trombones, one must remember that the tone of the bass trombone is always more or less prominent, especially if the first one is an alto trombone. (Example 129.)

129. SINFONIE FUNEBRE ET TRIOMPHALE, APOTHEOSE

Berlioz.

Allegro non troppo e pomposo.

Kl. Fl. in Des.
Terzflöten in Es.
Kl. Klar. in Es.
Klar. in B. I. II.
Oboen.
Hörner in Es I. II. in G III. IV. in D V. VI.
Tromp. in B. I. II. III. IV.
Kornetts in B. I. II. (mit Pist.)
Pos. (Alt od. Ten.) I. (Tenor) II. (Tenor) III.
Gr. Baßpos. (nicht obl.)
Ophikl. in C. in B.
Baßklar. in B.
Fag. I. II.
Kontrafag. (nicht obl.)
Viol. I. (20). Viol. II. (20). Violen (15). (nicht obligat.)
Vcelli. u. K. B.
(Mit den Schnarrsaiten oder ungedämpft.)
Trommeln I.
Trommeln II.
Halbmond. (Bei den Trommeln aufzustellen)
Becken und gr. Tr.
(Mit Schwammschlägeln)
Pauken in B. F. (nicht obl.)

cresc. poco a poco

Kl. Fl. in Des.
Terzfl. in Es.
Kl. Klar. in Es.
I.
Klar. in B.
II.
Ob.
in Es I. II.
Hrnr.
in G III. IV.
in D V. VI.
in F.
I. II.
Trp. in B.
III. IV.
Korn. I. II. in B.
Pos. I. II.
Pos. III.
Baßpos.
in C.
Oph.
in B.
Baßklar. in B.
Fag. I. II.
Kontrafag.
I.
Viol.
II.
Viola.
Vlc. u. K. B.
Trom. I.
Die Hälfte der zweiten Trommeln.
alle zweiten Trommeln.
Trom. II.
pp cresc. poco a poco
Hlbmd.
Becken u. gr. Tr.
Pkn.
cresc.
cresc. molto

Kl. Fl. in Des
Terzfl. in Es.
Kl. Klar. in Es.
I.
Klar. in B.
II.
Ob.
in Es I. II.
Hrnr.
in G III. IV.
in F V. VI.
I. II.
Trp. in B.
III. IV.
unis.
Korn. I. II. in B.
Pos. I. II.
Pos. III.
Baßpos.
in C.
Oph.
in B.
Baßklar. in B.
Fag. I. II.
Kontrafag.
I.
Viol.
II.
Viola.
Vlc. u. K. B.
Trom. I.
Trom. II.
Hlbmd.
Becken u. gr. Tr.
Pkn.

In a mezzoforte in the medium range, unisono or in harmony, the trombone assumes a religious character if the tempo is slow. Mozart has given us admirable models of this religious and solemn tone in the priests' choruses in "Die Zauberfloete" (Example 130).

130. DIE ZAUBERFLOETE, ACT II

The pianissimo of the trombones, employed in minor chords is gloomy, mournful—I might almost say, horrible. Especially if the chords are short and interrupted by rests, one can imagine strange monsters uttering groans of repressed rage from a gruesome darkness.

In my opinion no one has used this particular expression so dramatically as Spontini in his incomparable funeral march in "La Vestale", and Beethoven in the immortal duet of Leonore and the jailer in the second act of "Fidelio", while they are digging a grave for the prisoner condemned to die. (Examples 131 and 48, page 124.)

131. LA VESTALE, ACT III

Spontini.

The habit of some modern masters to form a quartet of three trombones and an ophicleide, assigning the actual bass to the latter, is rather objectionable. The penetrating and prominent tone of the trombones is by no means the same as that of the ophicleide. I consider it much better to use the ophicleide only for doubling the lowest part or at least to give the trombones the real bass by writing their three parts as if they were to be heard alone.

Gluck, Beethoven, Mozart, Weber, Spontini and several other composers have fully comprehended the high value of the trombones. They have ingeniously employed the different characteristics of this noble instrument to depict human passions as well as to reproduce the sounds of nature. They have faithfully preserved its power, its dignity and its poetry. But to force it—as the majority of contemporary composers does—to howl in a Credo crude phrases more fitting for a saloon than for a church; to play as if to celebrate Alexander's entry into Babylon, when there is actually nothing more than a dancer's pirouette; to strum the tonic and dominant of a song in which a guitar could furnish an adequate accompaniment; to join its Olympian voice with the trashy melody of a vaudeville duet or with the frivolous noise of a quadrille; to prepare in the tutti of a concerto the triumphant entry of an oboe or flute—all this means degrading a magnificent individuality, making a slave or a buffoon out of a hero, marring the sound of the orchestra, paralyzing all rational progress in instrumentation; it means destroying the past, present and future of art, committing a wanton act of vandalism and disclosing a lack of feeling for musical expression which comes close to stupidity.

Trombone mutes have been introduced recently with success. They are similar to the mutes of the horn and are—similarly to the trumpet mutes—easy to handle. In forte they give the trombones a rattling sound, in pp a tremendously gruesome, fantastic and gloomy one.

THE ALTO TROMBONE WITH VALVES

(With Pistons or Cylinders)

There are alto trombones in E♭ and F; one must therefore indicate precisely for which of these keys one is writing because this trombone is usually treated as a transposing instrument. It has no slide and is in certain respects a cornet with pistons in E♭ or F with a somewhat stronger tone than the real cornets.

The range of the alto valve trombone is the same as that of the ordinary alto trombone. It is written in the alto-clef or in the G-clef, transposing like the cornet:

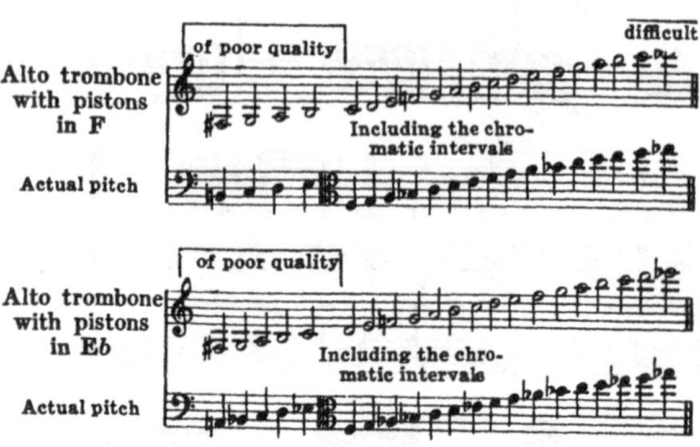

Since the valve trombone does not have the slide, it cannot produce the so-called pedal tones of the other trombones. Those trills of the alto trombone with a slide which are produced only by means of the lips can also be executed on the valve trombone. Several trills can also be played with the aid of the valves, but in general only minor trills are of good effect and can be executed rapidly. The following are the best:

The valves lend the trombones great agility, but reduce their purity of intonation a little. It is easily understood that the trombone, with its slide instantaneously obeying the slightest move, must be the purest of all wind instruments in the hands of a player who possesses a good ear; whereas the valve trombone, lacking the slide, becomes thereby an instrument with fixed intonation which can be modified very little by the lips. The alto trombone with valves is frequently employed for solo melodies. Well phrased, such a melody can display much charm; but it is an error to assume that the same melody would not sound just as well if played on a slide trombone—as has been frequently demonstrated with success by M. Dieppe. The advantage of purer intonation must be decisive for the composer, unless there are very rapid passages to consider.

In Germany there are tenor trombones with cylinders which descend as low as B♭ . In spite of this advantage I prefer the slide trombones.

Verdi's treatment of valve trombones and trumpets has been dealt with in the chapter on trumpets. I have only to add here that Wagner's manner of employing them for the expression of calm dignity and wisdom or of heroic, unrestrained vigor as in the Ride of the Valkyries corresponds much better with the true nature of the instrument.

THE TUBAS

To enrich the ensemble of brass instruments in his Nibelung cycle, Wagner devised, in addition to the bass trumpet, a quartet of tubas furnished with horn mouthpieces and to be played by horn players.

The tenor tubas are in B♭ and have a range from to (sounding one tone lower), the bass tubas are in F with a range from to (sounding a fifth lower), including all chromatic intervals. In his scores Wagner writes the tenor tubas in E♭, the bass tubas in B♭, for the sake of better legibility, as he says in a footnote—an explanation which is not very convincing.

Supported by the bass of the double-bass trombone and double-bass tuba, they serve almost everywhere in the scores of the "Ring" as the bearers of the solemn and majestic Walhall motif.

But their hoarse and rancorous tone can just as well symbolize Alberich's fierce hate and envy or the swelling vein of fury on Wotan's forehead (end of the second act of "Walkuere"); notice especially the sensible silence of the tubas—essentially legato instruments—during the two sharp final chords (Example 132).

132. WALKUERE, ACT II

Wagner.

Fl.
Ob.
Klar. in B.
Engl. Hrn.
Hrnr. in F.
Fag.
ff
Baßkl. in B.
3 Trp. in F.
Baßtrp. in D.
Pos.
più f
2 Ten.-Tub. in Es.
2 Baßtub. in B.
K.B.-Tub.
Pke I.
Viol. I. II.
Viola.
Vlc.
K.B.

Fl.
Ob.
Klar. in B.
Engl. Hrn.
Hrnr. in F.
Fag.
Baßkl. in B.
3 Trp. in F.
Baßtrp. in D.
Pos.
I. II.
III. IV.
2 Ten.-Tub. in Es.
2 Baßtub. in B.
K.B.-Tub.
Pke I.
Viol. I. II.
Viola.
Vlc.
K.B.
ff
f
più f
p
molto

Fl.
Ob.
Klar. in B.
Engl. Hrn.
Hrnr. in F.
Fag.
Baßklar. in B.
Trp. in F.
Baßtrp. in D.
Pos.
2 Ten.-Tub. in Es.
2 Baßtub. in B.
K.B.-Tub.
Pke I.
cresc.
Viol. I.
II.
Viola.
Vlc.
K.B.

Fl.
Ob
Klar. in B.
Engl. Hrn.
Hrnr. in F.
Fag.
Baßklar. in B.
Trp. in F.
Baßtrp. in D.
Pos.
2 Ten.-Tub. in Es.
2 Baßtub. in B.
K.B.-Tub.
Pke I.
Pke II.
Viol. I.
Viol. II.
Viola.
Vlc.
K.B.
a 2
più f
molto cresc.

THE BUGLE

We conclude the discussion of the wind instruments with a few words concerning the bugle family.

The simple bugle is written in the G-clef like the trumpet and has altogether eight tones:

The highest of these, C, can be produced almost only on the lowest bugle; and the lowest tone is of very poor quality. This instrument exists in three keys—B^b, C and E^b; other keys are very rare. The flourishes played on it, consisting exclusively of the three notes of the common chord, are necessarily of a boring uniformity bordering on vulgarity. The tone of this instrument is not very pleasant, it has no distinction, and it is hard to play on it in tune. Since it cannot execute diatonic successions, trills are of course impossible.

Bugles appear to me to hold no higher rank in the hierarchy of brass instruments than the fifes do among the wood-wind instruments. At best, both can serve the purpose of leading recruits to the parade, although in my opinion our soldiers—old or young—ought never to listen to such music; for there is no reason why they should become accustomed to the vulgar. However, since the tone of the bugle is very strong, there might be some occasion for using it in the orchestra; for instance, to reinforce some terrible outcry of simultaneously played trombones, trumpets and horns. This is probably the most that one could expect from it.

Since its tube is much shorter than that of the trumpet, the bugle has only the tones of the three lower octaves of the latter:

On account of the small length of its tube, these notes sound an octave higher and are therefore written as follows:

Conseqently the bugle in C is a non-transposing instrument; bugles in B^b and E^b are transposing and are written like trumpets in B^b and E^b:

THE KEY BUGLE

In cavalry music and even in some Italian orchestras one finds bugles with seven keys, which have a chromatic range of more than two octaves:

The bugle can execute trills on all tones of its scale, with the exception of:

It does not lack agility, and some artists play it excellently; but its tone is exactly like that of the plain bugle.

THE VALVE BUGLE

(With Pistons or Cylinders)

It has a lower range than the preceding. However, this is of no particular utility since its low tones are of very poor quality and respond easily only on the small bugle in E^b, which has therefore the greatest range:

This instrument is much better than the key bugle; it is quite suitable for rendering certain melodies of slow or at least moderate tempo. In lively or gay passages, however, it shows the same shortcomings which we pointed out in the valve cornets: it has no distinction, although this may be improved to a certain degree by the individual player's skill.

Beginning from the middle E: all major and minor trills are good on the valve bugle, with the exception of which is very difficult.

THE BASS OPHICLEIDE

Ophicleides are the altos and basses of the bugle. The bass ophicleide is excellent for sustaining the lowest part of massed harmonies; among the different ophicleides, it is the one most frequently used. It is written in the F-clef, and its range is three octaves and one tone:

A skillful player can execute the major and minor trills, beginning from the second C of its scale (as M. Caussinus has shown in his excellent textbook).

Formerly the low F# could be produced only very imperfectly with the lips and left much to be desired as regards intonation and steadiness. Thanks to the valve added to the instrument by M. Caussinus it now sounds as well as the other tones.

Diatonic and even chromatic passages up to a certain speed can be executed in the three higher octaves of the ophicleide; but below they are extremely difficult and of very inferior effect, e.g.:

Staccato passages are considerably more difficult and are scarcely practicable in fast tempo. There are bass ophicleides in two keys, C and B^b; now they are also made in A^b. The latter will be very useful because of the very low pitch of its lowest tones, which are in unison with the three-stringed double-bass. The ophicleide in B^b has already rendered important service in this respect. They are both written as transposing instruments:

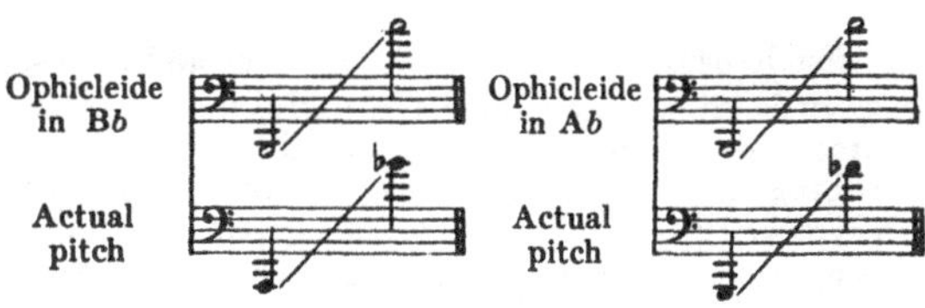

One can perceive that the first low G in the second example is in unison with the G of the double-bass. Unfortunately the ophicleide in A^b is still used very little.

The sound of these low tones is rough; but in certain cases, under a mass of brass instruments, it works miracles. The highest tones are of a ferocious character, which has not yet been utilized appropriately. The medium range, especially if the player is not skilled, recalls too closely the tone of the serpent and cornett; I believe that it should rarely be used without the cover of other instruments. Nothing is more clumsy—I could almost say, more monstrous—nothing less appropriate in combination with the rest of the orchestra than those more or less rapid passages played as solos in the medium range of the ophicleide in certain modern operas. They are like an escaped bull jumping around in a drawing-room.

THE ALTO OPHICLEIDE

There are alto ophicleides in F and in E♭; their range is the same as that of the bass ophicleide. Both are written in the G-clef, like the horns; and their pitch, like that of the horns, is an octave below the written notes. This C corresponds with this C of the F-clef and is the same as this C in the G-clef

The transpositions caused by the different keys of the instrument result in the following scales:

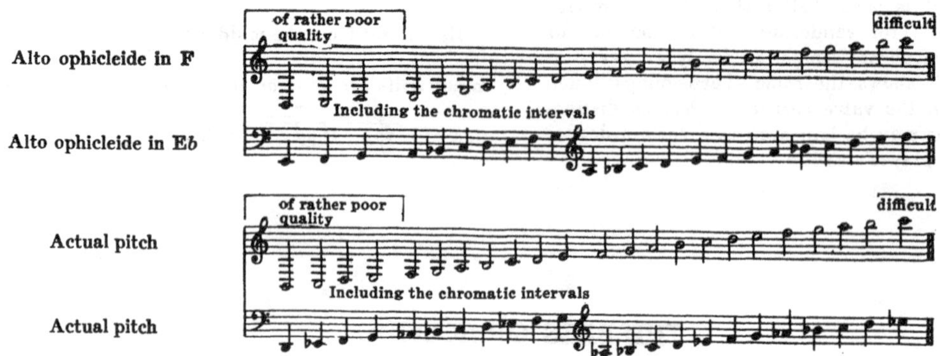

Alto ophicleides are used in some military bands for filling out the harmony and sometimes even for melodic passages; but their tone is generally unpleasant and rather commonplace and their intonation is inaccurate. This is probably the reason why these instruments have almost completely fallen into disuse.

THE DOUBLE - BASS OPHICLEIDE

The double-bass ophicleides, or monster ophicleides, are very little known. They might be useful in very large orchestras; but up to the present nobody in Paris has been willing to play them because of the volume of breath required. This surpasses the lung power of even the strongest man. They are in F and E♭, i.e. a fifth lower than the bass ophicleides and an octave lower than the alto ophicleides. In writing for them, one must not go above F:

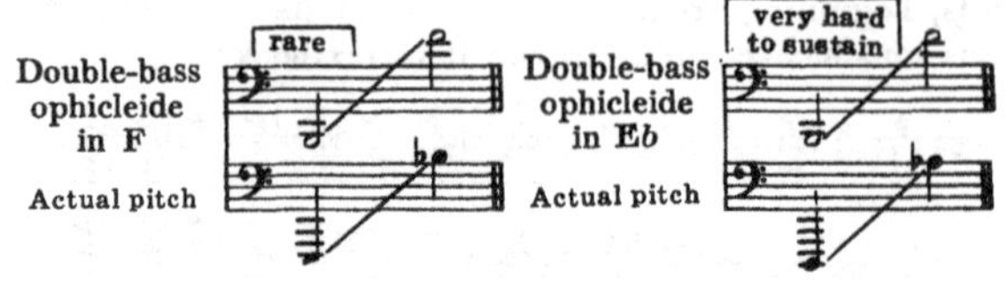

It goes without saying that trills and rapid passages are incompatible with the nature of such instruments.

THE BOMBARDON

This is an instrument of very low range, without keys but with three cylinders. Its timbre differs only little from that of the ophicleide. It is in F, with a range of two octaves and a sixth:

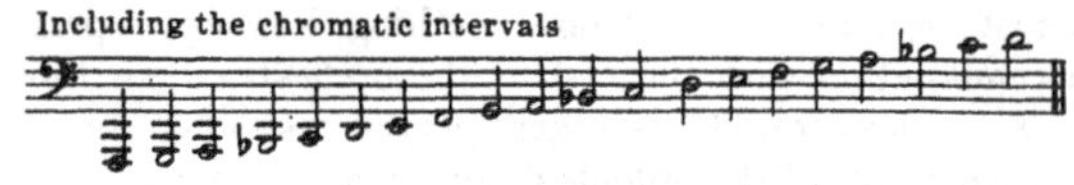

It has a few additional tones at both ends of this scale, but their emission is so uncertain that it is better to avoid them.

This instrument, whose tones are very powerful, can execute only passages of moderate speed. Rapid runs and trills are unplayable on it. It produces good effects in large orchestras in which wind instruments predominate. Its natural tones are those of the F-major scale, wherefore the instrument is called "in F". Nevertheless it is treated in Germany as a non-transposing instrument like the trombones and written in actual pitch.

THE BASS TUBA

(The double-bass of the wood-wind)

This is a kind of bombardon, whose mechanism has been improved by Herr Wieprecht, director of all music bands of the Royal Prussian guard regiments. The bass tuba, which is now widely used in northern Germany, especially in Berlin, possesses important advantages over all other low wind instruments. Its tone, incomparably more noble than that of the ophicleides, bombardons and serpents, has something of the vibrant timbre of the trombones. It is less agile, but more powerful than the ophicleides, and its range extends lower than that of any other instrument in the orchestra. Its tube, like that of the bombardon, produces the tones of the F-major chord; A. Sax now also makes bass tubas in E♭. Notwithstanding this difference, they are all treated in Germany as non-transposing instruments. The bass tuba has five cylinders, and its range is four octaves. (These instruments have been introduced in France some years ago, where they are written as transposing instruments —like the horns and trumpets.)

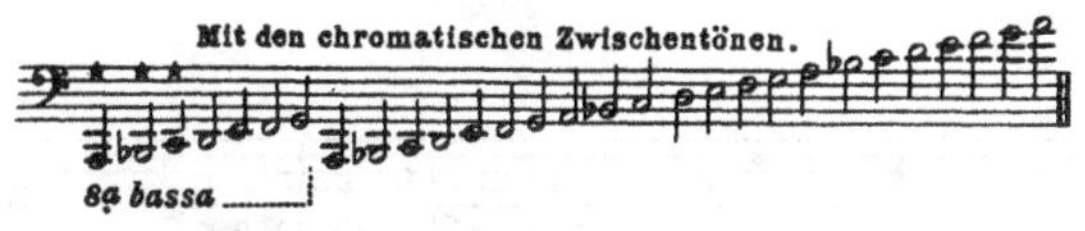

(In France this scale would be written a third lower.)

With the aid of the cylinders a few notes can be added above and even below this scale. Extremely high tones are very risky and extremely low ones hardly distinguishable. The tones marked * (A, B♭, C) are clearly audible only if doubled in the higher octave by another bass tuba, which imparts more sonority to these tones, and is in turn simultaneously reinforced by them.

Of course, this instrument is as unsuited to trills and rapid passages as the bombardon. It can play certain broad and slowly moving melodies. The effect of a great number of bass tubas in a large military band is beyond imagination. They sound like a combination of trombones and the organ.

The bass tuba was used by Wagner particularly for noble and gloomy melodies ("Eine Faust-Ouverture, Example 133), the double-bass tuba with special success as bearer of the Fafner motif in the second act of "Siegfried" (Example 134). In the B-major middle theme of the "Tannhaeuser" overture, however, the bass tuba, reinforcing the double-basses, is bearable only in large orchestras and if it is played not louder than *mf*. In the subsequently added bacchanal of the Venusberg scene, on the other hand, its expression of primitive sensuality has a marvelous effect (Example 135).

133. EINE FAUST-OUVERTURE

134. SIEGFRIED, ACT II

Wagner.

Klar. I.II. in B.
Hrnr. I.II. in F.
Fag. I.II.
Pos. II.III.
Baßtuba in B.
K.B.Tuba.
2 Paar Pkn. in As.
Viol. II.
Viola.
Vlc.
K. B.
pp
(immer p)
cresc.
sf
(in G.)
(get.)
pizz.
Klar. I.II. in B.
I. II.
Hrnr. in F.
III. IV.
(IV. allein)
Baßklar. in B.
Fag.
Baßtub. in B.
K. B. Tub.
2 Paar Pkn. in G.
Viol II.
Violen.
Vlc.
K.B.
ff
dim.
più p
(in A.)
pizz

in B.
Klar.
in A.
piu f
dim.
ff
piu p
I.II.
Hrnr.
in F.
IV.
Baßkl. in B.
Fag.
Baßtub.
in B.
K.B. Tub.
2. Paar Pkn.
in A.
Viol. II.
Viola.
(Bog.)
(trem.)
Vlc.
(get.)
K.B.
sf
pp
Klar. in B.
zu 2.
Baßkl. in B.
II. III.
cresc.
1. Paar Pkn.
in C.Fis.
pizz.
(Bog.)

(zu 3.)
3 Pos.
p (sehr bestimmt.)
K.B.Tub.
più p
1.Paar Pkn. in C, Fis.
più p
tr
pp
Viola.
pp
(Bog.)
K. B.
più p
pp
3 Pos.
molto cresc.
f dim.
pp
2 Ten.Tub. in Es.
sf
dim.
2 Baß-Tub. in B.
sf
dim.
K.B.Tub.
p
1.Paar Pkn.
tr
p
pizz.
(Bog.)
K.B.
p
(zu 3.)
3 Pos.
p
cresc.
f
dim.
p
2 Ten.Tub. in Es.
pp
cresc.
p
2 Baß-Tub. in B.
pp
cresc.
p
K.B.Tub.
1.Paar Pkn.
tr
p
(Violoncello.)
K.B.
più p
p

135. TANNHAEUSER, BACCHANAL

Gr. Fl.
Ob.
Klar. in A.
Hrnr. in E.
Fag.
I. Trp. in D.
Pos.
Baßtuba.
Pkn.
Triang.
Becken.
Tamb.
Kastagn.
I.
Viol.
II.
Viola.
Vlc.
K. B.
fz
p
a 2.
p molto stacc.
poco a poco
tr
pizz.
Klüften erschienen und drängen sich jetzt mit ihrem Tanze zwischen die Bacchanten und liebenden Paare.

Gr. Fl.
Ob.
Klar. in A.
Hrnr. in E.
Fag.
2 Trp. in E.
Baßtuba.
Pke.
Kastagn.
I.
Viol.
II.
Viola.
Vlc.
K.B.
p
cresc.
a2. stacc.
a2.
molto stacc.
poco a poco cresc.
pizz.

I myself have frequently written a single tenor tuba in B^b as the higher octave of the bass tuba; but performances have shown that, as a melodic instrument, the euphonium (frequently used in military bands) is much better suited for this than the rough and clumsy Wagner tubas with their demonic tone.

WIND INSTRUMENTS OF WOOD WITH MOUTHPIECE

THE SERPENT

This is a wooden instrument covered with leather, with a mouthpiece. It has the same range as the bass ophicleide, but less agility, purity and sonority. Among its tones there are three which are more powerful than the others: ; the player should try to smooth down this disturbing unevenness as much as possible. The serpent is in B♭ and must therefore be written a tone higher than the actual pitch, like the ophicleide in B♭.

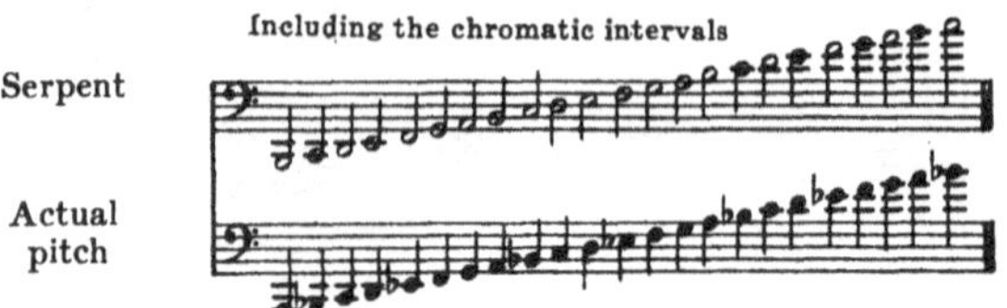

The truly barbaric tone of this instrument would be much better suited for the bloody cult of the Druids than for that of the Catholic church, where it is still in use—as a monstrous symbol for the lack of understanding and the coarseness of taste and feeling which have governed the application of music in our churches since times immemorial. Only one case is to be excepted: masses for the dead, where the serpent serves to double the dreadful choir of the Dies Irae. Here its cold and awful blaring is doubtless appropriate; it even seems to assume a character of mournful poetry when accompanying this text, imbued with all the horrors of death and the revenge of an irate God. The instrument might also be used in secular compositions based on similar ideas; but its use must be limited to this purpose only. Moreover, its tone blends poorly with the other timbres of the orchestra and of voices. As the bass of a great mass of wind instruments it cannot match the bass tuba or even the ophicleide.

THE RUSSIAN BASSOON

This is a low instrument related to the serpent. Its timbre is not very characteristic, and it lacks steadiness and hence purity of intonation. In my opinion it might be dropped from the family of wind instruments without the least injury to art. Its general range is:

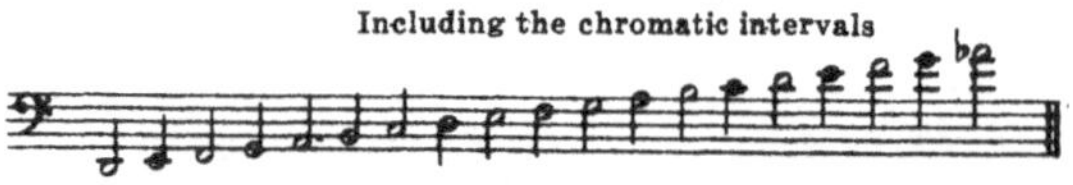

Some players can reach the low C and go up to the high D ; but these are exceptions which cannot be counted on in actual practice. The best tones of the Russian bassoon are D and E♭. Only extremely inferior effects can be expected from trills on this instrument. Russian bassoons are found in military bands. It is to be hoped that they will disappear forever as soon as the bass tuba becomes generally adopted.

VOICES

Voices are naturally divided into two great categories: the male (or low) and the female (or high) voices; the latter comprise not only women's voices but also those of children of both sexes and the voices of artificial sopranos and altos (castrati). Each of these two categories is subdivided into two classes, which, according to the generally accepted theory, have the same range but different pitch. The assumption customary in all Italian and German singing schools is that the low male voice—the bass—reaches from F under the stave of the F-clef to D and E♭ above the stave; and that the high male voice—the tenor—is a fifth above the bass and goes from C under the stave of the tenor-clef to A and B♭ above it. Women's and children's voices range in the same order, exactly an octave above the two men's voices: contralto (corresponding to the bass) and soprano (corresponding to the tenor). Hence the contralto can go (like the bass) from the low F to the high E♭ (almost two octaves), and the soprano (like the tenor) from low C to high B♭.

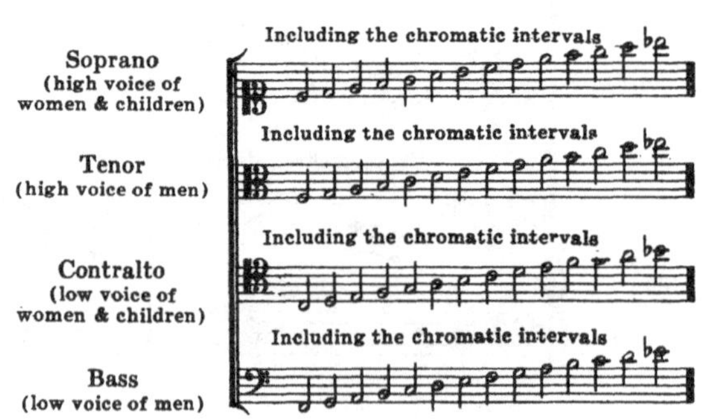

Doubtless this regular division of the four most easily distinguishable human voices is very tempting. But close examination shows that it is in many respects insufficient and harmful, since its rigid observance would deprive the choral composer of many precious voices. In reality nature does not proceed the same way in all climates.

While it is true that it produces many contralto voices in Italy, it cannot be denied that it is very sparing with them in France. Tenors who can easily reach high A and B♭ are plentiful in Italy and France; but they are rare in Germany, where—as a compensation—their low tones are more sonorous than in the other countries. Therefore, it appears to me very unwise to write choruses always in four real parts in accordance with the classical division into soprano, contralto, tenor and bass. In Paris, at any rate, the contralto in such a chorus (especially if it is numerous) would be so weak in relation to the other voices that the effect planned by the composer would be distorted. It is equally certain that the majority of tenors in Germany, and even in Italy and France, if kept within the traditional limits (that is, a fifth higher than the bass) would break down in passages where the composer requires them to go up to the high A or B♭; or else they would produce false, forced or ugly sounds. The case is exactly the opposite with the basses; most of them lose much of their sonority below C or B. It is therefore useless to write G and F for them. Since nature everywhere produces sopranos, tenors and basses, I consider it more prudent, more practical and even more musical—if one wants to give each voice the same importance—to write either for six parts: first and second soprano, first and second tenor, baritone and bass (or first and second bass); or for three parts, taking care to divide each part as the voice approaches the limits of its range: the first bass then takes the notes too low for the second bass, but a third, a fifth or an octave higher; notes too high for the first soprano or first tenor are given to the medium range of the second soprano or second tenor. It is less important to separate the first sopranos from the second if a phrase goes very low than in the opposite instance. It is true that high voices lose all their power and their peculiar character if forced to sing tones properly belonging to the contralto or to the second soprano; but at least they are not in danger of producing ugly sounds such as the second sopranos do when forced to go up too high. It is the same with the two other voices. The second soprano and the second tenor are usually a fourth below, and the first bass the same distance above the main voice whose name they bear, and they have almost the same range; this, however, applies more to the second soprano than to the second tenor and first bass. If the second soprano is assigned a range of an octave and a sixth, from B to G:

all the tones will sound well. It will not be quite the same with the second tenor if it is given a scale of the same length; its low D, C and B would have scarcely any sonority. Unless a special effect is intended, it is better to avoid these notes and to give them to the first or second basses, who can sing them with perfect ease. The opposite is found regarding the first basses or baritones: suppose they were a third above the second basses and their scale would consequently extend from the low A to the high G, then the low A would be dull and weak, the high G forced. Hence it follows that the second tenors and first basses have the smallest range: the second tenors can neither go as high as the first nor descend much lower; the first basses do not reach as low as the second and at the same time can scarcely go higher. In a chorus written—as I propose—in six parts, the real contraltos (a large chorus always includes a greater or smaller number of them) must necessarily sing the second-soprano part; where the part goes above the high F, they must be divided once more lest the lower, true contraltos be forced to scream notes too high for them.

{ (All this is very worthy of note.)

The following list shows the range of the most sonorous tones of the seven different voices found in most large choruses. Not included are the extremely high or low tones available only to a few singers. These should therefore be used only in exceptional cases.

Three-part women's choruses have an enchanting effect in compositions of a religious or tender character. They are divided into the voices just mentioned: first and second soprano and contralto. Sometimes a tenor part is added as a bass to these three women's voices. Weber has done so with success in his chorus of elves in "Oberon". But this is only advisable if a soft and quiet effect is intended, since such a chorus can obviously not have much power. On the other hand, choruses composed only of men's voices are very powerful, particularly when the voices are lower and less divided. Dividing the basses into first and second (to avoid high notes) is not so necessary if rough and wild effects are intended; for the forced tones (such as the high F and F#) are better suited because of their peculiar character than the natural tones of the tenors on the same notes. But these tones should be skillfully prepared; one must not jump abruptly from the medium or even the low range to the extreme upper register. Gluck, in his terrible chorus of Scythians in the second act of "Iphigénie en Tauride", lets all the basses, joined with the tenors, sing the high F# with the words, "Ils nous amènent des victimes"; but this F# is twice preceded by a D, and by binding the two notes on the syllable "nous" the voice is easily carried from the D to the F#.

The sudden unison of the tenors and basses gives the phrase so much sonority and emphasis that it is impossible to hear it without shuddering. Here we have another of those touches of genius that are to be found on almost every page in the scores of this giant of dramatic music.

Aside from a particular idea of expression which was apparently decisive in this case, simple considerations of vocal scoring may frequently necessitate such choral unisons. For instance, if a certain melody leads the first tenors up to the B (a dangerous tone, which should better be avoided), one can let the second soprano and contralto join the tenor just for this passage; they can sing easily in unison with the tenors, blending with them and supporting their intonation.

On the other hand, if the tenors are forced by the design of a melody to descend too low, the first basses serve to support and reinforce them, without changing the character of the sound conspicuously. It would be different, of course, if the tenors or—still worse—the basses were to support the contralto and second soprano voices; for the female voices would be overshadowed and their sound would be suddenly changed by the entry of the male voices so as to destroy completely the unity of such a passage. This method of supporting one voice by another must therefore not be employed indiscriminately for all voices if one wants to preserve the peculiar character of the voice carrying the melody and of the voice taking it over. For, I repeat, just as the contraltos in their middle register become lost when sustaining in unison the high register of the tenors, so, on the other hand, would the middle range of the tenors—joining the low register of the second sopranos—cover them so that the sopranos would be almost completely inaudible. If the composer simply wants to add the range of one voice to that of another in a descending melodic line, he must not let a mass of heavy timbres suddenly follow one of lighter quality because the joining-point would be too apparent. In such cases it is better to let the upper half of the high voices cease first and then to replace it by the upper half of the low voices, whereas the lower half enters a little later. For instance, let us assume a descending scale of considerable extent, beginning with the high G sung by the combined first and second sopranos; when the scale reaches E, a tenth below the initial G, the first sopranos stop and the first tenors enter on D (a tone below the last E of the high sopranos); the second sopranos continue the descending movement unisono with the first tenors, stopping only on the low B, whereupon the second tenors enter on A, in unison with the first tenors; then these cease on F, to be replaced by the first basses; the junction of the second basses with the second tenors takes place on the low D or C; and finally the two groups of basses descend together to the low G. The result for the hearer will be a descending scale of three octaves, during which the voices follow each other in such a way that the transitions are scarcely noticeable.

After these remarks the reader will easily understand that the composer has to adapt the choice of vocal registers to the character of the composition. For an Andante in sustained and soft tones he would employ only the tones of the medium register; they alone have the suitable timbre, they move with calmness and precision and can be sustained pianissimo without without the slightest effort. This is what Mozart did in his sublime prayer "Ave verum corpus" (Example 136).

136. AVE VERUM CORPUS

I.
Viol.
II.
Viola.
Chor.
Orgel u.Bässe.
- - ce pro ho - - mi - ne; cu - - jus la - tus
cru - ce pro ho - mi - ne; cu - - jus la - tus
cru - ce pro ho - - mi - ne; cu - - jus la - tus
cru - ce pro ho - - mi - ne; cu - - jus la - tus
I.
Viol.
II.
Viola.
Chor.
Orgel u.Bässe.
per - fo - - ra - tum un - - da flu - xit et san - - gui - ne; es - - to
per - - fo - ra - tum un - da flu - xit et san - - gui - ne; es - to
per - fo - - ra - tum un - - da flu - xit et san - - gui - ne;
per - - fo - ra - tum un - - da flu - xit et san - - gui - ne;
I.
Viol.
II.
Viola.
Chor.
Orgel u.Bässe.
no - bis prae - gus - ta - tum in mor - - - - tis ex - a - - mi - ne, in mor - - -
no - bis prae - gus - ta - tum in mor - - - - tis ex - a - - mi - ne, in
es - - to no - bis prae - gus - ta - tum in mor - tis ex - a - mi - ne, in
es - - to no - bis prae - gus - ta - tum in mor - tis ex - a - mi - - ne, in

Excellent effects can be obtained from the lowest tones of the bass—such as the E^b and even the D under the stave. Many voices can produce them easily if they have time to take them (i.e. if they are preceded by a rest for breathing) and if they coincide with sonorous syllables. On the other hand, choral pieces of brilliant, pompous or violent character should be written somewhat higher; but the high tones must not predominate continually nor must the singers be forced to pronounce a great number of words rapidly. The resulting fatigue would soon impair the execution; and such a succession of high tones on different syllables is also rather unpleasant from the listener's point of view.

Beethoven, in his inspired impetuosity, unfortunately did not avoid this mistake in his choral works (i.e. Ninth Symphony, Missa Solemnis). On the other hand, because of the recklessness of his magnificent choral polyphony, the great Johann Sebastian Bach often makes the voices (tenor, contralto and especially second soprano) descend so low that the most important fugue subjects can be imagined by the reader of the score, but not heard with clarity by the listener. For the sake of the polyphonic clarity of these wonderful creations it would almost be advisable to arrange Bach's great choral works according to Berlioz' ideas, bringing in a few tenors for important passages to support excessively low phrases of the sopranos, or a few basses (or baritones) for the support of alto or tenor melodies descending too low. The general imitation of this method is warmly recommended. A good example of beautiful treatment of the chorus is the a-capella prayer in the third act of "La Muette de Portici", where the unisono of the medium range of sopranos and contraltos produces an excellent effect.

We have not as yet spoken of the very high tones which are called *head tones* or *falsetto*. Those of the tenors are of great beauty and extend the normal range considerably; with the head voice some can reach E^b or even F above the stave without effort. These tones might be used more frequently and successfully in choruses if choral singers were more proficient in the art of singing. The head voice of basses and baritones is tolerable only in an extremely light style of music—such as the French comic operas; these high, feminine-sounding tones, so different from the natural tones of the low voices—the so-called *chest-voice*—have actually something repulsive about them, except in the case of musical jokes. There has never been any attempt to employ them in a chorus or vocal piece of noble style.

The point where the chest voice ends and the head voice starts cannot be determined exactly. Skillful tenors are able to produce certain high tones such as A, B and even C in forte with the chest or head voice, as they choose; but I believe that the high B^b should generally be considered the extreme limit of the chest voice of the first tenor. This again proves that the tenor voice is not strictly a fifth above the bass, as is stated in most school theories; for among twenty basses selected at random at least ten will be able to sing the high F# in chest voice after due preparation, whereas one cannot find among an equal number of tenors a single voice able to sing a tolerably good high C# in chest voice.

The old masters of French opera, who never employed the head voice, wrote for a voice which they called *haute-contre,* and which foreigners, deceived by the meaning of the Italian word *contralto,* often mistake for the low women's voice. However, this name indicates a male voice trained to sing almost exclusively the five high tones (including B) of the first tenor's compass in chest voice. It is generally assumed that the normal pitch was at that time a tone lower than at present; but this assumption does not seem to me to be irrefutable and entirely certain. If a high B occurs in a chorus nowadays, most tenors take it in head voice; only the very high tenors (the hautes-contre) use the chest voice without hesitation.

Children's voices are of excellent effect in large choirs. Boys' sopranos have something incisive and crystalline about them which is lacking in the timbre of women's sopranos. However, in soft, dignified and calm compositions the latter appear to me preferable because of their fuller and less strident sound. As for artificial sopranos and contraltos—to judge from those I have heard in Rome—it does not seem that their almost complete disappearance is to be regretted.

In northern Germany and in Russia there are basses of such low range that composers are not afraid to let them sustain the low D and C under the stave even without any preparation. These precious low voices contribute considerably to the wonderful effect of the choir in the Imperial Chapel in St. Petersburg—the foremost choir in the world according to the judgment of all who have heard it. In the high registers, however, these very low bass voices can scarcely reach B or C above the stave.

To employ the lowest tones of the bass voices appropriately, one must guard against giving them rapid successions of tones with too many words. Vocalizing (i.e. holding one vowel or syllable during several notes) o choruses in the low part of the scale is of extremely poor effect; it is not much better in the medium range.

In spite of the example set by most of the famous masters, let us hope that those ridiculous tonal roulades on the words "Kyrie eleison" or "Amen", which contribute toward making vocal fugues in church music an indecent and abominable tomfoolery, will be banned from any sacred composition aspiring to be worthy of its purpose. However, slow and soft vocalizations of sopranos accompanying a melody of lower voices have a pious and seraphic expression. One must not forget to intersperse them with short rests to give the singers time for breathing.

In performing a phrase which cannot be sung in one breath, a large chorus (e.g. a hundred sopranos) is divided so that four groups of twenty-five sopranos each breathe in four different places in the phrase. This is exactly the same method as that used in extended violin melodies where only one stroke of the bow is indicated.

The special kinds of voice production in men's voices called *mixed* and *dark* voice are very valuable and lend a peculiar character to solo as well as choral singing. The mixed voice combines, to a certain degree, the sound of the chest voice and the head voice. As with the latter, it is impossible to determine fixed upper and lower limits for the mixed voice. One voice can produce very high mixed tones; others cannot go so high. The dark voice—whose character is indicated by its name—depends not only on the manner of production, but also on the degree of force and on the expression of the singer. A chorus in not too fast tempo, which is to be sung softly (sotto voce), can very easily be executed in dark voice, provided that the singers possess a feeling for expression as well as experience in singing. This kind of execution always produces a great effect if contrasted with the powerful and brilliant tones of a forte in the high range.

As a magnificent example of this effect we can cite the chorus "Suis l'amour puisque tu le veux" in Gluck's "Armide". Its first two stanzas, sung in dark voice, lend even more power to the conclusion, sung in full voice and fortissimo on the repetition of the words "Suis l'amour". It is impossible to characterize any better the suppressed menace and the sudden outburst of wrath. Indeed, this is the way the spirits of hate and fury must sing! (Example 137.)

137. ARMIDE, ACT III

Ob.
Klar. in C.
Fag.
I. Viol. II.
Viola.
Chor.
mi - de! suis l'a-mour qui te gui - de dans un a-bîme af-freux, dans un a - bîme af -
rei - tet! Mag dein Wahn dich ver-der-ben, Ver-zweif-lung sei dein Los, Verzweif-lung sei dein
Vlc.
K. B.
f
sf
La Haine.
Der Haß.
Sur ces bords é-car-tés c'est en vain, que tu ca - - ches le hé -
Nimmer-mehr sei er-hört von dem tü-ckischen Got - - te! er zer-
freux!
Los!

I.
Viol.
II.
Viola.
Der Haß.
ros, dont ton coeur s'est trop lais-sé tou-cher; la gloire à qui tu l'ar-ra-
rei-ße dein Herz mit end-lo-ser Qual! Umsonst sei dein Fle-hen zu ihm,
Vlc.
K. B.
ches doit bien-tôt te l'ar-ra-cher: malgré tes soins, au mé-pris de tes lar-mes,
er ver-höh-ne dich im Schmerz, und al-le Pein, die er glü-hend er-schafft,
Ob.
Klar. in C.
Fag.
sf
p
Chor.
tu le ver-ras é-chap-per à tes char-mes! Suis l'a-mour puisque tu le
schleud're er grim-mig auf dei-ne Brust.
Nun so fol-ge unwürd'ger

Ob.
Klar. in C.
Fag.
I.
Viol.
II.
Viola.
Chor.
veux, in - for - tu - née Ar - mi - de! suis l'a - mour qui te gui - de dans un a - bîme af -
Glut, die dir nur Qual be - rei - tet! Mag dein Wahn dich ver - der - ben, Ver - zweif - lung sei dein
Vlc.
K.B.
f
sf
La Haine.
Der Haß.
Tu me rap - pel - le -
Dann rufst du mich zu -
freux, dans un a - bîme af - freux!
Los, Verzweif - lung sei dein Los!

I. Viol. II.
Viola.
Der Haß.
ras, peut - ê - tre, dès ce jour, et ton at - ten - te se - ra
rück! Wohl mir! es ist zu spät! Du wirst ver - geb - lich zu mir
Vlc.
K.B.
vai - ne. Je vais te quit-ter sans re - tour, je ne te puis pu - nir d'u - ne plus ru - de
fle - hen! Ich las - se dich froh seiner Macht, ich weihe dich dem schrecklichsten Ge-schick zur
pei - ne, que de t'a - ban - don - ner pour ja - mais à l'a - mour.
Beu - te, dich trifft mein schwerster Fluch, denn er selbst rä - chet mich.
Chor.
ff
Suis l'a-
Nun so
sf

Ob.
Klar. in C.
Fag.
I.
Viol.
II.
Viola.
Chor.
mour puis-que tu le veux, in - for - tu-née Ar - mi - de! suis l'a - mour qui te
fol - ge un-würd'-ger Glut, die dir nur Qual be - rei - tet! Mag dein Wahn dich ver -
Vlc.
K.B.
Ob.
Klar. in C.
Fag.
I.
Viol.
II.
Viola.
Chor.
gui - de dans un a - bîme af - freux, dans un a - bîme af - freux!
der - ben, Ver-zweif-lung sei dein Los, Verzweif-lung sei dein Los!
Vlc.
K.B.

So far we have only dealt with the voice as used in choral bodies. The art of writing for *solo* voices requires the consideration of so many varied points that it is difficult to enumerate them all; they vary with the peculiarities of each individual singer. One could show how it is best to write for Rubini, for Dubrez, for Haitzinger (three well-known tenors), but not how to write a tenor part equally suitable for all three.

Of all the voices the solo tenor is the one hardest to write for because of his three registers—chest voice, mixed voice and head voice—whose range and facility, as I have already stated, vary with the individual singer. One performer is particularly skilled in using the head voice and can give much sonority even to his mixed voice; another sings with ease high and sustained phrases in all dynamic shadings and in all degrees of rapidity, preferably on the vowels E and I; a third one produces head tones with difficulty and prefers to sing all the time in full and vibrant chest tones; a fourth one excels in passionate pieces, but because of a voice which is somewhat slow in responding, he requires moderate tempos; he will prefer open syllables and sonorous vowels like A, he will dread sustained high tones and consider a high G held for several bars difficult and risky. Thanks to the flexibility of his mixed voice, the first will be able to strike a high and loud tone without preparation; on the other hand, the second needs to have such a tone prepared gradually because he employs his chest voice for it, reserving the mixed and head tones exclusively for the mezzoforte effects and tender accents. Another, whose tenor belongs to the voices formerly called haute-contre in France, will not be afraid of high notes at all because he can take them with a full chest voice, without preparation and without danger.

The first soprano is less difficult to treat than the first tenor; its head tones are scarcely different from the rest of the voice. Still, in view of the inequalities in soprano voices, one should know exactly the singer for whom one writes. Some sopranos sound weak and pale in the medium or low register; the composer has to consider this in selecting the registers for the main notes of a melody.

The mezzo-soprano (second soprano) and contralto voices are generally more homogenous, and therefore easier to treat. However, these two voices should not be required to sing many words on high phrases, since this makes the pronounciation of syllables very difficult if not impossible.

The most convenient voice is the bass, because of its simplicity. Since head tones are not used, one need not worry about changes of timbre. The choice of syllables is also less important. Every singer possessing a true bass voice must be able to sing a reasonably written bass part ranging from the low G to E♭ above the stave. Some voices descend much lower, as for instance that of Levasseur, who can sing low E♭ and even D; some, like Alizard, rise to F# and even G without the slightest loss in purity of sound; but these are the exceptions. On the other hand, there are voices which without being able to go higher than E♭, have no sonority below C (within the stave); these are fragmentary voices, difficult to use—however great their power and beauty. Baritones in particular are frequently of this type; they have voices of very small range, moving almost always within a single octave (from medium E♭ to the higher E♭), which makes it very difficult for the composer to avoid a certain monotony.

The excellence or mediocrity of a vocal performance—choral as well as solo—depends not only on the art of using the registers, on the careful designation of breathing points and on the choice of words to be sung, but above all on the manner in which the composer arranges the instrumental accompaniment. Some accompaniments overwhelm the voices by an instrumental uproar which might be excellent before and after the vocal passage, but not while the singers are trying to make it heard. Others again, without unduly overloading the orchestra, take delight in displaying some single instrument by letting it play runs and unnecessarily complicated figures during an aria; thus they detract the listener's attention from the main subject and confound and annoy the singer instead of aiding and supporting him. This does not mean that the simplicity of accompaniments should be exaggerated and all expressive and musically interesting figures should be banned from the orchestra. They are very appropriate, particularly if interspersed with short rests which give the vocal movements a certain amount of rhythmic freedom and do not compress the measures with metronomic exactitude. Thus the sighing motive of the violoncellos in the pathetic aria in the last act of Rossini's "Guillaume Tell" ("Sois immobile")—whatever some great artists may say against it—has a touching and admirable effect. It expresses the idea of this complicated piece clearly without impeding the voice in the least, and enhances the affecting and sublime expression of the aria. (Example 138.)

138. GUILLAUME TELL, ACT III

A solo instrument playing a cantilena in the orchestra corresponding with the vocal melody and thus forming a kind of duet with the voice is also frequently of excellent effect. The horn solo in the second act of Spontini's "La Vestale", which joins Julia's voice in her sorrowful and passionate aria "Tois que j'implore", gives added intensity to the vocal part. Never has the mysterious, veiled and somewhat painful tone of the horn in F been used more ingeniously and more dramatically. (Example 139).

Another example is Recha's cavatina in the second act of Halévy's "La Juive", accompanied by a solo of the English horn. The weak and touching voice of this instrument joins in this scene most affectingly with the supplicating voice of the young girl.

139. LA VESTALE, ACT II

Spontini.

Fl.
Klar. in C.
Fag.
Hrnr. in Es.
Hrn. in F.
I. Viol. II.
Viola.
Vlc. u.K.B.
tr
ppp
Julia.
Toi que j'im - plo - - - re a -
Du, die mein Mund nur mit

Fl.
Klar. in C.
Fag.
Hrnr. in Es.
Hrn. in F.
I.
Viol.
II.
Viola.
Julia.
vec ef - froi, re - dou - ta - ble dé - es -
Be - ben nennt, ha - be Gna - de, Er - bar -
Vlc. u.K.B.
I.Solo.
pp
pp
se, que ta mal-heu-reu-se prê-tres-se ob-tien-ne grâ - ce de - vant toi.
men! Schenk Mitleid, o Göt-tin, der Armen, die reu-ig dir die Schuld be - kennt.
Vcello.

Runs, arpeggios and variations of a solo instrument during a vocal piece are, I repeat, so disturbing for the singer as well as for the hearers that it requires great art and a cogent reason to make them acceptable. At any rate, I must admit that I always find them insufferable —with the sole exception of the solo viola in Aennchen's aria in the third act of "Freischuetz". Notwithstanding the example set by Mozart, Gluck and the majority of ancient masters as well as some modern composers, it is seldom good to double the vocal part with an instrument, especially in an Andante. This is almost always superfluous, the voice being sufficient for the enunciation of a melody. Moreover, it is rarely agreeable; the inflections of the voice, its expressive nuances and subtle shadings would be merely burdened and weakened by the addition of a second melodic part. Finally, it is wearisome to the skilled singer, who will doubtless perform a fine melody better if the execution is left to him alone.

Sometimes a kind of vocal orchestra is formed in choruses or in large ensemble pieces; one part of the voices adopts an instrumental style and sings, beneath the melody, accompaniments of various forms and rhythms. This almost always results in the most charming effects; cf. the chorus during the ballet in the third act of "Guillaume Tell" by Rossini, "Toi que l'oiseau ne suivrait pas" (Example 140).

140. GUILLAUME TELL, ACT III

It remains to point out to composers that in pieces accompanied by instruments the vocal harmony should be complete, as if there were no accompaniment. The various timbres of the instruments are too dissimilar from those of the voices to supply basses for them, without which certain chord successions would appear defective. Gluck, in whose works many sixth chords are to be found, used them also in his priestess choruses in "Iphigénie en Tauride"; these are written for two soprano parts only. In these harmonic successions the second part is a fourth beneath the upper part; the effect of these series of fourths is softened only by the basses, which are a third below the medium part and a sixth below the upper part. Now, in these choruses by Gluck the sopranos execute the two upper parts and are written in series of fourths. The lower part, which completes the chords and renders them harmonious, is given to the instrumental basses, whose tone is entirely different from that of the sopranos. This difference is enhanced by their extreme depth and their distance from the singers. Conseqently, these successions of fourths sung on the stage sound like dissonances (or are, at least, extremely harsh) because of the apparently missing complementary sixths.

In the chorus "O songe affreux" in the first act of the same opera these chord successions serve to increase the dramatic effect; but this is not the case in the fourth act, when the priestesses of Diana sing the hymn "Chaste fille de Latone" with its ancient and yet so beautiful color. Here, purity of harmony is absolutely indispensable. The series of clearly audible fourths in the vocal part is a mistake on Gluck's part—a mistake which could have been avoided by adding a third vocal part under the second one, an octave above the orchestral basses. (Examples 141 and 142.)

141. IPHIGENIE EN TAURIDE, ACT I

142. IPHIGENIE EN TAURIDE, ACT IV

Viol. I.
Viol. II.
Viola.
Fag.
Chor.
Bassi.
Tout ce que l'E - rèbe en - ser - re à ton_ nom pâ - lit d'ef - froi.
al - les in_ des Or - kus Näch - ten schon vor dei - nem Wink er - bleicht.
dolce
En tout temps on te con - sul - te dans la paix, dans les com - bats,
Dir ist ganz die Zu - kunft hel - le, gleich der Zeit, die längst ver - rann;
et l'on t'off - re le seul cul - te ré - vé - ré dans ces cli - mats.
schon an dei - nes Tem - pels Schwel - le staunt dies Volk und be - tet an.
Da Capo.

Male choruses in the unison, introduced into dramatic music by the modern Italian school, are occasionally very effective; but they have been greatly misused. If certain masters continue using them, they do so out of mere laziness, or to please certain choral bodies which are unable to execute competently pieces in several parts.

On the other hand, double choruses are of remarkable richness and splendor. They are certainly not used too much at present.

The men's choruses in "Lohengrin" should be studied as models of clarity and expressive characterization.

It is to be regretted that the art of a-capella singing * (i.e. choral works without any instrumental accompaniment) is no longer practiced in Germany—with very few praiseworthy exceptions—whereas it is still cultivated in a few places abroad (e.g. in Holland, Russia and above all at the Orfeo Càtalà in Barcelona).

For our musicians who are always in a hurry—composers as well as performers—double choruses are too tiresome to write and to study. In fact, the ancient composers who made the most frequent use of them usually wrote only for two alternating choruses of four voices each; choruses of eight real parts are rather rare even with them. There are also compositions for three choruses; if their basic idea is worthy of such rich realization, such choral bodies, divided into twelve or at least nine real voices, produce unforgettable impressions and make choral music of the grand style the most powerful of all the arts.

PERCUSSION INSTRUMENTS

These are of two kinds: one comprises the instruments of fixed and musically determined pitch; the other, those whose sound has little musical value and can be ranked only among indefinite noises, is usable for special effects and for coloring the rhythm.

The kettledrums, the bells, the glockenspiel, the keyboard harmonica, the small ancient cymbals have fixed tones.

The bass drum, the tenor drum, the side drum, the tambourine, the cymbals, the gong, the triangle and the crescent produce only noises of various characters.

One can also include here the birch rod, the castanets and the rattle. The birch rod is used in Mahler's Third Symphony, the rattle in my "Till Eulenspiegel" (as a humorous imitation of the wild shrieks of market women suddenly stirred up from their rest).

KETTLEDRUMS

Of all the percussion instruments, I consider kettledrums the most valuable; at least they are in most general use, and modern composers have achieved the most picturesque and dramatic effects with them. The old masters used them almost exclusively in compositions of a brilliant and military character to sound the tonic and dominant in more or less common rhythms, combined almost always with the trumpets.

Modern composers still grossly misuse the kettledrums by employing them much too frequently.

In the majority of orchestras there are only two kettledrums, the larger of which produces the lower tone. They are usually given the first and fifth steps of the key in which the composition is written. Up to quite recent times, some masters had the habit of invariably writing for the kettledrums and merely indicating the actual tones at the beginning of the piece. They wrote, for instance, Timpani in D, in which case G and C meant ; or, Timpani in G, making G and C to mean These two examples will suffice to demonstrate the shortcomings of this method. The composite range of the two kettledrums is one octave, from to . That is to say, by means of the screws increasing or diminishing the tension of the skin (the so-called head), the lower kettledrums can be tuned in the following pitches:

and the higher kettledrums as follows:

*The activities of the German male choral societies are hardly worth considering, their artistic results being negligible—with the exception of a few very large societies, particularly of teachers.

Assuming that the kettledrums have to sound only the tonic and dominant tones, it is obvious that the dominant cannot have the same position in relation to the tonic in all keys; thus the kettledrums must sometimes be tuned in fifths and sometimes in fourths. In the key of C they will be tuned in fourths, the dominant necessarily taking the lower position because the high G is not available (although it might be). It will be the same in the keys of D♭, D, E♭ and E. In B♭ the composer is at liberty to have his kettledrums in the interval of the fifth or the fourth, i. e. to place the tonic above or below, because there are two Fs at his disposal. The tuning in fourths would produce a dull sound, since the heads of both kettledrums would have little tension; F in particular would be slack and of poor quality. For the opposite reason, the tuning in fifths produces a bright sound. Kettledrums in F also can be tuned in two ways: in fifths or in fourths On the other hand, in the keys of G, A♭ and A the tuning must necessarily be in fifths because there is no low D, E♭ or E. In this case it would be unnecessary to indicate the tuning in fifths because it is obvious that the player is limited to this interval. But would it not be absurd to write movements in fourths when the performer has to play movements in fifths, and to indicate to the eye that note as the lowest which actually sounds highest, and vice versa?

The main reason for this strange custom of treating the kettledrums as transposing instruments was apparently the idea that kettledrums should play only the tonic and dominant. As soon as composers realized that it was occasionally useful to give them other notes too, it became necessary to write the real tones. In fact, kettledrums are now tuned in all possible ways: in minor or major thirds, in seconds, in perfect or augmented fourths, in fifths, sixths, sevenths and octaves. Beethoven achieved excellent effects in his Eighth and Ninth Symphonies with the octave tuning

In the Eighth Symphony Hans von Buelow used the kettledrums with pedals to reinforce the insufficiently audible bass:

For many years composers complained about the impossibility of using the kettledrums in chords in which neither of their two tones appeared, because of the lack of a third tone. They had never asked themselves whether one kettledrummer might not be able to manipulate three kettledrums. At last, one fine day they ventured to introduce this bold innovation after the kettledrummer of the Paris Opera had shown that this was not difficult at all. Since then composers writing for the Opera have three kettledrum notes at their disposal. It took seventy years to reach this point! It would obviously be still better to have two pairs of kettledrums and two drummers: this is indeed the scoring used in several modern symphonies. But in theaters progress is not so rapid, and there it will probably take another score of years.

In strong tutti chords, the young Verdi did not mind letting the kettledrums sound tones of different harmony (e.g. in the first Finale of his "Ballo in Maschera"). This indifference is based on the practical experience that the sound of kettledrums is too indefinite to stand out disturbingly from a compact mass of harmonic tones. Nevertheless, this is not entirely to my taste.

One may employ as many kettledrummers as there are kettledrums in the orchestra, so as to produce at will rolls, rhythms and simple chords in two, three or four parts, according to the number of drums. With two pairs, for instance—one pair tuned in A and E♭ the other in C and F —four drummers could produce the following chords of two, three and four tones:

Moreover, enharmonic changes would tranform these tones:

into the following chord in D♭ minor:

or into this chord in C# minor:

This would also give the advantage of having at least one tone of all the chords which are not too remote from the principal key. Thus, to obtain a certain number of chords in three, four and five parts, more or less doubled, and furthermore to achieve the striking effect of very close rolls, I have employed in my grand Requiem Mass eight pairs of differently tuned kettledrums and ten drummers. (Example 143.)

143. REQUIEM, TUBA MIRUM

Berlioz.

Das Tempo ein wenig belebt.
Fl. Ob. Cl.
Bassoon
in Eb
Horns in F
in G
Corn. in Bb
Tenor Trom.
D.-b. Oph.
Trump. in F in Eb
Tenor Trom.
Trump. in Eb
Tenor Trom.
Trump. in low Bb
Tenor Tromb. & Oph. in C
Oph. in Bb
unis.
ff
Trp. in Es allein.
Trp. in F.

Fl. Ob. Cl.
Bassoon
in Eb
Horns in F
in G
Corn. in Bb
Tenor Trom.
D.-b. Oph.
Trump. in F in Eb
Tenor Trom.
Trump. in Eb
Tenor Trom.
Trump. in low Bb
Tenor Tromb. & Oph. in C
Oph. in Bb
ohne Oph.
Klar. allein.
unis.
Oph.

Fl. Ob. Cl.
Bassoon
in Eb
Horns in F
in G
Corn. in Bb
Tenor Trom.
D.-b. Oph.
Trump. in F in Eb
Tenor Trom.
Trump. in Eb
Tenor Trom.
Trump. in low Bb
Tenor Tromb. & Oph. in C
Oph. in Bb.
Kettledrums
Bass Drum in Bb
Bass Drum
Viol. I II
Violas
Chorus
Vlc. & D.-B.
cresc. molto
Trp. in F.
Trp. in Es.
Oph.
Mit Schwammschlägeln.
mf cresc.
Mit zwei Klöppeln abwechselnd von jeder Seite zu schlagen.
dim.
Vlc.
K.B.

Fl. Ob. Cl.
Klar. allein.
Bassoon
unis.
in Eb
Horns in F
in G
Corn. in Bb
Tenor Trom.
D.-b. Oph.
Trump. in F in Eb.
Tenor Trom.
Trump. in Eb
Tenor Trom.
unis.
Trump. in low Bb
Tenor Tromb. & Oph. in C
Pos.
Oph.
Oph. in Bb
Kettledrums
Bass Drum in Bb
Bass Drum
Viol. I II
Violas
Chorus
Et i - te - rum ven - tu-rus est cum glo-ri - a ju - di - ca - - - re
Vlc. & D.-B.

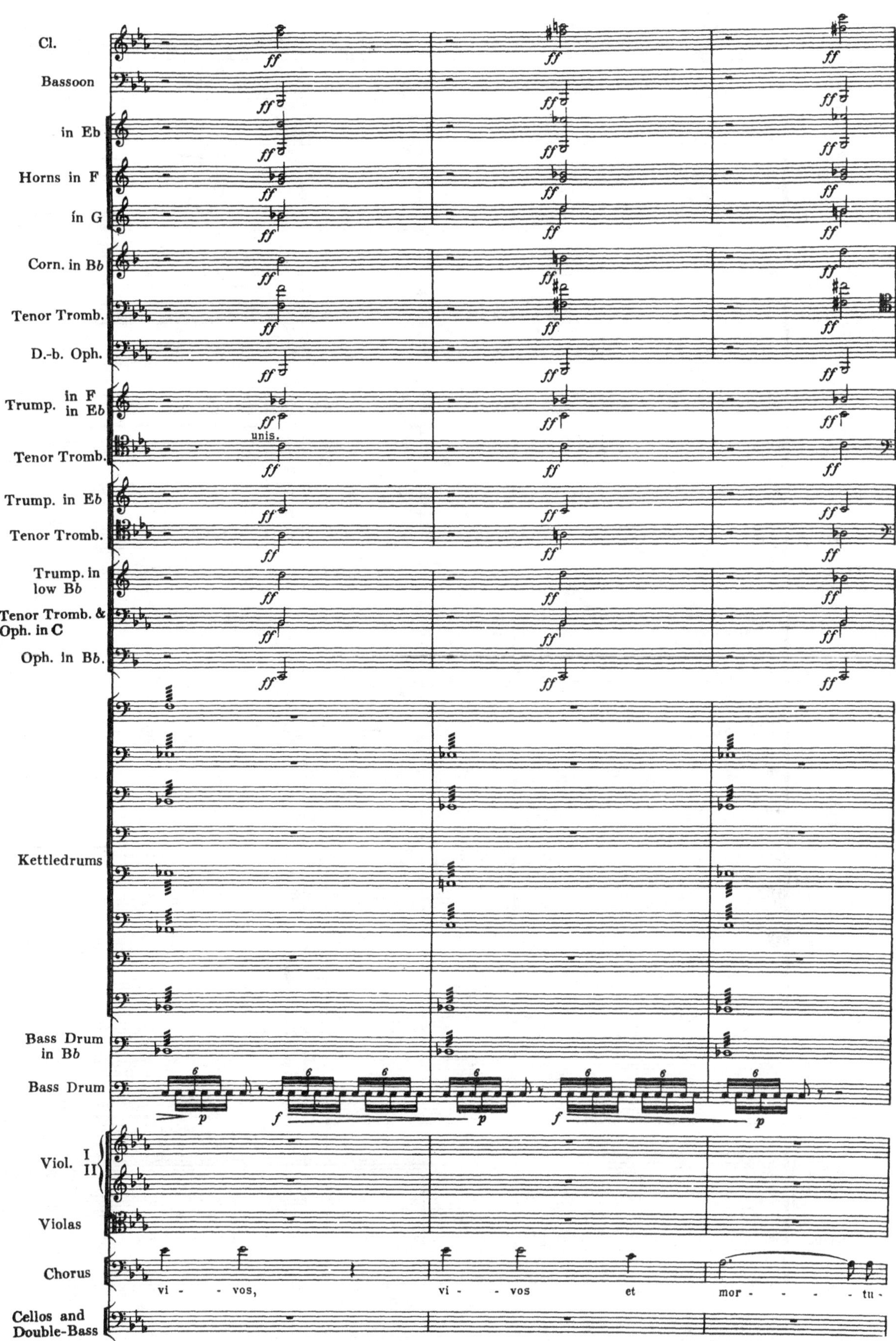

Cl.
Bassoon
in Eb
Horns in F
in G
Corn. in Bb
Tenor Tromb.
D.-b. Oph.
Trump. in F in Eb
unis.
Tenor Tromb.
Trump. in Eb
Tenor Tromb.
Trump. in low Bb
Tenor Tromb. & Oph. in C
Oph. in Bb.
Kettledrums
Bass Drum in Bb
Bass Drum
Viol. I II
Violas
Chorus
vi - - vos,
vi - - vos et
mor - - - - tu -
Cellos and Double-Bass

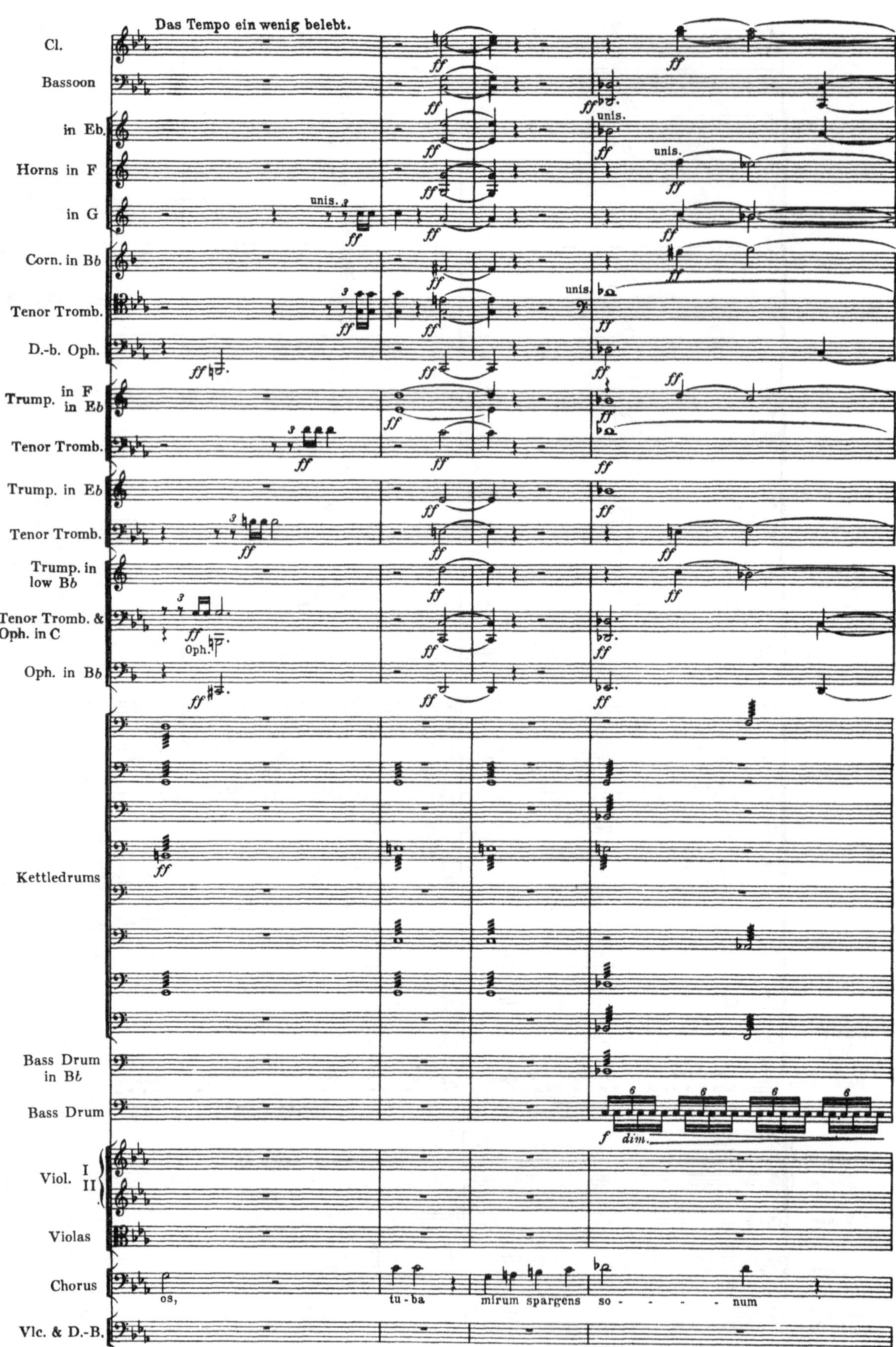
Das Tempo ein wenig belebt.
Cl.
Bassoon
in Eb.
Horns in F
in G
Corn. in Bb
Tenor Tromb.
D.-b. Oph.
Trump. in F in Eb
Tenor Tromb.
Trump. in Eb
Tenor Tromb.
Trump. in low Bb
Tenor Tromb. & Oph. in C
Oph. in Bb
Kettledrums
Bass Drum in Bb
Bass Drum
Viol. I II
Violas
Chorus
Vlc. & D.-B.
unis.
Oph.
dim.
os, tu-ba mirum spargens so - - - - num

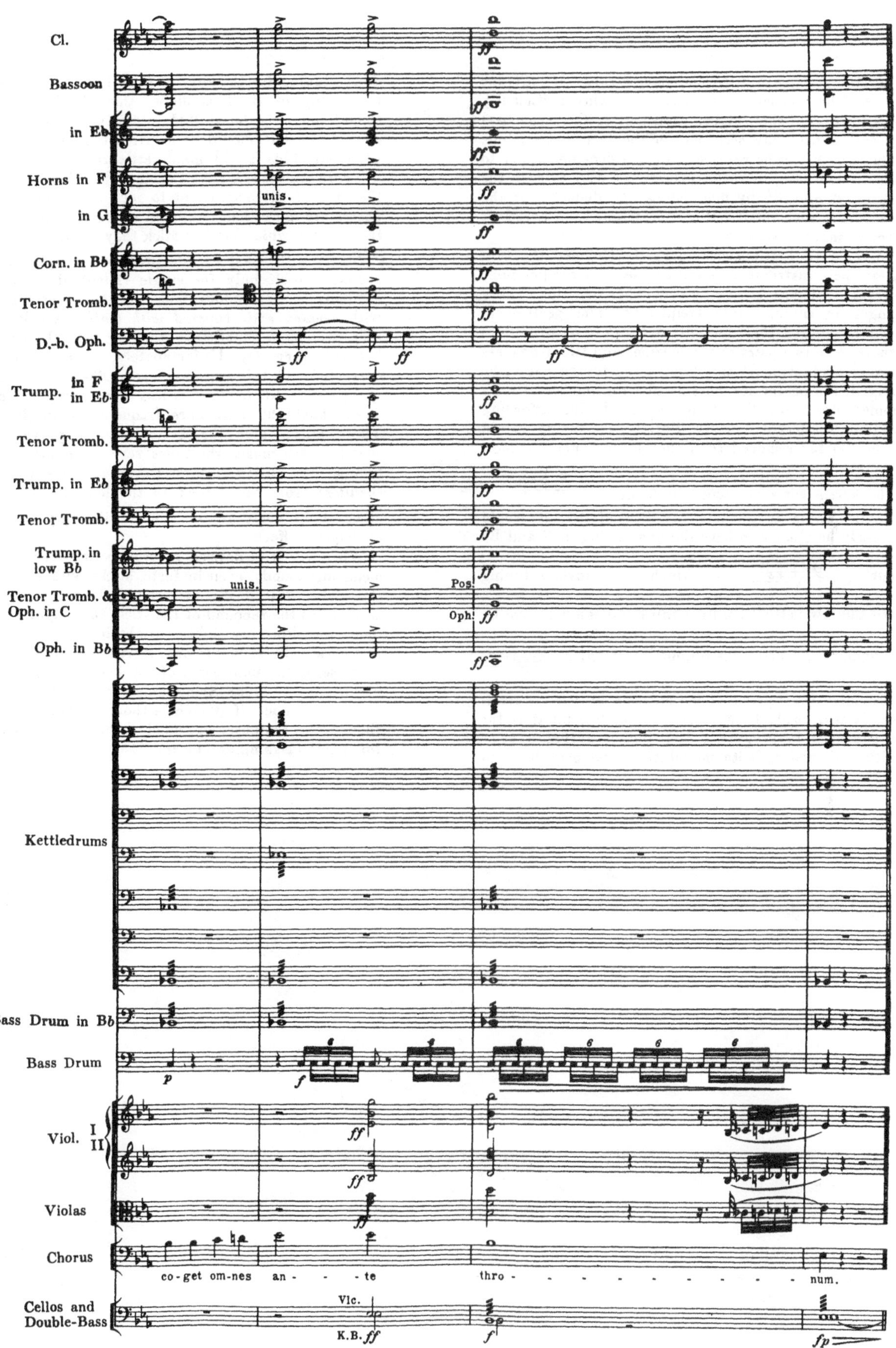
Cl.
Bassoon
in E♭
Horns in F
in G
unis.
Corn. in B♭
Tenor Tromb.
D.-b. Oph.
Trump. in F
in E♭
Tenor Tromb.
Trump. in E♭
Tenor Tromb.
Trump. in low B♭
Tenor Tromb. & Oph. in C
unis.
Pos.
Oph.
Oph. in B♭
Kettledrums
Bass Drum in B♭
Bass Drum
Viol. I II
Violas
Chorus
co-get om-nes an - - te thro - - - - - - - - - - - - - num.
Cellos and Double-Bass
Vlc.
K.B.

As stated above, kettledrums have a range of only one octave. The difficulty of obtaining skins sufficiently large to cover a shell bigger than that of the large bass kettledrum probably accounts for the fact that no tone lower than F can be reached. But this does not apply to high kettledrums; it would certainly be easy to gain the high G, A and B♭ by diminishing the diameter of the metal shell. Such small kettledrums might be of excellent effect in many instances.

In the past kettledrummers rarely changed the tuning of their instrument in the course of a composition; however, composers now do not hesitate to require changes in tuning quite frequently. The performers might be spared this difficult and awkward procedure if there were two pairs of kettledrums and two drummers in every orchestra. At any rate, if the tuning has to be changed, the performer must be given a number of rests commensurate with the change required, thus affording him time to effect it securely. Besides, the tuning should not be too far removed from the old one. For instance, if the kettledrums are tuned in A and E  and one wants to go into the key of B♭, it would obviously be clumsy to have the new tuning in F and B♭ (fourth)  , which would involve tuning down the low kettledrum by a third and the high one by an augmented fourth; the tuning B♭, F (fifth)  necessitates the raising of both drums by only a semitone. It will easily be understood how difficult it is for the drummer to prepare a new tuning during a composition abounding with modulations; he may have to do the tuning for the keys of C or F while the orchestra is playing in B. This shows that the kettledrummer should not only be skilled in the manipulation of the drumsticks, but should be a gifted musician with a sensitive ear. This is why good kettledrummers are so rare.

There are three kinds of drumsticks. Their use changes the tone of the instrument to such an extent that composers are more than negligent if they fail to indicate in their scores which kind of stick they desire.

Sticks with *wooden ends* produce a rough, dry, hard sound, suitable only for single violent blows or to accompany a tremendous noise in the orchestra. Sticks with *wooden ends covered with leather* are less hard; they produce a sound less startling than the preceding, but still very dry. Unfortunately, in many orchestras only sticks of this type are used. The best sticks have *sponge ends;* their effect is less noisy and more musical. They should be used more frequently than the others. These sticks give the kettledrums a grave, velvety sound, which makes the tones very clear and hence the tuning very distinct; they can render many different shadings from the softest to the loudest, such as the other sticks could produce only with ugly or at least inadequate effect.

Whenever it is desired to produce mysterious, darkly menacing sounds, even in forte, sticks with sponge ends should be prescribed. Since the elasticity of the sponge accelerates the rebound of the stick, the player need only touch the skin very lightly to obtain very delicate, soft and close rolls in pianissimo. Beethoven has made excellent use of the pianissimo of the kettledrums in his B♭-major and C-minor Symphonies; these admirable passages lose much if played without sponge heads, even though the composer specified nothing in his scores on this point (Examples 144 and 145.)

144. SYMPHONY IN B♭ MAJOR, 2nd MOVEMENT

Beethoven.

145. SYMPHONY IN C MINOR, TRANSITION TO THE FINALE

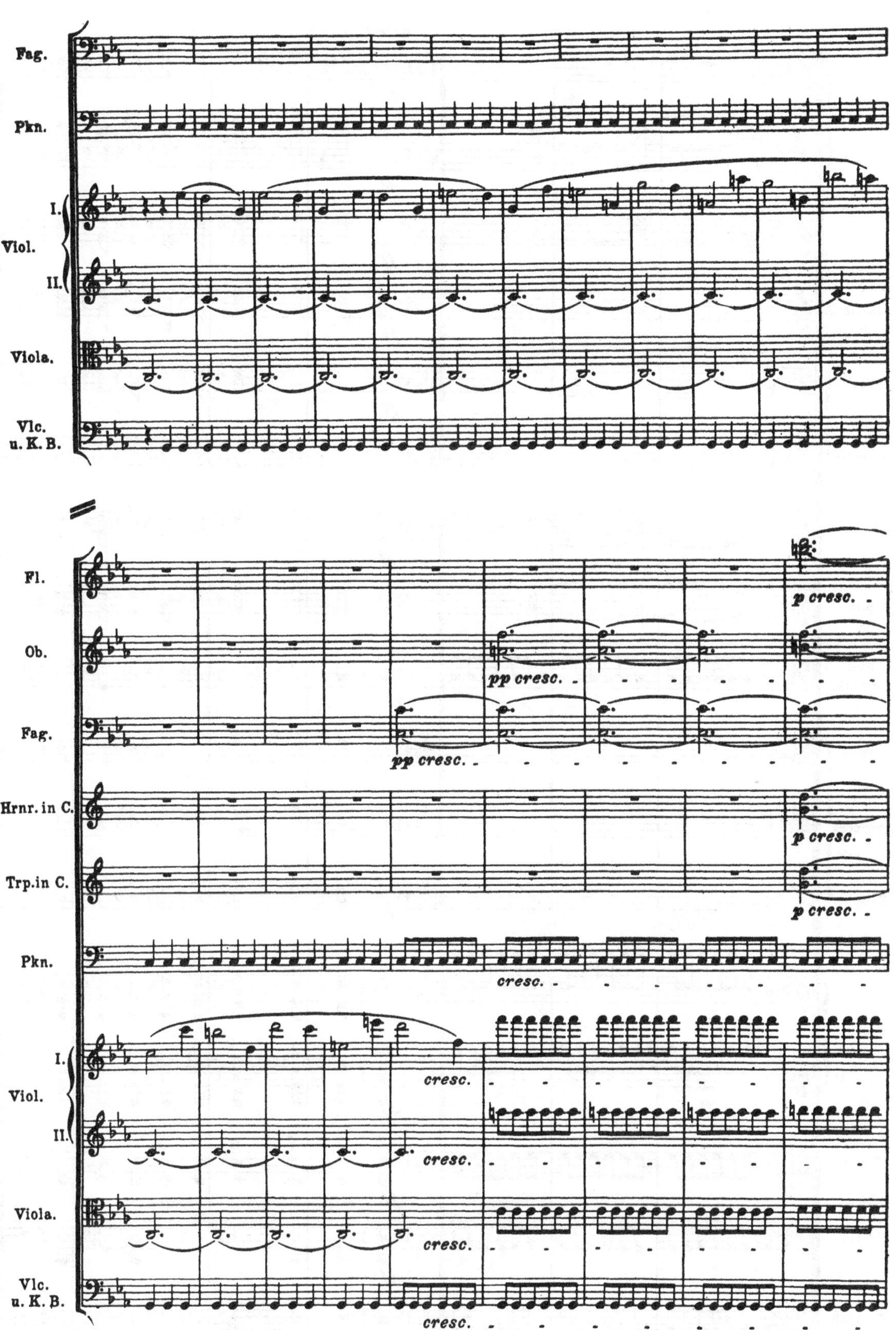
Fag.
Pkn.
I.
Viol.
II.
Viola.
Vlc.
u. K. B.
Fl.
p cresc.
Ob.
pp cresc.
Fag.
pp cresc.
Hrnr. in C.
p cresc.
Trp. in C.
p cresc.
Pkn.
cresc.
I.
cresc.
Viol.
II.
cresc.
Viola.
cresc.
Vlc.
u. K. B.
cresc.

Allegro.
Kl. Fl.
Gr. Fl.
Ob.
Klar. in C.
Fag.
Kontrafag.
Hrnr. in C.
Trp. in C.
Pkn. in C. G.
Altpos.
Tenorpos.
Baßpos.
I.
Viol.
II.
Viola.
Vcello.
Kontrab.
ff

Wagner employs a single anxious pulse beat of the kettledrum in "Walkuere" in Siegmund's monologue and the "Todesverkuendigung"—a sublime effect during the solemn silence of the entire orchestra.

There is a strange kettledrum passage in the second Finale of Beethoven's "Fidelio":

To make the repetition of beats in this rapid tempo possible, this passage is executed with crossed arms.

Particularly in the scores of the old masters, the indication *muffled* or *covered kettledrums* is frequently found. This means that the skin of the instrument is to be covered with a piece of cloth, which damps the sound and lends it a mournful expression. Drumsticks with sponge ends are preferable in this case. Sometimes it is advisable to indicate which notes the drummer should execute with two sticks and which with a single stick:

The nature of the rhythm and the position of the heavy accents should decide this choice.

The tone of the kettledrums does not extend very low. It sounds just the way it is written—in the F-clef; it is therefore in unison with the corresponding notes of the violoncellos and not an octave below them, as is sometimes assumed.

The pedal kettledrums, invented by Hans Schneller in Vienna, seem to have attained the facility of mechanism and the sensitivity in tuning which had been sought for such a long time. They permit rapid and precise changes in tuning by merely pressing a lever with the foot; at the same time they provide against irregular changes in the skin which are frequently caused by the weather.

BELLS

They have been introduced into instrumentation more for the sake of dramatic than of purely musical effects. The timbre of low bells is appropriate only for solemn and grandiose scenes. On the other hand, that of the high bells has a more serene character; it has something rustic and naive about it; this makes it particularly suitable for religious and pastoral scenes. For this reason Rossini has employed a little bell in high G to accompany the graceful chorus in the second act of "Guillaume Tell", whose refrain is "Voici la nuit"; whereas Meyerbeer used a bell in low F to give the signal for the massacre in the fourth act of his "Les Huguenots". At the same time the bassoons play a B - the diminished fifth of this F; together with the low tones of the two clarinets (in B^b and A) these create that ominous sound which spreads awe and horror in this immortal scene. (Example 146.)

146. LES HUGUENOTS, ACT IV

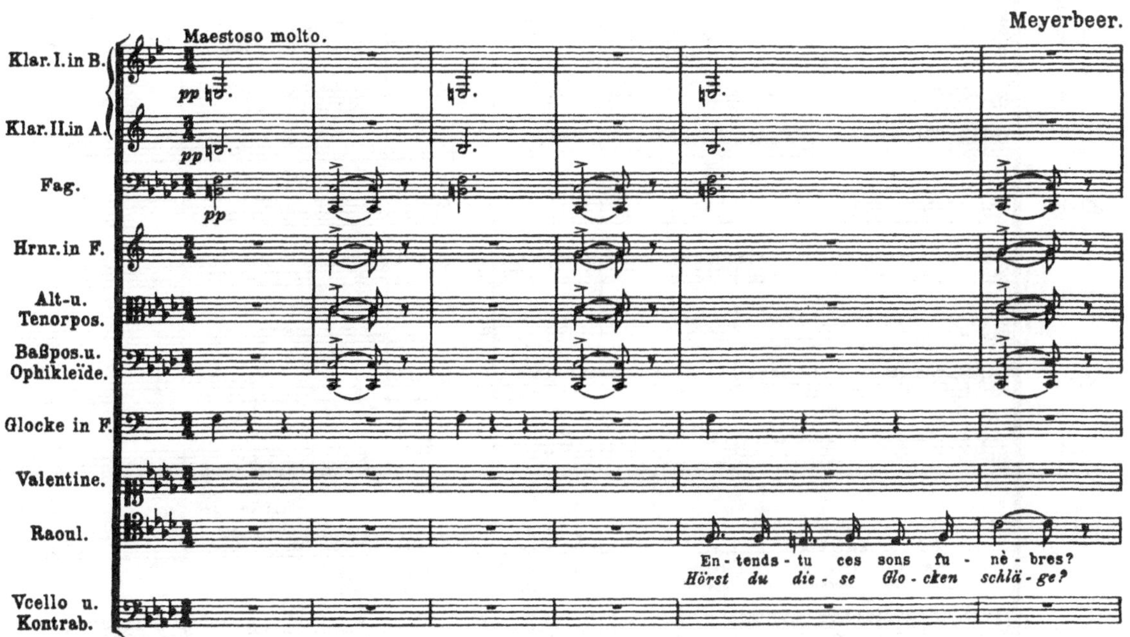

in B.
Klar.
in A.
Fag.
Hrnr. in F.
Pos.
u. Oph.
Glocke.
Val.
Ils me gla - cent de ter - reur!
Sie er - star - ren mir das Blut!
R.
Du sein des noi - res té - nè - bres s'é -
Durch nächt - lich Dun - kel er - schal - let der
Vcello u. Kontrab.
Fl. I.
Engl. H.
in B.
Klar.
in A.
Muta in B.
Fag.
Hrnr. in F.
Pos.
u. Oph.
Glocke.
I.
Viol.
II.
Viola.
Val.
Près de moi, cher Ra -
Hier bei mir, teu - rer
R.
lève un cri — de fu - reur; où donc é - tais - je?
Ra - che furchtbar Ge - schrei! O Gott, wo war ich?
Vlc.
K. B.

The wonderful application of the bells in "Parsifal" still meets with great difficulties, since real bells with this beautiful, low range are too heavy and expensive. Instead, large metal bars or several pianos combined with gongs have been used.

SETS OF SMALL BELLS

(Les Jeux de Timbres)

Very felicitous effects are obtained - especially in military bands - with a set of eight or ten very small bells fastened to an iron bar one above the other in diatonic sequence according to size, the highest tone being at the top of the pyramid and the lowest at the bottom. These chimes, which are struck with a little hammer, can execute melodies of moderate speed and small range. They are made in different keys; the highest ones are the best.

THE GLOCKENSPIEL

In his "Zauberfloete" Mozart wrote an important part for a keyboard instrument which he called the *Glockenspiel.* It doubtless consisted of a great number of small bells arranged in such a fashion that they could be sounded by a mechanism of keys. He gave it the following range:

Including the chromatic intervals

and wrote it on two staves and in two clefs, like the pianoforte. (Example 147.)

When the pasticcio "Les Mystères d'Isis", which contains more or less disfigured parts of the music of "Die Zauberfloete", was performed at the Paris Opera, they had a little keyboard instrument built for the Glockenspiel music; its hammers struck steel bars instead of bells. Its sound is an octave higher than the written notes. It is soft, mysterious and of extreme delicacy. It is suitable for the most rapid movements, and it is much better than the instrument with little bells.

147. ZAUBERFLOETE, ACT I, FINALE

Glockensp.
I.
Viol.
II.
Viola.
Chor.
Das klinget so herrlich, das klinget so schön; la ra la, la la
Vlc. u. K. B.
Glockensp.
I.
Viol.
II.
Viola.
Chor.
la ra la la la la ra la! Nie hab' ich so etwas ge - hört noch gesehn; la ra
Vlc. u. K. B.

Glockensp.
Viol.
I.
II.
Viola.
Chor.
la, la la la ra la la la la ra la! Nie hab' ich so et-was ge-
Vlc. u. K. B.
Glockensp.
Viol.
I.
II.
Viola.
Chor.
hört noch ge-sehn; la ra la, la la la ra la la la la ra la!
Vlc. u. K. B.

THE KEYBOARD HARMONICA

(Glass Harmonica)

This instrument is of the same type as the preceding; its hammers, however, strike glass plates. Its sound is of an extremely voluptuous delicacy and might be used in the most poetic effects. Its tone, like that of the keyboard with steel bars, is very weak. This fact should be kept in mind when it is to be combined with other orchestral instruments. The slightest forte accent of the violins would cover it completely. It would blend better with a light accompaniment in pizzicato or in harmonics, or with some very soft tones of the flutes in their medium range.

The keyboard harmonica sounds as it is written. It can scarcely be given a range of more than two octaves. All tones above the high E  are scarcely audible and those below D  are of poor quality and even weaker than the rest of the scale. This shortcoming might perhaps be remedied by using stronger glass plates for the low range.

Pianoforte manufacturers usually also build this charming and too little known instrument. It is written on two staves and in two G-clefs.

It should not be necessary to add that the manner of playing these two little keyboard instruments is the same as that on the pianoforte and that one can write for them (of course within the limits of their range) the same runs, arpeggios and chords as one would for a tiny pianoforte.

The *Celesta,* invented by Mustel in Paris, is an important addition to the orchestra. It may be considered an improved Glockenspiel, provided with a keyboard; its tone, produced by steel plates, is similar both to the Glockenspiel and to the harp. Its range is five octaves. Its beautiful sound is frequently utilized by modern French and Russian composers, but older works benefit by it as well (e.g. Papageno's aria in "Zauberfloete").

G. Charpentier in particular has combined it very subtly and effectively with other soft orchestral colors in his opera "Louise".

THE ANCIENT CYMBALS

They are very small. Their sound rises in pitch as they become thicker and smaller. I have seen some in the Pompeian Museum at Naples which were no larger than a piaster. Their tone is so high and weak that it is scarcely audible unless all other instruments are silent. In ancient times they served to mark the rhythm of certain dances, probably in the same fashion as our modern castanets.

In the fairy-like Scherzo of my "Romeo and Juliet" Symphony I have employed two pairs, equal in size to the largest of the Pompeian cymbals (i.e. somewhat smaller than a hand), and tuned in fifths. The lower one gives this B♭: , and the higher one this F:  To make them vibrate well, the players must not strike them together with their entire surfaces but only with the edges. Any bell maker can manufacture these small cymbals. They are cast in brass or copper and then tuned in the desired key by means of a lathe. They should be at least a third of an inch thick. They are delicate instruments similar to the keyboard harmonicas, but their tone is stronger and can be heard through a large orchestra playing piano or mezzoforte.

THE BASS DRUM

Among the percussion instruments with indefinite sound the bass drum is certainly the one which has done the greatest mischief and has been most misused in modern music. None of the great masters of the last century thought of introducing the bass drum into the orchestra. Spontini was the first to use it in the triumphal march in "La Vestale" and later in several pieces of his "Fernand Cortez"; there it was in its proper place. But it is really the height of folly to use this instrument in all ensembles, in every finale, in the most meaningless choruses, in dance tunes and even in cavatinas—as has been done during the past fifteen years; to call the matter by its right name—it is really sheer brutality. The composers do not even have the excuse of intending to accentuate a basic rhythm against other accidental rhythms. No—they senselessly beat the accented parts of each bar, they crush the orchestra, they choke the voices. No longer is there any melody, harmony, form or expression left; the prevailing key remains scarcely recognizable. And yet they naively think they have created an energetic instrumentation, something especially beautiful!

It is needless to add that in these cases the bass drum is almost never used without the cymbals—as if these two instruments were inseparable by nature. In some orchestras they are even played by the same musician; one of the cymbals is fastened on top of the bass drum, so that he can strike it with the other cymbal in his left hand while using the drumstick with his right hand. This economical procedure is intolerable; the cymbals lose their sonority and produce a noise similar to the sound of a falling bag full of old iron and broken glass. The resulting music is utterly trivial and devoid of any brilliance. It is perhaps suitable for the accompaniment of dancing monkeys, jugglers, mountebanks, swallowers of swords and snakes in public squares and at dirty street corners.

Nevertheless, the bass drum is of admirable effect if used skillfully. The entrance of the bass drum in a full orchestra can, for instance, redouble the force of a broad rhythm which has already been established and gradually reinforced by successive entrances of the most sonorous instrumental groups. In this instance it does wonders: the rhythmic power of the orchestra becomes immensely intensified; unbridled noise is transformed into music.

The pianissimo of the bass drum and cymbals together, struck at long intervals in an Andante is majestic and solemn. However, the pianissimo of the bass drum alone (if the instrument is well built and of large size) is gloomy and ominous; it resembles the distant sound of cannon.

In my Requiem I have used the bass drum in forte without cymbals and with two drumsticks. By striking the instrument alternately from both sides, the performer can produce a rather quick succession of sounds. Combined, as in this work, with kettledrum rolls in several parts and with an orchestration depicting anguish and terror, these sounds convey the idea of the strange and awful uproar accompanying great cataclysms of nature. (Example 143, p. 372).

In his mountain Symphony, Liszt also employed the bass drum very poetically to paint a solemn, distant rumbling.

I have used the bass drum in another instance in a symphony to obtain a hollow roll much lower in pitch than the lowest tone that the kettledrum could produce. The bass drum was placed upright like a military drum and was played simultaneously by two drummers.

THE CYMBALS

The cymbals are combined very frequently with the bass drum, but—as stated above—they can be used just as well by themselves. Their shrill and tingling sound stands out in a full orchestra. Combined with the high tones of the piccolo and with the strokes of the kettledrum, it is particularly suited to scenes of unbridled wildness or to the extreme frenzy of a bacchanalian orgy. The finest effect ever produced on cymbals is to be found in the chorus of Scythians in Gluck's "Iphigénie en Tauride" (Example 148).

148. IPHIGENIE EN TAURIDE, ACT I

Kl. Fl.
Ob. u. Klar. in C.
Trom.
Becken.
I.
Viol.
II.
Viola.
Chor.
Bassi.
Les dieux ap - pai - sent leur cour -
Be - sänf - tigt ist der Göt - ter
Les dieux ap - pai - sent leur cour -
roux, ils nous a - mè - nent des vic - ti - - - mes, les dieux ap -
Wut, da sie uns selbst das Op - fer sen - - - den; be - - sänf - tigt
roux, ils nous a - mè - nent des vic - ti - - - mes, les dieux ap -

Kl. Fl.
Ob. u. Klar. in C.
Trom.
Becken.
I. Viol. II.
Viola.
Chor.
pai - sent leur cour - roux, ils nous a - - mè - nent des vic -
ist der Göt - - ter Wut, da sie uns selbst das Op - fer
pai - sent leur cour - roux, ils nous a - - mè - nent des vic -
Bassi.
Kl. Fl.
Ob. u. Klar. in C.
Trom.
Becken.
I. Viol. II.
Viola.
Chor.
ti - - mes; à ces jus - tes ven - geurs des cri - - - mes que leur
sen - - den! Auf! ver - spritzt mit ge - weih - ten Hän - - den un - sern
ti - - mes; à ces jus - tes ven - geurs des cri - - - mes que leur
Bassi.

A wonderful, fantastic effect in "Rheingold" is the discreet symbolization of the gold by a pp roll on a freely suspended cymbal with a soft kettledrum stick. The cymbal stroke on the first chord of Liszt's "Mazeppa", similar to the crash of a whip, is of striking realism.

Vigorous and well-marked rhythms in a large choral piece or in an orgiastic dance gain greatly by the participation not of one pair of cymbals, but of four, six, ten and even more pairs of cymbals, according to the size of the concert hall and according to the number of other instruments and voices. The composer should always indicate the length of the cymbal sound exactly, if it is followed by a rest. If a prolonged sound is desired, long and sustained notes must be written with the indication "vibrato"; in the opposite case one should write eighth or sixteenth notes with the word "secco". The latter is excuted by holding the cymbals against the player's chest immediately after the stroke. Sometimes a drumstick with a sponge end or a bassdrum stick is used to vibrate a cymbal suspended by its leather strap. This produces a long, vibrant and sinister sound whose effect, however, is not quite as formidable as that of a gong.

THE GONG

The gong or tamtam is used only in compositions of a mournful character or in dramatic scenes of the utmost horror. Its powerful, vibrating sound combined with heavy chords of the bass (trumpets and trombones) has a truly awful effect. No less frightening are the lugubrious pianissimo strokes of a gong played almost alone. Meyerbeer has proved this in the magnificent scene of "Robert le Diable"—"The Resurrection of the Nuns" (Example 149).

149. ROBERT LE DIABLE, ACT III

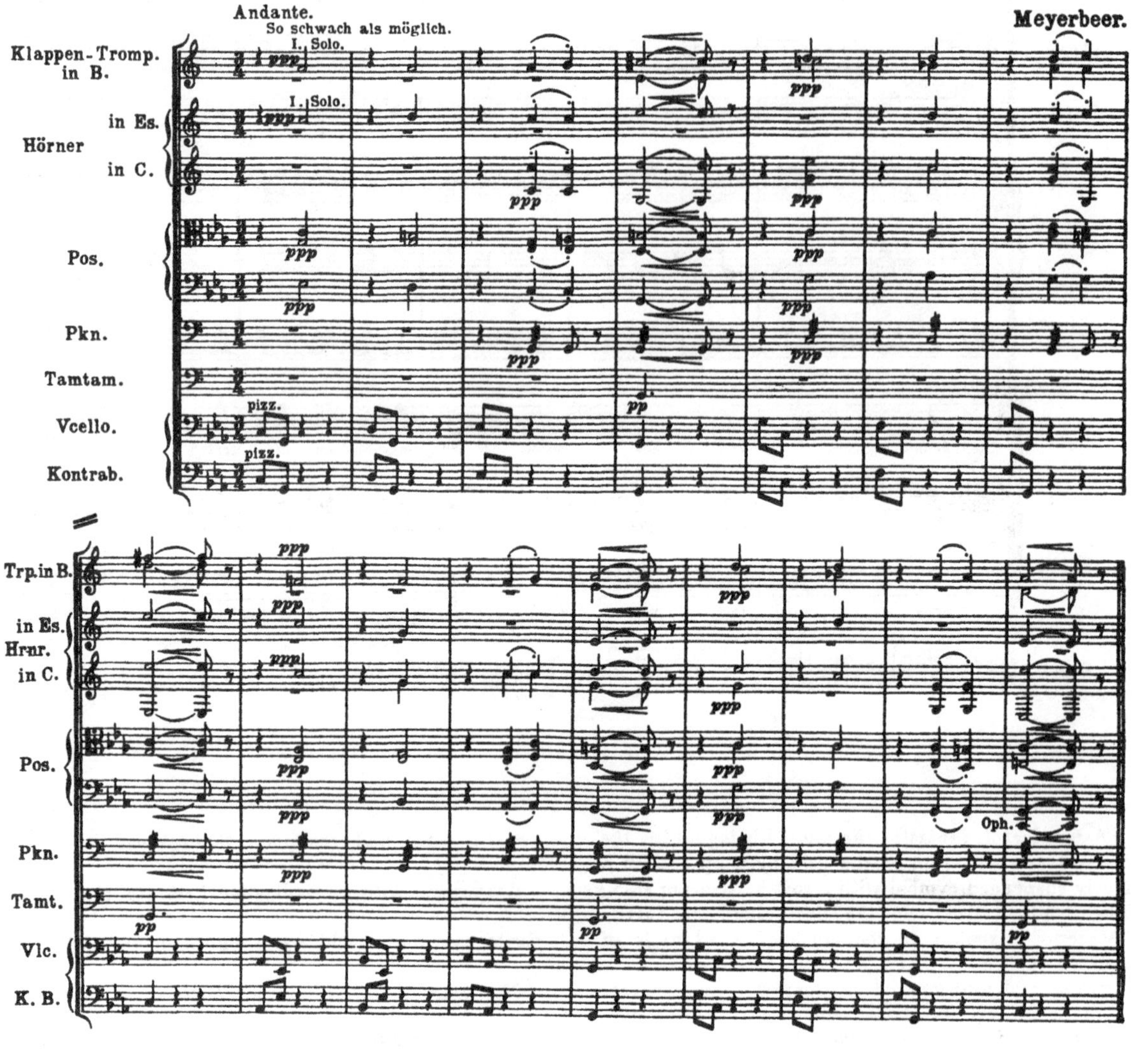

Andante. So schwach als möglich. Meyerbeer.

THE TAMBOURINE

This favorite instrument of Italian peasants, in whose festivities it plays an important role, is of excellent effect when employed in masses to stress the rhythm of a lively dance - similary to the cymbals or together with them. In the orchestra it is employed solo only to characterize peoples habitually using it, such as Gypsies, Basques, Italians from the Campagna, the Abruzzi and Calabria. It produces three very different kinds of sound. If it is simply struck with the hand, its sound is of little value and (except in masses) is audible only when not combined with other instruments. If the skin is rubbed with the fingertips, this causes a roll in which the sound of the jingles fastened around the edge of the instrument predominates; this is written: 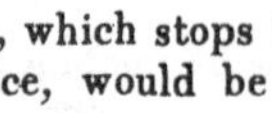 . This roll can be only of short duration because the finger rubbing the skin soon reaches the edge, which stops its action. A roll like this one, for instance, would be impossible:

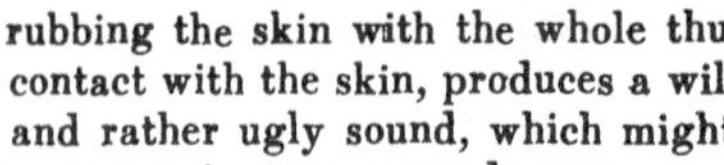

Finally rubbing the skin with the whole thumb, without quitting contact with the skin, produces a wild, strangely rattling and rather ugly sound, which might be used in special cases, e.g. in a masquerade scene.

THE SIDE DRUM

The drums proper are used almost exclusively in large bands. Their effect increases and becomes more noble in proportion to the number of drums employed. A single drum - particulary if used in an ordinary orchestra - has always appeared to me to sound low and vulgar. Yet it cannot be denied that Meyerbeer produced a peculiar and terrible effect through the combination of one drum with the kettledrums in the famous crescendo roll in the Consecration of the Swords in his "Huguenots". But eight, ten, twelve or still more drums executing rhythmic accompaniments or crescendo rolls in a military march serve as magnificent and powerful auxiliaries for the wind instruments. Simple rhythms without melody, harmony or key (i.e. without the elements which constitute music) but simply marking the step of soldiers, can have a stirring effect if executed by forty or fifty drums alone. This is probably the proper occasion to point out the peculiar charm to the ear created by a great number of instruments of the same kind played in unison or simultaneously producing a noise. In watching the drill of infantry soldiers, one can make the observation that at such commands as "shoulder arms" or "order arms" the slight click of the metal and the dull thud of the butts dropping to the ground are not conspicuous at all if only one, two, three or even ten or twenty men are exercising; but if the command is carried out by a thousand men, the thousandfold unison of a sound insignificant in itself produces a brilliant effect. It stirs and captivates the attention, it is not unpleasant; and I even find a vague and mysterious kind of harmony in it.

Drums are also used *muffled,* like the kettledrums. Instead of covering the head with a cloth, drummers simply loosen the snares or put a leather strap between them and the lower skin, thereby checking the vibration. This gives the drums a dim and hollow sound similar to that produced by muffling the upper skin — a sound appropriate only for compositions of a mournful or awe-inspiring character.

THE TENOR DRUM

The tenor drum is somewhat longer than the ordinary drum, and its body is made of wood instead of metal. Its sound is dull and similar to that of a drum without snares, i.e. of a muffled drum. It makes quite a good effect in military music, and its subdued rolls serve as a background for the other drums. It is a tenor drum which Gluck uses in the chorus of Scythians in his "Iphigénie en Tauride" for beating the barbarous rhythm of the continuous four eighths-notes (see Example 148, p.392).

Richard Wagner employed it magnificently in the Ride of the Valkyries to produce a wild roaring effect.

THE TRIANGLE

The triangle is frequently used just as poorly as the bass drum, the cymbals, the kettledrums, the trombones—in short, all the instruments that are loud and noisy. It is even more difficult to use it properly in the orchestra than the other instruments mentioned. Its metallic sound is appropriate in forte only for compositions of extremely brilliant character, and in piano for those of a certain wild bizarreness. Weber used the triangle felicitously in the gypsy choruses of his "Preciosa"; Gluck was even more successful in his use of the instrument in the D-major part of his terrible dance of Scythians in the first act of "Iphigénie en Tauride" (Example 150).

150. IPHIGENIE EN TAURIDE, ACT I

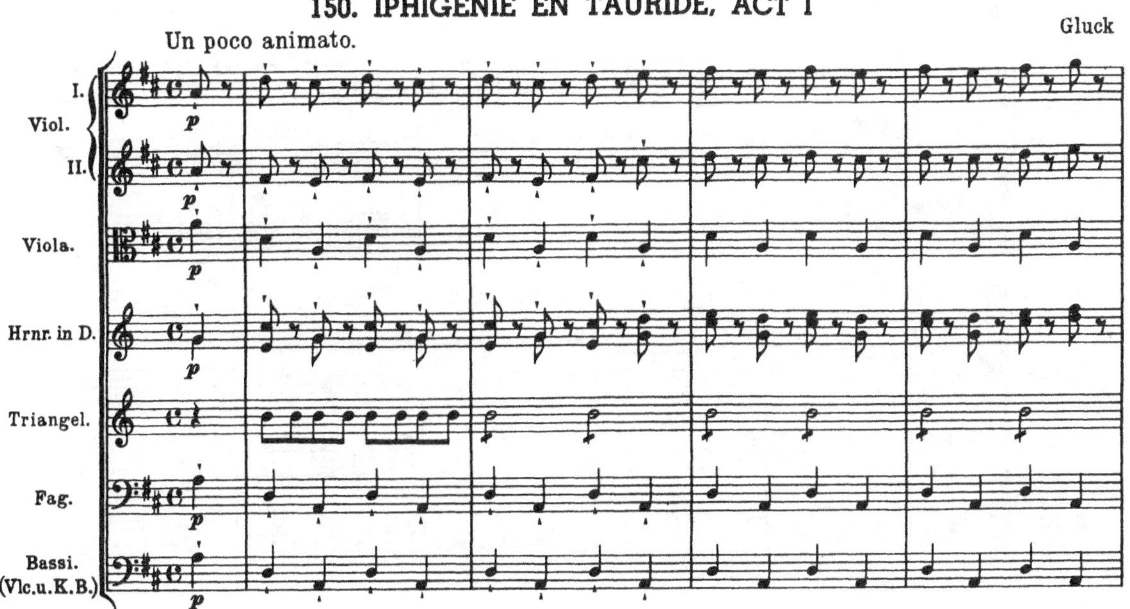

I.
Viol.
II.
Viola.
Hrnr. in D.
Triang.
Fag.
Bassi.
f
I.
Viol.
II.
Viola.
Hrnr. in D.
Triang.
Fag.
Bassi.
I.
Viol.
II.
Viola.
Hrnr. in D.
Triang.
Fag.
Bassi.

As a magnificent example of the wise application of the triangle we mention again the single triangle stroke at the end of the second act of "Siegfried"; its effect here is like that of a sun ray.

Gustav Mahler, too, employs all percussion instruments very ingeniously.

THE CRESCENT

With its numerous little bells it serves to lend added brilliance to display pieces and pompous marches of military bands. It can be shaken only at rather lengthy intervals, i.e. about twice in a bar of moderate speed.

Some more or less imperfect or unknown instruments such as the aeolidicon, the anemochord, the accordion, the Poikil organ, the ancient sistrum etc. will not be treated here. Readers desirous of knowing more about them are referred to scientific literature on the subject. Our object in this work is to acquaint the reader with only the instruments customarily used in modern music and to show him how to combine them harmoniously or to contrast them effectively, taking into account their expressive possibilities and individualities.

NEW INSTRUMENTS

The author does not consider it his duty to describe the enormous number of experiments made daily by manufacturers of musical instruments and their alleged, more or less abortive inventions; nor need he enumerate the useless objects which they try to introduce into the family of instruments. It is his duty, however, to point out to composers the really important inventions, particularly if their results have already had some general approval or practical application. The number of successful inventors is very small; Messrs. Adolphe Sax and Alexandre are outstanding among them.

M. Sax - whose creations shall occupy us first - has improved a number of older instruments (as has been mentioned frequently in the course of this work). He has also filled several gaps in the family of brass instruments. His principal contribution, however, lies in the creation of a new family of brass instruments with single reeds and clarinet mouthpieces which he completed only a few years ago.

These are the *saxophones*. These newly gained orchestral voices have rare and valuable qualities. In the high range they are soft yet penetrating; in the low range they are full and rich, and in the middle range they are very expressive. On the whole it is a timbre quite its own, vaguely similar to that of the violoncello, the clarinet and the English horn with a half-metallic admixture which gives it an altogether peculiar expression.

The body of the instrument is a parabolic cone of brass with a system of keys. Agile, suited just as well for rapid passages as for soft melodies and for religious and dreamy effects, saxophones can be used in any kind of music; but they are particulary suited to slow and tender compositions.

The high tones of low saxophones have a plaintive and sorrowful character; their low tones, however, have a sublime and, as it were, priestly calm. All saxophones, especially the baritone and bass, can swell and diminish their sound; this permits entirely new and quite peculiar sound effects in the extremely low range, which bear some resemblance to the tones of the "expressive organ". The sound of the high saxophones is much more penetrating than that of the clarinets in B♭ and C without having the sharp and often piercing tone of the small clarinet in E♭. The same can be said of the soprano saxophone. Ingenious composers are going to achieve wonderful, still unpredictable effects by joining the saxophones with the clarinet family or by means of other combinations.

The instrument can be played very easily, its fingering being similar to that of the flute and oboe. Players familiar with the clarinet embouchure will master its mechanism within a short time.

THE SAXOPHONES

There are six kinds: the *high, soprano, alto, tenor, baritone* and *bass* saxophones. M. Sax is about to produce a seventh one: the *double-bass* saxophone. The range of all these is about the same. The following list shows the extreme points of their scales, written—as proposed by Sax and already adopted by composers—in the G-clef for all instruments.

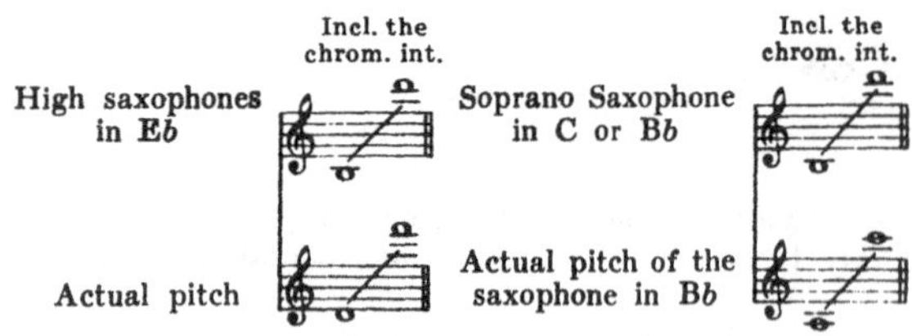

Major and minor thrills are practicable almost over the entire scale of the saxophones; only the following should be avoided:

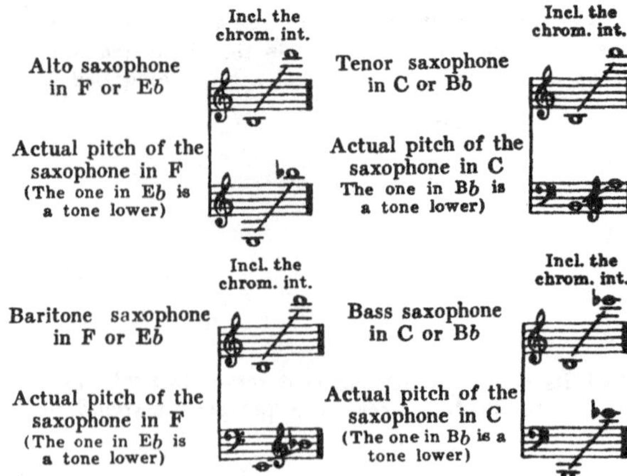

M. Sax also created the families of *saxhorns, saxotrombas* and *saxtubas,* brass instruments with cup-formed, wide mouthpieces and with a mechanism of three, four or five cylinders.

SAXHORNS

Their tone is round, pure, full and completely even over the whole range of their scale. The different keys of the saxhorn proceed, as those of the cornet, downwards from the main instrument - the small, very high saxhorn in C, an octave higher than the cornet in C. In France it is customary to write all these instruments, as well as the saxotrombas and saxtubas - the highest as well as the lowest - in the G-clef similary to the horns, with the sole difference that the actual sound of some very low Sax-instruments is not one octave lower than the note writen in the G-clef (as with the horn in low C), but two octaves lower.

The small, very high saxhorn exists in two keys, C and B♭:

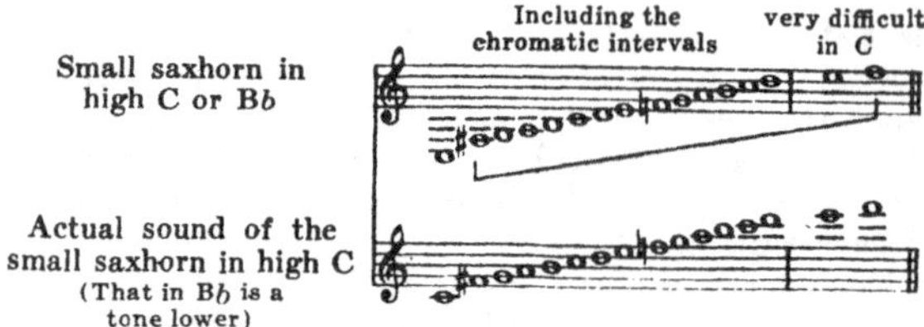

The extremely low tones do not sound well, and the instrument should hardly be used below the low A. On the other hand, all the tones of the higher octave are very brilliant, pure and - in spite of their power - free of any sharpness. Moreover, the tone of the small saxhorn is so clear and penetrating that a single high saxhorn stands out distinctly from the midst of a considerable number of other wind instruments. The high saxhorn in B♭ is more frequent than the one in C. Although it is a tone lower than the latter, its two highest tones

are rather difficult and require great care in playing. They should be used very sparingly and with caution.

The first tone of the other saxhorns (their lowest natural tone) is of such poor quality that it cannot be used. It has been omitted in the following table. We must also mention that the chromatic range of the soprano saxhorn is extended beyond F# down to C if instruments with four cylinders are used.

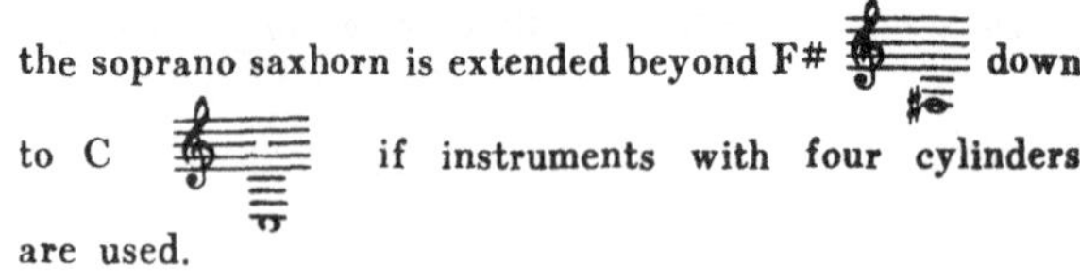

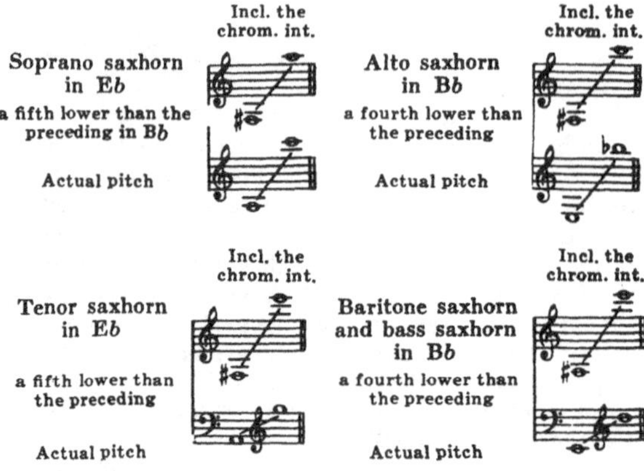

The baritone and bass saxhorns have the same upper range, but the tube of the baritone saxhorn is a little smaller. The bass saxhorn, which has almost always four cylinders, can reach the low tones more easily because of its wider tube.

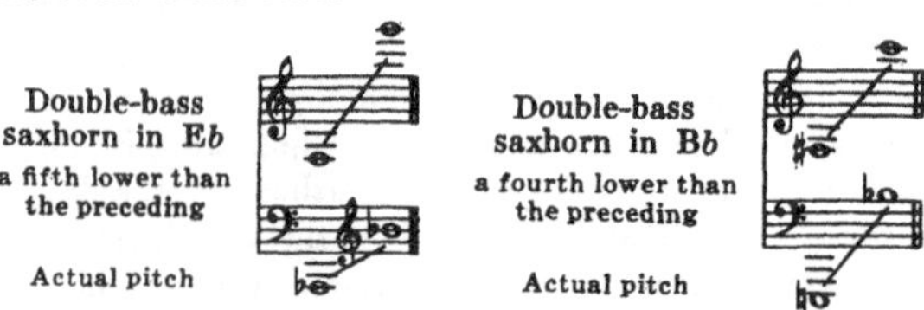

In addition, there is the double-bass saxhorn in low E♭ and the drone saxhorn in B♭, both an octave lower than the preceding ones; only their medium tones are usable, and those only in moderate tempo.

SAXOTROMBAS

These are brass instruments with cup-formed mouthpieces and three, four or five cylinders, like the preceding. Their narrower tube gives them a shrill timbre, somewhat similar to that of the trumpets and, at the same time, of the bugles.

The saxotromba family has as many members as that of the saxhorns. They stand in the same relation to each other and have the same range.

THE SAXTUBAS

These are instruments with cup-formed mouthpieces and a mechanism of three cylinders. They have tremendous sonority and their sound carries very far; hence, they are extremely effective in open-air bands.

They are to be treated exactly like saxhorns except that one must keep in mind the fact that the double-bass in E^b and the drone in B^b are missing. Their evenly rounded shape recalls that of the large ancient trumpets.

THE CONCERTINA

This is a small instrument with metal tongues which are vibrated by a stream of air. The *concertina* and later the *melodium* developed from the accordion, which was popular as a musical toy for a number of years. The timbre of the concertina is penetrating and soft at the same time; in spite of its weakness it carries quite far. It combines well with that of the harp and the pianoforte, and still better with that of the melodium, the present head of this family. This latter combination, however, would be of little use because the sound of the melodium is too similar to that of the concertina and produces the same effects as well as some additional ones not possible on the concertina.

The concertina is a small expansible box, held horizontally between both hands and compressed and expanded alternatingly. It is played by means of buttons which, when pressed with the finger tips, open valves which admit a stream of air to a series of metal tongues. The air is furnished by bellows between the two side-walls of the instrument, which carry the buttons on the outside and the vibrating tongues inside. The bellows, having no valve, can be filled and emptied only through the valves of the metal tongues, which inhale and exhale the air necessary for the vibration of these tongues.

Besides being related to the melodium, the concertina has a complete, small family of its own. There is a *bass, alto* and *soprano* concertina. The bass concertina has the range of the violoncello, the alto concertina that of the viola, and the soprano concertina that of the violin. The soprano concertina is almost the only one in use. Owing to the popularity of this instrument in England, it is also called the English concertina. In the first three octaves of the two chromatic scales—one of which is played on the right side, the other on the left side of the instrument (cf. the table of ranges below)—the manufacturer established enharmonic intervals between the A^b and G# and between E^b and D# by giving the A^b and E^b a somewhat higher pitch than the G# and D#; this is in accordance with acoustical theory but contrary to musical practice. It is a strange anomaly.

Being an instrument with fixed tones like the pianoforte, the organ and the melodium, the concertina should, of course, be tuned in equal temperament like these instruments. Because of the enharmonic tones it cannot be played in its present state together with these other instruments without producing dissonances as soon as the melodic phrase or the harmony cause unisons between the enharmonic A^b or G#, or E^b or D# of the concertina with the same, but well-tempered tones of the other instrument. On the instruments with equal temperament A^b and G# as well as E^b and D# are identical; not so on the concertina. Neither of the enharmonic tones A^b and G# of the concertina is in strict unison with the A^b or G# of the well-tempered instrument, which holds the mid-point between the two tones of the concertina.

The different tuning of a part of its scale becomes still more annoying if the concertina plays together with an instrument with movable tones such as the violin. Musical practice, musical feeling and the ear of all peoples cultivating modern music demand that in certain cases the leading tones, which are drawn upward to the higher tonic, become slightly higher than in the well-tempered scale, and that correspondingly the minor seventh and ninth, drawn downward toward the tones into which they resolve, are made slightly lower.

In the following passage, for instance,

the slightly sharp G# of the violin would not be in tune with the somewhat flat G# of the concertina. Likewise in this passage

the flat A^b of the violin would not correspond with the sharp A^b of the concertina (each player following a law diametrically opposed to that of the other - on the one hand the law of the calculation of vibrations and on the other the purely musical law). To effect strict unison, the violinist would have to adapt his tones to the fixed ones of the other instrument; he would have to play off pitch. This is actually done, but to a lesser degree—unconsciously and without offending the ear—when the violin plays with a pianoforte or with other well-tempered instruments. To be sure, the system of the English concertina might be reconciled with the system of raised leading tones and of lowered sevenths by a very odd procedure, namely, by doing the opposite of what acousticians think should be done about enharmonic tones: one would have to play A^b instead of G# and vice versa. The violinist, executing the following phrase musically,

would be almost in unison with the concertina playing according to this absurd notation:

The old presumption of acousticians to impose the results of their calculations upon the practice of art is no longer tenable; for musical practice is based above all on the study of the impressions by tones on the human ear.

It is certain that music must reject them if it wants to exist at all. It is equally certain that the customary modifications of intervals between two mutually attractive tones constitute extremely subtle shadings employed with the greatest care by virtuosos and singers and generally avoided by orchestral players, and that they require special treatment by composers.

Finally, it is certain that the great majority of musicians instinctively abstain from them in harmonic ensemble playing. Consequently, tones called incompatible by acousticians are entirely congenial in musical practice; relations found by calculation to be false are accepted as true by the ear, which completely disregards these very tiny differences—the opinions of mathematicians notwithstanding. There is hardly any modern score without melodic or harmonic passages written—to facilitate execution or for some other reason, frequently also without any reason at all—in a sharp key for one part of the orchestra and in a flat key for the other.

EXAMPLES:

Melodically:

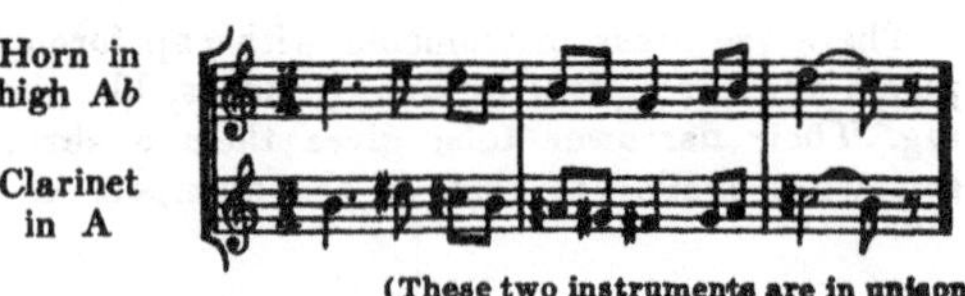

(These two instruments are in unison)

Seemingly in two different keys, of which only two tones are enharmonically related, as in this passage from Weber's "Freischuetz":

The violoncellos and double-basses seem to play in G minor with the trombones in B^b minor.

In the latter example one would doubtless notice if the violoncellos and double-basses played their F# too high and the trombones their G^b too low. But this must not happen in a good performance; the two tones will be in perfect unison in spite of their opposing tendencies. In these and many other cases the orchestra becomes one large well-tempered instrument without the players being aware of it.

In the celebrated chorus of demons in his "Orfeo," Gluck established an enharmonic relation between two parts in an indefinite key. I mean the passage about which J. J. Rousseau and others have written so much nonsense based on the supposed difference between G^b and F#.

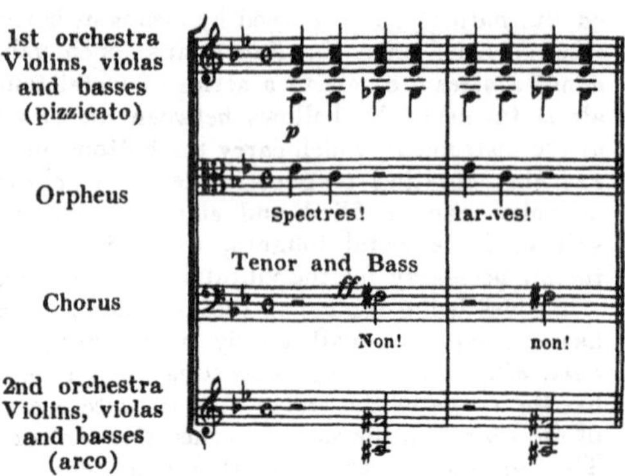

If it were a fact that the F# of the chorus and the pizzicato G^b of the basses are executed differently, an intolerable and unmusical dissonance, highly offensive to the ear, would result. In reality this phrase makes a deeply stirring and entirely musical impression upon the hearer, awakening in him feelings of terror and awe. It is true that he does not know what key he is hearing — B^b minor or G minor; but he does not care. His ear is by no means offended by the combination of the different instrumental and vocal parts. The tremendous effect of the F# of the chorus and orchestra is based on the unexpected introduction of this tone and on the strange character it has within an indefinite key, but not on the alleged, harsh dissonance with the G^b. It needs a naive ignorance of the effects of combined sounds not to understand that this dissonance cannot possibly be the cause of the impression, since the G^b, played pizzicato and piano by only a few basses, is necessarily covered or rather extinguished by the sudden entry of fifty or sixty men's voices in unison and by the entire body of stringed instruments playing the F# fortissimo (coll'arco).

These insipid discussions, this idle talk of littérateurs, these absurd deductions of theoreticians, all of whom are possessed with a mania of speaking and writing about an art concerning which they know nothing, can only amuse musicians. Nevertheless, it is a pity; erudition, eloquence and genius ought always to command the admiration and respect due to them.

After this long digression I return to the English concertina; this is its barbaric scale:

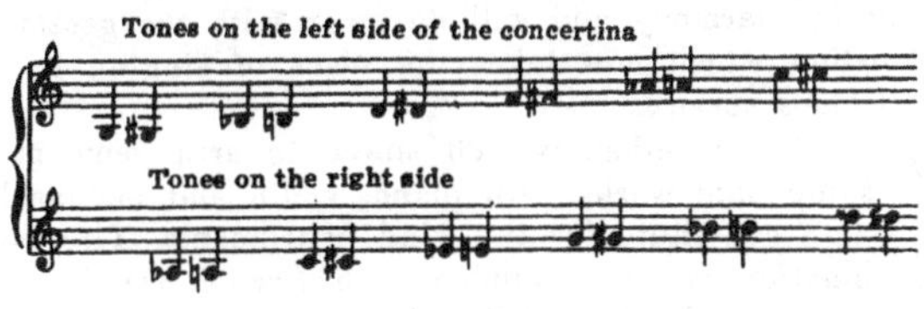

Notwithstanding the arrangement of the preceding example, the concertina is written on a single stave and in the G-clef. The trill is practicable on all steps of the scale, but it is more difficult in the lower range. The double trill (in thirds) is easy. Rather rapid diatonic, chromatic and arpeggiated passages can be executed on this instrument. It is possible to add to the main voice a second one moving approximately parallel with the melody, but not several complicated voices as on the pianoforte and organ. One can also play chords of four to six and even more tones:

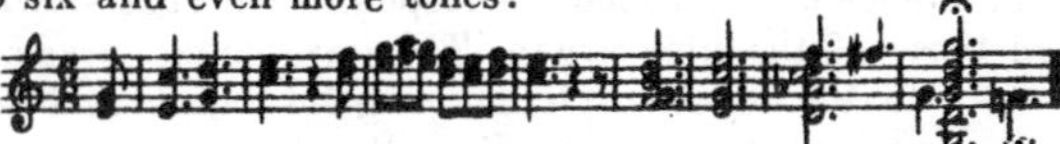

The *German* concertina—popular also in England—is not constructed according to the system of the preceding. Its scale, which extends lower, to C and B♭:

has no enharmonic intervals; it is tuned in equal temperament.

The range of concertinas depends on the number of buttons or keys, and this changes according to the manufacturer's whims. Finally, this instrument — like the guitar — requires that the composer who wants to use it successfully should know its mechanism thoroughly and be able to play it more or less adequately.

THE MELODIUM ORGAN BY ALEXANDRE

(The American Organ, The Harmonium)

This is a keyboard instrument, like the pipe organ. Its sound, like that of the concertina, is produced by delicate metal tongues over which passes a stream of air. This stream of air is caused by a bellows and set in motion by the player's feet. The tones of the instrument are stronger or weaker according to the force with which the feet act on the mechanism of the bellows.

Hence, the melodium organ possesses the crescendo and the decrescendo; it is *expressive*. One of its special mechanisms is therefore called "Régistre d'Expression." The fingering is the same as that on the organ and pianoforte. One writes for it on two or even three staves, as for the organ. It has a range of five octaves.

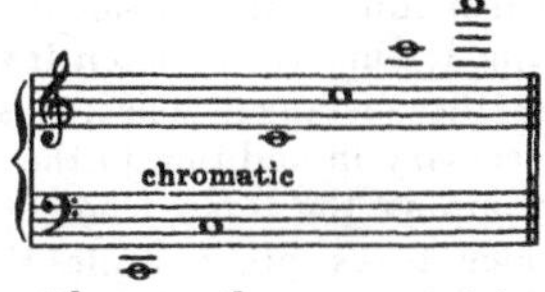

Melodiums with more than one register are not limited to this range. The number of registers varies considerably.

The simplest melodium with only one register, whose range we have just indicated, has two different kinds of tone—that of the *English horn* in the left half of the keyboard and that of the *flute* in the right half. The instruments with several registers may have—according to the intentions of the manufacturer—*bassoon, cornett, flute, clarinet, fife,* and *oboe* registers, so called because of their similarity with the instruments after which they are named; also the *Grand Jeu* (full organ), the *forte* and *expressive* registers. These give the melodium a range of seven octaves although its keyboard has only five.

The player puts these registers into action by means of a mechanism similar to that of the organ; it is arranged at both sides of the keyboard and has wooden handles which are pulled out by either hand. Several other stops are obtained by a similar mechanism beneath the body of the instrument, which is moved from right to left or from left to right by the knee of the performer.

The melodium does not possess the mixture stops of the organ, whose effect excites a traditional admiration in many people, while in reality they cause terrible confusion. The melodium has only single and double octave stops, by means of which each key can play, in addition to its own tone, the single and double octave, or the double octave without the single, or even the higher and lower octaves of this tone.

Many ignorant players and lovers of noise make lamentable use of these octave stops. This crude method is, to be sure, not as bad as the mischief done with the mixture stops of the organ; for there the two other tones of the common chord are heard at the same time (the major third and the fifth); but it remains crude just the same.

The resulting, unintended inversions of the chords introduce the most frightful disorder into the harmony (to say nothing of the thickening of the harmonic texture). Ninths are transformed into seconds and sevenths, seconds become sevenths and ninths, fifths become fourths and vice versa, and so on. To preserve true musical relations with these stops, they should be used only in pieces written in double counterpoint in the octave; but this is not done.

The introduction of these monstrosities into the organ is doubtless to be ascribed to the ignorance of the middle ages, groping blindly for the laws of harmony. They were preserved by senseless convention, and it is to be hoped that they will gradually disappear.

The tones of the melodium respond somewhat slowly, like those of the pipe organ. They are suited predominantly to the legato style of religious music and for slow, soft and tender melodies. Pieces with skipping rhythms or of violent character, written for the melodium or played on it, attest in my opinion to the ignorance of the composer or to the poor taste of the performer, or to the ignorance and tastelessness of both.

The real object aimed at and achieved by M. Alexandre was to give the melodium a dreamy, religious character and to endow it with all the shadings of the human voice and of most instruments.

The melodium is at once an instrument for the church and for the theater, for the drawing-room and for the concert hall. It occupies little space and is easily movable; hence, it is of indisputable utility to composers and amateurs. Since Meyerbeer, Halévy and Verdi have used the organ in their dramatic works, how many provincial theaters of France and even Germany have found difficulties in performing these works, and how many mutilations and more or less clumsy rearrangements of the scores have been caused by the lack of an organ! Nowadays theater managers have no longer an excuse to tolerate this, for the missing organ can be replaced easily and at moderate cost by the melodium.

The same applies to small churches where music hitherto has not been available at all. A melody played there by a sensitive musician can and will awaken a feeling for harmony and will do away with the grotesque howling which now takes the place of singing in the religious service.

The melodium is well suited to arrangements of symphonic works with piano, violin and violoncello, as a substitute for the wind instruments. This combination is very popular with French families for house music; it is definitely preferable to the piano duets customary in Germany.

PIANOFORTES AND MELODIUMS WITH PROLONGED SOUNDS

(By Alexandre)

The prolongation of sound is the most important invention by which keyboard instruments have been improved in recent times. It can be applied to the pianoforte as well as to the melodium and enables the player to prolong at will a tone, a chord or an arpeggio—within the entire range of the keyboard — after the hands have ceased pressing the keys. During this prolongation of a number of tones the performer can not only play with his free hands other tones which do not belong to the sustained chord, but can even replay the same sustained tones again. It is obvious how many different and charming combinations have been made possible by this invention on the melodium and pianoforte. These are real orchestral effects, similar in character to those produced by string instruments playing four or five different voices within a harmony sustained by wind instruments (flutes, oboes and clarinets) or, still better, like wind instruments playing a phrase in several voices during a sustained harmony of the divided violins, or finally like harmony and melody moving above or below a pedal point.

This prolongation of tones can take place in varying dynamic degrees, according to the register employed.

Under the keyboard of instruments furnished with this innovation two knee levers are attached so that they can be moved by slight pressure of the performer's knees; one, on the right side, effects the prolongation of tones on the right half of the keyboard; the other acts similarly on the left side. The motion of the knee must take place simultaneously with the pressing down of the keys whose tones are to be sustained, e.g.

A second pressure of the knee instantaneously stops the sustained tones:

Although the second pressure stops the prolongation produced by the first, it can at the same time start a new prolongation if one or several new keys are struck simultaneously.

If a single tone of a short chord is to be prolonged, the knee motion takes place only after the fingers have released the keys of the tones which are not to be sustained, while still holding for a moment the key of the tone to be sustained; only then the entire hand becomes free. To change the sustained tones, a series of these movements is necessary in addition to the supplementary movement for stopping the tones whose prolongation is not desired, which takes place while the key of the tone to be sustained is still pressed down.

This applies equally to both halves of the keyboard (by means of the left-hand and right-hand mechanism), and to the pianoforte as well as to the melodium.

When writing sustained tones for the pianoforte or for the melodium organ one must use at least three staves, sometimes even four. In the latter case, the upper stave is reserved for the high and medium sustained tones and the lowest stave for the low ones. The two middle staves serve for the parts executed by both hands.

THE OCTOBASS

M. Villaume, a violin maker in Paris, whose excellent violins are much in demand, has enriched the family of stringed instruments by a beautiful and mighty member: the octobass.

This instrument is not, as many people believe, the lower octave of the double-bass, but that of the violoncello; it can reach only the third below the E of the four-stringed double-bass.

It has only three strings, tuned in the fifth and fourth:

Since the fingers of the left hand are neither long nor strong enough to press down the strings (for the octobass is of colossal size), Villaume devised a system of movable keys which press the strings forcefully upon the frets placed on the neck of the instrument to produce whole tones and semitones. These keys are moved by levers which the left hand seizes and draws up and down behind the neck of the bass, and by seven other pedal keys which are moved by the players foot.

Of course, the octobass cannot execute rapid successions of tones and must be given a separate part, differing in many aspects from that of the double-basses. Its range is only an octave and a fifth.

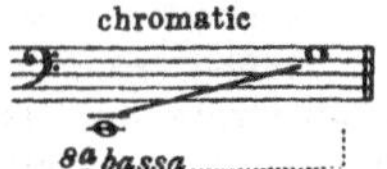

This instrument has tones of strange power and beauty, full and strong, without any roughness. It could produce extraordinary effects in a large orchestra. At least three should be available for music festivals if the number of instruments is greater than 150.

We shall not contest here the opinion of those who consider the new inventions of instrument makers harmful to musical art. These inventions exercise the same influence in their field as all other achievements of civilization. The fact that they can be and are frequently misused does not disprove their actual value.

THE ORCHESTRA

The orchestra may be considered a large instrument capable of playing a great number of different tones simultaneously or in succession; its power is moderate or gigantic according to the proportionate use of all or only part of the resources available to the modern orchestra, and according to the more or less propitious application of these resources in relation to acoustic conditions of various type.

It is also regulated by the degree to which the inner power of the themes involved not only justifies, but actually demands the full application of physical resources.

The performers of all sorts, constituting together the orchestra, are, so to speak, its strings, tubes, pipes, sounding boards—machines endowed with intelligence, but subject to the action of an immense keyboard played by the conductor under the direction of the composer.

I believe I have already stated my conviction that the invention of beautiful orchestral effects cannot be taught. Although this faculty can be developed by practice and rational observation, it belongs to those precious gifts which the composer, at once a poet and an inspired calculator, must have received from nature, similarly to talent for melody, expression, and even for harmony.

But it is certainly easy to indicate quite precisely *how to form an orchestra* capable of faithfully rendering compositions in all forms and dimensions.

A distinction should be made between theater and concert orchestras. In certain respects theater orchestras are inferior to concert orchestras.

The placing of the musicians is of great importance; whether they are arranged on a horizontal or an inclined platform, in a space enclosed on three sides, or in the middle of the hall; whether there are reflectors and whether these have hard surfaces (throwing back the sound) or soft ones (absorbing and breaking it); how close the reflectors are to the performers—all this is of extraordinary consequence.

Reflectors are indispensable. They are found, in various forms, in every enclosed place. The closer they are to the source of sound the greater is their effect. This is why there is no such thing as music in the open air. The largest orchestra, playing in a garden open on all sides—such as the Jardin des Tuileries—must remain completely ineffective. Even if it were placed close to the walls of the palace, the reflection would be insufficient; the sound would be immediately lost in all directions.

An orchestra of a thousand wind instruments and a chorus of two thousand voices, placed in an open plain, would be far less effective than an ordinary orchestra of eighty players and a chorus of a hundred voices arranged in the concert hall of the Conservatoire. The brilliant effect produced by military bands in some streets of big cities confirms this statement, in spite of the seeming contradiction. Here the music is by no means in the open air: the walls of high buildings lining the street on both sides, the avenues of trees, the facades of big palaces, near-by monuments—all these serve as reflectors. The sound is thrown back and remains for some time within the circumscribed space before finally escaping through the few gaps in the enclosure. But as soon as the band reaches an open plain without buildings and trees on its march from the large street, the tones diffuse, the orchestra disappears, and there is no more music.

The best way of placing an orchestra in a hall sufficiently large for the number of players used, is to arrange them in rows one above the other on a series of steps in such a fashion that each row can send its tones to the listeners without any intervening obstacles. Every well-directed orchestra should thus be arranged in echelons. If it plays on the stage of a theater the scene should be enclosed by wooden walls in the rear, at the sides and above.

Shells are bad if they seat only half the orchestra, while the other half is placed in front of the shell. Pear-shaped concert halls are the best.

On the other hand, if the orchestra is placed at one end of a hall or in a church and if, as frequently happens, the massive rear wall reflects with too much force and hardness the sound of the instruments closest to it, the excessive reverberation can easily be diminished by hanging a number of draperies or by placing other suitable objects there which serve to break the sound waves.

The architecture of our theaters and the requirements of dramatic representation make this ampitheatrical arrangement impossible for opera orchestras. Their members are condemmed to play at the lowest point of the hall, on a horizontal plane, immediately in front of the footlights; thus, they are deprived of most of the advantages resulting from the arrangement of the concert orchestra suggested by me. This is why so many effects are lost, so many fine shadings remain unnoticed in opera orchestras, in spite of the best execution. The difference is so great that composers must take it into account; they should not score their dramatic works in the same fashion as their symphonies, masses or oratorios.

In the past the number of string instruments in opera orchestras was always in correct proportion to that of the other instruments; but for some years this has no longer been the case. A comic-opera orchestra which had only two flutes, two oboes, two clarinets, two French horns, two bassoons, rarely two trumpets and hardly ever any kettledrums, was well balanced with nine first violins, eight second violins, six violas, seven violoncellos and six double-basses. Nowadays, however, with four horns, three trombones, two trumpets, a bass drum and kettledrums, but still with the same number of string instruments, the balance is completely destroyed. The violins are scarcely audible, and the total effect is extremely unsatisfactory.

The Bayreuth orchestra has 16 first violins, 16 second violins, 12 violas, 12 violoncellos and 8 double-basses.

The orchestra for grand opera which has—besides the wind instruments already named—two cornets and an ophicleide, various percussion instruments and sometimes six or eight harps, is equally unbalanced with 12 first violins, 11 second violins, 8 violas, 10 violoncellos and 8 double-basses. There should be at least 15 first violins, 14 second violins, 10 violas and 12 violoncellos, although not all of them need be used in works with very soft accompaniments.

The make-up of the comic-opera orchestra would be sufficient for a concert orchestra intended for the performance of Haydn's and Mozart's symphonies. A greater number of stringed instruments might even be too strong in some instances for the tender effects which these masters frequently assign to flutes, oboes and bassoons.

On the other hand, Beethoven's symphonies, Weber's overtures and more modern compositions in the monumental or passionate style require the number of stringed instruments just indicated for grand opera.

Yet the finest concert orchestra—for a hall scarcely larger than that of the Conservatoire, the most complete, the richest in shadings and tone colors, the most majestic, the most powerful and at the same time the most mellow, would be composed as follows:

21 first violins
20 second violins
18 violas
8 first violoncellos
7 second violoncellos
10 double-basses
4 harps
2 small flutes
2 large flutes
2 oboes
1 English horn
2 clarinets
1 basset-horn or 1 bass clarinet
4 bassoons
4 valve horns
2 valve trumpets
2 cornets with pistons (or cylinders)
3 trombones (1 alto, 2 tenor or 3 tenor trombones)
1 bass trombone
1 ophicleide in B♭ (or 1 bass tuba)
2 pairs of kettledrums with 4 drummers
1 bass drum
1 pair of cymbals

This has to be modified by including two English horns instead of one, eight valve horns instead of four, and perhaps two additional clarinets in D or E♭, a double-bass clarinet, a double-bassoon and four tubas.

It is generally indispensable to double the woodwind in forte or where it has important themes.

For a choral work such an orchestra would require:

46 sopranos (first and second)
40 tenors (first and second)
40 basses (first and second)

By doubling or tripling this mass of performers in the same proportion one could doubtless obtain a magnificent orchestra for a music festival. But it would be an error to assume that all orchestras must be composed according to this system, which is based on the preponderance of the strings; the opposite plan may bring very beautiful results, too. In this case the string instruments, too weak to dominate the mass of clarinets and brass instruments, serve as a harmonious link between the brilliant tones of the brass, sometimes softening their sharp sound, sometimes stimulating their movement with a tremolo which even transforms drumrolls into music by blending with them.

Commonsense tells us that the composer—unless he is forced to employ a particular kind of orchestra—must adapt the number of performers to the character and style of his work and to the principal effects demanded by its ideas. In a Requiem, for instance, I have employed four small bands (trumpets, trombones, cornets and ophicleides) placed seperately at the four corners of the main orchestra, in order to render musically the monumental images of the hymn of the dead. The main orchestra consists of an imposing body of stringed instruments, of the rest of the wind instruments doubled and tripled, and of eight pairs of differently tuned kettledrums played by ten drummers. It is certain that the peculiar effects achieved by this new kind of orchestra would be impossible with any other combination.

In this connection I want to mention the importance of the different points of origin of the tonal masses. Certain groups of an orchestra are selected by the composer to question and answer each other; but this design becomes clear and effective only if the groups which are to carry on the dialogue are placed at a sufficient distance from each other. The composer must therefore indicate in his score their exact disposition. For instance, the drums, bass drums, cymbals and kettledrums may remain together if they are employed, as usual, to strike certain rhythms simultaneously. But if they execute an interlocutory rhythm, one fragment of which is given to the bass drums and cymbals, the other to kettledrums and drums, the effect would be greatly improved and intensified by placing the two groups of percussion instruments at the opposite ends of the orchestra, i.e. at a considerable distance from each other. Hence, the constant uniformity of orchestral groups is one of the greatest obstacles to the creation of monumental and truly original works. This uniformity is preserved by composers more out of habit, laziness and thoughtlessness than for reasons of economy,

This situation is still the same even today.

although the latter motive is, unfortunately, also a rather important one. This is especially the case in France, where music is so far from forming a part of national life, where the government does everything possible for the theater but nothing for music itself, where capitalists readily pay fifty thousand francs and more for a painting by some great master (*because it represents a value*), but will not spare fifty francs to organize an annual music festival worthy of our nation, which would display the numerous musical resources which we own but do not use!

Yet it would be interesting to try once to combine all musical forces available in Paris for the performance of a work especially composed for such an occasion. If this combination were put at the disposal of a master, in a hall built for this purpose by an architect with a good knowledge of acoustics and music, the composer would have to determine the exact plan and arrangement of this gigantic orchestra and then design his work accordingly. Where such an immense body is to be used, it is obviously of the greatest importance to consider the greater or smaller distance of the various groups from each other. This is indispensable if one wants to derive full advantage from this orchestra and to calculate with certainty the scope of the different effects.

At past music festivals only ordinary orchestras and choruses were heard, quadrupled or quintupled according to the number of performers available. But the orchestra proposed here would be entirely different. The composer trying to employ the extraordinary and enormous resources of such an instrument would have to solve an entirely new problem.

Here, then, is how this could be achieved in Paris—with the necessary outlay of time, money and effort. The arrangement of the groups would be determined by the wishes and intentions of the composers. The percussion instruments, which exercise an irresistible influence on the rhythm and always lag when they are far from the conductor, should be placed as close to him as possible to be able to follow the slightest change of measure or tempo instantaneously and strictly.

120 violins, divided into two, three or four groups
40 violas, divided into first and seconds, if necessary; at least 10 of the players able to play the viola d'amore
45 violoncellos, divided into firsts and seconds, if necessary
18 double-basses with three strings, tuned in fifths (G, D, A)
15 other double-basses with four strings, tuned in fourths (E, A, D, G)
4 octobasses
6 large flutes
4 flutes in E*b*
2 octave piccolo flutes
2 piccolo flutes in D*b*
6 oboes
6 English horns
5 saxophones
4 tenoroons
12 bassoons
4 small clarinets (in E*b*)
8 clarinets (in C or B*b* or A)
3 bass clarinets in Bb
16 French horns (6 with valves)
8 trumpets
6 cornets
4 alto trombones
6 tenor trombones
2 bass trombones
1 ophicleide in C
2 ophicleides in B*b*
2 bass tubas
30 harps
30 pianofortes
1 very low positive organ with at least a 16′ stop
8 pairs of kettledrums (10 drummers)
6 drums
3 bass drums
4 pairs of cymbals
6 triangles
6 sets of small bells
12 pairs of ancient cymbals (in different keys)
2 large, very low bells
2 gongs
4 crescents

465 instrumentalists

40 children sopranos (first and second)
100 women sopranos (first and second)
100 tenors (first and second)
120 basses (first and second)

360 chorus singers

As one sees, the chorus does not predominate in this ensemble of 825 performers; even so, it would be difficult to assemble 360 suitable voices in Paris—so little is the study of singing cultivated in this city.

Every time this entire mass is put in action, a broad and monumental style must be adopted; tender effects, light and fast movements are assigned to smaller orchestras, which the composer can easily form out of this multitude and employ in musical dialogues.

Besides the radiant colors which this myriad of different sounds could conjure at any moment, unheard-of harmonic effects could be produced—as follows:

by dividing the 120 violins into eight or ten parts supported by the high tones of the forty violas—seraphic, ethereal expression in *pianissimo;*

by dividing the violoncellos and double-basses in the low range and in slow movements—melancholy, religious expression in *mezzoforte;*

by combining the lowest tones of the clarinet family into a small band—gloomy expression in *forte* and *mezzoforte;*

by combining the low tones of oboes, English horns, tenoroons and large flutes into a small band—expression of pious mourning in *piano;*

by combining the low tones of ophicleides, bass tubas and French horns into a small band, joined with the pedal tones of the tenor trombones, the lowest of the bass trombones and the 16′ stop of the organ—profoundly grave, religious and calm expression in *piano;*

by combining the highest tones of the small clarinets, flutes and piccolos into a small band—shrill expression in *forte;*

by combining the French horns, trumpets, cornets, trombones and ophicleides into a small band—pompous and brilliant expression in *forte;*

by combining the 30 harps with the entire mass of stringed instruments playing pizzicato into a large orchestra, thus forming a new gigantic harp with 934 strings—graceful, brilliant and voluptuous expression in all shadings;

by combining the 30 pianofortes with the 6 sets of small bells, the 12 pairs of ancient cymbals, the 6 triangles (which might be tuned in different keys like cymbals) and the 4 crescents into a metallic percussion orchestra—gay and brilliant expression in *mezzoforte;*

by combining the 8 pairs of kettledrums with the 6 drums and the 3 bass drums into a small, almost exclusively rhythmic percussion orchestra—menacing expression in all shadings;

by combining the 2 gongs, the 2 bells and the 3 large cymbals with certain chords of the trombones—sad and sinister expression in *mezzoforte.*

Who could envisage all the instrumental combinations which would result if each of these groups were joined with another similar or contrasting group?

There could be formed: grand duets between the wind instruments and the stringed instruments;

between one of these two and the chorus; between the chorus and the harps and pianofortes alone;

a grand trio between the chorus in unison and in the octave, the wind instruments in unison and in the octave, and the violins, violas and violoncellos likewise in unison and in the octave;

the same trio, accompanied by a rhythmic motif executed by all the percussion instruments, the double-basses, harps and pianofortes;

a single, double or triple chorus without accompaniment;

a melody for the combined violins, violas and violoncellos, or for the combined wood-wind, or for the combined brass, accompanied by a vocal orchestra;

a melody for the sopranos or tenors or basses, or for all voices in the octave, accompanied by an instrumental orchestra;

a small chorus, accompanied by the large chorus and some instruments;

a small orchestra, accompanied by the large orchestra and some voices;

a solemn melody executed by all bowed basses and accompanied above by the divided violins, the harps and pianofortes;

a solemn melody executed by the wind basses and the organ and accompanied above by flutes, oboes, clarinets and divided violins;

and so on, and so forth.

The method of rehearsal for such a gigantic orchestra would, of course, be the same as that employed for complex and monumental works offering difficulties in performance—i.e. the method of partial rehearsals. In this analytical task the conductor would have to proceed as follows:

I take for granted that he knows the work to be performed *thoroughly* and *in its minutest details*. First he would appoint two assistant conductors who are to beat the time during the general rehearsals, keeping their eyes continually upon him, in order to transmit the tempo to the groups too far removed from the center.

{ (The optical telegraph is still the best.)

Then he would designate coaches for each of the different instrumental and vocal groups.

He would now study with these coaches and instruct them how to rehearse the parts assigned to them.

The first coach would rehearse the first and second sopranos—first separately, then together.

The second coach would proceed with the first and second tenors in the same fashion; likewise the third with the basses. After this, three choruses will be formed, each composed of one-third of the entire chorus. Finally the entire chorus would rehearse together.

In these choral rehearsals an organ or a pianoforte supported by a few string instruments (violins and basses) could be used for the accompaniment.

The assistant conductors and coaches of the orchestra would rehearse separately in the same fashion:

1. the first and second violins—separately, then together;
2. the violas, violoncellos and double-basses—separately and together;
3. all the stringed instruments;
4. the harps alone;
5. the pianofortes alone;
6. the harps and pianofortes together;
7. the wood-wind instruments alone;
8. the brass instruments alone;
9. all the wind instruments together;
10. the percussion instruments alone, with special attention to the tuning of the kettledrums;
11. the percussion and wind instruments together;
12. finally the entire vocal and instrumental body together under the direction of the main conductor.

This procedure would, first, result in an excellent performance such as could never be obtained by the old method of rehearsing with all performers at once;

{ (now almost generally and rightly abandoned)

and, secondly, it would require each performer for not more than four rehearsals. As many tuning forks as possible should be distributed among the members of the orchestra; this is the only way in which the accurate tuning of such a multitude of instruments, so different in character and temperament, could be insured.

General prejudice charges large orchestras with being *noisy*. However, if they are well balanced, well rehearsed and well conducted, and if they perform truly good music, they should rather be called *powerful*. In fact, nothing is as different in meaning as these two expressions. A shabby, little vaudeville band may appear noisy, whereas a large orchestra, skillfully employed, will be extremely soft and of the greatest beauty of sound even in passionate outbursts. Three trombones, if clumsily employed, may appear noisy and unbearable; and the very next moment, in the same hall, twelve trombones will delight the listeners with their powerful and yet noble tone.

{ Very true and important!
Heavy brass sounds rather soft. Furthermore, a great mass of brass diminishes rather than increases the power. Two trumpets, stabbing sharply into a wood-wind and string orchestra, may occasionally produce more strident effects than a whole army of brass instruments which balance each other.

In fact, unisons are effective only if executed by many instruments. Thus, four first-rate violinists playing the same part will produce a rather unpleasant effect, whereas fifteen average violinists in unison would sound excellent.

{ Particularly the pp of a large orchestra is incomparable.

This is why small orchestras are of so little effect and hence of so little value, however accomplished the performance of the individual players.

On the other hand, the thousand combinations possible with the giant orchestra above described could produce a wealth of harmonies, a variety of sounds, an abundance of contrasts surpassing anything heretofore achieved in art. It could create, above all, an incalculable melodic, rhythmic and expressive power, a penetrating force of unparalleled strength, a miraculous sensitivity of gradations, in the whole or in any individual part. Its calm would be as majestic as an ocean in repose, its outbursts would recall tropical tempests, its explosive power the eruptions of volcanos. In it could be heard the plaints, the murmurings, the mysterious sounds of primeval forests, the outcries, the prayers, the triumphant or mourning chants of a people with an expansive soul, an ardent heart and fiery passions. Its silence would inspire awe by its solemnity. But its crescendo would make even the most unyielding listeners shudder; it would grow like a tremendous conflagration gradually setting the sky on fire.

ON CONDUCTING

Theory of the Art of Conducting

Music is probably the most exacting of all arts and certainly one of the most difficult to cultivate. Its works are rarely presented to us under conditions which allow their true value to be recognized and their character and meaning to be completely discerned.

Among creative artists the composer is almost the only one depending upon a host of intermediaries between him and the public—intermediaries who may be intelligent or stupid, friendly or hostile, diligent or negligent. It is in their power either to carry his work on to brilliant success or to disfigure, debase and even destroy it.

Singers are often considered the most dangerous of these intermediaries; I believe that this is not true. In my opinion, the conductor is the one whom the composer has most to fear. A bad singer can spoil only his own part, but the incapable or malevolent conductor can ruin everything. A composer must consider himself happy if his work has not fallen into the hands of a conductor who is both incapable and hostile; for nothing can resist the pernicious influence of such a person. The most excellent orchestra becomes paralyzed, the best singers feel cramped and fettered, all energy and unity are lost. Under such direction the noblest and boldest inspirations can appear ridiculous, enthusiasm can be violently brought down to earth; the angel is robbed of his wings, the genius is transformed into an eccentric or a simpleton, the divine statue is plunged from its pedestal and dragged in the mud. Worst of all, when new works are performed for the first time, the public and even listeners endowed with the highest musical intelligence are unable to recognize the ravages perpetrated by the stupidities, blunders and other offenses of the conductor.

For all the obvious shortcomings of a performance the conductor is not blamed; his victims shoulder the burden. If he misses the entry of the chorus in a finale, if he causes a wavering between the chorus and orchestra or between distant groups in the orchestra, if he drags or rushes the tempo, if he interrupts a singer before the end of a phrase, people say: "The chorus is terrible, the orchestra lacks assurance, the violins have spoiled the melodic line; nobody has vigor and fire, the tenor has made mistakes, he does not know his part; the harmonies are confused; the composer does not know how to write accompaniments for singers, etc., etc."

Only when he is listening to familiar and recognized masterworks can the intelligent listener distinguish the real culprit and do justice to the other partners in the performance. However, the number of such listeners is still so small that their opinion carries but little weight. Thus, the incapable conductor maintains himself with all the calm of a bad conscience in the presence of a public that would hiss an excellent singer pitilessly at the slightest vocal mishap.

Fortunately I am now speaking only of exceptions: capable or incapable conductors who are at the same time malevolent are very rare.

The conductor who is willing but incapable, on the other hand, is very common. There may be some doubt regarding the good faith of the many mediocre conductors who frequently have to conduct artists far superior to themselves. But nobody will accuse an author of conspiring against the success of his own work, and yet there are many composers who unknowingly ruin their best scores because they fancy themselves to be great conductors.

Beethoven, it is said, more than once spoiled performances of his symphonies, which he liked to conduct even at the time when his deafness had become almost complete. In order to keep together, the musicians finally agreed to follow the slight signs of the concertmaster and to ignore Beethoven's baton. Moreover, it should be remembered that conducting a symphony, an overture or any other composition with extended movements which contain few changes and contrasts is child's play in comparison with conducting opera and other works containing recitatives, arias, and numerous orchestral passages interspersed with irregular pauses. The example of Beethoven just cited shows that the direction of an orchestra, very difficult for a blind man, is entirely impossible for a deaf one, whatever may have been his technical skill before he lost his hearing.

The conductor must *see* and *hear,* he must be resourceful and energetic, he must know the nature and the range of the instruments and be able to read a score. Besides the specific talent whose component qualities we are going to discuss he must have other, almost indefinable gifts, without which the invisible contact between him and the performers cannot be established. Lacking these, he cannot transmit his feelings to the players and has no dominating power or guiding influence. He is no longer a director and leader, but simply a time-beater, provided he is able to beat and divide time regularly.

The players must feel that he feels, understands and is moved; then his emotion communicates itself to those whom he conducts. His inner fire warms them, his enthusiasm carries them away, he radiates musical energy. But if he is indifferent and cold, he paralyzes everything around him, like the icebergs floating in the polar sea, whose approach is announced by the sudden cooling of the atmosphere.

The conductor's task is very complex. He must not only be able to conduct a work with which the performers are familiar, according to the intentions of the composer, but also, in the case of a new work, to make them acquainted with it. During the rehearsals he has to point out to each of the performers his mistakes and errors. He must be able to employ the resources at his disposal so as to secure the greatest result from them in the shortest time possible; for, in most cities of Europe, musical art is in a sad plight. Musicians are poorly paid and the necessity of thorough study is so little understood that the economical utilization of time is one of the most imperative requisites of the conductor's skill. —Let us now see what constitutes the mechanical aspects of his art.

While not requiring particularly outstanding musical qualities, the art of beating time is nevertheless rather difficult to learn; very few people really possess it. The signs which the conductor makes are generally very simple, but they may occasionally become quite complicated by the divisions and subdivisions of the meter. The conductor must above all have a clear idea of the main features and the character of the work to be performed so that he can determine without hesitation and error the tempi planned by the composer. Unless he had the opportunity of receiving instructions directly from the composer or is familiar with the traditional tempi, he must consult the metronomic indications and study them thoroughly. Most modern composers mark compositions at the beginning and whenever there is a change of tempo. I do not mean to say by this that it is necessary to imitate the mathematical regularity of the metronome, which would give the music thus executed an icy frigidity; I even doubt whether it would be possible to maintain this rigid uniformity for more than a few bars. The metronome is nevertheless an excellent medium for determining the initial tempo of a piece and its main alterations.

If the conductor has neither the instructions of the composer nor traditional or metronomic tempo indications—as is frequently the case with works written before the invention of the metronome—he has no other guide than the customary, very vague tempo markings; for the rest he must rely on his own instinct and his feeling for the composer's style. To be sure, it cannot be denied that these guides are frequently insufficient or misleading. This is proved by the manner in which older operas are given in towns where the tradition for these works has been lost. Out of ten different tempi at least four will be wrong. I once heard a chorus from "Iphigénie en Tauride" performed in a German theater; instead of Allegro non troppo in 4-4 time it was played Allegro assai in 2-2 time, i.e twice as fast. I could quote an immense number of similar mistakes caused either by the ignorance and negligence of the conductor, or by the fact that sometimes it is really very difficult even for the most talented and careful man to discover the exact meaning of the Italian tempo marks. Of course, nobody will fail to distinguish a Largo from a Presto. If the Presto has two beats to a bar, an intelligent conductor, by examining the passages and melodic designs contained in the piece, will soon find the degree of speed intended by the author. But with a Largo in 4-4 time and of simple melodic design, what means has the unfortunate conductor of discovering the correct tempo? The different degrees of slow movement that may be used for such a Largo are very numerous; only the individual feeling of the conductor can be the guide in such a case, although what matters most is the composer's rather than the conductor's feelings. Therefore, composers ought not to neglect furnishing their works with metronomic indications, and it is the conductors' duty to study them closely. To neglect this study is equal to an act of dishonesty toward the composer.

We now assume that the conductor is thoroughly familiar with the tempi of the work to be performed or rehearsed. His next task is to impart the rhythmic feeling within him to the orchestral players, to determine the duration of each bar and to make all participants observe this duration uniformly. This precise and uniform collaboration of a more or less large orchestral or choral body can be attained only by means of certain signs given by the conductor.

These signs indicate the main divisions—the *beats* of each bar, and frequently also the subdivisions—the *half beats*. It is not necessary to explain the difference between the strong and weak beats; I assume that I am writing for musicians.

The orchestral conductor generally uses a small light stick, about 20 inches long (better white than of dark color, for the sake of visibility). He holds it in his right hand and distinctly marks with it the beginning, the divisions and the close of each bar. Some concertmasters use the violin bow for conducting, but it is less suitable than the baton. The bow is somewhat flexible; this lack of rigidity and the greater resistance it offers to the air because of the hair make its movements less precise.

The simplest of all meters—*two* in a bar—is indicated very simply. After raising the baton so that the hand is on a level with his head, the conductor marks the first beat by dropping the point of the baton perpendicularly (as far as possible by bending the wrist and not by moving the entire arm) and the second beat, in the opposite way, by raising it again:

The meter with *one* beat in a bar is, especially from the conductor's point of view, the same as a meter with two beats in a very rapid tempo; therefore, it is indicated like the preceding. The necessity of raising the point again after lowering it divides the movement in two anyway.

With *four* beats in the bar, it is customary to mark the first strong beat (the beginning of the bar) by a downward movement. The second movement of the baton diagonally upward from right to left marks the second (the first weak) beat. The third, horizontally from left to right marks the third (the second strong) beat and a fourth movement diagonally upward marks the fourth (the second weak) beat. These four movements result in this figure:

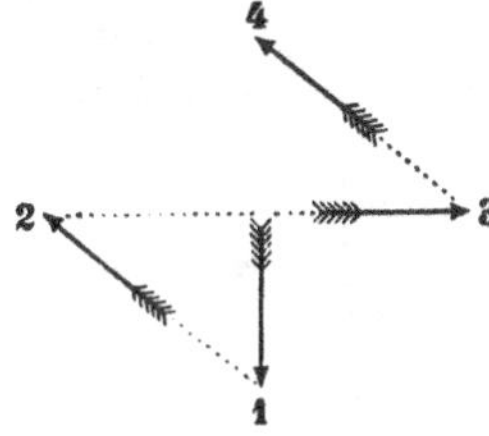

It is important that the conductor uses his arm as little as possible for these movements and consequently does not let the baton cover too much space; for each movement must be almost instantaneous or, at least, should occupy a moment so short as to be practically incommensurable. If the time interval becomes appreciable, it causes—since it is repeated many times— a retardation of the intended tempo and a very unpleasant heaviness in the orchestral performance. Moreover, this mistake has the result of needlessly tiring the conductor and of producing exaggerated; almost ridiculous movements of the body, which distract the attention of the listeners.

In a bar with *three* beats, the first downward movement is customary for marking the first beat; but there are two ways of marking the second. Most conductors beat from left to right:

some German conductors, however, do the contrary and carry the baton from right to left:

If the conductor has his back turned to the orchestra, as is customary in theaters, the latter method has a disadvantage in that only few players can see this very important marking of the second beat since the body of the conductor hides the movement of his arm. The other method is better because the second movement is outwards and the baton therefore remains perfectly visible to everybody, especially if the conductor raises it slightly above the level of his shoulders. If the conductor faces the orchestra, it is immaterial whether he makes the second movement to the right or to the left. The third beat is indicated in all cases by a diagonal, upward movement, like the last beat in 4-4 time:

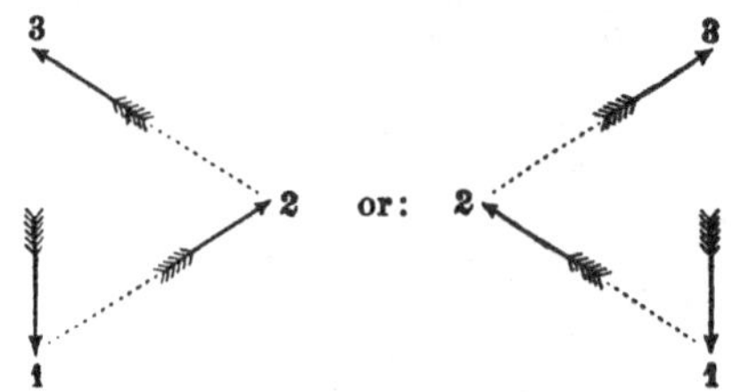

The meters with *five* and *seven* beats in a bar are not indicated by special series of gestures, but are treated as combinations of simple meters: the five beats as consisting of three and two beats, and the seven as four and three. They are therefore marked as follows:

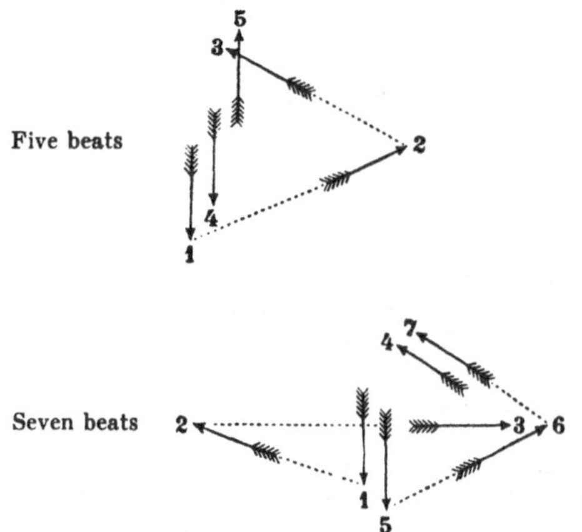

These divisions of the various meters are suited for moderate tempi. However, if the tempo is very fast or very slow, this method would be inadequate. As we have already seen, two beats in a bar can be marked only as shown above, however fast the tempo. On the other hand, if the tempo is exceptionally slow, the conductor has to subdivide each beat. A very rapid four in a bar should be marked by only two movements, since the four movements as used in moderate tempo would follow each other so rapidly that the eye could not follow them clearly; the players would be irritated rather than made secure. Moreover, and this is even more important, the conductor checks the rhythmic flow by the unnecessary four motions and loses all freedom of movement which he would retain with the simple division of the bar into two halves.

In such cases it is usually wrong for composers to indicate a 4-4 meter. When the tempo is very fast, they should always use the time signature ₵ and not **C**, which is misleading.

Triple time, i.e. rapid $3/4$ and $3/8$ meter, is treated similarly. The conductor does not mark the second beat, holding the first gesture for two periods and raising his baton only on the third beat:

It would be ridiculous to mark all three beats in a Beethoven Scherzo.

If the tempo is very slow, each beat must be subdivided; consequently, quadruple time is marked by eight movements, triple time by six movements, by repeating each of the previously indicated main movements in abbreviated form:

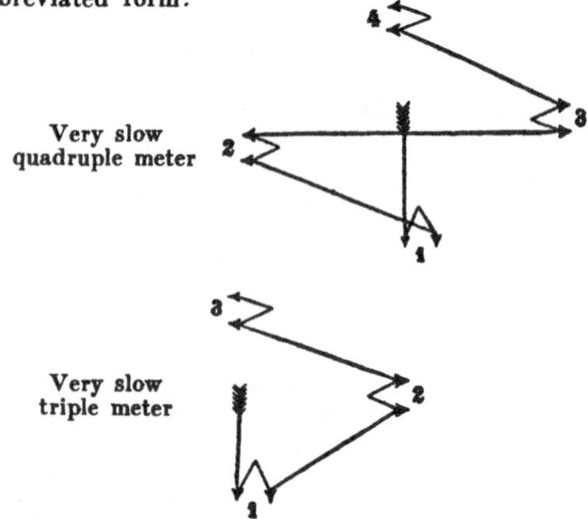

The arm should not take part in the short supplementary gestures marking the subdivisions of the bar; these are carried out by the wrist alone.

The purpose of this subdivision of the beats is to prevent rhythmic divergences which could easily arise in the orchestra during the intervals between two beats. If the conductor gives no sign at all during this long interval (which is unusually extended because of the slow tempo), the orchestra is left to itself for too long a time. Since not all players have the same rhythmic feeling, some will rush while others drag behind, and the ensemble will soon be destroyed. The only exception from this rule is a first-rate orchestra composed of virtuosos knowing each other very well and accustomed to play together, and who know the work to be performed almost by heart. Even then the carelessness of a single player may cause a mishap; why incur such a risk? I know that it hurts the vanity of some artists to be thus kept in leading-strings (like children, as they say); but with a conductor whose main aim is the excellence of the performance such considerations should have no weight. Even in a quartet the individual feeling of the players can rarely be allowed to follow its own paths. In a symphony the conductor's conception alone must rule. The quality of the performance depends on his conception and on the art of realizing it; the feelings of the individual players must never make themselves manifest.

Once this is clearly understood it becomes obvious that in very slow compound meters (such as 6/4, 6/8, 8/9, 12/8 etc.) the subdivision is even more important. These meters with triple time can be divided in various ways. If the tempo is rapid or moderate, only the simple beats are indicated according to the procedure adopted for the analogous simple meters. Hence, a 6/8 Allegretto or 6/4 Allegro requires a beat similar to duple meters (₵ or 2 or 2/4); 9/8 Allegro—like 3/4 Moderato or 3/8 Andantino; 12/8 Moderato or Allegro—like 4/4. But if the tempo is Adagio, Largo assai or Andante maestoso, all eighths-notes (or a quarter followed by an eighth-note) require beats, according to the form of the melody or the predominant figuration.

Larghetto grazioso.

In this triple meter it is unnecessary to mark all eighth-notes; the rhythm of a quarter plus an eighth-note to a beat is sufficient. One uses the little supplementary gestures indicated for subdivisions of simple meters, dividing each beat, however, into two unequal parts because it is necessary to mark the value of the quarter as well as of the eighth-note.

If the tempo is still slower, all eighth-notes require beats regardless of the meter; only thus can uncertainty be avoided and complete mastery assured.

With the indicated tempi, the conductor will beat in the 6/8 meter three eighths to each time unit, i.e. three beats down and three beats up:

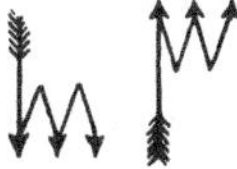

in the 9/8: three down, three to the right, three up:

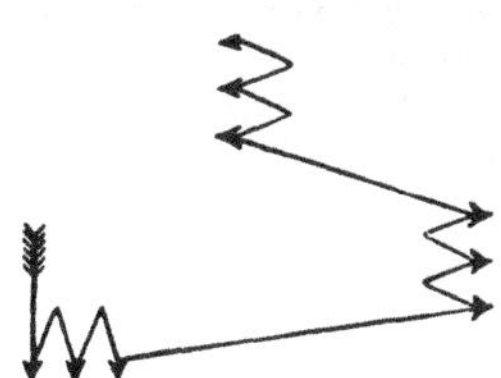

in the 12/8: three down, three to the left, three to the right, three up:

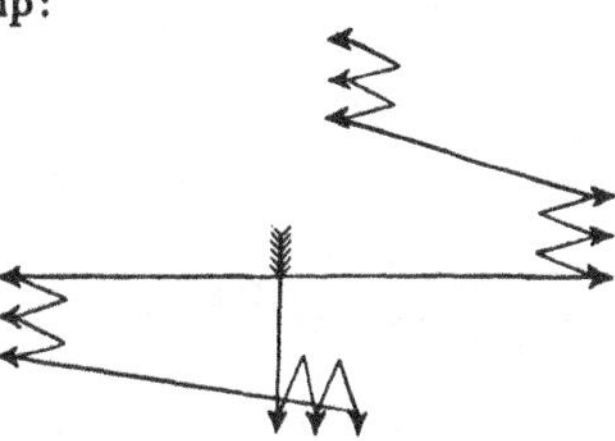

Sometimes a difficulty arises if certain voices in a score are given a triple rhythm for the sake of contrast, while the others continue in duple rhythm:

If the players of the wind instruments are very musical, there will be no need to change the manner of marking the bar and the conductor can continue to beat six or simply two. The majority of players, however, usually become uncertain when the syncopation begins and the triple rhythm clashes with the duple; they need assistance, which can be given to them in the following manner. The uncertainty in a group of performers caused by the sudden entry in a group of performers caused by the sudden entry of this unexpected rhythm conflicting with that of the rest of the orchestra always makes them look instinctively at the conductor, as if seeking his assistance. He should also look at them, turning a little toward them and marking the triple rhythm by small movements of his hand (as if this were the real meter); but this must be done in such a fashion that the violins and other instruments continuing the duple rhythm cannot see the altered beat, which would otherwise confound them completely. Thus, the new triple rhythm, being marked furtively by the conductor, is executed with assurance, while the duple rhythm, already firmly established, continues without difficulty although no longer indicated by the conductor.

On the other hand, in my opinion nothing is more objectionable and contrary to good musical sense than the application of this method where not two different and contrasting rhythms clash, but where simple syncopation is introduced. If the conductor divides the bar according to the number of accents in it, he destroys the effect of the syncopation for all listeners who see him, substituting an ordinary change of time for a rhythm of stimulating charm. Such is the case in the following passage from Beethoven's Pastoral Symphony if the conductor marks the accents instead of the beats:

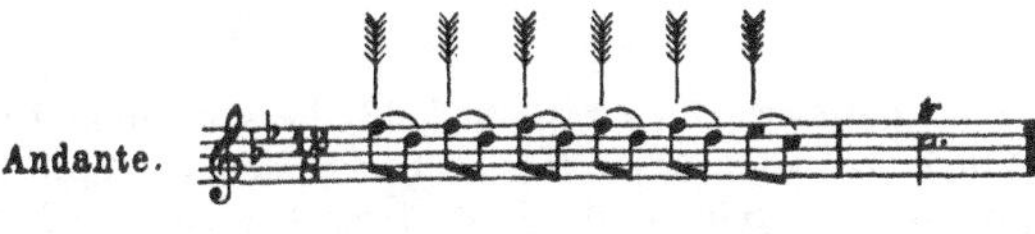

by making six movements to a bar, as indicated above the notes, instead of the four previously maintained; only the latter enable the listener to recognize and feel the syncopation clearly:

This voluntary submission to a rhythmical form which the composer actually intended to be resisted is one of the gravest stylistic mistakes a conductor can make.

Another difficulty, extremely troublesome to the conductor and requiring all his presence of mind, is caused by the combination of different meters. It is easy to conduct a duple meter, each of whose beats is subdivided in two, together with a superimposed duple meter whose beats are divided in three, if both have the same tempo. Their bars have the same duration and it is only necessary to divide them in half and to mark the two principal accents:

However, if a new, fast figure is introduced into a slow movement and if the composer has adopted for this new tempo the corresponding, short bar (either to facilitate the execution of the fast tempo or because it could not be written otherwise), two or even three of these short bars may then coincide with one bar of the slow movement:

It is the conductor's task to hold these unequal bars together. He will attain this in the quoted example by beginning to subdivide the beats from bar No. 1 of the Andante, which precedes the entrance of the Allegro 6/8, and then by continuing this division, perhaps even more markedly. The players of the Allegro 6/8 will understand that the two gestures represent the two beats of their short bar, while the players of the Andante take these same gestures merely for a divided beat of their long bar.

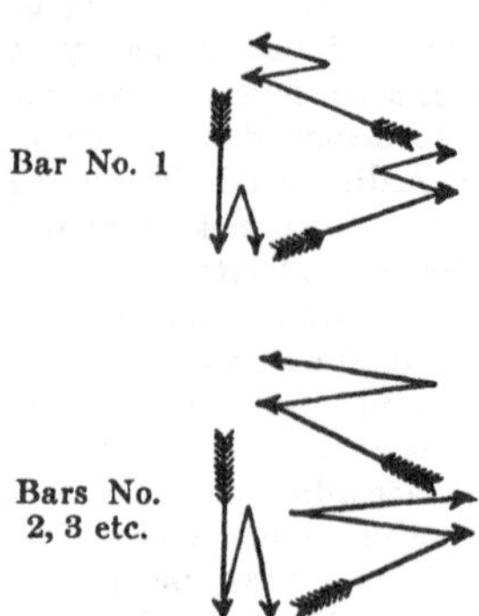

One sees, this is really quite simple because the divisions of the short bar coincide with the subdivisions of the long bar. The following example, however, in which a slow bar is superimposed over two short ones, but without this coincidence, offers greater difficulties:

Here the three bars of the Allegro assai preceding the Allegretto are conducted as usual, two to a bar. When the Allegretto begins, the conductor marks two *divided* beats for the long bar with two (unequal) movements down and two up:

The two large movements of the conductor divide the long bar in half and indicate its value to the oboes without confusing the violas, who maintain their fast movement supported by the shorter, subsidiary gestures dividing the short bar in half. From bar 3 on, the conductor ceases to divide the long bar in four because of the triple rhythm of the 6/8 melody entering here, with which this gesture would interfere. He confines himself to marking the two beats of the long bar. The violas, already accustomed to their fast rhythm, continue it without difficulty knowing that each movement of the baton marks the beginning of their short bar.

The preceding shows that subdividing a beat must be avoided if a part of the instruments or voices execute triplets on this beat. Such a division cutting through the second note of the triplet would make its execution insecure or actually impossible. The division should be avoided even a short time before the start of a triple rhythm or of a melody in triplets in order not to give the performers the feeling of a rhythm contrary to the one they are to execute.

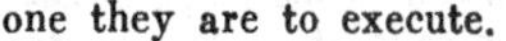

In this example it is advisable to divide the entire bar No. 1 in six, i.e. to subdivide each beat in two carrying out the following movements:

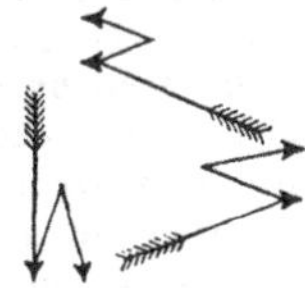

With the beginning of bar No. 2 it is necessary to omit the subdivision and to carry out only the simple movements:

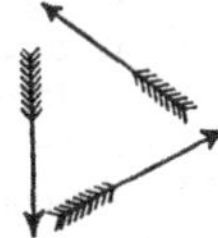

because of the triplets entering on the third beat, which would be impeded by the double movement. In the famous ball scene in Mozart's "Don Giovanni", where three orchestras in three different meters are combined, the difficulty of holding them together is not as great as might be assumed. It is sufficient to mark each beat of the Tempo di menuetto by a downward movement:

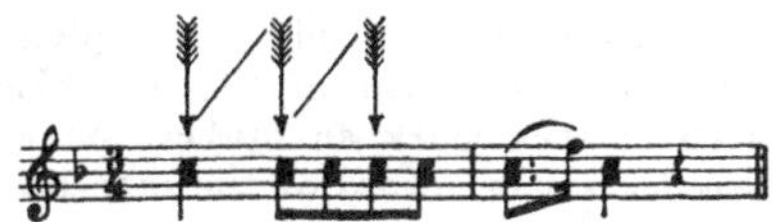

Once brought together, the two Allegros—the small one in 3/8 whose whole bar is a third (i.e. one beat) of the minuet bar, and the other in 2/4, whose bar is two thirds (i.e. two beats) of the minuet bar—fit together as well as with the main theme and proceed together without the slightest difficulty. The main thing is to make them enter correctly.

A gross fault that I have seen committed consists in slowing up the tempo of a piece in duple meter when triplets in half-notes occur:

The third note adds nothing to the duration of the bar, as some conductors seem to imagine. They may mark such passages with three beats if the tempo is slow or moderate, but the duration of the whole bar must remain exactly the same. If triplets occur in a very short bar in duple meter (Allegro assai), three beats would cause confusion. Only two should be marked—one down on the first note, the other up on the third. Owing to the quickness of the movement the two beats differ little from those of the bar with two equal beats and do not affect the execution of the parts continuing in duple meter.

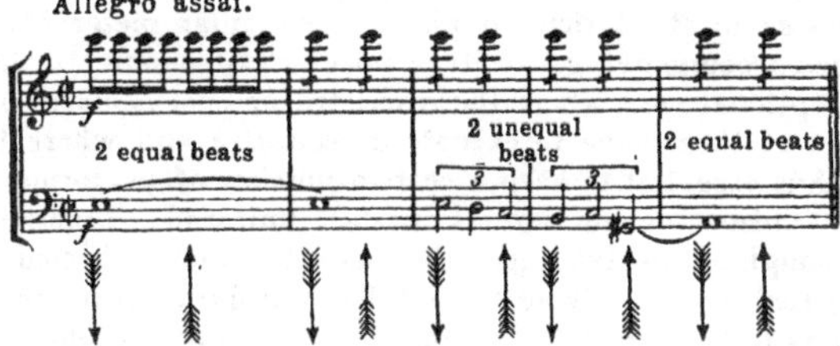

We shall now consider the method of conducting recitatives. Here the singer or instrumentalist is not confined to the regular divisions of the bar. The conductor must therefore follow their recitation attentively and must see to it that the chords and other instrumental passages inserted in the recitative are executed precisely and uniformly by the orchestra. If the recitative is accompanied by sustained notes or a tremolo in several voices and the harmony changes, he must indicate the change at the proper moment; sometimes the least conspicuous of the voices is the one whose progression changes the harmony and on which the conductor must therefore concentrate his attention.

In this example the conductor, while following the reciting, metrically free part, must also watch above all the viola part and make it move from F to E at the correct moment at the beginning of the second bar. Since this part is executed by several players, some might hold the F longer than others and thereby cause a momentary dissonance.

Many conductors have the habit of completely disregarding the written divisions of the bar when conducting recitative; they mark an up-beat on a heavy beat if it precedes a short chord of the orchestra, even if this chord comes on a weak beat:

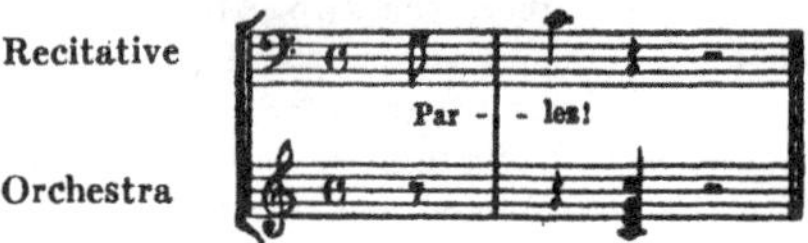

In a passage such as this they raise the baton on the quarter-rest at the beginning of the bar and lower it on the second beat to mark the entry of the chord. I cannot approve this absolutely unjustifiable method; it may frequently cause mishaps in the execution. I cannot see why in recitatives the bar should not be divided regularly and the real beats be marked in their proper place as in music played strictly according to meter. I therefore recommend marking the first beat in the preceding example with a downward motion, as usual, and to move the baton to the left with the entry of the chord on the second beat; and accordingly in other, similar cases, always dividing the bar regularly. It is also very important to divide it according to the tempo previously indicated by the composer; if it is an Allegro or Maestoso and the reciting voice has sung for some time without accompaniment, one must not forget when the orchestra re-enters to give each beat its proper value in an Allegro or Maestoso. If the orchestra plays by itself, it usually does so in strict time; it plays in irregular meter only when accompanying a reciting voice or instrument. In the exceptional case where the orchestra or chorus itself or part of them have to execute a recitative and where it is thus essential to keep a certain number of performers (in unison or in several parts) uniformly together although not in strict time, the conductor himself becomes the real reciter, giving to each bar the duration he considers to be correct. According to the form of the phrase, he sometimes marks the main beats, sometimes the subdivisions, sometimes the accents, sometimes the sixteenth-notes; in short, he designs with his baton the melodic form of the recitative. Of course the performers must know their music almost by heart and keep their eyes constantly on him; otherwise, no security or precision is possible.

Even with music in strict time, the conductor must generally insist that the players look at him as often as possible. *An orchestra which does not watch the conductor's baton has no conductor.* For instance, frequently after a pause the conductor is forced to wait before marking the re-entry of the orchestra until he sees the eyes of all performers fixed upon him. It is his task to accustom them during rehearsals to look at him simultaneously in all decisive moments.

Since in the preceding example the first note is indefinitely prolonged by the pause, the notes following it cannot be executed with the necessary verve and precision if this rule is disregarded; for without looking at the baton the performers cannot know when the conductor proceeds to the second beat and resumes the tempo momentarily suspended by the pause.

The obligation on the part of the performers to look at the conductor implies an equal obligation on his part to make himself visible to all of them. Whatever the arrangement of the orchestra may be, whether on steps or on a horizontal plane, the conductor must select his place so that he can be seen by everybody. The greater the number of performers and the larger the space occupied by them, the higher must be his place. His desk should not be too high lest the board carrying the score hide his face. For his facial expression has much to do with the influence he exercises. If a conductor practically does not exist for an orchestra unable or unwilling to look at him, he exists just as little for one unable to see him completely.

Noises caused by striking the desk with the stick or by stamping feet are to be banned completely; they are not only inexpedient, they are crude. Only if the chorus is unable to see the baton because of some stage action, the conductor is forced—for the sake of a secure entry by the chorus—to mark the beat preceding the entry by a slight tap of his baton on the desk. This is the only exception warranting the employment of an audible signal in conducting; even then the necessity of using it is to be regretted.

While speaking of choral singers and their operations on the stage we may mention that chorus masters often allow themselves to beat time backstage without being able to see the conductor's baton or even to hear the orchestra. Hence this arbitrary time, beaten more or less badly, cannot correspond with that of the conductor and causes a rhythmic discrepancy between the chorus and the orchestra; instead of aiding cooperation it impedes it.

There is another traditional barbarism which every intelligent and energetic conductor should abolish. For choral or instrumental pieces which are to be executed behind the scenes, sometimes without participation of the main orchestra, a second conductor is indispensable. If the main orchestra accompanies this group, the first conductor, who hears this music from the distance, is strictly bound to let himself be guided by the second conductor and to follow his lead by ear. But if—as frequently happens in modern music—the full sound of the large orchestra prevents him from hearing the backstage music, the application of a special mechanism transmitting the meter becomes necessary to establish an instantaneous communication between the conductor and the distant performers. For this purpose a number of more or less ingenious experiments have been carried out, whose results have not always met expectations. Only the electric metronome set up by Verbrugghe in the Brussels theater leaves nothing to be desired. It consists of copper wires attached to a voltaic pile placed beneath the stage; these wires connect the conductor's desk with a movable baton attached by a pivot in front of a board which is placed at any desired distance from the conductor. The desk is furnished with a copper key similar to a piano key, which has at its bottom a small protuberance of about a quarter of an inch. Immediately under this protuberance is a little copper cup filled with quicksilver. When the conductor wants to mark a beat, he presses the copper key with the forefinger of his left hand (his right hand holds the baton, as usual), whereby the protuberance makes contact with the quicksilver. The electrical connection thus effected makes the baton at the other end of the wires oscillate. The electrical contact and the movement of the baton take place simultaneously, regardless of the distance. The musicians behind the scenes watching the electric baton are thus practically under the immediate direction of the conductor, who might, if it were necessary, conduct from the middle of the Opéra orchestra in Paris a performance taking place in Versailles. It is only necessary to agree beforehand with the chorus singers or with their conductor (if there is one, as an additional precaution) on the manner of beating the time: whether the conductor is to mark all main beats or only the first beat in each bar. For the oscillations of the electric baton, taking place in only one direction, give no precise indication in this respect.

When I first used this valuable instrument in Brussels, its action disclosed one shortcoming. Every time the copper key was pressed down it touched another copper plate and, however soft the contact, there was a short noise which attracted the attention of the audience during the pauses of the orchestra, to the detriment of the musical effect. I pointed out the defect to M. Verbrugghe, who substituted for the copper plate the cup with quicksilver previously mentioned. The protuberance of the key enters into it without any disturbing noise. Only the electric spark emitted during the use of the instrument is still noticeable, but its crackling is so weak that the audience does not hear it. The installation of the metronome is not expensive. Large opera houses, churches and concert halls should have been provided with it long ago. Yet it is nowhere to be found except at the Brussels theater. This might appear unbelievable if the carelessness of many theater managers, to whom music is only a means toward an end, were not well known. We are only too well acquainted with their instinctive aversion to whatever is off the beaten track, with their indifference to the interests of art, their parsimony where an expenditure for the best of music is needed, and with the ignorance of the basic principles of our art among those in whose hands its fate rests.

Not all has been said as yet about those dangerous auxiliaries called chorus masters. Very few among them are really able to direct a musical performance so that the conductor can rely upon them. He must therefore supervise them closely when he needs their participation. Most to be dreaded are those whom high age has deprived of their energy and skill. The maintenance of any somewhat rapid tempo is impossible to them. However fast the initial tempo of a piece entrusted to their direction, little by little they slacken its pace until they have reached a certain degree of moderate slowness which corresponds with the blood circulation of their enfeebled organism. It must be added, however, that old men are not the only ones with whom composers run this risk. There are men in the prime of life, but with a sluggish temperament, whose blood seems to circulate *moderato.* If they have to conduct an Allegro assai, they gradually let it become a Moderato; if on the contrary, it is a Largo or Andante sostenuto of some length, they will have accelerated to a Moderato long before the end has been reached. Moderato is their natural pace, and they return to it as infallibly as a pendulum whose oscillations have been accelerated or retarded for a moment. These people are the born enemies of all characteristic music and the greatest destroyers of style. May orchestral conductors shun their cooperation at any price!

Once, in a large town which I will not name, a very simple chorus in 6/8 Allegretto was to be performed behind the scenes. The assistance of the chorus master was needed; and he was an old man. The tempo of the chorus was determined by that of the preceding orchestral introduction, and our Nestor followed it quite nicely during the first few bars; but soon he became so slow that it was impossible to continue without making a farce of the piece. It was started over again two, three, four times; half an hour was spent in increasingly irritating efforts, but always with the same result. The good man simply could not maintain an Allegretto. At last the orchestral conductor, out of all patience, asked him not to conduct any more, and made the chorus singers simulate a march movement by raising their feet alternatingly without moving from the place. This tempo corresponded exactly with the duple meter of the 6/8 Allegretto, and the singers, no longer hampered by their director, executed the piece correctly and without any slackening, as if they were singing on the march.

Nevertheless, I admit that some chorus masters or assistant conductors are really useful and even indispensable for the maintenance of unity among great masses of performers if it is absolutely necessary to place them so that a part of the instrumentalists or singers turn their backs on the conductor. He then needs a certain number of assistants placed in front of those performers who cannot see him to transmit his tempo indications to them. In order that this transmission is absolutely precise the assistant conductors must not take their eyes off the main conductor's baton for one moment. Should they cease to watch him for as little as three bars, to look at the score, there will immediately be a discrepancy between their tempo and his, and all will be lost.

At a music festival in Paris where 1200 performers were assembled under my direction, I employed five chorus conductors for the singers and two assistant conductors for the orchestra (one for the wind and one for the percussion instruments). I had urged them to look at me incessantly. They did not fail to do so, and our eight batons, rising and falling without the slightest rhythmic discrepancy, achieved a unity among the 1200 participants of a perfection never before experienced. With one or more electric metronomes this expedient will probably be no longer necessary. In fact, one can thus easily conduct a chorus placed with the back toward the conductor; but attentive and intelligent assistants are always preferable to a machine.

They must not only beat the time like a metronome, but they must also speak to the groups near them, drawing their attention to various shadings and giving them the cue for their re-entry after a rest. In a space arranged as a semicircular amphitheater the conductor alone can direct a considerable number of performers, since all participants can look toward him. I should nevertheless prefer to employ a number of assistant conductors, because of the great distance between the chief conductor and the performers placed at the extreme ends. The greater this distance, the smaller the conductor's influence upon the performers. It would be best to have several assistant conductors and several electric metronomes besides, marking the main beats of the bar before their eyes.

We now come to the question whether the conductor should stand or sit. In theaters, where works of tremendous length are performed, it is rather difficult for the conductor to endure the fatigue caused by standing the entire evening. On the other hand, it is obvious that the conductor loses part of his power by being seated, and that he cannot give free course to his temperament (if he has any).

Furthermore, should he conduct from the full score or from the first-violin part, as is customary in some theaters? He should doubtless use the full score. Conducting from a single part containing only the principal instrumental cues, the melody and the bass requires a needless effort of memory on the part of the conductor. Moreover, if he tells one of the performers whose part he does not have before him that he has made a mistake, he exposes himself to the risk of being answered: "what do you know about this?"

Placing and arranging the players and singers, especially for concerts, is also among the duties of the conductor. It is impossible to state categorically the best manner of grouping the performers in a theater or concert hall. Much depends on the size and shape of the particular place; the number of participants and sometimes the style of the composition to be performed must also be considered.

An amphitheater of eight or at least five different levels is generally indispensable for concerts. The semicircular form is best for the amphitheater. If the space is large enough to take in the entire orchestra, the instrumentalists will be arranged on the steps as follows: the first violins in front on the right, the second violins on the left, the violas in the middle between the two violin groups; the flutes, oboes, clarinets, horns, and bassoons behind the first violins; two rows of violoncellos and double-basses behind the wood-wind instruments; the harps in front, near the conductor; the kettledrums and other percussion instruments behind the brass; the conductor, his back toward the public, at the base of the amphitheater, near the front desks of the violins.

There should be a plane, more or less wide space in front of the first step of the amphitheater. Here the chorus singers are arranged in the form of a fan, their faces turned three-quarters toward the public so that they can comfortably watch the conductor. The grouping of the singers by voices varies according to the number of voices employed in a given work. In any case, the sopranos and the altos should take the front rows, seated; the tenors stand behind the sopranos and the basses behind the altos.

The soloists (singers as well as instrumentalists) occupy the center of the front space and should place themselves so that they can always see the conductor's baton by slightly turning their heads.

These indications, I repeat, are only approximate; they may be modified in many different ways, for various reasons.

In the Paris Conservatoire, where the amphitheater has only four or five steps (not forming a semicircle), the violins and the violas are on the stage, and only the basses and wind instruments occupy the steps; the chorus is seated in the front of the stage, looking toward the audience. All the sopranos and altos are unable to see the movements of the conductor, since their backs are turned directly toward him. The arrangement is very inconvenient for this part of the chorus.

It is always of the greatest importance that the chorus singers placed in front of the stage shall be lower than the violins, since they would otherwise greatly impair their sonority. If there are no additional steps for the chorus in front of the orchestra, it is necessary for the same reason that the women be seated and the men remain standing, so that the tenor and bass voices, issuing from a higher point than the sopranos and altos, can spread freely and are neither stifled nor intercepted.

As soon as the presence of the chorus in front of the orchestra is no longer necessary, the conductor should send them away, since this large number of human bodies diminishes the sonority of the instruments. The performance of a symphony would lose much if the orchestra were thus muffled.

There are some additional precautions concerning the orchestra which the conductor must observe to avoid certain defects in performance. The percussion instruments, placed on one of the last and highest rows of the amphitheater, have a tendency to drag the tempo. A series of strokes on the bass drum at regular intervals in a fast tempo, such as these:

will sometimes lead to the complete destruction of a fine rhythmic climax by checking the flow of the orchestra and ruining its unity. The drummer almost always gives the first stroke a little too late because he does not observe the conductor's first beat. This delay increases with each succeeding stroke and must eventually lead to a rhythmic discrepancy of fatal effect. The conductor will vainly try to restore unity in such a case. All he can do is to require the drummer to memorize the number of strokes in the passage and, instead of looking at his part, to watch the conductor's baton closely.

A similar retardation, but from different causes, frequently occurs in the trumpet part when it contains rapid passages such as the following:

The trumpeter, instead of taking breath before the beginning of the first bar, does so only during the eighth-rest. Not counting the time required for breathing he gives the rest its full value, thereby prolonging the first bar by an eighth. The resulting effect

is all the worse because the final accent, struck by the rest of the orchestra on the first beat of the third bar, comes too late in the trumpets, thus destroying the unity of execution in the final chord.

To prevent this, the conductor must point out in advance this inaccuracy to the players; for they are usually unaware of it. Then, while conducting, he must look at them at the decisive moment and give them, a little ahead of time, the first beat of the bar in which they have to enter. It is incredible how difficult it is to prevent the trumpeters from doubling such an eighth-rest.

Where the composer has indicated an extended *accelerando poco a poco* to pass from an Allegro moderato to a Presto, most conductors accelerate the tempo by jerks instead of enlivening it by a gradual and unnoticeable increase of speed. This mistake should be carefully avoided. This applies equally in the opposite instance; the smooth transition from a fast to a slow tempo is even more difficult.

Often a conductor demands from his musicians a certain exaggeration of the nuances indicated by the composer, either from a lack of delicate musical feeling or from a desire to give emphatic proof of his zeal. He does not understand the character and style of the work. The nuances become distortions, the accents turn into outcries. The intentions of the poor composer are completely disfigured; and those of the conductor, however honest they may be, are like the caresses of the ass in the fable, who killed his master by fondling him.

We now turn to some bad habits which can be found in almost all European orchestras—habits which reduce composers to despair, and whose early elimination is the duty of conductors.

Players of string instruments rarely take the trouble to produce a correct tremolo. They substitute for this very characteristic effect a mere repetition of notes, twice or even three times as slow as the real tremolo. Instead of sixty-fourth-notes they play thirty-second and even sixteenth-notes, i.e. instead of 64 notes to a bar (4-4, Adagio) they play only 32 or 16. The rapid motion of the arm necessary for the real tremolo is doubtless too great an effort for them. This laziness is intolerable!

Many double-bass players take the liberty of simplifying their part—either out of indolence or from fear of being unable to master certain difficulties. This system of simplification, generally accepted for the past forty years, can no longer be tolerated. The double-bass parts in older works are so simple that there is no reason for weakening them even more. Those in modern works are more difficuit, it is true; but, with very few exceptions, there is nothing impracticable in them. Composers who are masters of their art always write these parts with the greatest care and exactly as they should be performed. If the players simplify things out of laziness, the energetic conductor has sufficient authority to force them to do their duty; if they do it because of incompetence, he should dismiss them. It is in his own interest to rid himself of musicians who cannot play their instrument properly.

The flutists, accustomed to lead the other wind instruments and unwilling to play occasionally below the clarinets and oboes, frequently transpose entire passages to the higher octave. A conductor who does not read the score carefully and who does not know adequately the work to be performed, or one whose ear lacks acuteness, will not notice the strange liberty thus taken by the flutists. Many more examples of this kind could be cited; such abuses should no longer be tolerated.

It happens everywhere (I purposely do not say: in certain orchestras) that violinists, of whom usually ten, fifteen or twenty execute the same part, do not count the rests, but rely instead on the other players. The result is, of course, that scarcely half of them come in again at the right moment, while the others still hold their instrument under the left arm and stare in the air. The entry is thus weakened, if not entirely missed. I invoke the conductors' full attention and severity against this intolerable habit. However, it is so deep-rooted that the conductor will only succeed in eradicating it by making a large number of players liable for the fault of a single player, e.g. by fining a whole row if one of them misses coming in correctly. The amount of the fine may be small, but I warrant that each violinist will count his rests and see to it that his neighbor does the same, since the fine can be inflicted on the same player five or six times in the course of one performance.

An orchestra whose instruments are not in tune individually and in relation to each other is a tonal monstrosity. The conductor must therefore take great care that the musicians tune accurately. But this should not be done in the presence of the audience. Any kind of instrumental noise or of preluding during intermissions offends the ears of all refined listeners. One can immediately recognize the poor training and the musical mediocrity of an orchestra by this obnoxious noise made during the periods of quiet in an opera or concert.

It is also the conductor's duty to see to it that clarinetists do not always use the same instrument (usually the clarinet in B^b) without regard to the author's indications, as if the different clarinets, especially those in A and D, did not have their own individual character, whose special value is well kown to the intelligent composer. Moreover, the clarinet in A reaches a semitone lower than the one in B^b, namely to C# , which is of excellent effect. This C# represents the actual sound of the written note E , which on the clarinet in B^b produces D

Another habit, just as bad and even more dangerous, is found in many orchestras regarding the use of the valve horns. It consists in the execution as *open* tones (by means of the new mechanism) of those notes which are intended by the composer to be played as *stopped* tones (by introducing the right hand into the bell of the horn). Furthermore, horn players now use almost exclusively the horn in F (because of the facility of playing it in different keys by means of the valves), regardless of the key indicated by the composer. This habit causes a great many abuses, from which the conductor should preserve the works of composers *who know how to write*. As to the works of others, I must admit that there the damage is much less grave.

Furthermore, the conductor must resist the parsimonious custom, existing in certain theaters, of having the cymbals and the bass drum played by the same musician. The sound of these cymbals attached to the bass drum (the only way in which this economy is made possible) is only a vulgar noise fit for dance bands. Moreover, this custom leads mediocre composers into the habit of never using one of the two instruments alone and of considering it their sole purpose to stress the heavy beats very forcefully. This opinion caters to the predelection for vulgar noise and has brought upon us those ridiculous excesses which will sooner or later doom dramatic music unless a stop is put to them.

Finally, I must express my regret concerning the generally poor organization of rehearsals. Everywhere the system of mass rehearsals is retained for large vocal or orchestral works. All chorus singers as well as all instrumentalists are rehearsed together. Deplorable errors, innumerable mistakes, especially in inner voices, are the natural consequence—errors which neither the chorus master nor the orchestral conductor will notice. Once established, such errors grow into habits and become part and parcel of the performance.

The poor chorus singers receive the worst treatment of all with this type of rehearsal. They need an able *director,* who knows the correct tempi and is proficient in the art of singing, to beat the time and make critical observations; furthermore, they require a *good pianist,* playing from a *well-arranged* piano score on a *good* piano; and finally a good *violinist* to play in unison or in the octave with the voices as they study each part individually. Instead of these three indispensable artists they are given—at two-thirds of the European opera houses—a single instructor, a man who usually knows as little of conducting as of singing, who has scarcely any musical education and who is selected from among the worst pianists to be found, or who perhaps cannot play the piano at all; a pitiable invalid who, sitting before a battered and untuned instrument, tries to decipher a confused score which he does not know, plays false chords (minor instead of major and vice versa) and—under the pretext of conducting and accompanying at the same time—teaches the singers a wrong rhythm with his right hand and a wrong intonation with his left one.

One is carried back into the middle ages when he has to witness such an exhibition of barbarism for the sake of economy.

I firmly believe that a faithful, spirited and enthusiastic performance of a modern work, even by outstanding artists, can be achieved only by sectional rehearsals. Each choral part must be studied individually until the necessary security is reached; only then should it be rehearsed together with the other parts. One should proceed in the same fashion in rehearsing symphonies, if they are at all complicated. First the violins should be rehearsed alone, then the violas and basses, then the wood-wind (with a small group of strings to fill out the rests and to accustom the wind instruments to their cues); likewise the brass alone; sometimes it is even necessary to rehearse the percussion instruments by themselves; finally the harps—if they are numerous. The general rehearsals are then far more profitable and much faster, and one is assured of a fidelity of execution only too rare nowadays.

The performances obtained by the old method of rehearsing are never more than approximations of correct interpretations. Yet the conductor puts down his baton, after ruining another masterpiece, with a smile of satisfaction. Should he, nevertheless, feel some slight doubt whether he has fulfilled his task satisfactorily—and who can verify whether he has?—he murmurs to himself: "What of it? Vae victis!"

GLOSSARY OF GERMAN TERMS AND PHRASES USED IN THE FULL-SCORE EXAMPLES

1. NAMES OF INSTRUMENTS

Becken	cymbals	Kontrabass (K.B.)	double-bass
Dudelsack	bagpipe	Kontrafagott	double-bassoon
Fagott	bassoon	Orgel	organ
Grosse Trommel	bass drum	Pauke	kettledrum
Glocke	bell	Posaune	trombone
Halbmond	crescent	Ventilhorn,-hörner	valve horn(s)
Klappen-Trompete	keyed trumpet	Viola, Violen	viola(s)
Kleine Flöte	piccolo	Wirbeltrommel	side drum

2. PHRASES USED IN THE EXAMPLES

(Only those necessary for the understanding of the musical contents are listed. Phrases used repeatedly are included only once, at the place of their first occurrence).

Page		
3	sehr langsam	very slow
8	ein Vlc. allein	1 'cello alone
	2tes Pult	2nd desk
10	sehr bestimmt	very distinct
11	stürmisch	stormy
17	sehr lebhaft	very lively
	am Stege	near the bridge
	mit Dämpfer	con sordino
24	mässig	moderato
	allmählich immer etwas bewegter	gradually faster
25	ohne Dämpfer	senza sordino
30	wirklicher Klang	actual sound
	leichter Finger	finger touching
	fester Finger	finger pressing
39	mässig langsam	moderately slow
	auf dem Theater	on the stage
41	sehr schnell	very fast
56	immer langsamer	more and more slowly
58	sehr zart	very soft
65	vier einzelne Violinen	4 single violins
	sämtliche übrigen Violinen	all other violins
	in vier gleich starken Partien	in 4 equal groups
	durch Flageolet hervorzubringen	to be executed as harmonics
71	I. allein	1st (viola) alone
	die übrigen	the rest
79	A (tief)	low A
83	mässig bewegt	moderato
84	sehr ausdrucksvoll	with much expression
85	sehr ruhig und nicht schleppend	very calm, not dragging
	sehr weich	very soft
	etwas breit	somewhat broad
92	lebhaft, doch nicht zu schnell	animated, but not too fast
	Bog(en)	arco (with the bow)
100	nur die 6 zweiten Vlc.	only the six 2nd 'celli
104	zus(ammen)	together
113	nur 4-saitige Kontrabässe	only 4-stringed double-basses
118	allmählich schwindend	gradually fading
	sehr zögernd	very hesitatingly
124	dieses Stück wird durchaus sehr leise gespielt und die *sf* und *f* müssen nicht zu stark ausgedrückt werden	this piece is to be played very softly throughout; the *sf* and *f* must not be executed too strongly

Page		
129	Doppelgriff	double stop
134	ein wenig zurückhaltend	poco rit.
	allmählich wieder in etwas bewegterem früherem Zeitmass	gradually returning to the former, somewhat faster tempo
135	mit zunehmendem Ausdruck	with increasing expression
148	hinter der Szene	backstage
186	Pauke I in B, F hoch (Zwei Paukenschläger)	kettledrum I in high B♭, F (2 drummers)
	mit Schwammschlägeln	sticks with sponge heads
207	sehr gemächlich	molto moderato
215	fast wie nichts	almost inaudible
	auf zwei Saiten so sanft als möglich	on 2 strings, as soft as possible
223	die Stimme nachahmend	imitating the voice
239	bewegt	agitated
268	die 4 ersten	first 4 (double-basses)
	die 4 letzten	second 4 (double-basses)
269	das 5. Pult tritt hinzu	5th desk enters
276	ziemlich bewegt	rather fast
279	gedämpft	muted
280	die Fermaten sehr lang und bedeutungsvoll	very long and expressive pauses
	immer stärker	molto crescendo
	lustig und immer schneller und schmetternder	gay, increasingly fast and brassy
295	möglichst sanft und gebunden	as soft and legato as possible
324	nicht obligat	ad libitum
	bei den Trommeln aufzustellen	place with the drums
325	die Hälfte der zweiten Trommeln	half the 2nd drums
339	sehr gehalten	slow
340	träg und schleppend	heavy and dragging
372	diese grosse Trommel ist aufrecht zu stellen, die Wirbel sind mit zwei Paukenschlägeln auszuführen	this brass drum is to be placed upright, rolls are to be executed with 2 drumsticks
375	mit zwei Klöppeln abwechselnd von jeder Seite zu schlagen	beat with 2 sticks alternatingly from both sides

INDEX